Optimizing decision making in the apparel supply chain using artificial intelligence (AI)

The Textile Institute and Woodhead Publishing

The Textile Institute is a unique organisation in textiles, clothing and footwear. Incorporated in England by a Royal Charter granted in 1925, the Institute has individual and corporate members in over 90 countries. The aim of the Institute is to facilitate learning, recognise achievement, reward excellence and disseminate information within the global textiles, clothing and footwear industries.

Historically, The Textile Institute has published books of interest to its members and the textile industry. To maintain this policy, the Institute has entered into partnership with Woodhead Publishing Limited to ensure that Institute members and the textile industry continue to have access to high calibre titles on textile science and technology.

Most Woodhead titles on textiles are now published in collaboration with The Textile Institute. Through this arrangement, the Institute provides an Editorial Board which advises Woodhead on appropriate titles for future publication and suggests possible editors and authors for these books. Each book published under this arrangement carries the Institute's logo.

Woodhead books published in collaboration with The Textile Institute are offered to Textile Institute members at a substantial discount. These books, together with those published by The Textile Institute that are still in print, are offered on the Woodhead web site at: www.woodheadpublishing.com. Textile Institute books still in print are also available directly from the Institute's website at: www.textileinstitutebooks.com.

A list of Woodhead books on textile science and technology, most of which have been published in collaboration with The Textile Institute, can be found towards the end of the contents pages.

We are always happy to receive suggestions for new books from potential editors. To enquire about contributing to our Textiles series, please send your name, contact address and details of the topic/s you are interested in to sarah.lynch@woodheadpublishing.com. We look forward to hearing from you.

The Woodhead team responsible for publishing this book
Commissioning Editor: Kathryn Picking
Project Editor: Cathryn Freear
Editorial and Production Manager: Mary Campbell
Production Editor: Adam Hooper
Freelance Project Manager: Annette Wiseman
Copyeditor: Sue Clements
Proofreader: Jo Egre
Cover Designer: Terry Callanan

Woodhead Publishing Series in Textiles: Number 143

Optimizing decision making in the apparel supply chain using artificial intelligence (AI)

From production to retail

W. K. Wong, Z. X. Guo and S. Y. S. Leung

The Textile Institute

WP

WOODHEAD PUBLISHING

Oxford Cambridge Philadelphia New Delhi

Published by Woodhead Publishing Limited in association with The Textile Institute
Woodhead Publishing Limited,
80 High Street, Sawston, Cambridge CB22 3HJ, UK
www.woodheadpublishing.com
www.woodheadpublishingonline.com

Woodhead Publishing, 1518 Walnut Street, Suite 1100, Philadelphia,
PA 19102–3406, USA

Woodhead Publishing India Private Limited, G–2, Vardaan House,
7/28 Ansari Road, Daryaganj, New Delhi – 110002, India
www.woodheadpublishingindia.com

First published 2013, Woodhead Publishing Limited

British Library Cataloguing in Publication Data
A catalogue record for this book is available from the British Library.

Library of Congress Control Number: 2012952114.

ISBN 978-0-85709-779-8 (print)
ISBN 978-0-85709-784-2 (online)
ISSN 2042-0803 Woodhead Publishing Series in Textiles (print)
ISSN 2042-0811 Woodhead Publishing Series in Textiles (online)

The publisher's policy is to use permanent paper from mills that operate a sustainable forestry policy, and which has been manufactured from pulp which is processed using acid-free and elemental chlorine-free practices. Furthermore, the publisher ensures that the text paper and cover board used have met acceptable environmental accreditation standards.

Typeset by RefineCatch Limited, Bungay, Suffolk
Printed and bound in the UK by the MPG Books Group

Contents

	Woodhead Publishing Series in Textiles	*ix*
	Preface	*xvii*
1	Understanding key decision points in the apparel supply chain W. K. Wong, The Hong Kong Polytechnic University, China	1
1.1	Introduction	1
1.2	Selection of plant locations	1
1.3	Production scheduling and assembly line balancing control	2
1.4	Cutting room	3
1.5	Retailing	10
2	Fundamentals of artificial intelligence techniques for apparel management applications Z. X. Guo, Sichuan University, China and W. K. Wong, The Hong Kong Polytechnic University, China	13
2.1	Artificial intelligence (AI) techniques: a brief overview	13
2.2	Rule-based expert systems	17
2.3	Evolutionary optimization techniques	21
2.4	Feedforward neural networks (FNNs)	26
2.5	Fuzzy logic	32
2.6	Conclusions	38
2.7	References	39
3	Selecting the location of apparel manufacturing plants using neural networks W. K. Wong, X. H. Zeng and K. F. Au, The Hong Kong Polytechnic University, China	41
3.1	Introduction	41
3.2	Classification methods using artificial neural networks	42

3.3	Classifying decision models for the location of clothing plants	43
3.4	Classification using unsupervised artificial neural networks (ANN)	47
3.5	Classification using supervised ANN	49
3.6	Conclusion	52
3.7	Acknowledgements	53
3.8	References	53
3.9	Appendix: performance of back propagation (BP) and learning vector quantization (LVQ) with a different number of hidden neurons	54
4	Optimizing apparel production order planning scheduling using genetic algorithms Z. X. Guo, Sichuan University, China and W. K. Wong, S. Y. S. Leung, J. T. Fan and S. F. Chan, The Hong Kong Polytechnic University, China	55
4.1	Introduction	55
4.2	Problem formulation	57
4.3	Dealing with uncertain completion and start times	59
4.4	Genetic algorithms for order scheduling	61
4.5	Experimental results and discussion	66
4.6	Conclusions	74
4.7	Acknowledgement	74
4.8	References	74
4.9	Appendix 1: nomenclature	76
4.10	Appendix 2: Gantt charts	77
5	Optimizing cut order planning in apparel production using evolutionary strategies W. K. Wong and S. Y. S. Leung, The Hong Kong Polytechnic University, China	81
5.1	Introduction	81
5.2	Formulation of the cut order planning (COP) decision-making model	87
5.3	Genetic COP optimization	90
5.4	An example of a genetic optimization model for COP	95
5.5	Conclusions	101
5.6	Acknowledgement	101
5.7	References	101
5.8	Appendix: comparison between industrial practice and proposed COP decision-making model	103

6 Optimizing marker planning in apparel production using evolutionary strategies and neural networks 106
W. K. Wong and X. X. Wang, The Hong Kong Polytechnic University, China and Z. X. Guo, Sichuan University, China

6.1 Introduction 106
6.2 Packing method for optimized marker packing 109
6.3 Evolutionary strategy (ES) for optimizing marker planning 116
6.4 Experiments to evaluate performance 123
6.5 Conclusion 128
6.6 Acknowledgement 129
6.7 References 129

7 Optimizing fabric spreading and cutting schedules in apparel production using genetic algorithms and fuzzy set theory 132
W. K. Wong, C. K. Kwong, P. Y. Mok and W. H. Ip, The Hong Kong Polytechnic University, China

7.1 Introduction 132
7.2 Problem formulation in fabric-cutting operations 135
7.3 Genetic optimization of fabric scheduling 138
7.4 Case studies using real production data 142
7.5 Conclusions 149
7.6 Acknowledgement 150
7.7 References 150
7.8 Appendix: nomenclature 151

8 Optimizing apparel production systems using genetic algorithms 153
W. K. Wong, P. Y. Mok and S. Y. S. Leung, The Hong Kong Polytechnic University, China

8.1 Introduction 153
8.2 Problem formulation in sewing operations 155
8.3 Genetic optimization of production line balancing 156
8.4 Experimental results 163
8.5 Conclusions 166
8.6 Acknowledgement 167
8.7 References 167
8.8 Appendix: nomenclature 168

9 Intelligent sales forecasting for fashion retailing using harmony search algorithms and extreme learning machines 170
W. K. Wong, The Hong Kong Polytechnic University, China and Z. X. Guo, Sichuan University, China

9.1 Introduction 170
9.2 Hybrid intelligent model for medium-term fashion sales forecasting 174
9.3 Evaluating model performance with real sales data 180
9.4 Experimental results and analysis 182
9.5 Assessing forecasting performance 190
9.6 Conclusions 193
9.7 Acknowledgement 194
9.8 References 194

10 Intelligent product cross-selling system in fashion retailing using radio frequency identification (RFID) technology, fuzzy logic and rule-based expert system 196
W. K. Wong and S. Y. S. Leung, The Hong Kong Polytechnic University, China, Z. X. Guo, Sichuan University, China and Z. H. Zeng and P. Y. Mok, The Hong Kong Polytechnic University, China

10.1 Introduction 196
10.2 Radio frequency identification (RFID)-enabled smart dressing system (SDS) 200
10.3 Intelligent product cross-selling system (IPCS) 204
10.4 Implementation of the RFID-enabled SDS and IPCS 212
10.5 Evaluation of the RFID-enabled SDS 215
10.6 Assessing the use of RFID technology in fashion retailing 219
10.7 Conclusions 221
10.8 Acknowledgement 222
10.9 Notes 222
10.10 References 222

Index *225*

Woodhead Publishing Series in Textiles

1 **Watson's textile design and colour Seventh edition**
Edited by Z. Grosicki
2 **Watson's advanced textile design**
Edited by Z. Grosicki
3 **Weaving Second edition**
P. R. Lord and M. H. Mohamed
4 **Handbook of textile fibres Volume 1: Natural fibres**
J. Gordon Cook
5 **Handbook of textile fibres Volume 2: Man-made fibres**
J. Gordon Cook
6 **Recycling textile and plastic waste**
Edited by A. R. Horrocks
7 **New fibers Second edition**
T. Hongu and G. O. Phillips
8 **Atlas of fibre fracture and damage to textiles Second edition**
J. W. S. Hearle, B. Lomas and W. D. Cooke
9 **Ecotextile '98**
Edited by A. R. Horrocks
10 **Physical testing of textiles**
B. P. Saville
11 **Geometric symmetry in patterns and tilings**
C. E. Horne
12 **Handbook of technical textiles**
Edited by A. R. Horrocks and S. C. Anand
13 **Textiles in automotive engineering**
W. Fung and J. M. Hardcastle
14 **Handbook of textile design**
J. Wilson
15 **High-performance fibres**
Edited by J. W. S. Hearle
16 **Knitting technology Third edition**
D. J. Spencer
17 **Medical textiles**
Edited by S. C. Anand
18 **Regenerated cellulose fibres**
Edited by C. Woodings

19 **Silk, mohair, cashmere and other luxury fibres**
Edited by R. R. Franck
20 **Smart fibres, fabrics and clothing**
Edited by X. M. Tao
21 **Yarn texturing technology**
J. W. S. Hearle, L. Hollick and D. K. Wilson
22 **Encyclopedia of textile finishing**
H-K. Rouette
23 **Coated and laminated textiles**
W. Fung
24 **Fancy yarns**
R. H. Gong and R. M. Wright
25 **Wool: Science and technology**
Edited by W. S. Simpson and G. Crawshaw
26 **Dictionary of textile finishing**
H-K. Rouette
27 **Environmental impact of textiles**
K. Slater
28 **Handbook of yarn production**
P. R. Lord
29 **Textile processing with enzymes**
Edited by A. Cavaco-Paulo and G. Gübitz
30 **The China and Hong Kong denim industry**
Y. Li, L. Yao and K. W. Yeung
31 **The World Trade Organization and international denim trading**
Y. Li, Y. Shen, L. Yao and E. Newton
32 **Chemical finishing of textiles**
W. D. Schindler and P. J. Hauser
33 **Clothing appearance and fit**
J. Fan, W. Yu and L. Hunter
34 **Handbook of fibre rope technology**
H. A. McKenna, J. W. S. Hearle and N. O'Hear
35 **Structure and mechanics of woven fabrics**
J. Hu
36 **Synthetic fibres: nylon, polyester, acrylic, polyolefin**
Edited by J. E. McIntyre
37 **Woollen and worsted woven fabric design**
E. G. Gilligan
38 **Analytical electrochemistry in textiles**
P. Westbroek, G. Priniotakis and P. Kiekens
39 **Bast and other plant fibres**
R. R. Franck
40 **Chemical testing of textiles**
Edited by Q. Fan
41 **Design and manufacture of textile composites**
Edited by A. C. Long
42 **Effect of mechanical and physical properties on fabric hand**
Edited by H. M. Behery

43 **New millennium fibers**
T. Hongu, M. Takigami and G. O. Phillips
44 **Textiles for protection**
Edited by R. A. Scott
45 **Textiles in sport**
Edited by R. Shishoo
46 **Wearable electronics and photonics**
Edited by X. M. Tao
47 **Biodegradable and sustainable fibres**
Edited by R. S. Blackburn
48 **Medical textiles and biomaterials for healthcare**
Edited by S. C. Anand, M. Miraftab, S. Rajendran and J. F. Kennedy
49 **Total colour management in textiles**
Edited by J. Xin
50 **Recycling in textiles**
Edited by Y. Wang
51 **Clothing biosensory engineering**
Y. Li and A. S. W. Wong
52 **Biomechanical engineering of textiles and clothing**
Edited by Y. Li and D. X-Q. Dai
53 **Digital printing of textiles**
Edited by H. Ujiie
54 **Intelligent textiles and clothing**
Edited by H. R. Mattila
55 **Innovation and technology of women's intimate apparel**
W. Yu, J. Fan, S. C. Harlock and S. P. Ng
56 **Thermal and moisture transport in fibrous materials**
Edited by N. Pan and P. Gibson
57 **Geosynthetics in civil engineering**
Edited by R. W. Sarsby
58 **Handbook of nonwovens**
Edited by S. Russell
59 **Cotton: Science and technology**
Edited by S. Gordon and Y-L. Hsieh
60 **Ecotextiles**
Edited by M. Miraftab and A. R. Horrocks
61 **Composite forming technologies**
Edited by A. C. Long
62 **Plasma technology for textiles**
Edited by R. Shishoo
63 **Smart textiles for medicine and healthcare**
Edited by L. Van Langenhove
64 **Sizing in clothing**
Edited by S. Ashdown
65 **Shape memory polymers and textiles**
J. Hu
66 **Environmental aspects of textile dyeing**
Edited by R. Christie

67 **Nanofibers and nanotechnology in textiles**
Edited by P. Brown and K. Stevens
68 **Physical properties of textile fibres Fourth edition**
W. E. Morton and J. W. S. Hearle
69 **Advances in apparel production**
Edited by C. Fairhurst
70 **Advances in fire retardant materials**
Edited by A. R. Horrocks and D. Price
71 **Polyesters and polyamides**
Edited by B. L. Deopura, R. Alagirusamy, M. Joshi and B. S. Gupta
72 **Advances in wool technology**
Edited by N. A. G. Johnson and I. Russell
73 **Military textiles**
Edited by E. Wilusz
74 **3D fibrous assemblies: Properties, applications and modelling of three-dimensional textile structures**
J. Hu
75 **Medical and healthcare textiles**
Edited by S. C. Anand, J. F. Kennedy, M. Miraftab and S. Rajendran
76 **Fabric testing**
Edited by J. Hu
77 **Biologically inspired textiles**
Edited by A. Abbott and M. Ellison
78 **Friction in textile materials**
Edited by B. S. Gupta
79 **Textile advances in the automotive industry**
Edited by R. Shishoo
80 **Structure and mechanics of textile fibre assemblies**
Edited by P. Schwartz
81 **Engineering textiles: Integrating the design and manufacture of textile products**
Edited by Y. E. El-Mogahzy
82 **Polyolefin fibres: Industrial and medical applications**
Edited by S. C. O. Ugbolue
83 **Smart clothes and wearable technology**
Edited by J. McCann and D. Bryson
84 **Identification of textile fibres**
Edited by M. Houck
85 **Advanced textiles for wound care**
Edited by S. Rajendran
86 **Fatigue failure of textile fibres**
Edited by M. Miraftab
87 **Advances in carpet technology**
Edited by K. Goswami
88 **Handbook of textile fibre structure Volume 1 and Volume 2**
Edited by S. J. Eichhorn, J. W. S. Hearle, M. Jaffe and T. Kikutani
89 **Advances in knitting technology**
Edited by K-F. Au
90 **Smart textile coatings and laminates**
Edited by W. C. Smith

91 **Handbook of tensile properties of textile and technical fibres**
Edited by A. R. Bunsell
92 **Interior textiles: Design and developments**
Edited by T. Rowe
93 **Textiles for cold weather apparel**
Edited by J. T. Williams
94 **Modelling and predicting textile behaviour**
Edited by X. Chen
95 **Textiles, polymers and composites for buildings**
Edited by G. Pohl
96 **Engineering apparel fabrics and garments**
J. Fan and L. Hunter
97 **Surface modification of textiles**
Edited by Q. Wei
98 **Sustainable textiles**
Edited by R. S. Blackburn
99 **Advances in yarn spinning technology**
Edited by C. A. Lawrence
100 **Handbook of medical textiles**
Edited by V. T. Bartels
101 **Technical textile yarns**
Edited by R. Alagirusamy and A. Das
102 **Applications of nonwovens in technical textiles**
Edited by R. A. Chapman
103 **Colour measurement: Principles, advances and industrial applications**
Edited by M. L. Gulrajani
104 **Fibrous and composite materials for civil engineering applications**
Edited by R. Fangueiro
105 **New product development in textiles: Innovation and production**
Edited by L. Horne
106 **Improving comfort in clothing**
Edited by G. Song
107 **Advances in textile biotechnology**
Edited by V. A. Nierstrasz and A. Cavaco-Paulo
108 **Textiles for hygiene and infection control**
Edited by B. McCarthy
109 **Nanofunctional textiles**
Edited by Y. Li
110 **Joining textiles: Principles and applications**
Edited by I. Jones and G. Stylios
111 **Soft computing in textile engineering**
Edited by A. Majumdar
112 **Textile design**
Edited by A. Briggs-Goode and K. Townsend
113 **Biotextiles as medical implants**
Edited by M. King and B. Gupta
114 **Textile thermal bioengineering**
Edited by Y. Li

115 **Woven textile structure**
B. K. Behera and P. K. Hari
116 **Handbook of textile and industrial dyeing Volume 1: Principles, processes and types of dyes**
Edited by M. Clark
117 **Handbook of textile and industrial dyeing Volume 2: Applications of dyes**
Edited by M. Clark
118 **Handbook of natural fibres. Volume 1: Types, properties and factors affecting breeding and cultivation**
Edited by R. Kozłowski
119 **Handbook of natural fibres. Volume 2: Processing and applications**
Edited by R. Kozłowski
120 **Functional textiles for improved performance, protection and health**
Edited by N. Pan and G. Sun
121 **Computer technology for textiles and apparel**
Edited by J. Hu
122 **Advances in military textiles and personal equipment**
Edited by E. Sparks
123 **Specialist yarn and fabric structures**
Edited by R. H. Gong
124 **Handbook of sustainable textile production**
M. I. Tobler-Rohr
125 **Woven textiles: Principles, developments and applications**
Edited by K. Gandhi
126 **Textiles and fashion: Materials design and technology**
Edited by R. Sinclair
127 **Industrial cutting of textile materials**
I. Viļumsone-Nemes
128 **Colour design: Theories and applications**
Edited by J. Best
129 **False twist textured yarns**
C. Atkinson
130 **Modelling, simulation and control of the dyeing process**
R. Shamey and X. Zhao
131 **Process control in textile manufacturing**
Edited by A. Majumdar, A. Das, R. Alagirusamy and V. K. Kothari
132 **Understanding and improving the durability of textiles**
Edited by P. A. Annis
133 **Smart textiles for protection**
Edited by R. A. Chapman
134 **Functional nanofibers and applications**
Edited by Q. Wei
135 **The global textile and clothing industry: Technological advances and future challenges**
Edited by R. Shishoo
136 **Simulation in textile technology: Theory and applications**
Edited by D. Veit

137 **Pattern cutting for clothing using CAD: How to use Lectra Modaris pattern cutting software**
M. Stott

138 **Advances in the dyeing and finishing of technical textiles**
M. L. Gulrajani

139 **Multidisciplinary know-how for smart textile development**
T. Kirstein

140 **Handbook of fire resistant textiles**
Edited by F. Selcen Kilinc

141 **Handbook of footwear design and manufacture**
Edited by A. Luximon

142 **Textile-led design for the active ageing population**
Edited by J. McCann and D. Bryson

143 **Optimizing decision making in the apparel supply chain using artificial intelligence (AI): From production to retail**
W. K. Wong, Z. X. Guo and S. Y. S. Leung

144 **Mechanisms of flat weaving technology**
V. Choogin, P. Bandara and E. Chepelyuk

145 **Innovative jacquard textile design using digital technologies**
F. Ng and J. Zhou

146 **Advances in shape memory polymers**
J. Hu

147 **Clothing manufacture management: A systematic approach to planning, scheduling and control**
J. Gersak

148 **Anthropometry, apparel sizing and design**
D. Gupta and N. Zakaria

Preface

Practitioners in manufacturing and retail enterprises in the fashion industry, ranging from senior to front line management, constantly face complex and critical decisions. These decisions include site selection for manufacturing plant, production planning and scheduling, marker planning, cut order planning, production line balancing control, sales forecasting, recommendations about fashion trends and so on. Traditionally, such decisions depended on their experience and judgement. However, as the market has shifted to short production runs to meet rapidly changing demand, and costs have been squeezed in favour of just-in-time production methods, these decisions have become more complex. At the same time, apparel processing has become more automated and integrated, allowing greater control of the supply chain.

Recently, artificial intelligence (AI) techniques have received increasing attention from both practitioners and researchers in the apparel industry, and have been utilized to handle a variety of decision-making processes in apparel supply chain operations. A number of AI techniques, such as neural networks, genetic algorithms, fuzzy logic and evolutionary strategies, have been applied successfully. The ten chapters of this book provide a detailed coverage of the fundamentals and application of various artificial intelligence techniques to assist decision makers in tackling key problems in the apparel supply chain. Chapter 1 discusses a range of key problems faced by apparel enterprises in apparel supply chain operations. Chapter 2 introduces the fundamentals of the main AI techniques which have been used in solving decision-making problems. The remaining eight chapters show how key problems in the apparel supply chain can be solved and solutions optimized by use of AI techniques.

The authors wish to express their sincere thanks to K.F. Au, S.F. Chan, J.T. Fan, W.H. Ip, C.K. Kwong, P.Y. Mok, X.X. Wang and X.H. Zeng for their contributions of material to individual chapters.

Dr Calvin Wong
Associate Professor
Institute of Textiles and Clothing
The Hong Kong Polytechnic University
Hunghom, Kowloon
Hong Kong
China
E-mail: calvin.wong@polyu.edu.hk

1
Understanding key decision points in the apparel supply chain

W. K. WONG, The Hong Kong Polytechnic University, China

DOI: 10.1533/9780857097842.1

Abstract: In the apparel supply chain, a range of key decisions are always faced by apparel enterprises. These decisions, including site selection for establishing manufacturing plant, production planning and scheduling, line balancing, sales forecasting, etc., rely on the experience and subjective assessment of management and decision makers. As the apparel industry is characterized by short product life cycles, volatile customer demands and tremendous product varieties, such decisions have become more complex. This chapter will discuss these key decision points.

Key words: plant location, production planning and scheduling, marker planning, cut order planning, spreading, cutting, line balancing, sales forecasting, cross-selling and up-selling.

1.1 Introduction

Apparel manufacturers and retailers in the fashion industry face a range of key decisions, including selection of plant locations, production planning and scheduling, marker planning, cut order planning, apparel assembly line balancing, retail sales forecasting and marketing. Traditionally, such decisions depended on the experience and judgement of key staff. However, as the market has shifted to short production runs to meet rapidly changing customer demands, and costs have been squeezed in favour of just-in-time production methods, these decisions have become more complex. At the same time, production has become more automated and integrated, allowing greater control of the supply chain. In this chapter, key decisions in the apparel supply chain will be discussed.

1.2 Selection of plant locations

Apparel manufacturers' direct investment and joint ventures in developing regions have grown rapidly in the past few decades. The choice of plant locations for foreign direct investment is an important decision. Non-optimized selection can adversely affect a plant's performance in terms of productivity, manufacturing and logistics costs. Selection of a proper plant location is thus crucial. In the case of establishing overseas plants, apparel manufacturers should consider costs, profits and other intractable factors, such as social environment, political stability, legality, technology, and micro-environmental factors, including customers, competitors and suppliers. Most manufacturers have difficulties in decision making due to vague and subjective measures, particularly for variables not represented by objective values, such as country risk and community facilities. The decision of plant locations thus mostly relies on the intuition and assessment of manufacturers.

1.3 Production scheduling and assembly line balancing control

The current competitive market environment causes difficulties in scheduling and line balancing control in the modern apparel industry.

1.3.1 Production scheduling

In today's apparel industry, fashion products require a significant amount of customization due to differences in body measurements, diverse style preferences and replacement cycles. Apparel manufacturers are usually given a short production lead-time, tight delivery dates and small quantities with frequent style changes. To cope with the increasing demand for product customization, the quantity of garments per production order tends to be smaller and thus the number of production orders is higher.

It is necessary for apparel supply chains to be responsive to the ever-changing fashion markets by producing smaller jobs in order to provide customers with timely and customized products. Because of ever-increasing global market competition, apparel manufacturers have to improve their production performance continuously to be more competitive. Effective production planning and scheduling (PPS) plays a significant role in maximizing resource utilization and shortening the production lead time. As PPS decisions mostly rely on production planners' *ad hoc* assessment and intuition, they may not be consistent or optimized even under similar conditions. All this makes it more difficult for manufacturers to make effective PPS decisions.

In the real-life production environment, various uncertainties often occur, such as customer orders and processing time. An estimate not conforming to industrial practice can lead to an unsatisfactory scheduling solution. Without considering uncertainties, it is difficult to produce an optimized production schedule and thus hard to achieve optimal performance. For example, if a schedule fails to factor in possible future orders, rush orders can disrupt the production of orders which have already been scheduled.

Some commercial PPS systems only provide a platform for conducting PPS arrangements, but cannot automatically provide scientific and optimized solutions. PPS decisions in the apparel industry still rely heavily on production schedulers' experience, intuition and assessment rather than a scientific and systematic approach.

1.3.2 Assembly line balancing control

The assembly sewing process is the most labour-intensive part of apparel manufacturing. The progressive bundle unit system is common in sewing room design. Recently, many manufacturers have installed unit production systems as a means to improve efficiency and effectiveness. Assembly involves a set of workstations in which a specific task of a pre-defined sequence is processed.

In order to achieve a balanced line before production, sewing line supervisors usually assign one or more sewing operatives to each task based on the standard time required to complete the task. However, it is difficult to achieve a perfectly balanced line because the production rate of each workstation is different. Imbalance occurs due to various factors, including fluctuation in operative efficiency, frequent changes of product styles, order size, prior experience and unexpected factors, such as absenteeism and machine breakdown. Line balancing control is required to smooth away bottlenecks.

The balance control of an apparel assembly line relies heavily on the shop-floor expert's knowledge, experience and intuition. The effectiveness of a decision depends on the subjective and *ad hoc* assessment of production line supervisors. Small order size and frequent changes of styles can make the matter even worse for optimal production control. With the recent development and adoption of real-time shop-floor data capture systems, real-time production statistics and progress reports can be generated to assist production line supervisors in line balancing control and bottleneck elimination. However, their decisions may not be consistent even under similar conditions and may thus be non-optimal.

1.4 Cutting room

The key decision points in the cutting room of apparel manufacture include cut order planning, marker planning, and spreading and cutting scheduling.

1.4.1 Cut order planning

In apparel supply chains, fabric is the single largest contributor to garment costs. Approximately 50–60% of manufacturing costs can be attributed to fabric. Apart from fabric, labour and factory operation costs have also been continuously increasing while selling prices of apparel products have been falling, which presents a great challenge to apparel manufacturers to adopt quick response strategies to manufacture and deliver apparel products to retailers while maximizing fabric utilization rates (i.e. minimizing material costs) and minimizing labour and manufacturing costs.

Cut order planning (COP) is the first stage in the production workflow of a typical apparel manufacturing company upon receiving a production order from a client (Fig. 1.1). It is the process to determine the number of markers needed, the

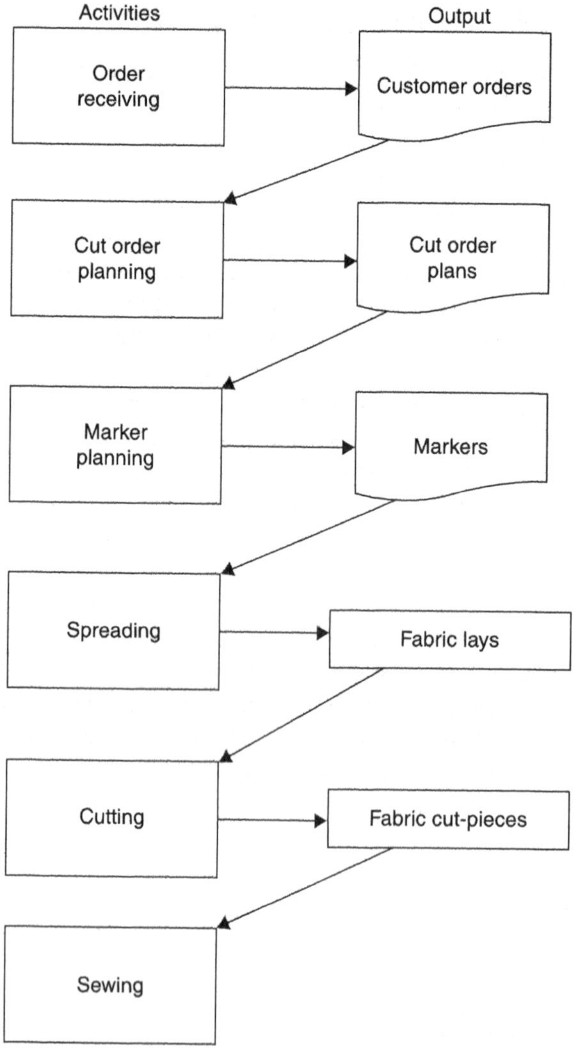

1.1 Schematic workflow of activities of a fabric-cutting department of a typical apparel manufacturing company.

number of garment sizes in each marker, and the number of fabric plies to be cut from each marker. Markers are the output of marker planning, which is the operation following COP. Figure 1.2 shows a marker planning process using commercial computing to arrange all patterns of component parts of one or more garments on a piece of marker paper (Fig. 1.3). The third operation is fabric-spreading, in which fabric pieces are superimposed to become a fabric lay on a cutting table (Fig. 1.4). The last operation is fabric-cutting. Garment pieces are cut out of fabric lays according to the pattern lines of component parts of one or more

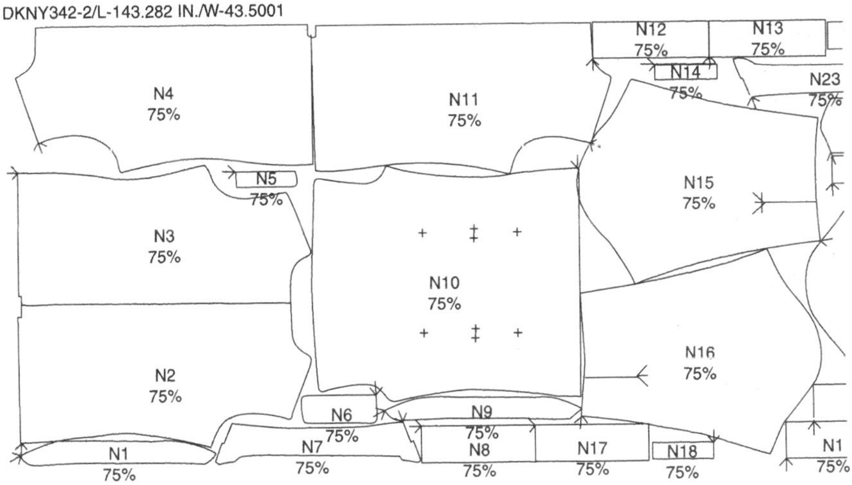

1.2 Example of marker paper.

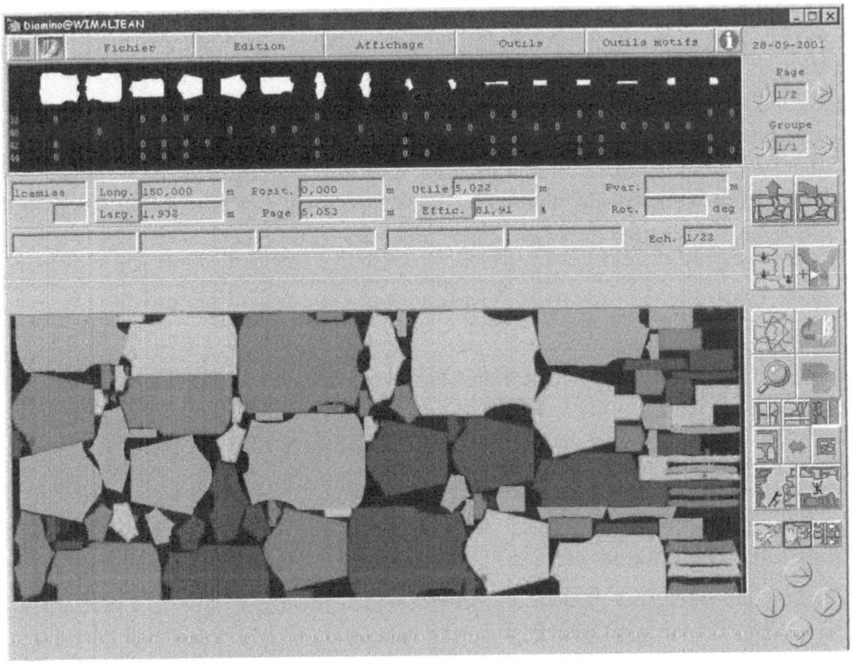

1.3 Marker planning process using commercial computing software.

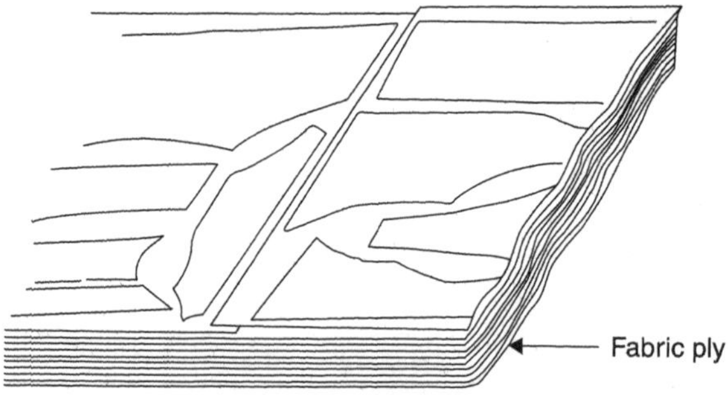

1.4 Fabric lay composed of fabric plies after spreading.

garments on the marker, and then assembled by the sewing department as a finished garment.

COP, the most upstream activity in apparel manufacturing, plays a significant role in affecting fabric and manufacturing costs in the cutting department. Based on the requirements of customer orders in terms of style, quantity, size and colour, it seeks to minimize total production costs by developing cutting orders with respect to material, machinery and labour.

After COP and marker planning, spreading and cutting are executed in the cutting room, and time and costs required for these two operations are determined by COPs. A good plan can improve fabric utilization rates.

The COP usually begins with a retail order comprising quantities, sizes and colours of garments to be manufactured. The following example demonstrates how a COP is derived. For simplicity, only quantities and sizes of garments are considered. The details of the customer order are as follows:

Size	Small	Medium	Large
Quantity (in pieces)	300	600	400

The constraints on fabric lay dimensions are:

- Maximum number of plies for each lay: 75
- Maximum number of garments marked on each marker: 5

The maximum number of garments produced per lay is 5 × 75 = 375 pieces and the number of garments required by the customers is 300 + 600 + 400 = 1300 pieces. Therefore, the theoretical minimum number of lays is 1300/375 = 3.47, which gives a practical minimum of four lays to cut the order. If the order is cut at the lowest cost, the lays need to be as long and deep as possible. One of the possible solutions is:

Small	Small	Small	Small	Small	Lay 1: 60 plies
Medium	Medium	Medium	Large	Large	Lay 2: 75 plies
Medium	Medium	Medium	Large	Large	Lay 3: 75 plies
Medium	Medium	Medium	Large	Large	Lay 4: 50 plies

An alternative to lay 1 is to have a 4-garment marker and spread 75 plies, which could reduce cutting costs but is rejected on the grounds of fabric costs, since there would be 15 more plies and high fabric end loss occurring on both ends of each fabric ply (more plies mean greater end loss). This solution demonstrates that sizes Medium and Large are in the ratio of 3:2. The marker for lay 2 can also be used for lays 3 and 4, thus reducing marker making costs.

This example shows that numerous possible COP solutions can be generated. The COP becomes more difficult when the numbers of garments and sizes increase, and can be further complicated when the parameter of colour is considered in the plan. In addition, labour is needed to operate spreading and cutting machines. As cut-pieces are transported to the sewing room for garment assembly, COP needs to consider the fulfilment of quantities of cut-pieces demanded from the downstream sewing room.

Current industry approaches to generating the COP range from manual *ad hoc* procedures by cut order planners to commercial software. However, many apparel manufacturers still use rather primitive methods and rely on planners' expertise and assessment to produce plans. Therefore, an optimal COP cannot always be guaranteed. Commercial COP software is available for use, but COP heuristics are usually kept confidential by proprietors. Apart from generating a COP with the right garment quantity, size and colour, there is little room for minimizing material, machine and labour costs.

1.4.2 Marker planning

In an apparel manufacturing workflow, marker planning is a critical operation in the cutting room, in which garment pattern pieces of different sizes and styles are laid out on a sheet of paper with fixed width and arbitrary length in order to achieve the highest marker efficiency. The layout is called a *marker* (Fig. 1.2) and always contains areas of unusable fabric due to the irregular shapes of pattern pieces. Therefore, minimization of fabric wastage is crucial to costs reduction. Current automated marker planning systems fall short of human performance by 5–10% in marker efficiency. Such ineffective performance, compared with a human expert, makes the adoption of automatic marker planning uneconomical because a 0.1% difference in marker efficiency implies an annual increase of millions of dollars in material costs. Most textile and clothing manufacturers thus abandon automatic marking and use only interactive approaches to high marker efficiency. Figure 1.3 shows a marker planning process using commercial computing to arrange all patterns of component parts of one or more garments on a piece of marker paper. Experience and skills are thus the critical factors in marker efficiency. Time, effort and resources are required to train a skilful marker planner even when a computerized marker planning system is in place.

1.4.3 Spreading and cutting scheduling

In an apparel manufacturing workflow, spreading and cutting are the two operations following COP and marker planning. Effective upstream fabric spreading and cutting operations ensure the smoothness of downstream operations, such as sewing, finishing and packaging, and are therefore important to the overall efficiency of apparel manufacturing and thus the supply chain.

Between the late 1960s and the early 1970s, apparel equipment suppliers introduced computerized cutting technology. The continuing demands by apparel manufacturers for greater accuracy in the cutting room, faster throughput and greater cost savings made computerized cutting machines popular in these two decades. However, the computerized cutting system may not be managed in the most efficient way. Once a decision is made to install automatic spreading and computerized cutting machines, more time and effort must be invested in scheduling of spreading and cutting, since the throughput time of spreading and cutting operations becomes shorter. Thus, it is significant to have an optimized sequence for spreading fabric lays; otherwise, idle time can appear on spreading and cutting machines. However, the production schedule is always determined in a heuristic way by cutting-room management, who solve scheduling problems in such a way that solutions are feasible but not necessarily optimal. In order to achieve daily production targets, operators and machines have to work overtime, which in turn increases overall production costs.

The procedure of a computerized cutting system (Fig. 1.5) is to spread a fabric lay on a spreading table and move it to the cutting machine for cutting. Once the fabric lay is cut, the cut fabric is moved to a bundling table. The cutting machine is then moved laterally from the existing spreading table to another table for cutting another fabric lay. In a real-life environment, a computerized cutting machine is set up to serve two to four spreading tables, since the cutting time of a fabric lay by a computerized cutting machine is less than a quarter to a third of the spreading time of the same fabric lay. Since each fabric lay has different quantities of plies to be spread and different numbers of garment sizes on the marker, the standard spreading time and cutting time vary with each fabric lay and thus the progress of each spreading table is different. With the constraint on spreading

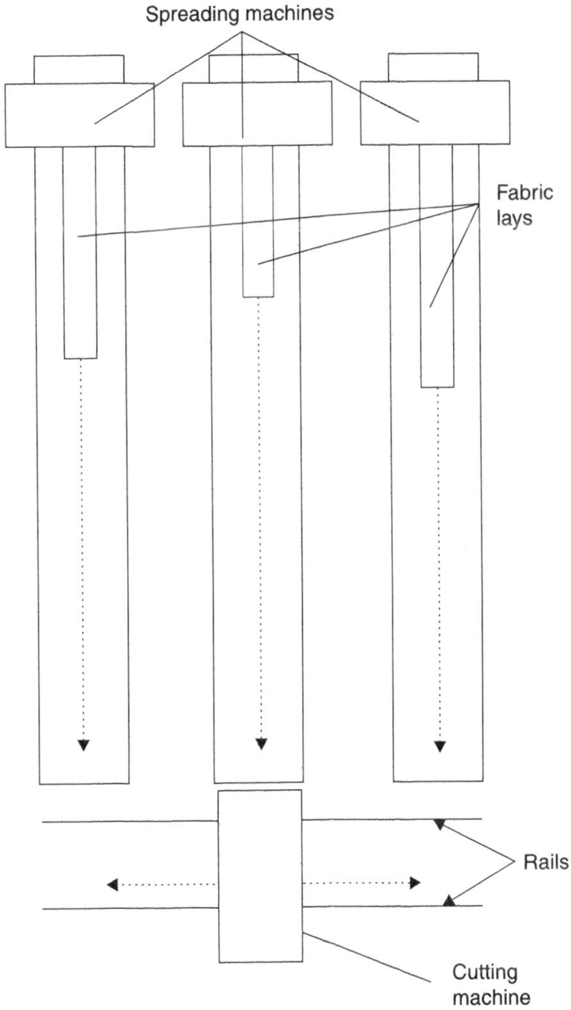

1.5 Operating procedures of a computerized cutting system.

space of each spreading table, line balancing always happens between spreading and cutting. In the absence of a good spreading and cutting schedule, there exists a scenario in which many spread fabric lays occupy all spreading tables waiting to be cut and there is no more space on spreading tables for another spread. Another scenario is that no fabric lay is ready for cutting and thus the cutting machine is idle, especially when some large fabric lays with a greater number of fabric plies are spread on three spreading tables at the same time. Thus, a good spreading and cutting sequence is vital to a smooth production flow and machine utilization in the cutting room.

1.5 Retailing

Fashion retailers need to forecast sales accurately as well as expand their customer base and increase profit from existing customers.

1.5.1 Fashion sales forecasting

Sales forecasting is the foundation for various phases of operation planning. It is a significant task in supply chain management under current dynamic market demands and thus greatly affects fashion retailers in various ways. Without accurate and reliable sales forecasts, operations can only respond retroactively, which causes poor production planning, lost orders, inadequate customer services, and poorly utilized resources. Recent research has shown that effective sales forecasting enables improvement in supply chain performance. Because of ever-increasing global competition, sales forecasting plays an increasingly prominent role in supply chain management when profitability and long-term viability rely on effective and efficient sales forecasts. With regard to the fast-expanding Chinese market, the approximately 10% growth rate each year leads to a great increase in disposable income, which attracts more and more fashion retailing companies to enter this potential market, and thus the fashion retail industry becomes a blooming business.

The fashion retail business is characterized by short product life cycles, volatile customer demands and tremendous product varieties. Most fashion items are of strong seasonality. Uncertain customer demands in a frequently changing market environment and numerous explanatory variables that influence fashion sales cause an increase in irregularity or randomicity of sales data. Such distinct characteristics increase the complexity of sales forecasting in the fashion retail industry. For most fashion products, market demand is uncertain until the selling season has started. When the actual demand deviates from the forecast, fashion retailers may not have time to respond to changes. Stock outages may occur for certain styles or sizes of fashion products and thus affect the profitability for fashion retailers.

In fact, most fashion retailers still rely on forecasting professionals' assessment and experience for production planning and stocking decisions before the launch of their products. And, when these professionals (i.e. fashion buyers) leave, their replacements may fail to develop reliable sales forecasts without their predecessors' know-how. Currently, fashion retail enterprises usually make sourcing budgets on an annual and/or seasonal basis by forecasting the total sales amount of each fashion item. Then fashion buyers determine which items need to be purchased or produced in each fashion item category, which consists of multiple items with common attributes. In an enterprise, categories are usually unchanged, while items in each category frequently change in different selling seasons.

1.5.2 Cross-selling and up-selling

Today, the competition in fashion retail business is keener than ever. Fashion retailers realize the importance of retaining existing customers and gaining new ones. However, customers are likely to switch from one fashion brand to another in response to attractive and competitive offers. The competition for customers, particularly in mature markets, turns retailers into a revolving door of acquiring and losing customers. Fashion retailers currently adopt different strategies to retain customers, including better service quality, better business decisions, and identifying customers' purchasing behaviour through analysing transaction data. Various types of customer relationship management systems using data mining techniques have been developed to cater for the needs of these retailers, and allegedly enable retailers to make decisions concerning replenishment, inventory control, and marketing and promotion strategies. Through the use of data mining techniques, customers' purchasing behaviour can be analysed and new knowledge about retail business discovered. However, adoption is still limited, since the systems are not tailor-made for the fashion industry with its characteristic short cycles of fashion trends, volatile customer demands, and tremendous product and style varieties.

Fashion retailers are well aware that, in addition to expanding their customer base, they need to increase profitability obtained from their existing customers. It is suggested that cross-selling and up-selling strategies can increase the number of transactions per customer and consequently lead to growth of profits and customer loyalty. Cross-selling refers to sales of additional items to a customer in relation to items that he has already purchased. Up-selling is a process through which a customer is persuaded (usually by a salesman) to purchase an upgrade of his target item. To actualize these strategies, retailers inevitably make use of historical transaction data to identify customers' preferences and rely on sales staff for successful execution. However, historical data can become outdated and poorly reflect customers' tastes. Quality of salesmanship also varies widely between salesmen.

Recently, radio frequency identification (RFID) has emerged as a technology for data collection by reading tags from a distance without making contact, and thus is a powerful tool to collect customer data. An RFID system consists of three major components, namely RFID tags (transponders), an antenna and an RFID reader, and is usually interfaced to a computer database where product information is stored. Tags are attached to products and activated when the products are brought close to an antenna, and product codes are transmitted to the RFID reader. By relating received product codes to product details stored in the computer database, users can identify products and make use of the information for many business and management purposes.

In 2002, the New York Prada became the first documented RFID user to interact with in-store customers. The RFID technology was used in the fitting rooms by using a near-range reader to detect the RFID tag on each garment. The garments were located at a specific location inside the fitting room so that the detection devices, concealed behind walls, could read the signals from the tags. Then production information or a video clip showing a model wearing the garment on the catwalk was provided to customers inside the fitting rooms.

2

Fundamentals of artificial intelligence techniques for apparel management applications

Z. X. GUO, Sichuan University, China and W. K. WONG,
The Hong Kong Polytechnic University, China

DOI: 10.1533/9780857097842.13

Abstract: The fundamentals of artificial intelligence (AI) techniques are introduced briefly in this chapter. The definition, significance and classification of AI techniques are presented first. Some representative AI techniques, especially those which have been used in solving decision-making problems in the apparel supply chain operations, are then introduced to help readers understand AI techniques used in subsequent chapters. These techniques include rule-based expert systems, evolutionary optimization techniques, feedforward neural networks and fuzzy logic. Their relevant fundamentals are introduced, including their origins, fundamental characteristics, possible applications and the procedures of implementation.

Key words: expert system, evolutionary computation, neural network, fuzzy logic.

2.1 Artificial intelligence (AI) techniques: a brief overview

Artificial intelligence (AI) is a multidisciplinary subject which has attracted researchers from a variety of fields, such as computing, psychology, neuroscience, mathematics and linguistics. The popularity of AI techniques has been increasing rapidly in recent years; they currently cover a large variety of subfields in science and engineering, from general-purpose areas, such as decision-making, perception and logical reasoning, to specific tasks, such as robot control and disease diagnosis. AI techniques have received increasing attention from participants and researchers in the fashion industry over the last two decades, and have been utilized to handle a variety of decision-making processes in fashion supply chain operations, such as plant location selection, sewing assembly line balancing, production scheduling, marker making, sales forecasting and fashion recommendation.

2.1.1 Definition of AI

There is no precise definition of AI. Researchers from different fields define AI differently. Researchers from computer science are usually interested in the creation of intelligent systems and programs capable of reproducing human-like behavior, such as understanding languages and learning from experience. On the other hand, engineering researchers place more emphasis on using AI as a problem solver.

Russell and Norvig (1994) reviewed the definitions of AI and classified them into four categories, including systems that (1) think like humans; (2) act like humans; (3) think rationally; and (4) act rationally. According to these definitions, AI techniques have the abilities (1) to artificially simulate the human brain; (2) to act intelligently as a human; (3) to actively learn and adapt as a human; (4) to process languages and symbols; and (5) to perform general intelligent action.

In this book, AI is defined as the study of how computer programs (systems) simulate intelligent processes, including learning, reasoning, associative memory, and understanding symbolic information in context.

2.1.2 Uses of AI

Problem-solving techniques can be roughly classified as either traditional or AI. It is necessary to develop AI techniques because traditional techniques do not always solve scientific problems effectively due to ongoing scientific exploration. For example, they are ineffective in solving optimization problems with high problem complexity or large solution space.

Song *et al.* (1996) pointed out that 'the engineering goal of AI is to solve real-world problems using AI as a tool to simulate human problem-solving capabilities'. AI techniques promise effective solutions to various problems due to their abilities to emulate intelligent processes, as opposed to traditional techniques. AI is also an effective supplement to natural intelligence because it builds intelligence into computer systems. The systems can effectively execute particular tasks, such as robot control, which can reduce human labor and mistakes.

AI techniques have the capability to tackle a wide range of real-world problems, including modeling, classification, optimization and forecasting. These problems involve a large variety of application domains, including manufacturing and service industries, business and finance, computer science and telecommunications. Some real-world problems are very complex and intractable, such as production order planning, sewing assembly line balancing, and fashion sales forecasting.

2.1.3 Classification of AI techniques

AI techniques can be roughly divided into two categories: symbolic AI and computational intelligence. The former focuses on development of knowledge-based systems while the latter focuses on development of a set of nature-inspired computational approaches. The latter primarily includes evolutionary computations, artificial neural networks and fuzzy logic systems. A brief introduction to these techniques begins on the next page.

Knowledge-based systems

Knowledge consists of data and information, which are indispensable for drawing inferences and reaching conclusions. It can be implicit (e.g. practical skill or expertise) or explicit (e.g. theoretical understanding of a domain or a subject). Once knowledge is organized and represented in such a way that it can be identified by computer programs, it often generates decision-making solutions as good as or even better than human experts. Knowledge-based systems were developed on the basis of this concept.

Knowledge-based systems are tools for establishing applications that make logical inferences and decisions from their stored knowledge of the problem domain (Hembry, 1990), aiming at supporting human decision-making, learning and action. To construct a knowledge-based system, one needs to focus on the acquisition, accumulation, representation and use of knowledge specific to a particular task. From the perspective of the end user, a knowledge-based system consists of three core components:

- Knowledge base: contains highly specialized and problem-related knowledge, such as rules, frames, cases, facts and heuristics.
- Knowledge inference mechanism: provides solution recommendations for decision makers and problem solvers.
- User interface: bridges the gap between end users and the system, and entices more people to use the system with its user-friendliness.

There are two types of knowledge-based systems, expert systems and case-based reasoning systems, which have been widely applied in various fields, such as fashion matching recommendation, software engineering, computer vision, computer-aided design and production management. We will introduce the most popular knowledge-based system, the rule-based expert system, in Section 2.2.

Evolutionary computation

Evolutionary computation is an umbrella term for a range of evolutionary optimization techniques mainly inspired by optimum-seeking mechanisms from the real world, such as natural selection and genetic inheritance, which simulate evolution processes on a computer to iteratively improve the performance of solutions until an optimal (or feasible at least) solution is obtained.

Evolutionary optimization techniques make few or no assumptions about the problem being optimized. They are powerful in addressing complex optimization problems with large solution spaces and randomness, when traditional techniques fail to do so. These techniques are one of the fastest-growing areas of computer science and engineering, and are being increasingly widely applied to a variety of problems, ranging from practical applications in industry to leading-edge scientific research, such as large-scale production scheduling and stochastic combinatorial optimization.

Broadly speaking, evolutionary computation includes evolutionary algorithms, such as genetic algorithms and evolution strategies, and swarm intelligence, such as ant colony algorithms, particle swarm optimization, artificial immune systems and harmony search. We will introduce several representative evolutionary optimization techniques in the field of evolutionary computation in Section 2.3.

Neural network

An artificial neural network, usually called neural network (NN), is a computational model inspired by research into biological neural networks. An NN consists of a number of interconnected neurons (or nodes), which are analogous to biological neurons in the brain, according to some patterns of connectivity. In most cases, an NN is an adaptive system, which discovers the relationships between inputs and associated outputs by adjusting the network setting in terms of data patterns of training samples.

The history of NNs can be traced back to 1943, when physiologists McCulloch and Pitts established the model of a neuron as a binary linear threshold unit (McCulloch and Pitts, 1943). One of the most well-known features of NNs is that they can be used as universal approximators (Scarselli and Tsoi, 1998; Zhang *et al.*, 2012). In view of this feature, NNs have been widely applied to a variety of related problems, such as forecasting, modeling, classification and clustering.

To construct an NN, one needs to decide the following three issues:

- Network architecture, including the number of input neurons, the number of hidden layers and hidden neurons, the number of output neurons, and the interconnections among these neurons.
- Activation function, which determines the relationship between input and output of a neuron.
- Learning algorithm, which determines the connection weights among network neurons.

According to different settings of the above issues, there exist many types of NN, such as feedforward NNs (FNNs), recurrent NNs and random NNs. We will introduce FNNs in Section 2.4.

Fuzzy logic

The term 'fuzzy logic' emerged in the development of the fuzzy set theory by Professor Lofti Zadeh (1965) at the University of California. Fuzzy logic has two distinct meanings. In a narrow sense, it is a generalization of various many-value logics that have been investigated in the area of mathematical logic. In a broad sense, fuzzy logic serves mainly as a system of concepts, principles, and methods for handling modes of reasoning with imprecise information. The purpose of researching fuzzy logic in the narrow sense is to provide fuzzy logic in the broad sense with a sound foundation.

Fuzzy logic is often referred to as 'reasoning with uncertainty', and provides a mechanism to handle vague or imprecise data in human reasoning and communication so that precise deductions can be made. Natural languages have a position of centrality in human reasoning and communication, which are pervasively imprecise and involve various vague linguistic terms. Vagueness of a linguistic term is a kind of uncertainty caused by imprecise meaning instead of information deficiency. Fuzzy logic provides the capability of expressing imprecision in vague terms, which allows for approximate values and inferences as well as fuzzy or incompletely defined data as opposed to depending on crisp data, and also provides approximate solutions to problems that are hard for non-fuzzy methods to solve.

Fuzzy logic has achieved great success in a variety of applications over the last three decades. The most well-known applications have been in the area of control, ranging from simple control systems in consumer products (e.g. intelligent washing machines, air conditioners) to highly challenging control systems (e.g. voice-controlled robot helicopters). In addition, successful applications of fuzzy logic can also be found in manufacturing, transportation, image processing and computer vision, expert systems, decision-making, biological science and many other engineering and science areas.

2.2 Rule-based expert systems

Expert systems are computer programs that perform sophisticated decision tasks by emulating the decision-making abilities of human experts, and are built from explicit pieces of knowledge extracted from human experts. The extracted knowledge is a mixture of factual knowledge and heuristic knowledge, comprising intuition, judgement and logical inferences. Different representations have been proposed to represent knowledge effectively in an expert system, such as rules, semantics and frames, among which rules are the most commonly used. Expert systems using rules to represent knowledge are called rule-based expert systems.

2.2.1 Structure of rule-based expert systems

A general rule-based expert system consists of six components: knowledge base, knowledge acquisition facility, database, inference engine, explanation facility and user interface. A functional integration of these components is shown in Fig. 2.1. The functions of these components are described on the next page.

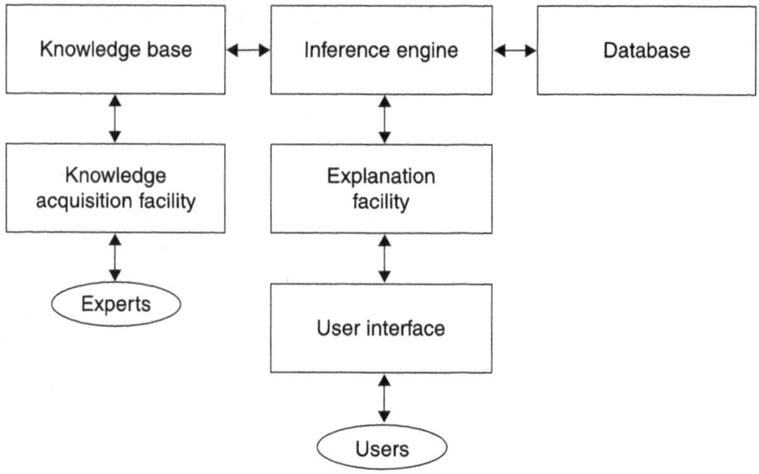

2.1 Architecture of a rule-based expert system.

- **Knowledge base**: A knowledge base stores knowledge, such as problem-solving rules and intuition, which a human expert might use in solving problems in a given problem domain. A knowledge base can combine the knowledge of multiple human experts. In a rule-based expert system, knowledge is represented as a set of IF-THEN rules. A rule is a conditional statement that links given conditions to conclusions or actions. Once the condition part of a rule is satisfied, the rule is fired and the conclusion part is executed.
- **Knowledge acquisition facility**: This component provides a convenient and efficient means for capturing all IF-THEN rules and stores them into the knowledge base. In some expert systems, it also provides an interactive way to enable a domain expert to input knowledge directly in runtime.
- **Database**: This component stores a set of facts which are used to match the IF-THEN rules stored in the knowledge base.
- **Inference engine**: This component carries out reasoning processes whereby the expert system reaches a solution, and links rules in the knowledge base with facts in the database. An inference engine decides which rules are satisfied, prioritizes them and executes those of the highest priority.
- **Explanation facility**: It enables a user to understand how the expert system arrives at its conclusions. Keeping track of the fired rules, the component presents a trace of reasoning that leads to a certain conclusion.
- **User interface**: It provides a mechanism to support communication between the user seeking a solution and the system. It is determined at the time of system design.

2.2.2 Rule-based knowledge representation

In a rule-based expert system, rules provide a formal way of representing expert knowledge, which can represent relations, recommendations, directives, strategies and heuristics (Durkin, 1994). A rule consists of two parts: the IF part, called the antecedent (premise or condition), and the THEN part, called the consequent (conclusion). The basic syntax of a rule is:

IF <antecedent>
THEN <consequent>

The antecedent and consequent of a rule consist of two parts: an object and its value, which are linked by an operator. The operator identifies an object and assigns a value. Operators, such as is, are, is not and are not, are usually used to assign a symbolic value to a linguistic term. Mathematical operators can also be used to define an object as numerical and assign it a numerical value. For example,

IF the tardiness of materials >10 days
THEN production rescheduling is required.

A rule can have multiple antecedents joined by logic operators AND (conjunction), or OR (disjunction), and multiple consequents joined by AND. For example,

IF the shirt color is white AND the pants are black
THEN the mix-and-match change is not required.

IF the tardiness of materials >5 days
THEN production rescheduling is required
AND penalty weight =100%.

2.2.3 Inference techniques

In a rule-based expert system, the inference engine models and performs the reasoning of a human expert by using a collection of IF-THEN rules. To achieve this, an inference technique is used to determine when rules should be fired and what solution can be finally reached. The inference technique compares each IF-THEN rule in the knowledge base with facts stored in the database. When the condition (IF) part of a rule matches a fact, the rule is fired and its action (THEN) part is executed. Inference techniques aim at forming several rules in succession to construct a logical sequence of deduction, which is known as chaining. Two types of inference technique are commonly used, including forward chaining and backward chaining, which are introduced on the next page.

Forward chaining

Forward chaining is a technique for gathering information and then inferring from it whatever can be inferred. The steps involved in forward chaining are described as follows.

- ***Step 1:*** Obtain problem information from the user and put it in the database.
- ***Step 2:*** Scan the rules in the knowledge base in pre-specified order to search for one whose antecedent (condition) matches the facts in the database.
- ***Step 3:*** Check if the rule is found in Step 2. If so, the rule is fired and the rule's conclusion part is added to the database.
- ***Step 4:*** Go to Step 2 to search for new matches until a solution is found or no further rules can be found.

It is clear that the order in which rules are fired is determined by the facts available to the inference engine at that stage. Thus, forward chaining is data-driven reasoning, which works well when a problem naturally begins by gathering information and then examining what can be deduced from it. However, in forward chaining, many rules may be fired even though they have nothing to do with the expected goal because forward chaining has no effective mechanism of recognizing and selecting which rules should not be used.

Backward chaining

Backward chaining is the opposite of forward chaining. It is goal-driven reasoning. In backward chaining, the rule-based expert system has a goal (a hypothetical solution) and the inference technique needs to find evidence to prove it. The steps involved in backward chaining are described as follows.

- ***Step 1:*** Search the rules in the knowledge base and look for one (or more) that contains the goal in its THEN part. This type of rule is called goal rule.
- ***Step 2:*** Check if the goal rule's IF (antecedent) part is listed in the database. If so, go to Step 5; otherwise, go to Step 3.
- ***Step 3:*** Set the antecedent not listed in the database as a new goal (also called subgoal) for proof.
- ***Step 4:*** Go to Step 1 until the system finds an antecedent that is not supported by any rule.
- ***Step 5:*** The rule is fired and the original goal is proved. The iterative process stops.

In backward chaining, the reasoning keeps the focus on the goal because it starts at the final step of a possibly long chain of reasoning. Backward chaining works well when the problem naturally starts by informing a hypothesis and examining if it can be proven.

In forward chaining and backward chaining, it is possible that no effective chaining can be formed to infer the original goal, which means that existing information (facts and rules) is insufficient and more facts or rules need to be provided. In addition, forward chaining and backward chaining can be combined to perform an inference task, which is usually used in applications where different tasks are naturally performed in either a data-driven or a goal-driven manner.

2.3 Evolutionary optimization techniques

The processes of optimum-seeking have been remarkably successful in lots of real-world phenomena, such as human evolution, food-seeking of ant colonies, and improvisation of musicians. By using stochastic heuristic individual searches and generation processes, these phenomena work toward a perfect individual to fill a particular environmental niche. It is naturally expected that evolutionary optimization processes can be created by modeling the behaviors of these phenomena. The evolutionary optimization techniques were thus developed to perform this function, which mimics the optimum-seeking processes of these phenomena in a computer program.

This section will introduce several representative evolutionary optimization techniques, including genetic algorithms (GA), evolution strategies (ES) and harmony searches (HS).

2.3.1 Optimum-seeking mechanism of evolutionary optimization techniques

Evolutionary optimization techniques have a similar optimum-seeking mechanism although they are inspired by different real-world phenomena. A general flowchart of evolutionary optimization techniques is shown in Fig. 2.2. The procedures involved are described as follows.

1. Generate initial individual population: Each solution individual is usually generated randomly based on pre-specified solution representation and population size.
2. Evaluate solution individual: Evaluate the performance (fitness) of solutions newly generated on the basis of a given performance measure.
3. Check stopping criteria: Check if stopping criteria are met. If so, return the best individual as the optimal solution; otherwise, go to the next loop for generating new individuals.
4. Generate new individuals: Each new individual is generated based on one or more individuals in the current population. Different evolutionary optimization techniques generate new individuals.
5. Form next individual population: A specified number of individuals are selected from the newly generated individuals and the current population to form the next population (also called offspring population).

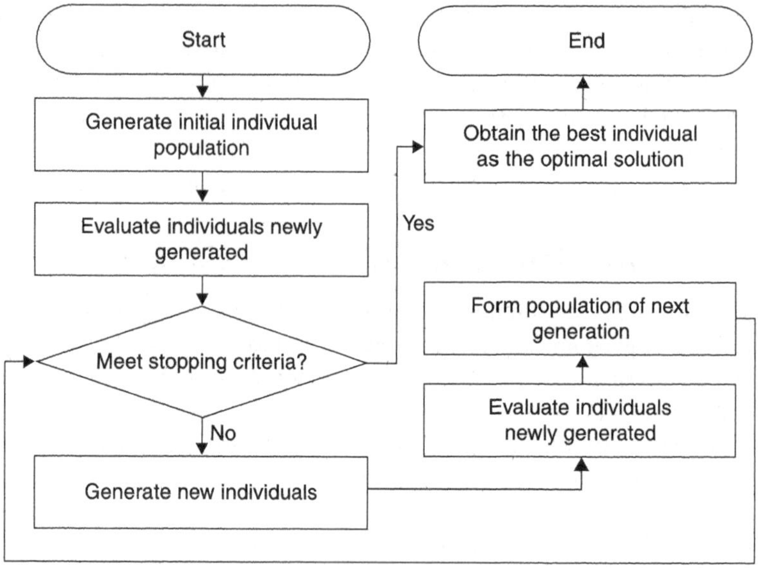

2.2 General flowchart of evolutionary optimization techniques.

To design and develop an evolutionary optimization technique for tackling a problem, one needs to make a variety of design decisions, such as:

- choosing a particular paradigm that is suited for the problem
- choosing an appropriate solution representation and population size
- choosing an appropriate method to generate new individuals
- choosing an appropriate mechanism to form the next population
- choosing an appropriate performance measure to evaluate individuals
- choosing an appropriate stopping criterion.

2.3.2 Brief introduction to genetic algorithm

The GA is the most popular technique in the family of evolutionary computation, which is inspired by the principles of genetics and natural selection – Darwin's 'survival of the fittest' theory. The origin of the GA can be traced back to the early 1950s, when several biologists used computer programs to perform simulations of biological systems (Goldberg, 1989). However, the popularization of GAs is accredited to the work (Holland, 1975) done in the late 1960s and early 1970s under the direction of John Holland.

The optimum-seeking mechanism of a GA is analogous to the biological evolutionary process. The GA operates on a population of chromosomes (also called individuals). Each chromosome represents a feasible solution to the problem investigated. Different representations have been developed to represent chromosomes, such as real-coded representation and order-based representation. According to evolutionary theories, only the chromosomes adapting to the environment in the parental population are likely to survive and generate offspring by transmitting their biological heredity to the offspring population (next population). The offspring chromosomes are generated by using a set of biologically inspired genetic operators, including selection, crossover and mutation. The offspring are supposed to inherit excellent genes from their parents so that the average quality of solutions is better than in previous generations.

Figure 2.3 shows the flowchart of a canonical GA. GAs work iteratively. Each single iteration is called a generation. In each generation, the fitness of each chromosome is evaluated and determined by the fitness function. When the fitness function value of a chromosome is larger, the chromosome becomes fitter, indicating that the chromosome has a bigger opportunity to survive in the next generation. This evolution process is repeated until some stopping criteria are met. Selection operators determine which chromosomes are selected for mating from the current generation. Crossover and mutation operators are employed to create offspring chromosomes based on chromosomes selected by selection operators. The entire set of generations is called a run. At the end of a run, one or more chromosomes with the highest fitness values are taken as optimal solutions.

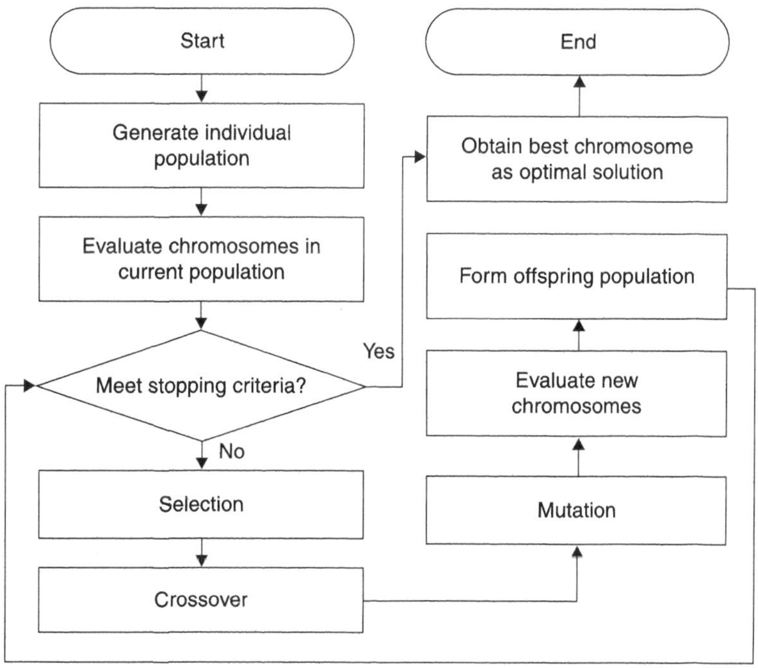

2.3 Flowchart of a canonical genetic algorithm (GA).

2.3.3 Brief introduction to evolution strategy

The evolutionary strategy (ES) is another intelligent optimization technique of mimicking natural evolution, which was invented by Ingo Rechenberg and Hans-Paul Schwefel in the early 1960s (Rochenberg, 1965; Schwefel, 1975) to solve parameter optimization problems.

The general flowchart of an ES is shown in Fig. 2.4, which is very similar to that of a GA. The only difference is that an ES uses only one genetic operator (mutation). The earliest ES model, termed as $(1+1)$-ES, was based on a population having one individual (chromosome) only. Generally ESs are based on the population of μ ($\mu > 1$) individuals, which makes them less prone to getting stuck in the local optima (Hansen and Kern, 2004). In these ESs, a new (offspring) individual is generated by randomly selecting a parental individual to undergo mutation. In each generation, λ offspring are generated. ESs can be classified into (μ,λ)-ES and $(\mu+\lambda)$-ES. The two types use different strategies to generate populations of the next offspring generation:

(μ,λ)-ES: The next population consists of μ best individuals from the population of λ newly generated offspring.

$(\mu+\lambda)$-ES: The next population consists of μ best individuals from μ parents and λ newly generated offspring.

The ES is modified to handle combinatorial optimization problems, although it was initially developed for continuous optimization. In addition, some researchers extended the ES to recombination, which leads to more general notation $(\mu/\rho,\lambda)$-ES. ρ refers to the number of parents involved in the generation of one offspring

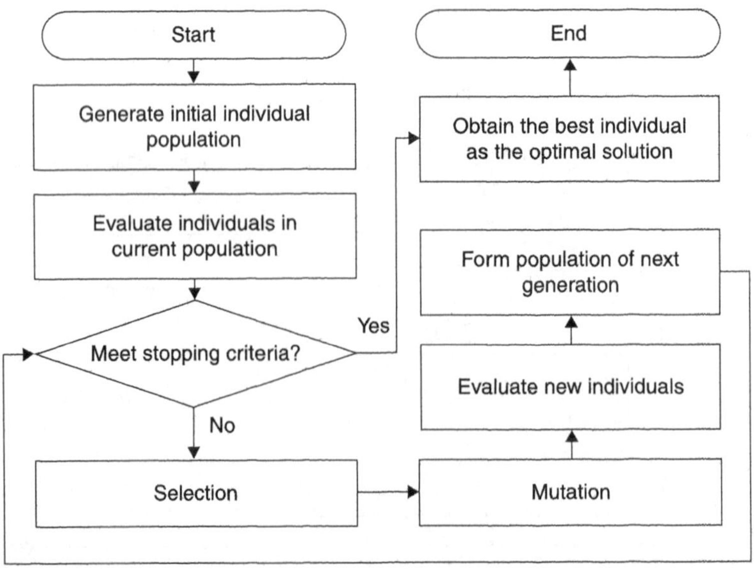

2.4 Flowchart of a canonical evolution strategy (ES).

(mixing number). For $\rho=1$, we have ES cases (μ,λ) and $(\mu+\lambda)$ without recombination. For $\rho>1$, we have ES cases with recombination. Like GAs facing different optimization problems, different individual representations and evolutionary operators in ESs are required to adapt themselves to these problems.

2.3.4 Brief introduction to harmony search

Some evolutionary optimization techniques do not originate in natural evolution. The HS is a relatively new evolutionary optimization algorithm developed by Geem *et al.* (2001), which is inspired by musicians' improvisation of their instruments' pitches to search for perfect harmony.

The HS generates a new individual (solution vector) by considering all existing vectors, whereas traditional evolutionary algorithms (such as ES and GA) only consider one or two parental individuals. This distinct feature of the HS increases the algorithm's flexibility so that it can generate better solutions than conventional mathematical methods or GA- and ES-based approaches (Lee and Geem, 2004; Mahdavi *et al.*, 2007).

The flowchart of an HS is shown in Fig. 2.5. The initial harmony memory is generated randomly, in which each harmony (individual, solution vector) v represents a distinct feasible solution of all decision variables. That is, v = $[v_1, v_2, \ldots, v_p]$. The performance (fitness) of each harmony is evaluated and determined by the fitness function. When the fitness function of a harmony is larger, the performance of the harmony is better. This evolution process is repeated until

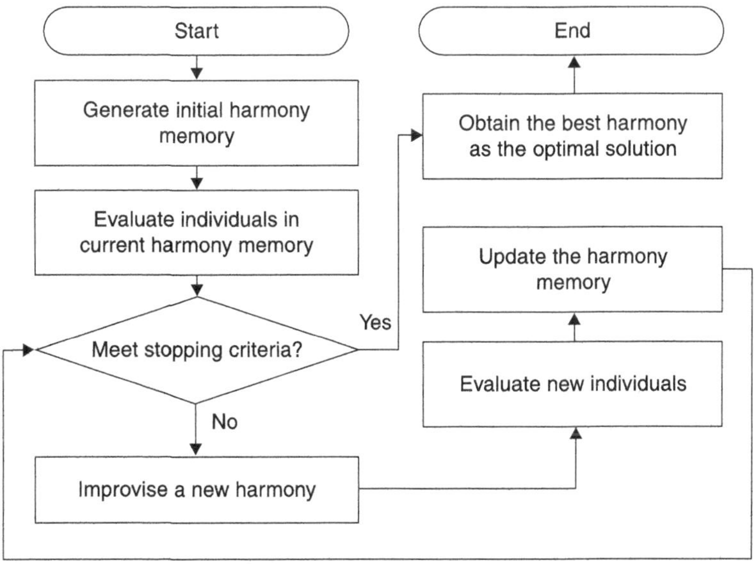

2.5 Flowchart of a harmony search (HS).

some stopping criteria are met. After the fitness values of all individuals in the population are calculated, two HS procedures, memory consideration and pitch adjustment, are used to improvise a new harmony (or generate a new solution vector). Generating a new harmony is called improvisation.

2.4 Feedforward neural networks (FNNs)

Feedforward neural networks (FNNs) are the most common type of NN, which have been used in a wide variety of real-world applications, including pattern recognition and classification, system identification and control, and forecasting. Applications of FNNs in fashion supply chain operations involve prediction, classification and model identification (Guo *et al.*, 2011).

2.4.1 Brief introduction to FNN

FNNs are a type of NN in which connections among units do not travel in a loop but in a single directed path. Typically, an FNN consists of an input layer of neurons (nodes), one or more hidden layers of neurons, and an output layer of neurons. The input layer and output layer form bookends for hidden layers of neurons. Signals are propagated from the input layer to hidden neurons and then onto output neurons, which output responses of the network to outside users. That is, signals only move in a forward direction on a layer-by-layer basis. Figure 2.6 shows a typical FNN with one hidden layer.

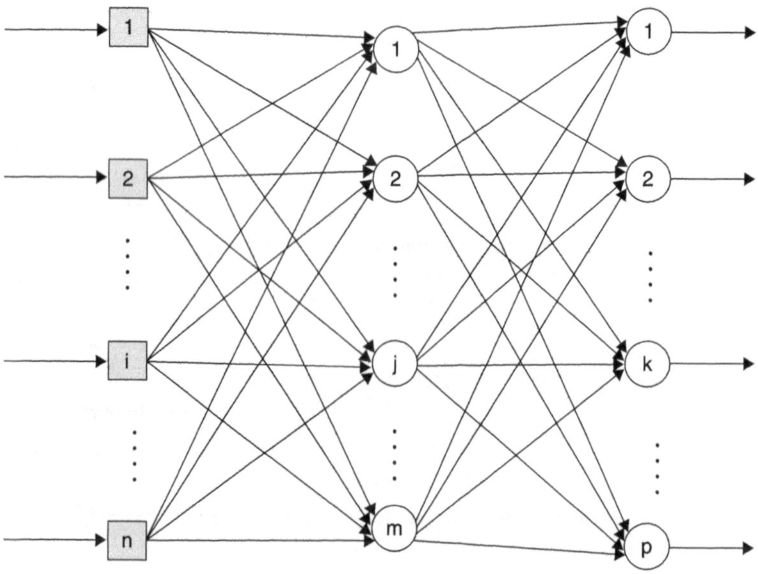

2.6 Feedforward neural network (FNN) with one hidden layer.

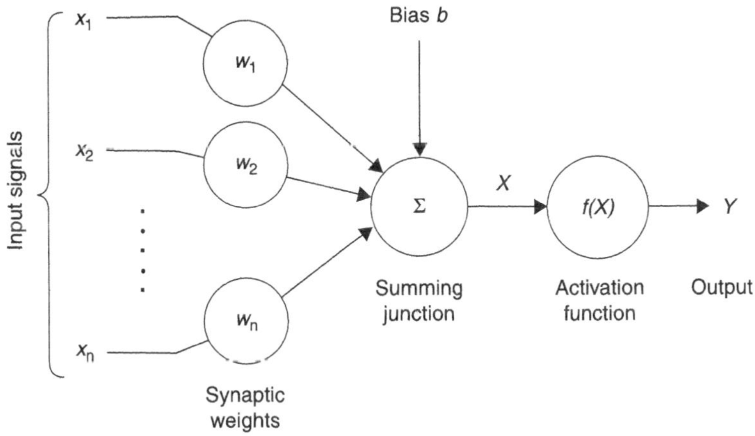

2.7 Diagram of a neuron.

In the NN, a neuron is a mathematical function conceived as abstraction of biological neurons. Figure 2.7 shows a typical neuron. A neuron receives signals from its inputs x_i ($i=1, \ldots, n$) (representing one or more dendrites) and an externally applied bias b. The weighted summation $X(X=\sum_{i=1}^{n} x_i w_i + b)$ of these input signals is then passed through activation function $f(X)$ to generate output signal Y (representing a biological neuron's axon). It is clear that

$$Y = f(X) = f\left(\sum_{i=0}^{n} x_i w_i\right).$$

In this equation, the effect of the bias is considered by: (1) adding a new input signal fixed at +1, and (2) adding a new synaptic weight equal to bias b. That is, $x_0 = 1$, $w_0 = b$. The input signal $x_i(i=1, \ldots, n)$ can be raw data or outputs of other neurons. Output signal Y can be either a final solution to the problem or an input to other neurons. It should be noted that, for simplicity, the NN shown in Fig. 2.6 does not include bias signals, which is feasible in practical applications.

Various FNNs have been presented, including backpropagation networks, extreme learning machine networks, learning vector quantization networks, self-organizing map networks and radial basis function networks. These FNNs are capable of approximating generic classes of functions (Scarselli and Tsoi, 1998; Zhang *et al.*, 2012) and are constructed in terms of different settings from the following three perspectives.

Network architecture: In traditional FNNs, neurons are by default fully connected between neighboring layers (Fig. 2.6) in order to simplify the network design, although fully connected NNs are biologically unrealistic (Wong *et al.*, 2010). To simplify the network structure and improve the generalization capability of FNNs, some partially connected FNNs have been developed (Wong *et al.*,

2010; Elizondo and Fiesler, 1997). However, fully connected FNNs are still dominant because designing partially connected FNNs is complicated and usually data-dependent. In FNNs, backpropagation networks can have more than one hidden layer, while ELM networks and radial basis function networks have only one hidden layer each.

Activation function: Every neuron has its own activation function and generally only two activation functions are used in a particular NN. Neurons in the input layer use the identity function as the activation function. That is, the output of an input neuron equals its input. The activation functions of hidden and output layers can be differentiable and non-linear in theory. Several 'well-behaved' (bounded, monotonically increasing and differentiable) activation functions are commonly used in practice, including: (1) the sigmoid function $f(X) = (1 + \exp(-X))^{-1}$; (2) the hyperbolic tangent function $f(X) = (\exp(X) - \exp(-X))/(\exp(X) + \exp(-X))$; (3) the sine or cosine function $f(X) = \sin(X)$ *or* $f(X) = \cos(X)$; (4) the linear function $f(X) = X$; (5) the radial basis function. Among them, the sigmoid function is the most popular, while the radial basis function is only used for radial basis function networks.

Learning algorithm: Traditionally, NN learning is an algorithmic procedure whereby parameters (such as weights) of an NN are estimated. Within this framework, two categories of learning are considered: supervised learning and unsupervised learning. Learning can be 'supervised' since an NN should fulfill a function known in some or even all points: a 'teacher' provides sample data of inputs and corresponding outputs of a task that an NN should perform. The most popular supervised learning algorithm is the backpropagation algorithm. In contrast to supervised learning, unsupervised learning does not require a 'teacher'. During the learning process, an NN receives a number of input patterns, discovers significant features in these patterns and learns how to classify input data into categories appropriately. The most popular unsupervised learning algorithm is the self-organizing map.

2.4.2 Backpropagation network

The backpropagation (BP) network is the most commonly used FNN. Its structure is the same as that shown in Fig. 2.6 except that it can contain more than one hidden layer. A BP algorithm is used for BP network learning, which is described in detail below.

Given a desired output response vector $d = [d_1, d_2, \ldots, d_p, \ldots, d_P]$, the learning algorithm performs an optimization process to find optimal connection weights so that each output error e_p, defined as the error between the desired output d_p and the output of network o_p, is minimized. That is, $\min_{w \in R^n} E(w)$
where

$$E(w) = \frac{1}{2}\sum_{p=1}^{P}[d_p - o_p]^2 = \frac{1}{2}\sum_{p=1}^{P} e_p^2.$$

Consider an FNN with L–1 (L>2) hidden layers. Let $neuron(i,l)$ be the ith neuron in layer l, and w^l_{ji} be the connection weight between $neuron(j,l)$ and $neuron(i,l-1)$. I^l_{ji} denotes the ith input of $neuron(j,l)$, which is equal to the output o^{l-1}_i of $neuron(i,l-1)$ (i.e. $I^l_{ji} = o^{l-1}_i$). The BP algorithm can be implemented on the basis of the following steps:

- ***Step 1:*** Set a learning rate η $(0 \le \eta \le 1)$.
- ***Step 2:*** Set all connection weights $w^l_{ji}(0)$ to random numbers uniformly distributed inside a small range. A feasible empirical range (Haykin, 1994) is $(-2.4/N^l_j, +2.4/N^l_j)$, where N^l_j is the total number of inputs of neuron$(j,1)$.
- ***Step 3:*** Select a random input pattern with its corresponding target output.
- ***Step 4:*** Assign to each neuron in the input layer the appropriate value in the input vector. Feed this input to all neurons in the first hidden layer.
- ***Step 5:*** For $neuron(j,l)$ in hidden and output layers (i.e. $2 \le l \le L$), calculate its total input net^l_j,

$$net^l_j = \sum_i I^l_{ji} w^l_{ji}$$

where I^l_{j0} equals 1, w^l_{j0} equals the bias b^l_j applied to $neuron(j,l)$. The output of this neuron is $f(net^l_j)$. $f(\cdot)$ is the activation function that can be any function with bounded derivatives.

- ***Step 6:*** Calculate the error signal at output neuron $neuron(k,L)$,

$$\delta^L_k = -\frac{\partial E}{\partial net^L_k} = -\frac{\partial E}{\partial o^L_k} \cdot \frac{\partial o^L_k}{\partial net^L_k} = (d^L_k - o^L_k) \cdot f'(net^L_k).$$

- ***Step 7:*** Calculate the error signal for each neuron $neuron(j,l)$ in hidden layers $(2 \le l \le L-1)$,

$$\delta^l_j = -\frac{\partial E}{\partial net^l_j} = -\frac{\partial E}{\partial o^l_j} \cdot \frac{\partial o^l_j}{\partial net^l_j} = f'(net^l_j) \sum_k \delta^{l+1}_k w^{l+1}_{kj}.$$

- ***Step 8:*** Update the weights for all layers $w^l_{ji}(n+1) = w^l_{ji}(n) + \eta \delta^l_j I^l_{ji}$.
- ***Step 9:*** Continue at Step 3.

2.4.3 Extreme learning machine network

The major drawback of the BP network is its slow convergence speed caused by the local minima. The extreme learning machine (ELM) network has the capability of providing better generalization and much faster learning speed than BP networks. The ELM network is a type of novel FNN, which was developed by Huang *et al.* at Nanyang Technological University, Singapore, in 2004 (Huang *et al.*, 2004). Compared with BP networks, ELM networks contain only one hidden layer and use ELM algorithms as learning algorithms.

The structure of the ELM network is shown in Fig. 2.6. It is assumed that the ELM network with m hidden neurons and activation function $f(x)$ is trained to approximate N distinct samples (u_i, y_i) with zero error means, where u_i is the input of samples and $u_i = [u_{i1}, u_{i2}, \ldots, u_{in}]^T \in R^n$, y_i is the output of samples and $y_i = [y_{i1}, y_{i2}, \ldots, y_{ip}]^T \in R^p$. In ELM networks, input weights and hidden biases are generated randomly. Non-linear ELM networks can thus be converted into the following linear system.

$M\beta = T$, (1) where $M = \{h_{ij}\}$ ($i = 1, \ldots, N$ and $j = 1, \ldots, m$) denotes the hidden-layer output matrix, $h_{ij} = f(w_j \cdot u_i + b_j)$ is the output of the jth hidden neuron $neuron(j,2)$ with respect to u_i; $w_j = [w_{j1}, w_{j2}, \ldots, w_{jn}]^T$ is the weight vector connecting $neuron(j,2)$ and input neurons, and b_j denotes the bias of $neuron(j,2)$; $w_j \cdot u_i$ denotes the inner product of w_j and u_i; $\beta = [\beta_1, \ldots, \beta_j, \ldots, \beta_m]^T$ ($j = 1, \ldots, m$) is the matrix of output weights and $\beta_j = [\beta_{j1}, \beta_{j2}, \ldots, \beta_{jp}]^T$ denotes the weight vector connecting $neuron(j,2)$ and output neurons; $Y = [y_1, y_2, \ldots, y_N]^T$ is the matrix of targets (desired outputs).

The determination of output weights between hidden and output layers is to find the least-square solution to the given linear system. The minimum norm least-square solution to linear system (1) is $\hat{\beta} = M^{\dagger}Y$, where $M^{\dagger}$ is the Moore–Penrose generalized inverse of matrix M. The minimum norm least-square solution is unique and has the smallest norm among the least-square solutions.

Compared with BP algorithms, ELM has much faster learning and convergence speed because its network weights are obtained by using random generation and a least-mean squares method based on a Moore–Penrose's generalized inverse, instead of using iterative weight adjustment. In addition, ELM can avoid difficulties experienced by BP algorithms, such as selection of stopping criteria, learning rate and learning epochs, due to its distinct learning mechanism.

2.4.4 Learning vector quantization network

Learning vector quantization (LVQ) is a supervised learning technique invented by Teuvo Kohonen (1988; 1990). The LVQ network is the precursor of the self-organizing map NN. Both of them are based on the Kohonen layer, which is capable of sorting items into categories of similar objects with the aid of training samples, and are widely used for classification.

Topologically, an LVQ network consists of an input layer, a single Kohonen layer (also known as competitive or hidden layer) and an output layer. Figure 2.8 shows the structure of an LVQ network. The Kohonen layer contains a number of neurons placed in the nodes of a lattice, which maps input vectors into clusters that are found by the network during training. The output layer merges groups of previous layer clusters into classes defined by target data. Unlike traditional FNNs, the neurons between the Kohonen layer and the output layer are not fully connected.

LVQ procedures are intuitively clear and easy to implement. The classification of data is based on a comparison with a number of so-called prototype vectors.

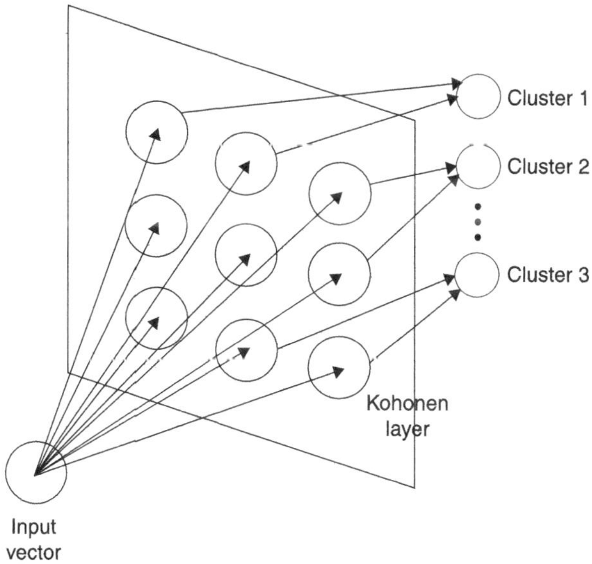

2.8 Structure of learning vector quantization (LVQ) network.

Prototypes are determined in training from labeled examples and can be interpreted in a straightforward fashion as they directly represent typical data in the same input space, in contrast with adaptive weights in FNNs, which do not allow immediate interpretation easily.

The procedures of LVQ permit only the update of winning prototypes (i.e. the closest prototype of the LVQ network). The prototype vector **w** is moved in the direction of the input vector **x** if the class of the input vector and that of the prototype vector match. Otherwise, the prototype vector **w** is moved away from the direction of the input vector **x**. LVQ proceeds as follows:

- ***Step 1. Initialization:*** Initialize the prototype vectors $\{\mathbf{w}_j(0) \mid j = 1,2, \ldots, N\}$. by setting them equal to the first N exemplar input vectors $\{\mathbf{x}_i \mid i = 1,2, \ldots, L\}$. Usually, $L > N$.
- ***Step 2. Sampling:*** Draw a sample (vector) **x** from the input data; **x** represents the new pattern input for LVQ.
- ***Step 3. Similarity Matching:*** Find the best matching prototype vector $\mathbf{w}_j$ at time **n** based on the minimum-distance Euclidean criterion:

$$\arg\min_j \| \mathrm{x}(n) - \mathrm{w}_j(n) \|, \quad j = 1,2,\ldots,N.$$

- ***Step 4. Adaptation:*** Adjust only the best matching prototype vector, while the others remain unchanged. It is supposed that a prototype vector $\mathbf{w}_c$ is the closest to the input vector $\mathbf{x}_i$. Let C_{w_c} denote the class associated with the prototype vector $\mathbf{w}_c$, and $C_{\mathbf{x}_i}$ denote the class label of the input vector $\mathbf{x}_i$. The prototype vector $\mathbf{w}_c$ is adapted as follows:

$$\mathbf{w}_c(n+1) = \begin{cases} \mathbf{w}_c(n) + \alpha_n[\mathbf{x}_i - \mathbf{w}_c(n)], & C_{\mathbf{w}_c} = C_{\mathbf{x}_i} \\ \mathbf{w}_c(n) - \alpha_n[\mathbf{x}_i - \mathbf{w}_c(n)], & C_{\mathbf{w}_c} \neq C_{\mathbf{x}_i} \end{cases}.$$

The learning constant α_n $(0 < \alpha_n < 1)$ is chosen as a function of the discrete time parameter n. It is desirable for the learning constant α_n to decrease monotonically with the number of iterations n.

- ***Step 5. Termination Checking:*** Stop if there are no noticeable changes in the above procedures. Otherwise, go to Step 2.

One of the advantages of LVQ is that it creates prototypes that are easy for experts to interpret in the respective application domain. The key issue of LVQ is to choose an appropriate measure of similarity for training and classification. The original method relies on the Euclidean distance corresponding to the assumption that data can be represented by isotropic clusters. To provide more general metric structures, some alternative techniques have been proposed (Schneider *et al.*, 2009), such as relevance adaptation in generalized LVQ (GLVQ) and matrix learning in GLVQ.

2.5 Fuzzy logic

Fuzzy logic is not logic that is fuzzy, but a kind of precise logic of imprecision and approximate reasoning. Humans usually rely on practical knowledge and judgement to solve problems. Human knowledge is often vague and ambiguous. For example, a piece of practical knowledge might be: 'Though the material delivery is slightly delayed, the production schedule can remain unchanged.' It is unclear how many days constitute a slight delay. Fuzzy logic attempts to model human reasoning with imprecise and incomplete knowledge. Through fuzzy logic, a system cannot only represent such imprecise concepts as slow, late and expensive, but also use these concepts to make precise deductions with imprecise data.

2.5.1 Uses of fuzzy logic

The real world is pervaded with fuzziness. Most human knowledge is described in natural languages for describing perceptions. Due to the intrinsic impreciseness of human perceptions, natural languages are pervasively imprecise in the sense that almost everything admits of degrees therein. For example, linguistic terms, such as distance, area, speed and temperature, are all expressed on a sliding scale. The distance between Hong Kong and London is very far. The area of Russia is very large. Rabbits run very fast. The boiler temperature is very high. The values of these linguistic terms are vague and imprecise. Classical Boolean or conventional logic is not capable of capturing and expressing the vagueness of linguistic terms.

Boolean logic uses sharp distinctions and forces us to separate members of a class from non-members. For example, one may regard lower than 180 cm as short and higher than 180 cm as tall. Based on this standard, Mike, who is 178 cm, is short. However, Boolean logic cannot decide whether Mike is really short or the standard is just arbitrarily set. Such absurdities can be avoided by using fuzzy logic.

Unlike two-valued Boolean logic, fuzzy logic is an extension of multi-valued logic. Instead of just completely true or false, fuzzy logic accepts that things can be partly true and partly false at the same time, which is consistent with human reasoning. Fuzzy logic also deals with degrees of truth by using the continuum of logical values between 0 (completely false) and 1 (completely true). Therefore, fuzzy logic is more accurate than Boolean logic in dealing with fuzzy reality.

2.5.2 Fuzzy set

Fuzzy set representation

The fuzzy set theory is an outgrowth of the classical set theory. First, recall the classical set theory, which views the world as either black or white. Let X be the universe of discourse and x be its elements. According to the classical set theory, crisp set A of X is defined by the characteristic function $f_A(x)$ of set A.

$$f_A(x): X \rightarrow 0, 1$$

where

$$f_A(x) = \begin{cases} 1, & if\ x \in A \\ 0, & if\ x \notin A \end{cases}$$

Based on the fuzzy set theory, fuzzy set A of X is defined by its membership function $\mu_A(x)$

$$\mu_A(x): X \rightarrow [0, 1]$$

where

$$\mu_A(x) = \begin{cases} 1, & if\ x\ is\ totally\ in\ A; \\ 0, & if\ x\ is\ not\ in\ A; \\ u\ (0 < u < 1), & if\ x\ is\ partly\ in\ A. \end{cases}$$

For any element x of universe X, membership function $\mu_A(x)$ equals the degree to which x is an element of set A. This degree represents the degree of membership, also known as the membership value of element x in set A. The most commonly used membership functions are triangular, trapezoidal, piecewise linear and Gaussian functions because they are easily prepared and computationally fast. The choice of membership functions is largely arbitrary because there is no theoretical justification for using one rather than another. The number of membership functions is dependent on users. More membership functions can achieve greater resolution but also cause greater computational complexity.

Linguistic variables and hedges

The idea of linguistic variables is essential to development of the fuzzy set theory. Fuzzy logic is primarily associated with quantifying and reasoning out imprecise or vague terms that appear in our languages. These terms are referred to as linguistic or fuzzy variables. For example, the statement 'the completion date is late' implies that the linguistic variable 'completion date' takes on the linguistic value 'late'.

The range of possible values of a linguistic variable represents the variable's universe of discourse. For example, the universe of discourse of the linguistic variable 'completion date' might have the range between 1 and 10 days, and include fuzzy subsets such as early, normal and late.

A linguistic hedge is an operation that modifies the meaning of a fuzzy set, which can be understood as terms that modify the shapes of fuzzy sets by using adverbs such as *very*, *quite*, *more*, *less* and *slightly*. It is assumed that we have already defined a fuzzy set to describe a late completion date. If we need to talk about how late the completion date is, we can use a hedge to change the fuzzy set. For example, *very late*, *moderately late* and *slightly late* are examples of hedges applied to the fuzzy set of the late completion date.

Figure 2.9 shows an application of hedges (very). The universe of discourse – men's heights – consists of five fuzzy sets: *very short*, *short*, *average*, *tall* and *very tall*. For example, a man 180 cm tall is a member of the *tall* set with a degree of membership of 0.5 and a member of the *very tall* set with a degree of membership of 0.2.

Fuzzy set operations

Fuzzy set operations are a generalization of crisp set operations, each of which is a fuzzy set operation. In fuzzy logic, three operations, including fuzzy complement, fuzzy intersection and fuzzy union, are the most commonly used. Let fuzzy sets *A*

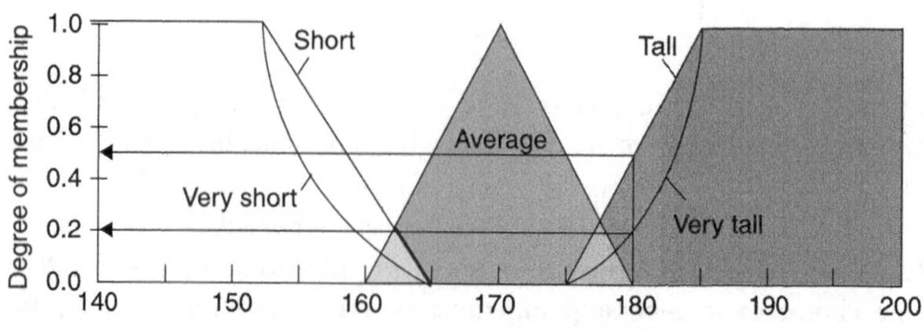

2.9 Fuzzy sets with hedge.

and *B* be described by their membership functions $\mu_A(x)$ and $\mu_B(x)$. The three fuzzy set operations are defined below.

- **Fuzzy complement:** The complement of a fuzzy set is the opposite of the set in question. The fuzzy complement of fuzzy sets *A* can be represented as

  $$\mu_{\sim A}(x) = 1 - \mu_A(x).$$

- **Fuzzy intersection:** Fuzzy intersection is the fuzzy operation for creating the intersection of fuzzy sets *A* and *B* on the universe of discourse X, which can be obtained as:

  $$\mu_{A \cap B}(x) = \min(\mu_A(x), \mu_B(x)) = \mu_A(x) \cap \mu_B(x), \text{ where } x \in X.$$

- **Fuzzy union:** The union of two fuzzy sets is the reverse of their intersection. That is, the fuzzy union is the largest membership value of the element in either set. The fuzzy union for forming the union of fuzzy sets *A* and *B* on the universe of discourse X can be given as:

  $$\mu_{A \cup B}(x) = \max(\mu_A(x),\mu_B(x)) = \mu_A(x) \cup \mu_B(X), \text{ where } x \in X.$$

2.5.3 Fuzzy rule

In one of his most influential papers, Lotfi Zadeh presented an outline of a new approach to analysis of complex systems and decision processes (Zadeh, 1973). He suggested using fuzzy rules to capture and express human knowledge. Human knowledge is usually in the form of 'if-then' rules, which can be easily implemented by fuzzy conditional statements.

A fuzzy rule is defined as a conditional statement in the form:

IF *x* is *A* THEN *y* is *B*

where *x* and *y* are linguistic variables; *A* and *B* are linguistic values determined by fuzzy sets on the universes of discourse *X* and *Y*, respectively.

Fuzzy reasoning involves two parts: evaluating the rule antecedent (the IF part of the rule) and applying the result to the consequent (the THEN part of the rule). Like the rules in expert systems, a fuzzy rule can have multiple antecedents joined by fuzzy operators AND or OR, or multiple consequents joined by fuzzy operator AND. For example:

IF the delivery date is late AND the tardiness penalty is high, THEN the production cost is high.

IF the material delivery date is late, THEN the completion date is late AND the tardiness penalty is high.

2.5.4 Fuzzy logic system

A fuzzy logic system maps crisp inputs into crisp outputs using the theory of fuzzy sets. In a fuzzy logic system, an inference engine works with fuzzy rules.

The engine takes inputs, some of which may be fuzzy, and generates outputs, some of which may be fuzzy. The fuzzy core of the inference engine is bracketed by one step that can convert crisp data into fuzzy data, and another step that does the reverse. Figure 2.10 shows the general procedures involved in a fuzzy logic system as follows.

Fuzzification of input data

The first step is to take the crisp input x and determine the degree to which the input belongs to each of the appropriate fuzzy sets.

Fuzzification is the process of mapping crisp input $x \in U$ into fuzzy set $A \in U$. This is achieved with three different types of fuzzifier, including singleton fuzzifiers, Gaussian fuzzifiers, and trapezoidal or triangular fuzzifiers. These fuzzifiers map crisp input x into fuzzy set A with different membership functions $\mu_A(x)$ listed below.

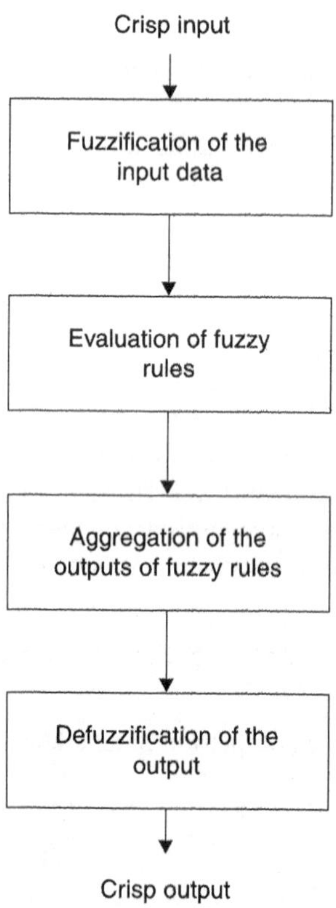

2.10 The general structure of a fuzzy logic system.

Membership function of singleton fuzzifier:

$$\mu_A(x) = \begin{cases} 1 & \textit{if } x = x' \\ 0 & \textit{otherwise} \end{cases}.$$

Membership function of Gaussian fuzzifier:

$$\mu_A(x) = e^{-(\frac{x_1 - x_1'}{a_1})^2} \ldots e^{-(\frac{x_n - x_n'}{a_{n1}})^2}$$

where $\{a_i, i = 1, \ldots, n\}$ are positive parameters.

Membership function of triangular fuzzifier:

$$\mu_A(x) = \begin{cases} \left(1 - \frac{|x_1 - x_1'|}{b_1}\right) \ldots \left(1 - \frac{|x_n' - x_n'|}{b_n}\right) & \textit{if} \quad |x_i - x_i'| \le b_{i,} i = 1, 2, \ldots, n \\ 0 & \textit{otherwise} \end{cases}$$

where $\{b_i, i = 1, \ldots, n\}$ are positive parameters.

Evaluation of fuzzy rules

After input data are fuzzified and their membership values obtained, the next step involves application of them to the antecedents of fuzzy rules. If a given fuzzy rule has multiple antecedents, a fuzzy operator (AND or OR) is used to obtain a single number that represents the result of antecedent evaluation. This number is then applied to a consequent membership function.

AND is used to evaluate the conjunction of rule antecedents. Typically, fuzzy logic systems utilize the classical fuzzy operation intersection to implement this operation. Consider fuzzy rule 1:

If x is A AND y is B, then z is C.

Assume $\mu_A(x) = 0.1$, $\mu_B(y) = 0.6$, then we have $\mu_C(z) = \min[\mu_A(x), \mu_B(y)] = 0.1$.

Similarly, OR is used to evaluate the disjunction of rule antecedents, which is implemented by the classical fuzzy operation union in fuzzy logic systems. Consider fuzzy rule 2:

If x is A OR y is B, then z is C.

Assume $\mu_A(x) = 0.1$, $\mu_B(y) = 0.6$, then we have

$$\mu_C(z) = \max[\mu_A(x), \mu_B(y)] = 0.6.$$

Aggregation of outputs of fuzzy rules

Several fuzzy rules often provide fuzzy information about the same variable and different outputs must be combined. Aggregation is the unification of outputs of all fuzzy rules. That is, aggregation takes membership functions of all rules' consequents and combines them into a single fuzzy set. Fuzzy set operations, such as union and intersection, can be used to implement aggregation.

Defuzzification of the output

The last step in a fuzzy logic system is defuzzification. As the name suggests, defuzzification is the opposite of fuzzification, which produces crisp output y' for a fuzzy logic system from the aggregated output of fuzzy set B. A number of defuzzifiers have been developed; the most popular is the centroid defuzzifier, which finds a vertical line and divides an aggregated set into two equal portions. Mathematically the center of gravity (COG) can be defined by:

$$y' = COG = \frac{\int_a^b \mu_B(y)\,y\,dy}{\int_a^b \mu_B(y)\,dy}.$$

In addition to centroid defuzzifiers, maximum defuzzifiers and means of maxima defuzzifiers are also commonly used.

- **Maximum Defuzzifier:** This defuzzifier chooses y' as the point at which associated membership functions achieve their maximum values.
- **Mean of Maxima Defuzzifier:** This defuzzifier examines fuzzy set B, determines values for which associated membership functions achieve their maximum values and computes the mean of these values as its output y'.

2.6 Conclusions

This chapter provides a brief introduction to the family of AI techniques so that readers can gain a basic understanding of the AI family and various AI techniques, and understand the subsequent chapters more easily. This chapter introduces the definition of artificial intelligence and presents a brief overview of artificial intelligent techniques. Some representative AI techniques are briefly introduced, all of which have been used for decision making in the fashion supply chain. We also discuss the origins of these techniques, fundamental characteristics, and possible applications as well as the procedures to implement them.

A number of research outputs show the effectiveness of AI techniques for decision making in the fashion industry, as well as their superiority over classical approaches (Guo *et al.*, 2011). The subsequent chapters will introduce several representative applications of AI in the fashion supply chain.

The fashion supply chain is characterized by short product life cycles, volatile and unpredictable customer demands, tremendous product variety, labor-intensive production, and long supply processes. These distinct features increase the complexity of decision making in the fashion supply chain. As a result, research on AI applications in the fashion industry is still limited, although great research advances have been made so far. A great number of issues are worthy of research, for example, production planning and control with unreliable material supplies and dynamic customer demands, and retail replenishment with uncertain delivery dates by apparel manufacturers.

2.7 References

Durkin, J., 1994. *Expert Systems Design and Development*, Englewood Cliffs, NJ: Prentice Hall.

Elizondo, D. and Fiesler, E., 1997. A survey of partially connected neural networks. *International Journal Neural Systems*, 8 (5–6), 535–558.

Geem, Z., Kim, J. and Loganathan, G., 2001. A new heuristic optimization algorithm: Harmony search. *Simulation*, 76 (2), 60–68.

Goldberg, D.E., 1989. *Genetic Algorithms in Search, Optimization and Machine Learning*, Reading, MA: Addison-Wesley.

Guo, Z.X., Wong, W.K., Leung, S.Y.S. and Li, M., 2011. Applications of artificial intelligence in the apparel industry: A review. *Textile Research Journal*, 81 (18), 1871–1892.

Hansen, N. and Kern, S., 2004. *Evaluating the CMA Evolution Strategy on Multimodal Test Functions*. Berlin Heidelberg: Springer-Verlag.

Haykin, S., 1994. *Neural Networks: A Comprehensive Foundation*, New York: Macmillan College Publishing Company.

Hembry, D.M., 1990. Knowledge-based systems in the AD/cycle environment. *IBM Systems Journal*, 29 (2), 274–286.

Holland, J., 1975. *Adaptation in Natural and Artificial Systems*, Ann Arbor, MI: University of Michigan Press.

Huang, G.B., Zhu, Q.Y. and Siew, C.K., 2004. Extreme learning machine: a new learning scheme of feedforward neural networks, *Proceedings of the International Joint Conference on Neural Networks (IJCNN2004)*, pp. 25–29. Budapest, Hungary.

Kohonen, T., 1988. Learning vector quantization. *Neural Networks*, 1 (1), 303.

Kohonen, T., 1990. Improved versions of learning vector quantization, *Proceedings of the International Joint Conference on Neural Networks*, Vols 1–3, pp. A545–A550. Washington, USA.

Lee, K. and Geem, Z., 2004. A new structural optimization method based on the harmony search algorithm. *Computers & Structures*, 82 (9–10), 781–798.

Mahdavi, M., Fesanghary, M. and Damangir, E., 2007. An improved harmony search algorithm for solving optimization problems. *Applied Mathematics and Computation*, 188 (2), 1567–1579.

McCulloch, W.S. and Pitts, W.H., 1943. A logical calculus of the ideas immanent in nervous activity. *Bulletin of Mathematical Biophysics*, 5, 115–133.

Rochenberg, I., 1965. *Cybernetic Solution Path of an Experimental Problem*, Ministry of Aviation, Royal Aircraft Establishment, UK.

Russell, S. and Norvig, P., 1994. *Artificial Intelligence: A Modern Approach*, Prentice Hall.

Scarselli, F. and Tsoi, A., 1998. Universal approximation using feedforward neural networks: A survey of some existing methods, and some new results. *Neural Networks*, 11 (1), 15–37.

Schneider, P., Biehl, M. and Hammer, B., 2009. Adaptive relevance matrices in learning vector quantization. *Neural Computation*, 21 (12), 3532–3561.

Schwefel, H.P., 1975. *Evolutionsstrategie und numerische Optimierung*, Dissertation, TU, Berlin, Germany.

Song, Y.H., Johns, A. and Aggarwal, R., 1996. *Computational Intelligence Applications to Power Systems*, Beijing: Science Press, Kluwer Academic Publishers.

Wong, W.K., Guo, Z.X. and Leung, S.Y.S., 2010. Partially connected feedforward neural networks on Apollonian networks. *Physica A – Statistical Mechanics and its Applications*, 389 (22), 5298–5307.

Zadeh, L., 1965. Fuzzy sets. *Information and Control*, 8 (3), 338–353.

Zadeh, L., 1973. Outline of a new approach to the analysis of complex systems and decision processes. *IEEE Transactions on Systems, Man and Cybernetics*, 3 (1), 28–44.

Zhang, R., Lan, Y., Huang, G.B. and Xu, Z.B., 2012. Universal approximation of extreme learning machine with adaptive growth of hidden nodes. *IEEE Transactions on Neural Networks and Learning Systems*, 23 (2), 365–371.

3

Selecting the location of apparel manufacturing plants using neural networks

W. K. WONG, X. H. ZENG and K. F. AU,
The Hong Kong Polytechnic University, China

DOI: 10.1533/9780857097842.41

Abstract: The direct investment and joint ventures of clothing manufacturers in developing regions have grown rapidly over the last few decades. Manufacturers have encountered difficulties when selecting the plant location however, because their decisions are based on subjective judgments and inconsistent assessments rather than on a clear classification system. Variances between potential plants cannot always be represented in terms of objective value, such as country risk and community facilities. Clothing manufacturers must also consider more intangible factors such as the social environment and political stability when deciding the most appropriate site for production. Classification methods are a more efficient and less time-consuming way of organizing a number of sites into different levels of appropriateness, thereby allowing clothing manufacturers to make more informed and objective decisions about plant locations. This chapter investigates two recent types of classification technique; unsupervised and supervised artificial neural networks. The limitations of the adaptive resonance theory of the unsupervised artificial neural network are demonstrated in this chapter and a comparison of the performance of the three types of supervised artificial neural network, back propagation, learning vector quantization and probabilistic neural network are presented. The supervised artificial neural network has proved to be an effective classifier in which the probabilistic neural network performs better than in the other networks on the site selection problem.

Key words: clothing manufacture, artificial neural network, plant location.

3.1 Introduction

In clothing manufacture, decisions about using overseas production sites are regarded as complicated because of numerous location factors as well as the complexity caused by trade agreements instituted with trade blocs such as NAFTA, EU or AGOA. The changing market dynamics have forced companies to consider macro-environmental factors including economic, social, political, legal and technological issues as well as micro-environmental factors such as customers, competitors and suppliers (Uncu *et al.*, 2002). Plant location decisions for foreign direct investment have therefore created problems for clothing manufacturers.

Different decision-making techniques have been developed to assist with the selection of plant locations. These techniques include: scaling (ranking or scoring) methods (Hoffman and Schniederjans, 1994); the analytic hierarchy process (Yurimoto and Masui, 1995); mathematical programming (Brimberg and Revelle, 1999; Schmidt and Wilhelm, 2000); heuristic algorithms (Ronnqvist, 1999; Verter and Dasci, 2002) and simulation (Chakravarty, 1999). Various types of artificial intelligence techniques (Liang and Wang, 1991; Yurimoto and Masui, 1995; Kuo *et al.*, 2002; Au *et al.*, 2006) have also been used to search for optimal sites.

These techniques depend on the subjective judgement of the manufacturer and therefore rely heavily on their knowledge and experience. Additionally, in cases where sites have only slightly different scores, it is difficult to conclude that site A is really better than site B at a particular moment or under different conditions. Classification methods are an efficient and less time-consuming way of organizing a number of sites into different levels of location appropriateness so that clothing manufacturers can make their selection more easily.

3.2 Classification methods using artificial neural networks

Several recently proposed classification techniques, which use artificial neural networks (ANN) and fuzzy logic, are very promising candidates for decision-making applications. These techniques can be divided into two general categories: (a) supervised techniques in which labeled training samples are used for optimizing the design parameters of the classification system; and (b) unsupervised techniques, or automatic classification using data clustering algorithms. Different types of ANN can act as the classifier, including back propagation (BP), learning vector quantization (LVQ), and probabilistic (P) networks, which are supervised techniques, as well as adaptive resonance theory (ART) and self-organizing feature maps (SOFM), which are unsupervised ones. Supervised neural networks use an omniscient input which is presented during training in order to learn what the correct answer should be. This type of neural network performs well in a multiple criteria decision-making problem. Contrastingly, the unsupervised neural network has no knowledge of the correct answer and cannot know exactly what the correct response should be. This type of unsupervised neural network has some limitations in multiple criteria decision-making. The details of these techniques are further discussed in Section 4.

3.2.1 Back propagation networks

Back propagation is a supervised learning technique, which is capable of computing a functional relationship between its input and output. In general, the BP network is multilayered, fully connected and most useful for feed-forward networks. The first and last layers are called the input and output layers, respectively. The layer/s between the input layer and the output layer is/are called the hidden layer/s.

Several researchers have demonstrated that during training, a BP network tends to develop internal relationships between the nodes so as to organize the training data into classes of patterns (Freeman and Skapura, 1992). The key concept of the BP network is that given the training inputs, there is an internal representation to generate the desired outputs. This same internal representation can be applied to inputs that were not used during training. The BP network will classify these previously unseen inputs according to the features they share with the training examples.

3.2.2 Learning vector quantization networks

The learning vector quantization network was developed by Teuvo Kohonen in the mid-1980s (Teuvo, 1995). It is known as a kind of supervised ANN model and is mostly used for statistical classification or recognition. Topologically, the LVQ network contains an input layer, a single LVQ layer and an output layer. The network can be trained to classify inputs while preserving the inherent topology of the training set. LVQ not only offers ways to interpret behavior, but can also be trained using an appropriate distance measure. The architecture of the LVQ network means that it can perform more accurate classifications in many types of problem (Luo *et al.*, 2003).

3.2.3 Probabilistic networks

The probabilistic network is a non-linear and non-parametric pattern recognition algorithm, originally introduced by Donald Specht in the 1980s. The P network operates by defining a probability density function (PDF) for each data class based on the training set data and the optimized kernel width parameter (Specht, 1990). It is a three-layer network, composed of the input layer, the radial basis layer, and the competitive layer. The radial basis layer of the P network is the core of the algorithm. During the training phase, the pattern vectors in the training set are simply copied to the radial basis layer of the P network. Unlike other types of ANN, the P network has only a single adjustable parameter. This parameter, termed sigma (σ), or kernel width, along with the members of the training set, defines the PDF for each data class. Each PDF is composed of exponential-shaped kernels of width σ located at each pattern vector. The PDF essentially determines the boundaries for classification (Hammond *et al.*, 2004).

3.3 Classifying decision models for the location of clothing plants

The proposed decision model for classifying clothing plant location using neural networks can be separated into two sequential phases: the learning (preference assessing) phase and the executing (decision-making) phase. The goal of the learning phase is to train the neural network with the prior knowledge in terms of the experts' experience, whereas the goal of the executing phase is to obtain the most desirable alternative based on the constructed neural network model. The flow chart of the proposed classification decision model is shown in Fig. 3.1.

Unlike the conventional methods of location selection, this model does not require that the weight of each factor be determined, which is often a very difficult and time-consuming task. Instead, classification of the selected alternatives with associated preference relations according to the prior knowledge is required. The ANN is therefore essentially used to establish the classification decision rule about locating a clothing plant based on only a limited number of the selected sites. Figure 3.2 illustrates the learning process of the ANN classification model. The ANN can thus act as a rational proxy on behalf of the decision-maker to evaluate and classify any alternatives.

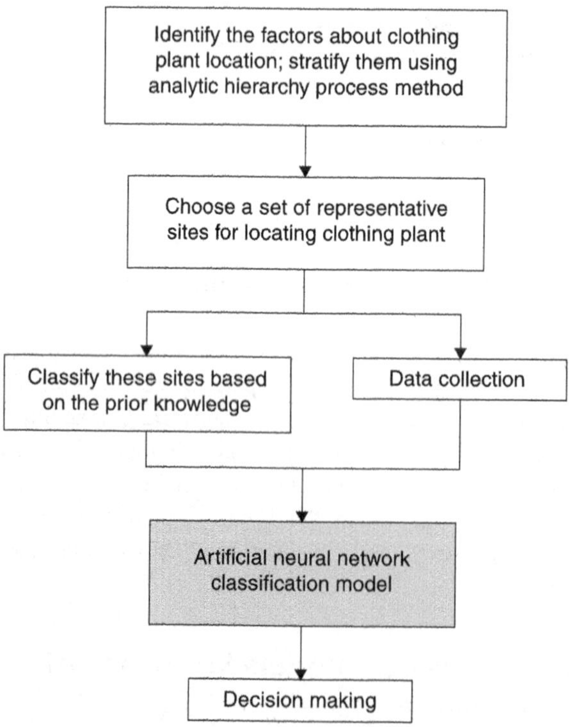

3.1 Flow chart of the classification decision model of site selection for clothing plant.

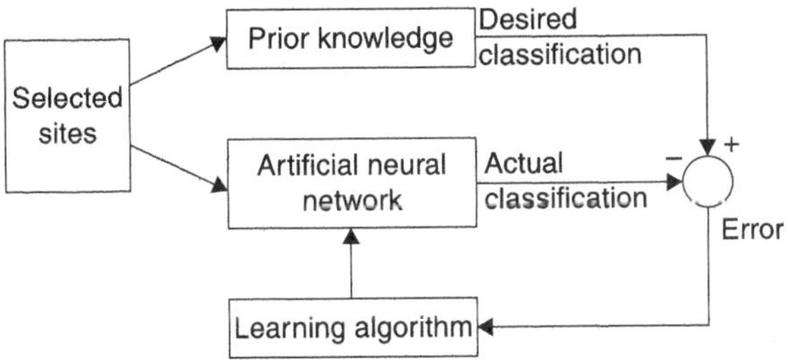

3.2 Learning process of artificial neural network.

3.3.1 Identification of location factors

The analytic hierarchy process (AHP) is one of the most extensively used multi-criteria decision-making methods. One of the main advantages of this method is that it is able to relatively easily handle multiple criteria. After reviewing the information in related publications and ascertaining the experts' opinion of the industry, we established 10 important factors on level 1 of the AHP, which we further divided into 16 related sub-factors at level 2 in the clothing plant location problem, each with appropriate evaluation indices. Figure 3.3 shows the hierarchical structure of location factors in the selection of clothing production sites. After identifying the location factors, a set of representative sites for locating clothing plants would be chosen for classification. This study focuses on 20 sites and is mostly concerned with Hong Kong clothing suppliers. Quantitative measures of all factors for each site were collected and computed based on *The World Competitiveness Yearbook* (International Institute for Management Development, 2002) and related government publications.

3.3.2 Classification based on multi-attribute utility model

The next step was to produce rank ordered lists of the sites based on their suitability for locating clothing production sites. Although we can refer the classification of the chosen sites to the experts by questionnaire, the multi-attribute utility (MAU) model, a traditional systematic model for scoring, is more suitable for dealing with this classification problem, which will be utilized to benchmark the relative performance of the proposed ANN classification decision model. The MAU model can be mathematically stated as follows:

$$S_j = \sum_{i=1}^{n} w_i x_{ij}, j = 1, \cdots, m \qquad \text{where}$$

$$\sum_{i=1}^{n} w_i = 1,$$

S_j = suitability index calculated for country
j = candidate country number
i = location factor number
w_i = weight assigned to factor i
x_{ij} = normalized value assigned to factor i for country j
n = number of location factors
m = number of candidate locations

The resultant suitability indices of the alternative candidates for locating clothing manufacturing sites are shown in Table 3.1. The sites are classified into four groups based on a subjective grouping of the suitability indices.

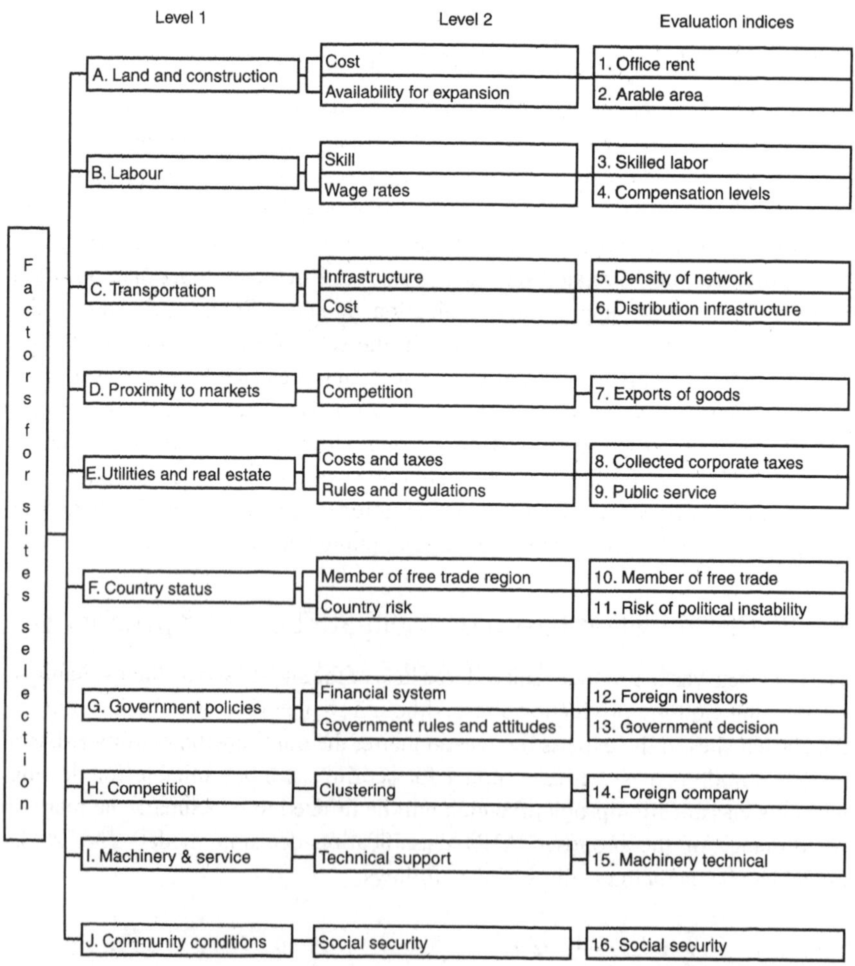

3.3 Hierarchical representation of location factors for clothing manufacturing sites selection.

Table 3.1 Grouping and suitability indices for locating clothing manufacturing sites

Group	Suitability index	Candidate site
A	0.6894	China
	0.6831	Pakistan
	0.6622	India
	0.6482	Thailand
	0.6419	Sri Lanka
B	0.5973	Philippines
	0.5803	Cambodia
	0.5777	Mauritius
	0.5750	Myanmar
	0.5724	Vietnam
	0.5715	Bangladesh
	0.5698	Indonesia
	0.5663	South Africa
C	0.5543	Malaysia
	0.5359	Mexico
	0.5305	Taiwan
	0.5218	Turkey
D	0.4854	Israel
	0.4518	Brazil
	0.3839	Argentina

3.4 Classification using unsupervised artificial neural networks (ANN)

Gaber and Benjamin utilized the adaptive resonance theory (ART2), a typical unsupervised ANN, in classifying US manufacturing plant locations (Gaber and Benjamin, 1992). In their study, the ART2 yielded results similar to those obtained using the MAU model and its' performance was very encouraging. However, this method has limitations when dealing with classification decision problems as demonstrated in the following example:

Assuming that seven sites (S1, S2, S3, S4, S5, S6 and S7) were chosen, they should be classified based on their suitability for establishing a clothing plant. In order to assess the ability of ART2 for classifying the sites, the MAU model was first employed for classification. To elaborate this example clearly, four factors F1, F2, F3 and F4 to assess the sites were defined. The tentative scores of the seven sites are shown in Table 3.2.

To calculate the suitability indices of the seven sites, the weight of four factors should randomly be assigned first. Five random cases of the weights of the four factors were assumed as shown in Table 3.3. Table 3.4 illustrates the resultant suitability indices in each case after computation. Based on the suitability indices of the five cases, the seven sites could be classified into three groups, namely

Table 3.2 Tentative scores for the seven sites

Sites	F1	F2	F3	F4
S1	0.8	0.8	0.8	0.8
S2	0.2	0.4	0.8	0.8
S3	0.2	0.4	0.1	0.6
S4	0.4	0.2	0.8	0.5
S5	0.1	0.1	0.1	0.1
S6	0.3	0.8	0.6	0.1
S7	0.8	0.1	0.6	0.3

Table 3.3 Five cases of the weights of the four factors

	F1	F2	F3	F4
Case 1	0.25	0.25	0.25	0.25
Case 2	0.4	0.1	0.1	0.4
Case 3	0.85	0.05	0.05	0.05
Case 4	0.05	0.05	0.85	0.05
Case 5	0.05	0.85	0.05	0.05

Table 3.4 Resultant suitability indices of the five cases

Sites	Case 1	Case 2	Case 3	Case 4	Case 5
S1	0.8000	0.8000	0.8000	0.8000	0.8000
S2	0.5500	0.5200	0.2700	0.7500	0.4300
S3	0.3250	0.3700	0.2250	0.1450	0.3850
S4	0.4750	0.4600	0.4150	0.7350	0.2550
S5	0.1000	0.1000	0.1000	0.1000	0.1000
S6	0.4500	0.3000	0.3300	0.5700	0.7300
S7	0.4500	0.5100	0.7300	0.5700	0.1700

Groups A, B, and C. Those sites with scores greater than 0.70 were classified as Group A, those with scores ranging from 0.40 to less than 0.70 were classified as Group B and those sites with scores less than 0.40 were classified under Group C, as shown in Table 3.5.

In Table 3.5, the variance of the weights of the factors has a great influence on the classification results, which could lead to an opposite result. For example, the classification results of site 'S7' is Group A, B and C in cases 3, 4 and 5, respectively. On the other hand, after using ART2, the seven sites were classified based on the data stated in Table 3.2. The result is shown in Table 3.6.

Table 3.5 Classification results of the seven sites of the five cases

Sites	Case 1	Case 2	Case 3	Case 4	Case 5
S1	A	A	A	A	A
S2	B	B	C	A	B
S3	C	C	C	C	B
S4	B	B	B	A	C
S5	C	C	C	C	C
S6	B	C	C	B	A
S7	B	B	A	B	C

Table 3.6 Classification result using ART2

Sites	Group
S1	A
S2	C
S3	C
S4	B
S5	A
S6	A
S7	B

Comparing the results of the ART2 in Table 3.6 with that of the MAU model in Table 3.5, the following points can be addressed:

1. The classification result of ART2 only produced a unique result due to its automatic classification characteristic. This implies that ART2 cannot reflect the influence of different levels of importance of the factors on the suitability indices.
2. Though both vectors S1 and S5 differ only in amplitude in Table 3.2, they are classified into different groups which can seen in Table 3.5. In Table 3.6, they are classified into the same group since one of ART2 characteristics is that vectors that are just simple multiples of each other are treated as the same group.

Based on the above analysis, it can be concluded that the unsupervised ANN is inappropriate for solving the classification decision problem. The performances of several supervised ANN were thus investigated for their use in the proposed model.

3.5 Classification using supervised ANN

3.5.1 Classification using the back propagation network

The first ANN classifier used in the proposed model was a two-layered feed-forward network trained with the BP. The network received 16 real values

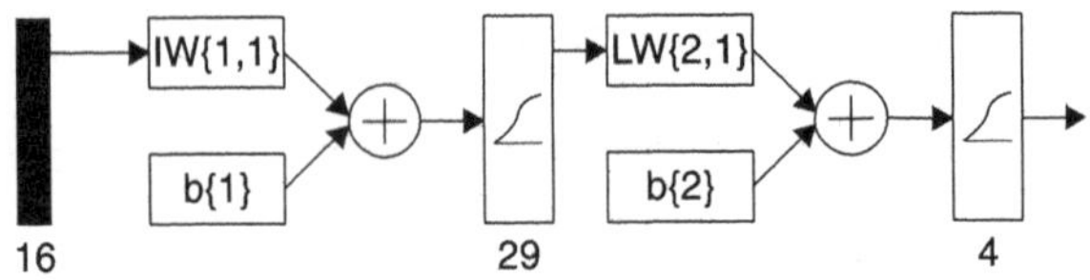

3.4 Notation of the architecture of BP network.

of the sub-factors as a 16-element input vector in order to identify the sites by responding with a 4-element output vector representing 4 classes of site suitability. The network responded with a value of 1 in the position of the site being presented to the network, while all other values in the output vector would be 0. The architecture of BP is shown in Fig. 3.4.

The network was formulated as a two-layered log-sigmoid/log-sigmoid network in which the log-sigmoid transfer function was employed since its output range was perfect for learning the output bipolar values, i.e. 0 and 1. The hidden layer had 29 neurons after trial test (for details, please see Table A1.1 in the Appendix). In order to identify the class for each input vector, the network was trained to output a value of 1 in the correct position of the output vector and fill the rest of the output vector with 0's. Since the exact 1's and 0's could not be produced by the output of the network during the simulation process, it was necessary to pass the output through the competitive transfer function 'compete' in order to ensure that the output value must be 1 while the others have a value of 0.

Among the 20 sites, 15 sites were selected randomly as training samples and the other 5 sites were used for testing. Table 3.7 summarizes the results of the correct classification of the five testing sites. The percentage shown in the table represents the number of correct classification times out of 1000 trials in which random initial weights were used in each trial. In each trial, the network was trained until the squared error was less than 0.000001.

Table 3.7 Percentage of the correct classification using BP network

Testing site	Original group	Percentage of times of the correct classification
Sri Lanka	A	81.2%
Philippines	B	97.6%
South Africa	B	88.5%
Malaysia	C	90.0%
Brazil	D	93.5%

3.5.2 Classification using the learning vector quantization network

The second type of ANN classifier used in the classification decision model was the learning vector quantization (LVQ) network, which had a competitive and linear layer. The proposed LVQ network had a 16-element input neuron (16 location factors at level 2 for clothing manufacturing sites selection in Fig. 3.3) and a 4-element output neuron (4 classified groups). The number of the hidden layer had 10 neurons, which was also determined by trial test (for details, please see Table A1.2 in the Appendix). The architecture of the LVQ network is shown in Fig. 3.5. In order to train the LVQ network, the LVQ2 learning rule (Kohonen, 1997) was applied to improve the performance. Similar to the former BP method, 1000 trials were conducted to classify the sites. In each trial, the training epoch was set at 200. The percentage of correct classification of the five testing sites is presented in Table 3.8.

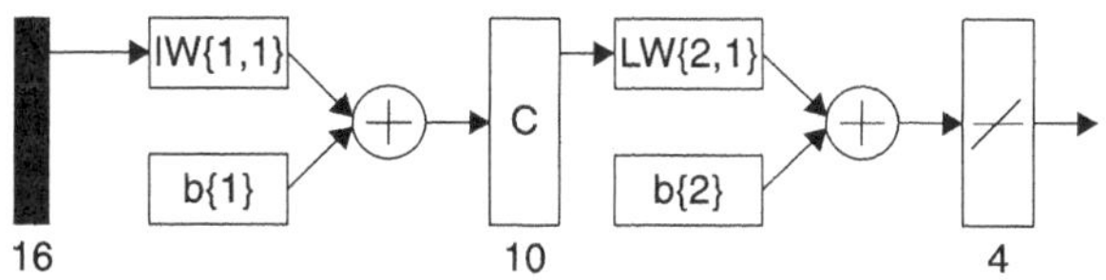

3.5 Abbreviation notation of the architecture of LVQ network.

Table 3.8 Percentage of the correct classification using LVQ network

Testing site	Original group	Percentage of times of the correct classification
Sri Lanka	A	100%
Philippines	B	100%
South Africa	B	83%
Malaysia	C	100%
Brazil	D	100%

3.5.3 Classification using the probability network

The last type of ANN classifier employed is the probabilistic (P) network, which is a feed-forward neural network in which a Bayesian decision strategy for classifying input vectors is implemented (Freeman, 1994). The P network has a 16-element input neuron and a 4-element output neuron. Figure 3.6 depicts the architecture of a P network.

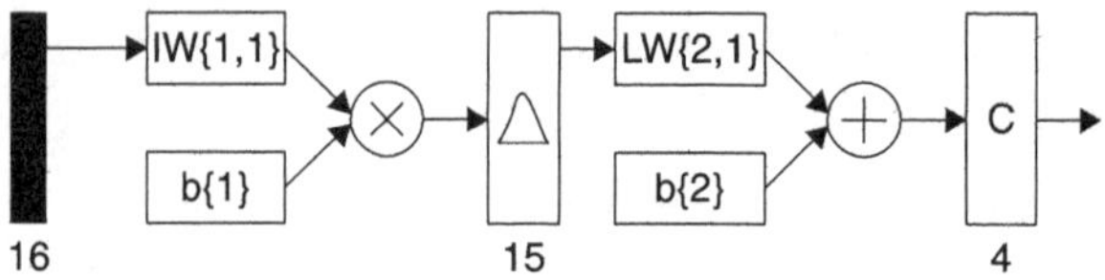

3.6 The abbreviation notation of the architecture of P network.

Table 3.9 Percentage of the correct classification using P network

Testing site	Original group	Percentage of times of the correct classification
Sri Lanka	A	100%
Philippines	B	100%
South Africa	B	100%
Malaysia	C	100%
Brazil	D	100%

In Fig. 3.4, the transfer functions of this network in the first and second layer are the common 'radbas' and 'compet' function, respectively. The hidden layer had 15 neurons which were set by the algorithm of the probabilistic neural network being equal to the number of the testing samples. Table 3.9 indicates that after 1000 trials were conducted, the percentage of correct classification of the 5 testing sites is 100 which outperformed the BP and LVQ network.

3.6 Conclusion

In this chapter, the limitations of adaptive resonance theory of unsupervised artificial neural network were demonstrated and it was concluded that this classification technique is inappropriate for solving the classification decision problem. Three types of supervised artificial neural network, including back propagation, learning vector quantization and probabilistic neural network were compared. The results in Tables 3.7, 3.8 and 3.9 indicate that these three supervised artificial neural network yielded over 80 % of the correct classification, which is benchmarked with the result generated from the multi-attribute utility model. The supervised artificial neural network is thus proved to be a competent and effective classifier for use in the decision-making domain. Of the three supervised artificial neural network methods, the probabilistic network performs best since it is based on probability. Better and possibly even optimal classification results could be acheived by further investigation and by trying to combine the strengths of various types of classifiers.

3.7 Acknowledgements

The authors would like to thank The Hong Kong Polytechnic University for the financial support in this research project (Project A/C Code: A-PE11).

3.8 References

Au, K.F., Wong, W.K. and Zeng, X.H., 2006. Decision model for country site selection of overseas clothing plants, *International Journal of Advanced Manufacturing Technology*, 29(3–4), 408–417.

Brimberg, J. and Revelle, C., 1999. A multi-facility location model with partial, satisfaction of demand, *Studies in Locational Analysis*, 13, 91–101.

Chakravarty, A.K., 1999. Profit margin, process improvement and capacity decisions in global manufacturing, *International Journal of Production Research*, 35(7), 1891–1910, 1999.

Freeman, J.A., 1994. *Simulating Neural Networks with Mathematica*, Addison-Wesley, Reading, MA.

Freeman, J.A. and Skapura, D.M., 1992. *Neural networks: algorithms, applications, and programming techniques*, Addison-Wesley, Reading, MA.

Gaber, M.T. and Benjamin, C.O., 1992. Classifying US manufacturing plant locations using an artificial neural network, *Computers and Industrial Engineering*, 23, 101–104.

Hammond, M.H., Riedel, C.J., Rose-Pehrsson, S.L. and Williams, F.W., 2004. Training set optimization methods for a probabilistic neural network, *Chemometrics and Intelligent Laboratory Systems*, 71, 73–78.

Hoffman, J.J. and Schniederjans, M.J., 1994. A two-stage model for structuring global facility site selection decisions. *International Journal of Operations and Production Management*, 14(4), 79–96.

International Institute for Management Development (IIMD), 2002. *The World Competitiveness Yearbook*, Lausanne, Switzerland.

Kohonen, T., 1997. *Self-Organizing Maps*, Second Edition, Berlin: Springer-Verlag.

Kuo, R.J., Chi, S.C. and Kao, S.S., 2002. A decision support system for selecting convenience store location through integration of fuzzy AHP and artificial neural network, *Computers in Industry*, 47, 199–214.

Liang, G.S. and Wang, M.J., 1991. A fuzzy multi-criteria decision-making method for facility site selection, *International Journal of Production Research*, 29(11), 2313–2330.

Luo, X.C., Singh, C.A. and Patton, A.D., 2003. Power system reliability evaluation using learning vector quantization and Monte Carlo simulation, *Electric Power Systems Research*, 66(2), 163–169.

Ronnqvist, M., 1999. A repeated matching heuristic for the single source capacitated facility location problem, *European Journal of Operational Research*, 116(1), 51–68.

Schmidt, G. and Wilhelm, W.E., 2000. Strategic, tactical and operational decisions in multi-national logistics networks: a review and discussion of modelling issues, *International Journal of Production Research*, 38(7), 1501–1523.

Specht, D.F., 1990. Probabilistic neural networks, *Neural Networks*, 3, 109–118.

Teuvo Kohonen, 1995. *Self-Organizing Maps*, Springer-Verlag, Heidelberg.

Uncu, S., Hodge, G., Jones, M. and Oxenham, W., 2002. An analysis of the current methodologies for international plant location selection, *Proceedings of the IFFTI International Conference*, The Hong Kong Polytechnic University, pp. 750–772.

Verter, V. and Dasci, A., 2002. The plant location and flexible technology acquisition problem, *European Journal of Operational Research*, 136, 366–382.
Yurimoto, S. and Masui, T., 1995. Design of a decision support system for overseas plant location in the EC, *International Journal of Production Economics*, 41, 411–418.

3.9 Appendix: performance of back propagation (BP) and learning vector quantization (LVQ) with a different number of hidden neurons

Table A1.1 Performance of BP with different number of hidden neurons

	Number of hidden neurons			
	9	19	29	49
Train MSE	1.01e-06	1.28e-06	1.14e-06	1.37e-06
Test MSE	0.15	0.101	0.064	0.069

Note: The mean squared error of training is 0.000001

Table A1.2 Performance of LVQ with different number of hidden neurons

	Number of hidden neurons			
	5	8	10	15
Train MSE	0.075	0.089	0.058	0.021
Test MSE	0.138	0.058	0.034	0.068

Note: The training epoch is set at 200

4

Optimizing apparel production order planning scheduling using genetic algorithms

Z. X. GUO, Sichuan University, China and W. K. WONG, S. Y. S. LEUNG, J. T. FAN and S. F. CHAN, The Hong Kong Polytechnic University, China

DOI: 10.1533/9780857097842.55

Abstract: In this chapter the order scheduling problem at the factory level is investigated. Various uncertainties are considered and described as random variables. A mathematical model for this order scheduling problem is presented with the objectives of maximizing the total satisfaction level of all orders and minimizing their total throughput time. Uncertain completion time and beginning time of production process are derived from probability theory. A genetic algorithm is developed to seek after the optimal order scheduling solution. Experiments are conducted to validate the proposed algorithm by using real-world production data. The experimental results show the effectiveness of the proposed algorithm.

Key words: order scheduling, uncertain processing time, probability theory, genetic algorithms.

4.1 Introduction

Faced with ever-increasing global market competition, today's manufacturers have to continuously improve their production performance so as to be more competitive in the market. Effective production scheduling plays a significant role in maximizing resource utilization and shortening production lead times. A large number of studies have been published on production scheduling. These have focused mostly on the scheduling for various types of production systems at the shop-floor or assembly-line level, such as job shop scheduling (Adam *et al.*, 1993; Fayad and Petrovic, 2005; Guo *et al.*, 2006; Kondakci and Gupta, 1991), flow shop scheduling (Ishibuchi *et al.*, 1994; Iyer and Saxena, 2004; Morita and Shio, 2005; Nagar *et al.*, 1996), machine scheduling (Baek and Yoon, 2002; Dimopoulos and Zalzala, 2001; Fowler *et al.*, 2003; Liu and Tang, 1999), assembly line scheduling (Guo *et al.*, 2008; Kaufman, 1974; Vargas *et al.*, 1992; Zhang *et al.*, 2000), etc.

Ashby and Uzsoy (1995) have presented a set of scheduling heuristics to solve the order release and order sequencing problem in a single-stage production system. Axsater (2005) has discussed the order release problem in a multi-stage assembly network by an approximate decomposition technique. Their studies only focused on determining the starting times for different processes of each production order. Chen and Pundoor (2006) have considered order assignment and scheduling in the supply chain, focusing on assigning orders to different factories and finding a schedule for processing the assigned orders at each factory. However, multiple shop floors and multiple assembly lines are set up in most factories. The order scheduling problem at the factory level, involving scheduling the production process of each order to the appropriate assembly line, has not been reported so far.

The great majority of previous studies on production scheduling are based on the deterministic estimation of the processing time of each production process and the arrival time of each order. In real-life production environments, various uncertainties often occur, such as uncertain customer orders, uncertain estimation of processing time, and so on. Deterministic estimation does not reflect industrial practice and will lead to an unsatisfactory scheduling solution. Moreover, without considering these uncertain factors, it is difficult to achieve an optimized production schedule in a real-life production environment. As an example, if a schedule is generated without considering possible orders in the future, new rush orders may interrupt those already scheduled, causing serious disruption of due dates.

This chapter will investigate the order scheduling problem at the factory level, in which each production process corresponds to a unique shop floor comprising one or multiple assembly lines. The objectives are first to maximize the total satisfaction level of orders' actual competition times, and also to minimize these orders' total throughput time by determining which assembly line to use and when the production process of each order should be processed. In a make-to-order manufacturing environment, it is very important to predict whether the due date can be satisfied before receiving a new order from the customer and to schedule the production of each process in different assembly lines. A typical example is apparel manufacturing.

Some possible uncertainties in order scheduling will also be investigated in this chapter. We consider the uncertain processing time as a continuous random variable, and uncertain orders as well as arrival times as discrete random variables. On the basis of the stochastic processing time, the stochastic beginning time and completion time of processes are derived using the probability theory approach. The genetic algorithm (GA) will be adopted to solve the order scheduling problem, in which a novel process order-based representation with variable length of sub-chromosome is presented.

The rest of this chapter is organized as follows. Section 4.2 defines the notations which are used in this chapter. A detailed problem formulation for the order scheduling problem is presented first in Section 4.3. Section 4.4 explains how to calculate the stochastic beginning time and completion time. The proposed GA to solve the addressed order scheduling problem is introduced in Section 4.5. In Section 4.6 experiments are conducted to validate the effectiveness of the proposed methodology using real production data from an apparel manufacturing factory. Lastly, concluding remarks are presented and further research is suggested in Section 4.7.

4.2 Problem formulation

This section explains the formulation of the order scheduling problem in an order-based manufacturing factory. Production processes of each order should be performed in different types of shop floors respectively. Each type of shop floor comprises one or more assembly lines. According to a pre-determined production flow, production processes involved in each order must be completed on an assembly line of the corresponding shop floor. For simplicity, we assume that there is no work in progress (WIP) in each shop floor.

The real-life manufacturing environment is subject to the following constraints:

- Arrival constraint: Order P_i cannot be started until the arrival of this order, i.e.

$$A_i \le B_{i1}. \tag{4.1}$$

- Allocation constraint: Production process R_{ij} can be only processed in the corresponding shop floor which can process it, i.e.

$$\sum_{kl, L_{kl} \notin SAL_{ij}} X_{ijkl} = 0. \tag{4.2}$$

- Each production process must be performed, i.e.

$$\sum_{kl} X_{ijkl} \ge 1. \tag{4.3}$$

- Process precedence constraint: For one order, each process cannot start before its preceding process is completed and the order is transported to the corresponding assembly line, i.e.

$$C_{ij} + ET_{ij} \le B_{ij'}, R_{ij} \in SP(R_{ij'}). \tag{4.4}$$

- Processing time constraint: Process R_{ij} must be assigned processing time, i.e.

$$C_{ij} = B_{ij} + T_{ijkl}. \tag{4.5}$$

In this chapter, T_{ijkl} is represented as a random variable whose probability density function is defined as

$$f(T_{ijkl}) = \begin{cases} k_1 \cdot T_{ijkl} + b_1 & t_L < T_{ijkl} \le t_L + \tau/2 \\ -k_1 \cdot T_{ijkl} + b_2 & t_L + \tau/2 < T_{ijkl} \le t_L + \tau. \\ 0 & otherwise \end{cases} \tag{4.6}$$

A graph of $f(T_{ijkl})$ is shown in Fig. 4.1, in which the values of t_L, τ, p_L and p_U are predetermined constants. The four constants can decide uniquely the proposed probability distribution of processing time, and the vector form (t_L, τ, p_L, p_U) can thus be used to represent the probability density function of this type. Based on

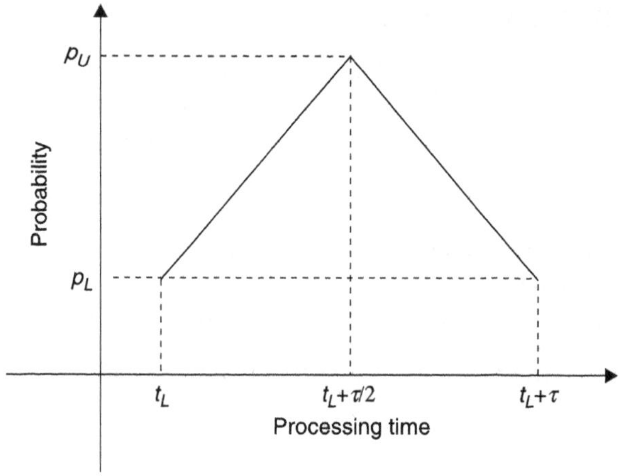

4.1 Probability distribution of processing time.

the given vector, the values of k_1, b_1 and b_2 in Eq. 4.6 can be obtained easily. Moreover, since the total probability in the sample space is 1, the following relationship exists:

$$(p_L + p_U) \cdot \tau = 2. \qquad [4.7]$$

Because order P_i can be uncertain or have uncertain arrival and/or processing times, the above constraints 1–4 are required to be satisfied for each possible realization to accurately model the uncertainties.

In the make-to-order factory, one of the most important production objectives is to meet the due dates of production orders. Since the processing time of production process is uncertain probabilistically, the completion time of each production order is also uncertain. It is difficult to evaluate directly whether the due dates are met. In this chapter, the total satisfactory level *SL* is used to evaluate the performance of all orders to meet their due dates, which is expressed as follows:

$$SL = \frac{1}{m}\sum_{i=1}^{m}\int_0^{\infty} f(C_i)\cdot s(C_i)d(C_i) \qquad [4.8]$$

where $f(C_i)$ is the probability density function of the actual completion time C_i of order P_i. $s(C_i)$ describes the relationship of C_i with its satisfactory level, which is defined as

$$s(C_i) = \begin{cases} k_3 \cdot C_i + b_3 & t_L < C_i \le D_i \\ k_4 \cdot C_i + b_4 & D_i < C_i \le t_U. \\ 0 & otherwise \end{cases} \qquad [4.9]$$

A graph of $s(C_i)$ is shown in Fig. 4.2. The values of k_3, k_4, b_3 and b_4 can be obtained based on the given three coordinates in this figure. These coordinate values are determined by the decision maker. The closer C_i is to its due date, the higher the satisfactory level of C_i. Moreover, the decrease of the satisfactory level is faster when $C_i > D_i$ than when $C_i < D_i$. This is because the former will lead to tardiness penalties, which are greater than the earliness penalties generated by the latter.

The primary objective of the addressed problem is to maximize the total satisfactory level SL, which is expressed as

$$Obj1 : \max SL(B_{i1}, X_{ijkl}) = \max\left(\frac{1}{m}\sum_{i=1}^{m}\int_{0}^{\infty} f(C_i)\cdot s(C_i)d(C_i)\right). \quad [4.10]$$

Based on the optimized total satisfactory level, the secondary objective of the addressed problem is to minimize the expected value of total throughput time TT of all orders, which is expressed as follows:

$$Obj2 : \min TT(B_{i1}, X_{ijkl}) = \min\left(E\left(\sum_{i=1}^{m}(C_i - B_{i1})\right)\right) \quad [4.11]$$

where $C_i - B_{i1}$ is the throughput time of order P_i and $E(\cdot)$ denotes the expected value of a random variable.

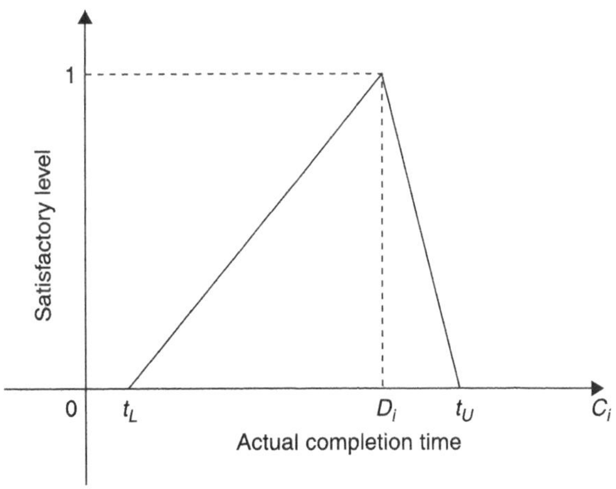

4.2 Relationship between C_i and its satisfactory level.

4.3 Dealing with uncertain completion and start times

In a real-life apparel manufacturing environment, uncertain start time and completion time of operations invariably occur and must be dealt with.

4.3.1 Completion time of production process

The completion time C_{ij} of process R_{ij} is determined by its beginning time and processing time. Since the beginning time and the processing time are independent, the probability density function of C_{ij} is equal to the convolution of probability density functions of its beginning time and processing time according to the theory of probability.

4.3.2 Start time of production process

Since both the processing time and the completion time of process R_{ij} are uncertain, the beginning time of $R_{i,j+1}$, the subsequent process of R_{ij}, is also uncertain. Consider a production situation: production processes R_{12} and R_{22} are assigned to assembly line L_{21} for processing, and the probability density functions of the completion time of R_{12} and R_{21} are determined by vectors $(t_{L1}, \tau_1, p_{L1}, p_{U1})$ and $(t_{L2}, \tau_2, p_{L2}, p_{U2})$, respectively, which are shown in Fig. 4.3 (assume $t_{L1} \leq t_{L2}$). R_{22} is the subsequent process of R_{21}. Process R_{22} cannot begin until processes R_{12} and R_{21} are both completed.

The probability density function of the beginning time B_{22} of R_{22} is computed as follows:

If $t_{L1} + \tau_1 \leq t_{L2}$, B_{22} is determined by the completion time of R_{21} and has the same probability density function as the completion time C_{21} of R_{21}.

If $t_{L1} + \tau_1 > t_{L2} \geq t_{L1}$, B_{22} is determined by the completion times of R_{12} and R_{21}. The beginning time B_{22} will locate between t_{L2} and $t_{L2} + \tau_2$, and its cumulative probability distribution functions $F(B_{22})$ in several different intervals are respectively as follows:

$$F(B_{22}) = \begin{cases} P_{21}^1 - P_{21}^1 \cdot P_{12}^3 & t_{L2} \leq B_{22} < t_X \\ P_{21}^2 + P_{21}^1 \cdot P_{12}^3 & t_X \leq B_{22} < t_{L1} + \tau_1 \\ P_{21}^3 & t_{L1} + \tau_1 \leq B_{22} < t_{L2} + \tau_2 \end{cases} \quad [4.12]$$

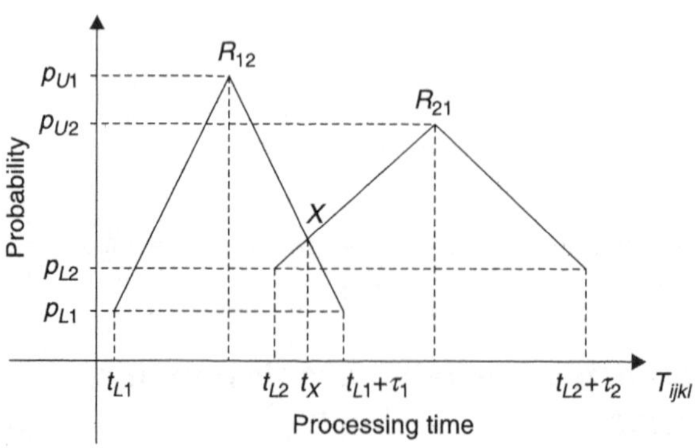

4.3 Probability distributions of processing times of processes R_{12} and R_{21}.

where P^1_{21}, P^2_{21}, P^3_{21} are the cumulative probability distributions of the completion time C_{21} of R_{21} falling into (t_{L2}, t_X), $(t_X, t_{L1} + \tau_1)$ and $(t_{L1} + \tau_1, t_{L2} + \tau_2)$, respectively, and P^3_{12} is the cumulative probability distribution of the completion time C_{12} of R_{12} falling into $(t_X, t_{L1} + \tau_1)$.

The probability density function $f(B_{22})$ of B_{22} is

$$f(B_{22}) = \begin{cases} g(B_{22}) - g(B_{22}) \cdot h(B_{22}) & t_{L2} \le B_{22} < t_X \\ g(B_{22}) + g(B_{22}) \cdot h(B_{22}) & t_X \le B_{22} < t_{L1} + \tau_1 \\ g(B_{22}) & t_{L1} + \tau_1 \le B_{22} < t_{L2} + \tau_2 \end{cases} \quad [4.13]$$

where $g(\cdot)$ is the probability density function of the completion time of R_{21} and $h(\cdot)$ is the probability density function of the completion time of R_{12}.

4.4 Genetic algorithms for order scheduling

The order scheduling problem addressed here is categorized as the combinational optimization problem of NP-hard type (Ross and Corne, 2005) and the number of its possible solutions grows exponentially with the number of assembly line, orders and processes. It is very difficult for the classical technique to solve this type of problem. Since the GA has been proven to be very powerful and efficient in finding heuristic solutions from a wide variety of applications (Goldberg, 1989), it is adopted in this chapter.

The GA was first introduced by Holland (1975). It is a global heuristic search technique whose mechanism is based on the simplifications of evolutionary processes observed in nature. It is an iterative procedure which maintains a population of chromosomes representing different possible solutions to a problem. Each single iteration is called a generation. In each generation, the fitness of each chromosome is evaluated, which is decided by the fitness function, and some chromosomes are selected as the parental chromosomes. Based on the parental chromosomes, new chromosomes, called offspring (also called child chromosomes), are reproduced by two genetic operators, crossover and mutation. The offspring are supposed to inherit the excellent genes from their parents, so that the average quality of solutions is better than that in the previous generations. This evolution process is repeated until some termination criterion is met. The following sub-sections describe in detail how the GA is developed to solve the addressed order scheduling problem.

4.4.1 Representation

The first step in constructing the GA is to define an appropriate genetic representation (coding). A good representation is crucial because it significantly affects all the subsequent steps of the GA. In this research, a process order-based representation with variable length of sub-chromosome is developed. Each chromosome is composed of some sub-chromosomes. Each sub-chromosome represents an assembly line and the value of each gene in the sub-chromosome represents a process which the corresponding assembly line performs. The length of sub-chromosome, i.e. the number of genes in the sub-chromosome, is variable. If one sub-chromosome comprises multiple genes, it indicates that the corresponding assembly line performs multiple processes according to the gene sequence in the sub-chromosome.

Figure 4.4 shows two examples of this representation which describe 16 processes from 5 orders to be assigned to 6 assembly lines of 4 shop floors. As shown in Fig. 4.4, each chromosome includes 6 sub-chromosomes which are separated by brackets. The lengths of the sub-chromosomes corresponding to assembly line 1 of shop floor 1 are different (3 and 2, respectively). Two feasible solutions corresponding to the two chromosomes, represented as an array of length 16, are:

$$[(R_{11}, R_{41}, R_{51}) (R_{21}, R_{31}) (R_{12}, R_{32}, R_{52}) (R_{13}, R_{23}, R_{43}) (R_{24}, R_{34}, R_{54}) (R_{14}, R_{44})]$$

and

$$[(R_{11}, R_{41}) (R_{21}, R_{31}, R_{51}) (R_{12}, R_{32}, R_{52}) (R_{13}, R_{23}, R_{43}) (R_{24}, R_{34}, R_{54}) (R_{14}, R_{44})]$$

Based on each solution, we can obtain the process assignment for different assembly lines and the processing sequence of these processes. For example, according to the first sub-chromosome of chromosome 1, three processes, R_{11}, R_{41} and then R_{51}, will be performed in order in the assembly line 1 of shop floor 1.

4.4.2 Initialization

The GA starts with an initial population of chromosomes. Either heuristic procedures or random creations can be used to generate feasible chromosomes that form the initial population. Anderson and Ferris (1994) have mentioned that the performance of the GA scheme is not as good from the pre-selected starting

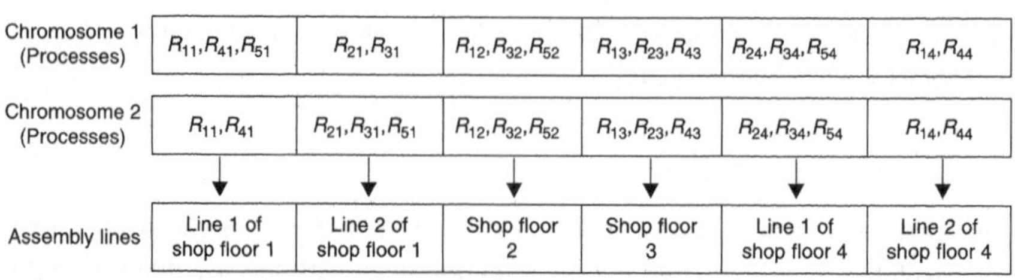

4.4 Sample of the chromosome representation.

population as it is from a random start. In this research each chromosome is randomly initialized by assigning the processes of all orders to the assembly lines which can handle it. The initialization process can be described as follows:

- ***Step 1.*** Initialize parameters: index $i = 1$, a population size u, population $POP = \{\varphi\}$.
- ***Step 2.*** Randomly generate a chromosome CHR_i, $POP = POP \cup CHR_i$.
- ***Step 3.*** Set $i = i + 1$. If $i > u$, STOP, else go to Step 2.

The procedure for randomly generating a chromosome is as follows:

- ***Step 1.*** Initialize parameters: the number of assembly lines in shop floor S_k is LQ_k, the number of shop floors in the factory is SQ, and shop floor index k is equal to 1.
- ***Step 2.*** Randomly divide the processes of all orders, which need be performed in shop floor S_k, into LQ_k set of processes. Each set of processes forms a sub-chromosome.
- ***Step 3.*** Place the generated sub-chromosomes into the corresponding positions of the chromosome in turn.
- ***Step 4.*** Set $k = k + 1$. If $k > SQ$, STOP, else go to Step 2.

4.4.3 Fitness and selection

Fitness function is defined as the fitness of each chromosome to determine which will reproduce and survive into the next generation, which is relevant to the objective functions to be optimized. The value of fitness function of a chromosome, fitness, represents the probability of its survival. The greater the fitness of a chromosome, the greater the probability it will survive.

In this research, objective functions 4.10 and 4.11 can be combined as below:

$$OBJ(B_{i1}, X_{ijkl}) = \max\left(\gamma \cdot \frac{SL(B_{i1}, X_{ijkl})}{TT(B_{i1}, X_{ijkl})}\right) \quad [4.14]$$

where γ denotes the objective weight used to adjust the weighted relationship between the satisfaction level objective and the throughput time objective, and it can be adjusted according to the policy of the factory and the experience of the decision maker. The fitness function *fitness* can thus be defined as

$$fitness = \gamma \cdot \frac{SL(B_{i1}, X_{ijkl})}{TT(B_{i1}, X_{ijkl})}. \quad [4.15]$$

The selection in the GA is the process of selecting chromosomes for the next generation in terms of their fitness. Many selection schemes have been reported (Bäck, 1994). The tournament selection (Goldberg, 1989) is commonly utilized because it is simple to implement and provides good solutions. In this research, this scheme is used and its procedure can be described as follows:

- ***Step 1.*** Set a tournament size $k \geq 2$.
- ***Step 2.*** Generate a random permutation of the chromosomes in the current population.
- ***Step 3.*** Compare the fitness value of the first k chromosomes listed in the permutation, and copy the best one into the next generation. Discard the strings compared.
- ***Step 4.*** If the permutation is exhausted, generate another permutation.
- ***Step 5.*** Repeat Steps 3 and 4 until no more selections are required for the next generation.

The scheme can control the population diversity and selective pressure by adjusting the tournament size k. A larger value of k will increase the selection pressure while decreasing the population diversity.

4.4.4 Genetic operators

Genetic operators are used to combine existing solutions into others and to generate diversity. The former can be implemented by crossover, and the latter can be implemented by mutation.

In the order scheduling problem addressed, each process must be carried out in the corresponding type of assembly line. Thus, the genes of chromosomes for different types of process should be independent and the genetic operations can only be performed among genes with the same assembly line type. Therefore, for the sub-chromosomes of each assembly line type, we perform the corresponding genetic operators. The detailed descriptions of the two operators are as follows.

Crossover

The crossover operation is a random process with a probability of crossover, which breeds a pair of child chromosomes from a pair of parental chromosomes. The typical probability of the crossover operator is between 0.6 and 1.0. A large number of crossover operators have been proposed (Poon and Carter, 1995). Uniform order crossover (Davis, 1991) is commonly utilized because it has the advantage of preserving the position of some genes and the relative sequence of the rest. It is adopted in this research and its procedure is as follows:

- ***Step 1.*** Create a bit string with same length as the chromosomes.
- ***Step 2.*** Copy the genes from Parent 1 wherever the bit code is '1' and fill them in the corresponding positions on Child 1. (Now we have Child 1 filled in wherever the bit code is '1' and we have gaps wherever the bit code is '0'.)
- ***Step 3.*** Select out the genes from Parent 1 wherever the bit code is '0'.

- ***Step 4.*** Permute these genes so that they appear in the same order as they appear in Parent 2.
- ***Step 5.*** Fill these permuted genes in order in the gaps on Child 1.
- ***Step 6.*** To make Child 2, carry out a similar process according to Steps 2–5.

Figure 4.5 shows an example of the uniform order crossover operator.

Mutation

The mutation operation is critical to the success of the GA since it diversifies the search directions and avoids convergence to local optima. It is used to transform the chromosome by the means of randomly changing the genes. Only some offspring take part in the mutation operation. The size is determined by the probability of mutation (the typical value is between 0.0015 and 0.03). In this research, the inversion mutation operator (Holland, 1975) is adopted, which is implemented by simple inversion of the genes between two randomly selected genes of a chromosome. Figure 4.6 shows an example of this mutation operator.

4.4.5 Termination criterion

The GA is controlled by a specified number of generations and by using a diversity measure to stop the algorithm. The diversity of the GA is defined by the standard deviation of the fitness values of all chromosomes of a population in a certain generation. The standard deviation should be less than a certain value, which

Parent 1	R_{11}	R_{41}	R_{51}	R_{21}	R_{31}
Parent 2	R_{21}	R_{31}	R_{11}	R_{41}	R_{51}
Random bit string	1	0	0	1	0
Child 1	R_{11}	R_{31}	R_{41}	R_{21}	R_{51}
Child 2	R_{41}	R_{31}	R_{11}	R_{21}	R_{51}

4.5 Sample of uniform order crossover operator.

Original chromosome	R_{11}	R_{41}	R_{51}	R_{21}	R_{31}
Mutated chromosome	R_{11}	R_{31}	R_{21}	R_{51}	R_{41}

4.6 Sample of inversion mutation operator.

corresponds to the lowest allowed diversity of the population. If either of these two termination criteria is satisfied, the mechanism of the GA is terminated. For example, assume that the specified maximal number of generations is 100 and the lowest allowed standard deviation value is 0.2. Once the standard deviation is less than 0.2, whichever generation the GA is running at, it will be terminated.

4.5 Experimental results and discussion

To evaluate the performance of the proposed algorithm for the order scheduling problem, a series of experiments have been conducted. The experimental data were collected from a make-to-order apparel manufacturing factory producing outerwear and sportswear. This section highlights three of these experiments in detail. Each example includes several cases. In each case, the order scheduling result generated by the proposed method is compared with that of the practical method from industrial practice. In industrial practice, all random variables are replaced by their means and the subsequent deterministic problems are usually solved by using precedence diagrams and trial-and-error method (Bhattacharjee and Sahu, 1987).

The investigated factory comprises seven shop floors, and each shop floor is composed of one or two assembly lines. Each shop floor processes different production processes. Each production process can only be performed in the assembly line(s) of the corresponding shop floor. In this chapter, each production process can only be assigned to one assembly line, and the uncertain processing time obeys the probability distribution presented in Section 4.2 with $\tau = 2$. Moreover, the transportation times between different assembly lines are also negligible because they are much less than the processing times in assembly lines.

4.5.1 Experiment 1: order scheduling with uncertain processing time

In this experiment, three different cases are presented, which are described in detail as follows.

- *Case 1:* five production orders are scheduled in five shop floors performing processes 1 to 5 respectively. The processing time of process 4 of each order is stochastic.
- *Case 2:* five production orders are scheduled in seven shop floors performing processes 1 to 7 respectively. The processing time of process 5 of each order is stochastic.
- *Case 3:* seven production orders are scheduled in seven shop floors performing processes 1 to 7 respectively. The processing time of process 5 of each order is stochastic.

Processes in each case should be performed based on the specified processing sequence; the process with lower process number should be performed earlier.

The relevant data for the three cases are shown in Tables 4.1–4.3 respectively. In these tables, the first column (Order no.) shows the order number, the 'Arrival time' column shows the arrival time of each order, the 'Due time' column shows the due time of each order, and other columns show the mean of processing time of each production process in the corresponding assembly line. For example, the value 4 in the second column and the row of 'Order 1' represents that the average processing time of process R_{11}, the first process of order 1, is 4 units of time in assembly line 1 of shop floor 1. Moreover, in the investigated factory, shop floors 1 and 5 are both composed of two assembly lines, and other shop floors comprise only one assembly line.

In this chapter, the order scheduling solutions for all cases of the different experiments are shown in Fig. 4.7. Based on the order scheduling solutions and the processing time of each process, the Gantt chart of processes being performed in different assembly lines can be obtained. Figure 4.8 shows the Gantt charts for

Table 4.1 Data for case 1 of experiment 1

Order no.	Processing time of process in the corresponding assembly line							Arrival time	Due time
	Shop floor 1		Shop floor 2	Shop floor 3	Shop floor 5		Shop floor 7		
	Line 1	Line 2			Line 1	Line 2			
Order 1	4	6	2.5	2	5	5.5	2	0	17
Order 2	3	4.5	/	4	4	4.5	1.5	0	18.5
Order 3	6	7	3	/	5.5	6.5	2.5	2	27
Order 4	5	5.5	/	3	5	6	2	4	24
Order 5	5.5	7	4	/	6	6.5	2	8	31

Table 4.2 Data for case 2 of experiment 1

Order no.	Processing time of process in the corresponding assembly line									Arrival time	Due time
	Shop floor 1		Shop floor 2	Shop floor 3	Shop floor 4	Shop floor 5		Shop floor 6	Shop floor 7		
	Line 1	Line 2				Line 1	Line 2				
Order 1	3	2.5	2.5	1.5	/	5.5	5.5	1	0.5	0	14
Order 2	4	3	/	4	1.5	4	4.5	1.5	1	0	20
Order 3	5.5	5	4.5	/	/	6	6.5	1	1.5	0	24
Order 4	6	5.5	/	3	2	5	6	1.5	1.5	5	28
Order 5	2	1.5	/	/	/	2.5	3	0.5	1	8	24

Table 4.3 Data for case 3 of experiment 1

Order no.	Processing time of process in the corresponding assembly line									Arrival time	Due time
	Shop floor 1		Shop floor 2	Shop floor 3	Shop floor 4	Shop floor 5		Shop floor 6	Shop floor 7		
	Line 1	Line 2				Line 1	Line 2				
Order 1	3.5	4	4	3.5	/	5	5	1.5	1	0	24
Order 2	5	4.5	/	4	1.5	4	4.5	1.5	1	0	18
Order 3	4	4.5	4.5	/	/	6.5	6	1	1.5	0	26
Order 4	5.5	5	/	2	3	5.5	6	2	1.5	7	35
Order 5	2	2	1.5	/	2	2.5	2	0.5	1	10	27
Order 6	4.5	4.5	/	/	/	2.5	2.5	1	1	16	33
Order 7	3	3.5	/	3	/	3	2	1	1.5	20	32

Table 4.4 Order scheduling results for case 1 of experiment 1

		Order 1	Order 2	Order 3	Order 4	Order 5
Proposed method	Mean of completion time	16	18.07	26	23.5	30
	Satisfaction level	99.00%	99.01%	99.00%	99.09%	99.00%
	Throughput time	16	18.07	21.5	19.5	21
Practical method	Mean of completion time	16	18	24.5	26.5	30
	Satisfaction level	99.00%	99.09%	97.50%	75.00%	99.00%
	Throughput time	16	18	20.5	22	20

case 1 of experiment 1 based on the solutions generated by the proposed method and the practical method. For other cases in this chapter, the Gantt charts can be found in Appendix 2.

The order scheduling results of the three cases are shown in Tables 4.4–4.6. Consider the order scheduling results of case 1 shown in Table 4.4. According to the results of the proposed method, the mean of the completion time of each order is equal or very close to the desired due time and the total satisfaction level of all orders is 99.02%. The total satisfaction level of the practical method is 5.1% less than that of the proposed method because the completion time of order 4 has

Experiment No.	Case No.	Methods	Line 1 of shop floor 1	Line 2 of shop floor 1	Shop floor 2	Shop floor 3	Shop floor 4	Line 1 of shop floor 5	Line 2 of shop floor 5	Shop floor 6	Shop floor 7
Experiment 1	Case 1	M1	R_{11}, R_{41}, R_{51}	R_{21}, R_{31}	R_{12}, R_{32}, R_{52}	R_{13}, R_{23}, R_{43}	/	R_{24}, R_{34}, R_{54}	R_{14}, R_{44}	/	$R_{15}, R_{25}, R_{45}, R_{35}, R_{55}$
		M2	R_{11}, R_{31}, R_{51}	R_{21}, R_{41}	R_{12}, R_{32}, R_{52}	R_{13}, R_{23}, R_{43}	/	R_{24}, R_{34}, R_{54}	R_{14}, R_{44}	/	$R_{15}, R_{25}, R_{35}, R_{45}, R_{55}$
	Case 2	M1	R_{11}	$R_{31}, R_{21}, R_{41}, R_{51}$	R_{12}, R_{32}	R_{13}, R_{23}, R_{43}	R_{24}, R_{44}	R_{25}, R_{55}	R_{15}, R_{35}, R_{45}	$R_{16}, R_{26}, R_{56}, R_{36}, R_{46}$	$R_{17}, R_{27}, R_{37}, R_{57}, R_{47}$
		M2	R_{21}, R_{41}	R_{11}, R_{31}, R_{51}	R_{12}, R_{32}	R_{23}, R_{13}, R_{43}	R_{24}, R_{44}	R_{15}, R_{35}	R_{25}, R_{55}, R_{45}	$R_{16}, R_{26}, R_{56}, R_{36}, R_{46}$	$R_{17}, R_{27}, R_{57}, R_{37}, R_{47}$
	Case 3	M1	R_{31}, R_{41}	$R_{21}, R_{11}, R_{51}, R_{61}, R_{71}$	R_{32}, R_{12}, R_{52}	$R_{23}, R_{13}, R_{43}, R_{73}$	R_{24}, R_{44}, R_{54}	R_{35}, R_{15}, R_{45}	$R_{25}, R_{65}, R_{55}, R_{75}$	$R_{26}, R_{36}, R_{16}, R_{56}, R_{76}, R_{66}, R_{46}$	$R_{27}, R_{17}, R_{37}, R_{57}, R_{77}, R_{67}, R_{47}$
		M2	$R_{11}, R_{31}, R_{51}, R_{71}$	R_{21}, R_{41}, R_{61}	R_{12}, R_{32}, R_{52}	$R_{23}, R_{13}, R_{43}, R_{73}$	R_{24}, R_{54}, R_{44}	$R_{25}, R_{35}, R_{65}, R_{75}$	R_{15}, R_{55}, R_{45}	$R_{26}, R_{16}, R_{36}, R_{56}, R_{46}, R_{56}, R_{76}$	$R_{27}, R_{17}, R_{37}, R_{57}, R_{47}, R_{67}, R_{77}$
Experiment 2	Case 1	M1	R_{11}, R_{41}	R_{21}, R_{31}	R_{12}, R_{32}	R_{13}, R_{23}, R_{43}	/	R_{24}, R_{34}	R_{14}, R_{44}	/	$R_{15}, R_{25}, R_{45}, R_{35}$
		M2	R_{11}, R_{31}	R_{21}, R_{41}	R_{12}, R_{32}	R_{13}, R_{23}, R_{43}	/	R_{24}, R_{34}	R_{14}, R_{44}	/	$R_{15}, R_{25}, R_{35}, R_{45}$
	Case 2	M1	R_{11}, R_{41}	R_{31}, R_{21}	R_{12}, R_{32}	R_{13}, R_{23}, R_{43}	R_{24}, R_{44}	R_{25}	R_{15}, R_{35}, R_{45}	$R_{16}, R_{26}, R_{36}, R_{46}$	$R_{17}, R_{27}, R_{37}, R_{47}$
		M2	R_{21}, R_{41}	R_{11}, R_{31}	R_{12}, R_{32}	R_{23}, R_{13}, R_{43}	R_{24}, R_{44}	R_{15}, R_{35}	R_{25}, R_{45}	$R_{16}, R_{26}, R_{36}, R_{46}$	$R_{17}, R_{27}, R_{37}, R_{47}$
Experiment 3	Case 1	M1	R_{11}, R_{31}, R_{51}	R_{21}, R_{41}	R_{12}, R_{32}, R_{52}	R_{13}, R_{23}, R_{43}	/	R_{24}, R_{44}, R_{54}	R_{14}, R_{34}	/	$R_{15}, R_{25}, R_{45}, R_{35}, R_{55}$
		M2	R_{11}, R_{31}, R_{51}	R_{21}, R_{41}	R_{12}, R_{32}, R_{52}	R_{13}, R_{23}, R_{43}	/	R_{24}, R_{34}, R_{54}	R_{14}, R_{44}	/	$R_{15}, R_{25}, R_{35}, R_{45}, R_{55}$
	Case 2	M1	R_{11}, R_{31}	R_{21}, R_{41}, R_{51}	R_{12}, R_{32}	R_{13}, R_{23}, R_{43}	R_{24}, R_{44}	R_{55}, R_{35}	R_{15}, R_{25}, R_{45}	$R_{16}, R_{26}, R_{56}, R_{36}, R_{46}$	$R_{17}, R_{27}, R_{37}, R_{57}, R_{47}$
		M2	R_{21}, R_{41}	R_{11}, R_{31}, R_{51}	R_{12}, R_{32}	R_{23}, R_{13}, R_{43}	R_{24}, R_{44}	R_{15}, R_{35}	R_{25}, R_{55}, R_{45}	$R_{16}, R_{26}, R_{56}, R_{36}, R_{46}$	$R_{17}, R_{27}, R_{57}, R_{37}, R_{47}$

M1-Proposed method, M2-Practical method

4.7 Order scheduling solutions for all cases of three experiments.

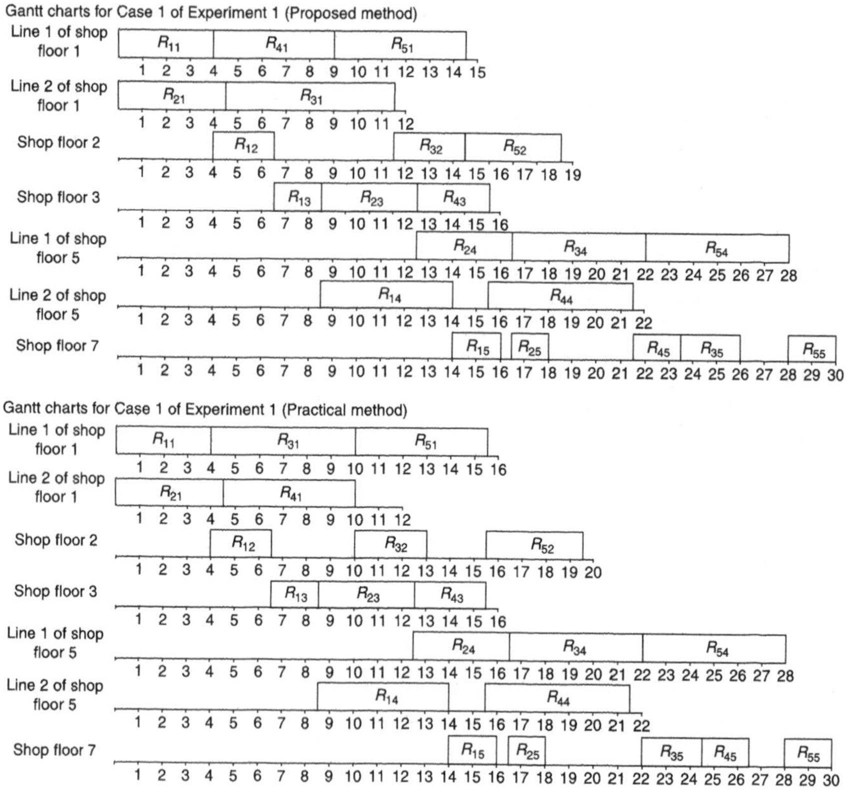

4.8 Gantt charts for case 1 of experiment 1.

about 2.5 time units of tardiness and its satisfaction level is only 75%. Moreover, the total throughput times generated by the proposed method and the practical method are 96.05 and 96.5, respectively. Obviously, the performance of the proposed method is better in this case.

As shown in Tables 4.5 and 4.6, the satisfaction levels of order 1 in cases 2 and 3 are both less than 79% in the practical method, while the satisfaction levels of all orders in the proposed method are greater than 97.80%. Moreover, the total throughput time of the proposed method outperforms that of the practical method in case 2. Regarding the total throughput time in case 3, the result of the proposed method is slightly inferior to that of the practical method. This is because the proposed method generates the scheduling result from the viewpoint of global optimization. These three cases demonstrate that the proposed method can obtain better optimization performance than the practical method from industrial practice.

Table 4.5 Order scheduling results for case 2 of experiment 1

		Order 1	Order 2	Order 3	Order 4	Order 5
Proposed method	Mean of complction time	14	20	23	28	24
	Satisfaction level	97.80%	99.00%	99.00%	99.00%	99.00%
	Throughput time	14	15	23	20	10.5
Practical method	Mean of completion time	16.5	18.5	23.5	26	19.5
	Satisfaction level	75%	97.50%	99.09%	97.00%	94.50%
	Throughput time	16.5	18.5	21	21	11.5

Table 4.6 Order scheduling results for case 3 of experiment 1

		Order 1	Order 2	Order 3	Order 4	Order 5	Order 6	Order 7
Proposed method	Mean of completion time	23.5	17	25	34.58	26.57	32.57	31.5
	Satisfaction level	99.09%	99.00%	99.00%	99.58%	99.57%	99.57	99.09%
	Throughput time	19	17	25	27.58	16.57	16.57	11
Practical method	Mean of completion time	19.5	16.5	22.5	28.5	23.5	29.5	31.5
	Satisfaction level	78.66%	98.50%	96.50%	93.50%	96.50%	96.50%	99.09%
	Throughput time	19.5	16.5	19	21.5	13.5	13.5	11.5

4.5.2 Experiment 2: order scheduling with uncertain order

In each case of this experiment, some existing orders and an uncertain order are scheduled. The data for case 1 and case 2 are similar to cases 1 and 2 of experiment 1 respectively, except that order 5 is uncertain. In cases 1 and 2 of experiment 1, order 5 arrives on time 8. But, in this experiment, order 5 may come on time 8 with probability 0.3, or it may not come at all. That is, two different production events may occur in each case. If order 5 comes, five orders will be scheduled; otherwise only four orders are scheduled.

In the proposed method, two possibilities of each case are scheduled respectively. If order 5 does not come, based on the proposed method, the order scheduling results of the two cases are shown in the 'Proposed method' rows of Tables 4.7–4.8 respectively. In each case, the total satisfaction level is equal to the probability expectation of the satisfaction levels under different possibilities. Take case 1 as an example. If order 5 comes, the total satisfaction level of 5 orders is 99.02%. If it does not come, the total satisfaction level of four orders is 99.03%. Therefore, the total satisfaction level of case 1 is $99.02\% \cdot 0.3 + 99.03\% \cdot 0.7 = 99.027\%$. Similarly, we can obtain that the total satisfaction level of case 2 is 98.575%, and the total throughput times of cases 1 and 2 are 81.37 and 76.34, respectively.

In the practical method, the uncertain order, order 5, is treated as never arriving. The order scheduling considers only four orders and the scheduling results of the two cases are shown in the 'Practical method' rows of Tables 4.7–4.8, respectively. The total satisfaction levels of cases 1 and 2 are 92.65% and 91.90%, respectively. The total throughput times of the two cases are 82.5 and 80.1 respectively, which are inferior to the results from the proposed method. It follows from the discussion above that, in this experiment, the order scheduling results generated by the proposed method are also better than those generated by the practical method when four orders are scheduled.

Table 4.7 Order scheduling results for case 1 of experiment 2

		Order 1	Order 2	Order 3	Order 4
Proposed method	Mean of completion time	16	18.07	26	23.5
	Satisfaction level	99.00%	99.01%	99.00%	99.09%
	Throughput time	16	18.07	21.5	19.5
Practical method	Mean of completion time	16	18	24.5	26.5
	Satisfaction level	99.00%	99.09%	97.50%	75.00%
	Throughput time	16	18	20.5	22

Table 4.8 Order scheduling results for case 2 of experiment 2

		Order 1	Order 2	Order 3	Order 4
Proposed method	Mean of completion time	14	20	21.7	28
	Satisfaction level	97.80%	99.00%	97.70%	99.00%
	Throughput time	14	15	21.7	23
Practical method	Mean of completion time	16.5	18.5	23.5	25
	Satisfaction level	75.00%	97.50%	99.09%	96.00%
	Throughput time	16.5	18.5	21	20

4.5.3 Experiment 3: order scheduling with uncertain arrival times

In this experiment, the arrival times of some orders are uncertain. The data for case 1 and case 2 are also similar to cases 1 and 2 of experiment 1, respectively, except that two orders have uncertain arrival times. In case 1, the arrival time for order 4 is random: either time 4 with probability 0.2 or time 5 with probability 0.8. In case 2, the arrival time for order 3 is random: either time 0 with probability 0.3 or time 3 with probability 0.7.

In the proposed method, the uncertain arrival time should be considered according to all its possible arrival times. The above two cases both have two possible circumstances. For each case, the scheduling results of one possible circumstance have been presented in experiment 1. The scheduling results of other possible circumstances are shown in the 'Proposed method' rows in Tables 4.9–4.10. Taking case 1 as an example, the total satisfaction level is 99.02% if the arrival time of order 4 is time 4, and the total satisfaction level is 98.92% if its arrival time is time 5. Therefore, the expectation of the total satisfaction level of case 1 is 98.94%. Similarly, the total satisfaction level of case 2 can be obtained, which is 98.64%.

In the practical method, the uncertain arrival time of the order is replaced by its mean. That is, the arrival time of order 4 in case 1 is considered as 4.8 and the arrival time of order 3 in case 2 is considered as 2.1. Their scheduling results are shown in the 'Practical method' rows of Tables 4.9–4.10. The total satisfaction levels of the two cases are 93.92% and 95%, respectively. These results are also worse than those generated by the proposed method.

In the above experiments, the order scheduling performance generated by the proposed method outperforms that of the practical method because the former meets the production objectives better. The optimized results in this chapter are obtained based on the following parameter settings: the population size and the maximum number of generations of the proposed GA are 100 and 50, respectively;

Table 4.9 Order scheduling results for case 1 of experiment 3

		Order 1	Order 2	Order 3	Order 4	Order 5
Proposed method	Mean of completion time	16	18.07	26	23.5	29.5
	Satisfaction level	99.00%	99.01%	99.00%	99.09%	98.50%
	Throughput time	16	18.07	22	15.5	19.5
Practical method	Mean of completion time	16	18	24.5	26.5	30
	Satisfaction level	99.00%	99.09%	97.50%	75.00%	99.00%
	Throughput time	16	18	20.5	18.5	20

Table 4.10 Order scheduling results for case 2 of experiment 3

		Order 1	Order 2	Order 3	Order 4	Order 5
Proposed method	Mean of completion time	14	19.5	23	26.07	24
	Satisfaction level	99.00%	99.09%	99.00%	98.07%	97.80%
	Throughput time	14	19.5	20	21.07	13.5
Practical Method	Mean of completion time	16.5	18.5	23.5	26	19.5
	Satisfaction level	85%	98.50%	99.09%	98.00%	95.50%
	Throughput time	16.5	18.5	20.5	21	11.5

the tournament size $k=2$; the objective weight $\gamma=1$; and the proportional parameters k_3 and k_4 in Eq. 4.9 are 0.01 and 0.1, respectively.

4.6 Conclusions

This chapter has dealt with a multi-objective order scheduling problem at the factory level, where uncertainties are described as continuous or discrete random variables. The objectives were to maximize the total satisfaction level of all orders and minimize their total throughput time. These are particularly helpful to meet the due dates of orders and reduce the WIP in each shop floor.

Uncertain processing time (including beginning and completion times) has been derived from probability theory. The GA with a novel process order-based representation has been developed to explore order scheduling solutions. Experiments have been conducted to evaluate the effectiveness of the proposed algorithm. The experimental results showed that the proposed algorithm is substantially better than the practical method and can solve the addressed problem well. Our further research will investigate the uncertainties on scheduling in the level of job shop or assembly line, such as unpredictable machine breakdown, operator absenteeism, and shortage of materials.

4.7 Acknowledgement

The authors would like to thank the Innovation and Technology Commission of the government of the Hong Kong SAR and Genexy Company Limited for financial support of this research project (Project No. UIT/62).

4.8 References

Adam, N., Bertrand, W., Morehead, D. and Surkis, J., 1993. Due-date assignment procedures with dynamically updated coefficients for multilevel assembly job shops. *European Journal of Operational Research*, 68(2), 212–227.

Anderson, E.J. and Ferris, M.C., 1994. Genetic algorithms for combinatorial optimization: the assembly line balancing problem. *ORSA Journal on Computing*, 6(2), 161–173.

Ashby, J. and Uzsoy, R., 1995. Scheduling and order release in a single-stage production system. *Journal of Manufacturing Systems*, 14(4), 290–306.

Axsater, S., 2005. Planning order releases for an assembly system with random operation times. *OR Spectrum*, 27(1–2), 459–470.

Bäck, T., 1994. Selective pressure in evolutionary algorithms: a characterization of selection mechanisms. In *Proceedings of the First IEEE Conference on Evolutionary Computation* (Fogel, D. ed.), pp. 57–62. IEEE Press, Orlando, USA.

Baek, D. and Yoon, W., 2002. Co-evolutionary genetic algorithm for multi-machine scheduling: coping with high performance variability. *International Journal of Production Research*, 40(1), 239–254.

Bhattacharjee, T.K. and Sahu, S., 1987. A critique of some current assembly line balancing techniques. *International Journal of Operations and Production Management*, 7(6), 32–43.

Chen, Z. and Pundoor, G., 2006. Order assignment and scheduling in a supply chain. *Operations Research*, 54(3), 555–572.

Davis, L., 1991. *Handbook of Genetic Algorithms*. Van Nostrand Reinhold, New York.

Dimopoulos, C. and Zalzala, A., 2001. Investigating the use of genetic programming for a classic one-machine scheduling problem. *Advances in Engineering Software*, 32(6), 489–498.

Fayad, C. and Petrovic, S., 2005. A fuzzy genetic algorithm for real-world job shop scheduling. *Innovations in Applied Artificial Intelligence*, 3533, 524–533.

Fowler, J., Horng, S. and Cochran, J., 2003. A hybridized genetic algorithm to solve parallel machine scheduling problems with sequence dependent setups. *International Journal of Industrial Engineering-Theory Applications and Practice*, 10(3), 232–243.

Goldberg, D.E., 1989. *Genetic Algorithms in Search, Optimization and Machine Learning*. Addison-Wesley, Massachusetts.

Guo, Z.X., Wong, W.K., Leung, S.Y.S., Fan, J.T. and Chan, S.F., 2006. Mathematical model and genetic optimization for the job shop scheduling problem in a mixed- and multi-product assembly environment: A case study based on the apparel industry. *Computers and Industrial Engineering*, 50(3), 202–219.

Guo, Z.X., Wong, W.K., Leung, S.Y.S., Fan, J.T. and Chan, S.F., 2008. A genetic-algorithm-based optimization model for scheduling flexible assembly lines. *International Journal of Advanced Manufacturing Technology*, 36(1–2), 156–168.

Holland, J.H., 1975. *Adaptation in Natural and Artificial Systems*. University of Michigan Press, Michigan.

Ishibuchi, H., Yamamoto, N., Murata, T. and Tanaka, H., 1994. Genetic algorithms and neighborhood search algorithms for fuzzy flowshop scheduling problems. *Fuzzy Sets and Systems*, 67(1), 81–100.

Iyer, S. and Saxena, B., 2004. Improved genetic algorithm for the permutation flowshop scheduling problem. *Computers and Operations Research*, 31(4), 593–606.

Kaufman, M., 1974. Almost optimal algorithm for assembly line scheduling problem. *IEEE Transactions on Computers*, 23(11), 1169–1174.

Kondakci, S. and Gupta, R., 1991. An interactive approach for a dual constraint job shop scheduling problem. *Computers and Industrial Engineering*, 20(3), 293–302.

Liu, J. and Tang, L., 1999. A modified genetic algorithm for single machine scheduling. *Computers and Industrial Engineering*, 37(1–2), 43–46.

Morita, H. and Shio, N., 2005. Hybrid branch and bound method with genetic algorithm for flexible flowshop scheduling problem. *JSME International Journal Series C-Mechanical Systems Machine Elements and Manufacturing*, 48(1), 46–52.

Nagar, A., Heragu, S. and Haddock, J., 1996. A combined branch-and-bound and genetic algorithm based approach for a flowshop scheduling problem. *Annals of Operations Research*, 63(1–4), 397–414.

Poon, P. and Carter, J., 1995. Genetic algorithm crossover operators for ordering applications. *Computers and Operations Research*, 22(1), 135–147.

Ross, P. and Corne, D., 2005. Evolutionary scheduling: A review. *Genetic Programming and Evolvable Machines*, 6, 191–220.

Vargas, J., Pishori, R., Natu, R. and Kee, C., 1992. Expert system mixed-model assembly line scheduling. *Expert Systems with Applications*, 5(1–2), 79–85.

Zhang, Y., Luh, P, Yoneda, K., Kano, T. and Kyoya, Y., 2000. Mixed-model assembly line scheduling using the Lagrangian relaxation technique. *IIE Transactions*, 32(2), 125–134.

4.9 Appendix 1: nomenclature

The following notations are used in developing the mathematical model of order scheduling discussed in this chapter:

A_i, arrival time of order P_i

B_{ij}, beginning time of process R_{ij}

C_i, completion time of order P_i

C_{ij}, completion time of process R_{ij}

D_i, due date of order P_i

ET_{ij}, transportation time between assembly lines processing process R_{ij} and its following process

L_{kl}, lth assembly line of shop floor S_k

P_i, ith production order $(1 \leq i \leq m)$

R_{ij}, jth production process of order P_i

SAL_{ij}, set of assembly lines which can perform process R_{ij}

S_k, kth shop floor

SL, total satisfactory level which is used to evaluate the grade of the due dates of all orders being met

$SP(R_{ij})$, set of the preceding processes of process $R_{ij'}$

T_{ijkl}, processing time of R_{ij} on assembly line L_{kl}

TT, expected value of total throughput time of all orders

X_{ijkl}, indicates that if process R_{ij} is assigned to assembly line L_{kl}, X_{ijkl} is equal to 1, otherwise it is equal to 0.

4.10 Appendix 2: Gantt charts

The following Gantt charts show the results generated by the proposed method and the practical method in different cases of 3 experiments. For other cases in this chapter please refer to Section 4.5.

Gantt charts for Case 2 of Experiment 1 (Proposed method)

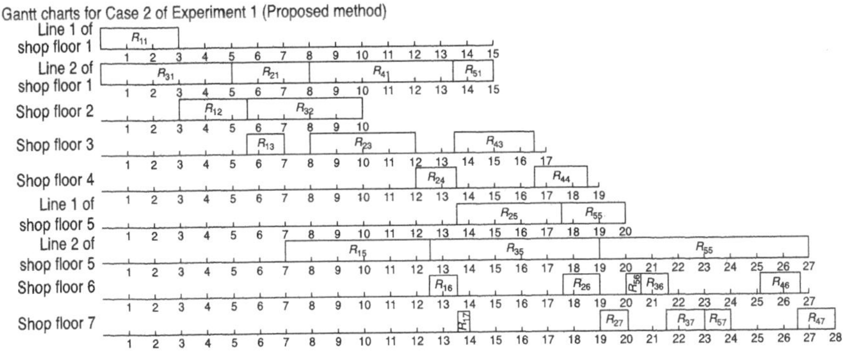

Gantt charts for Case 2 of Experiment 1 (Practical method)

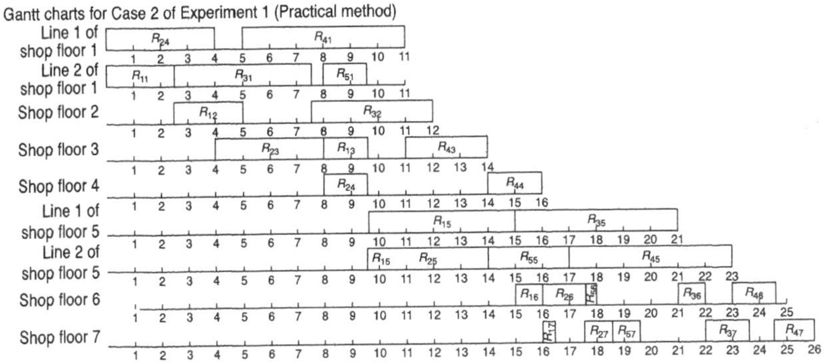

Gantt charts for Case 3 of Experiment 1 (Proposed method)

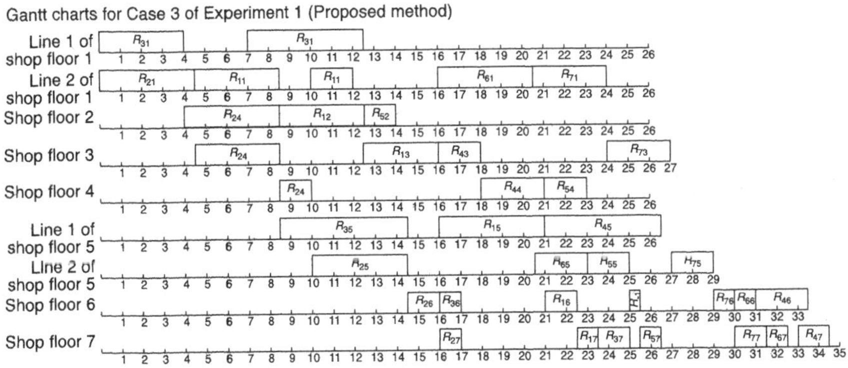

Gantt charts for Case 3 of Experiment 1 (Practical method)

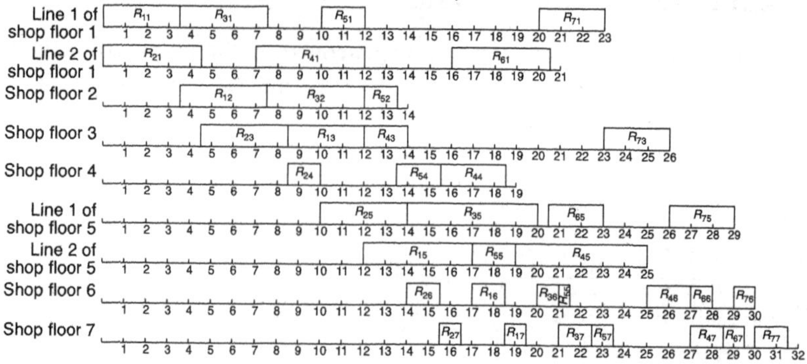

Gantt charts for Case 1 of Experiment 2 (Proposed method)

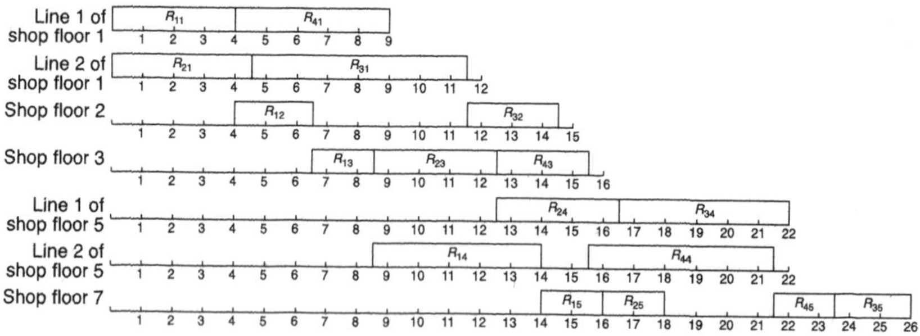

Gantt charts for Case 1 of Experiment 2 (Practical method)

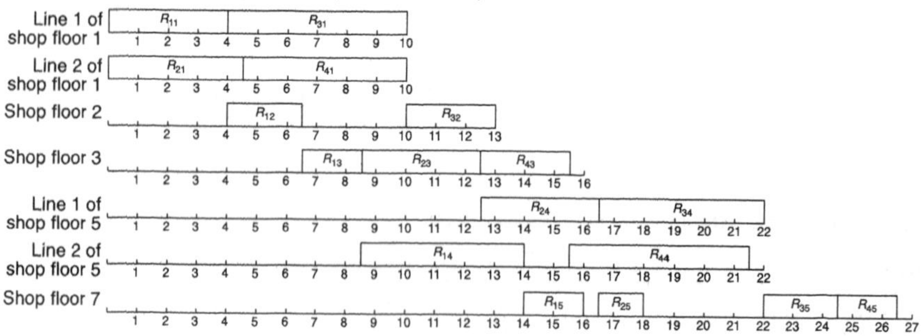

Gantt charts for Case 2 of Experiment 2 (Proposed method)

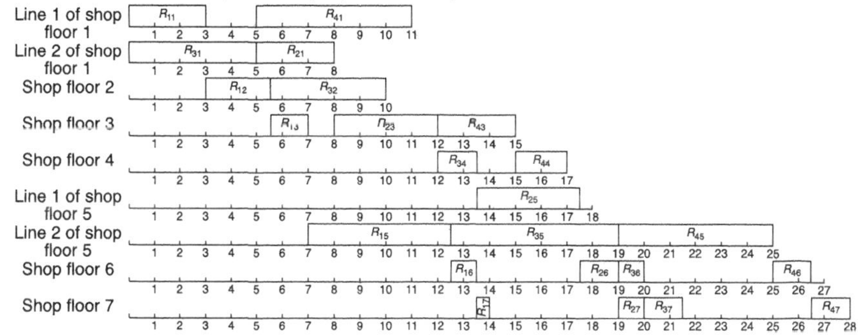

Gantt charts for Case 2 of Experiment 2 (Practical method)

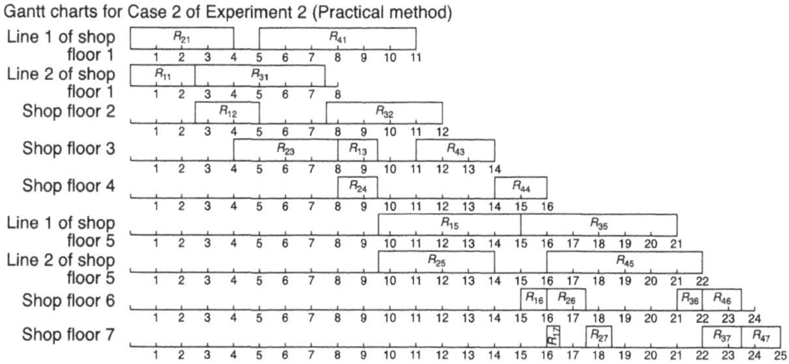

Gantt charts for Case 1 of Experiment 3 (Proposed method)

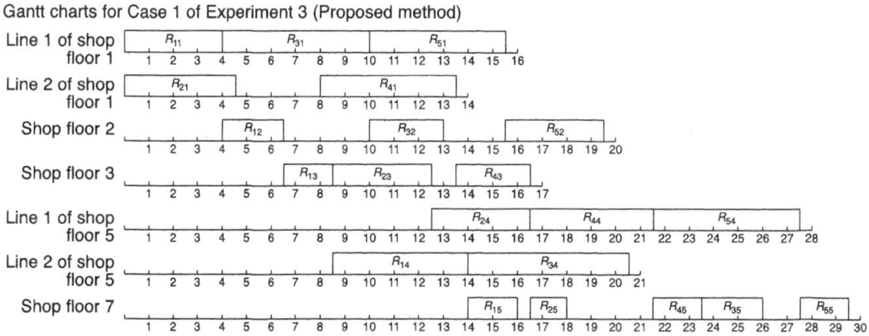

Gantt charts for Case 1 of Experiment 3 (Practical method)

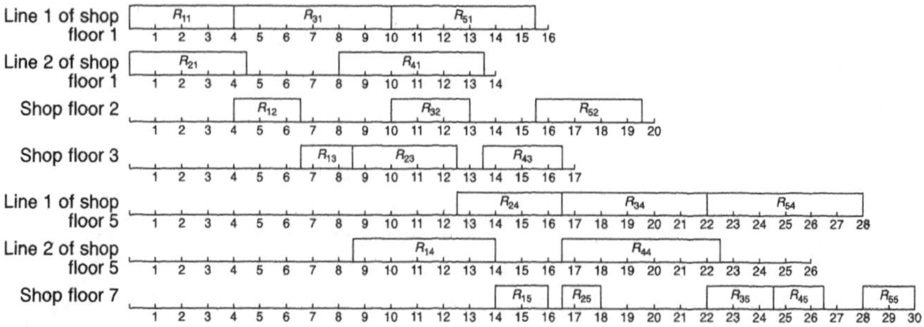

Gantt charts for Case 2 of Experiment 3 (Proposed method)

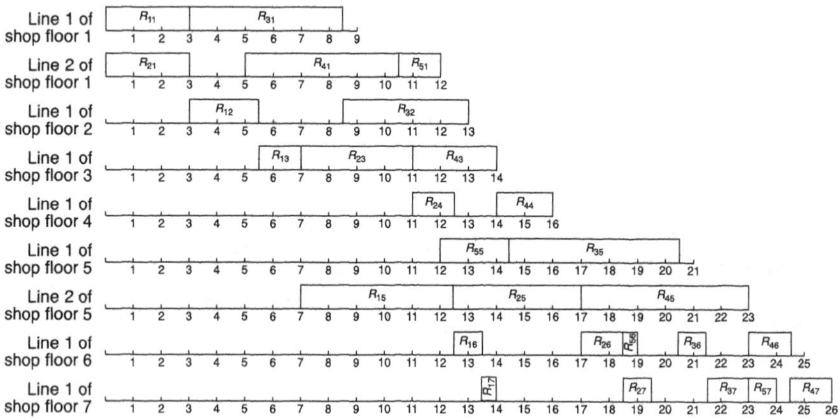

Gantt charts for Case 2 of Experiment 3 (Practical method)

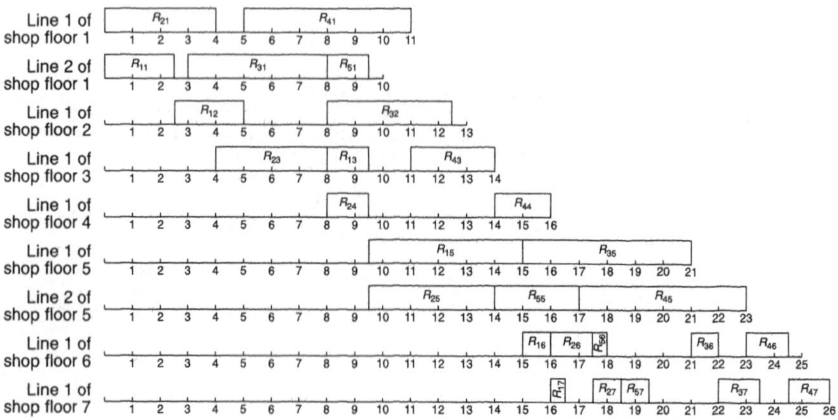

5

Optimizing cut order planning in apparel production using evolutionary strategies

W. K. WONG and S. Y. S. LEUNG,
The Hong Kong Polytechnic University, China

DOI: 10.1533/9780857097842.81

Abstract: Cut order planning (COP) plays a significant role in managing the cost of materials. COP seeks to minimize the total manufacturing costs by developing feasible cutting order plans with respect to material, machine and labour. In this chapter, a genetic optimized decision-making model using adaptive evolutionary strategies is devised for COP. Four sets of real production data were collected to validate the proposed method. The experimental results demonstrate that the proposed method can reduce both the material costs and the production of additional garments while satisfying time constraints. Although the total operation time used is longer than that using industrial practice, this is outweighed by the benefits of reduction in fabric cost and extra garments.

Key words: evolutionary strategies, optimization, decision support, resource utilization.

5.1 Introduction

In today's apparel industry, fashion products require a significant amount of customization due to differences in body measurements, diverse preferences for style and replacement cycles. It is necessary for apparel supply chains to be responsive to the ever-changing fashion markets by producing smaller jobs in order to provide customers with timely and customized fashion products. In apparel supply chains, fabric is the single largest material in the cost of a garment; approximately 50–60% of the manufacturing cost can be attributed to fabric. Apart from the fabric, labour and factory operation costs have also been continuously increasing while the selling price of apparel merchandise has been falling. Adopting quick response strategies to manufacture and deliver apparel products to the retailers while maximizing the fabric utilization rate (in other words, minimizing the material cost) and minimizing the labour and manufacturing cost becomes a great challenge to apparel manufacturers.

5.1.1 Cut order planning

Cut order planning (COP) is the first stage in the production workflow of a typical apparel manufacturing company, as shown in Fig. 5.1. It is a planning process to determine how many markers are needed, how many of each size of garment

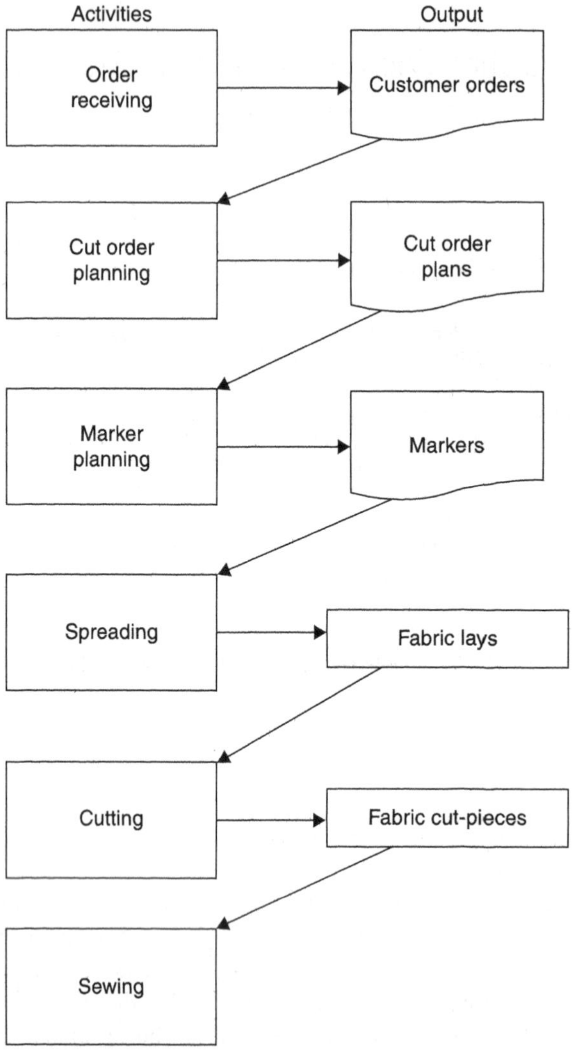

5.1 Schematic workflow of activities of a fabric-cutting department of a typical apparel manufacturing company.

should be in each marker, and the number of fabric plies that will be cut from each marker. Marker is the output of the process of marker planning, which follows cut order planning. Figure 5.2 illustrates a marker planning process using commercial computing to arrange all patterns of the component parts of one or more garments on a piece of marker paper, as shown in Fig. 5.3. Following marker planning, the third operation is fabric spreading, the process by which fabric pieces are superimposed to become a fabric lay on a cutting table, as shown in Fig. 5.4.

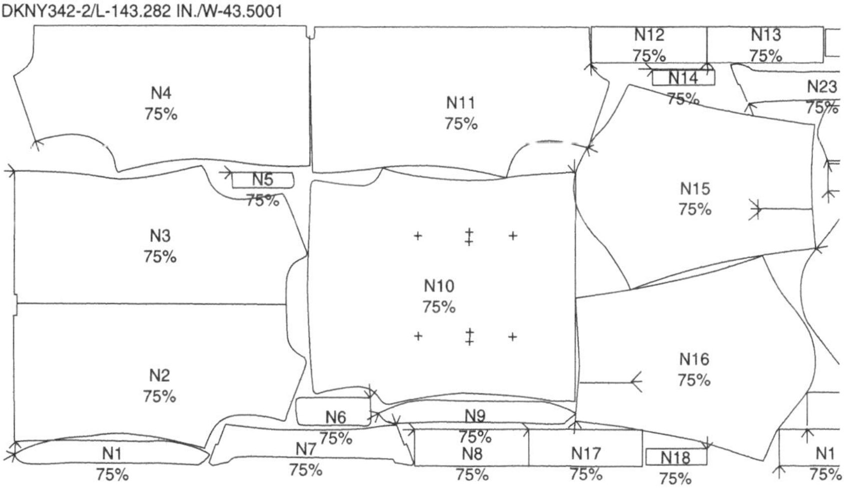

5.2 Example of a marker paper.

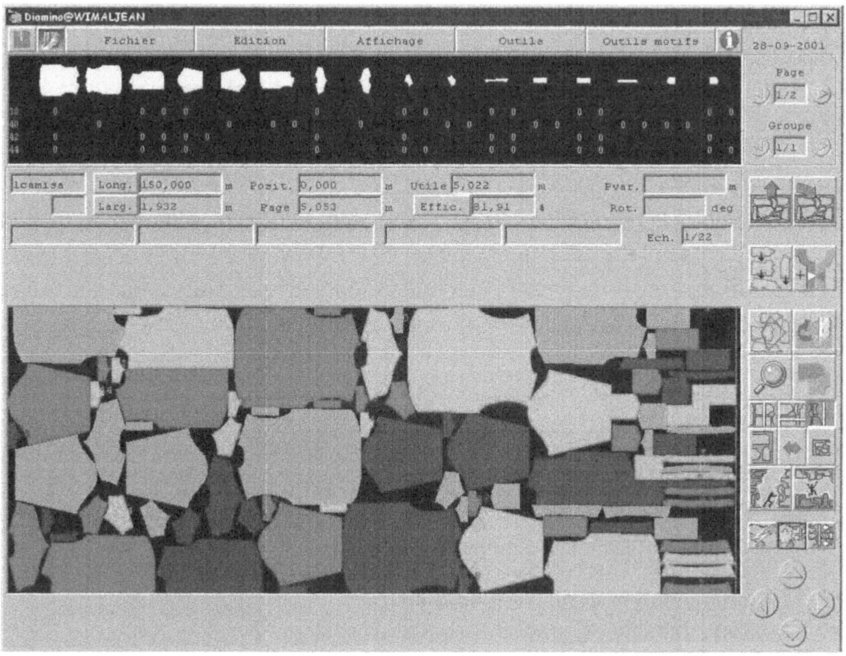

5.3 Marker planning process using commercial computing software.

The last operation is fabric cutting. Garment pieces are cut out of the fabric lay following the pattern lines of the component parts of one or more garments on the marker, and then transported to the sewing department for assembly into a finished garment.

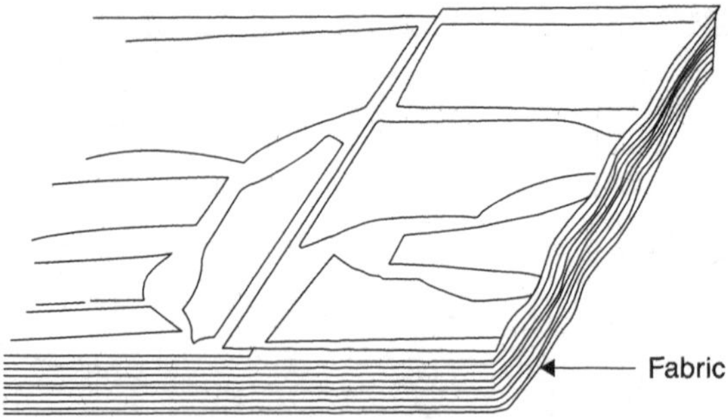

5.4 Fabric lay composed of fabric plies after spreading.

COP, the most upstream activity, plays a significant role in affecting the material cost and the manufacturing cost in the cutting department. Based on the requirements of customer orders in terms of style, quantity, size and colour, it seeks to minimize the total production cost by developing cutting orders with respect to material, machine and labour. In the cutting room, after the completion of COP and marker planning, spreading and cutting are then executed, and the time and costs required for these two operations will be affected by the quality of the cut order plans being developed. A good plan can improve the rate of fabric utilization.

The COP usually begins with a retail order comprising the quantities, sizes and colours of garments to be manufactured. The following example demonstrates how a cut order plan is derived. For simplicity, only the quantities of garments and sizes are considered. The details of the customer order are as follows:

Size	Small	Medium	Large
Quantity (in pieces)	300	600	400

The constraints on fabric lay dimensions are:

- Maximum number of plies for each lay: 75
- Maximum number of garments marked on each marker: 5

The maximum number of garments produced per lay is $5 \times 75 = 375$ pieces and the number of garments required by the customers is $300 + 600 + 400 = 1300$ pieces. Therefore, the theoretical minimum number of lays equals $1300/375 = 3.47$. This gives a practical minimum of four lays to cut the order. If the order is to be cut at the lowest cost, the lays need to be as long and deep as possible. One of the possible solutions is:

Small	Small	Small	Small	Small	Lay 1: 60 plies
Medium	Medium	Medium	Large	Large	Lay 2: 75 plies
Medium	Medium	Medium	Large	Large	Lay 3: 75 plies
Medium	Medium	Medium	Large	Large	Lay 4: 50 plies

An alternative to lay 1 is to have a four-garment marker and to spread 75 plies. This would reduce the cutting cost, but was rejected because of the fabric cost, since there would be 15 more plies and high fabric end loss occurring on both ends of each fabric ply (more plies mean greater end loss). This solution has demonstrated that sizes Medium and Large are in the ratio of 3:2. The marker for lay 2 can also be used for lays 3 and 4, thus reducing the costs of marker making.

This example shows that numerous other possible COP solutions can be generated. The COP problem becomes more difficult when the numbers of garments and sizes increase. The problem will be further complicated when the parameter of colour is also considered in the plan. In addition, labour is needed to operate the spreading and cutting machines. As the fabric cut pieces will be transported to the sewing room for garment assembly, COP needs to consider the fulfilment of the demand quantity of cut-piece from the downstream sewing room.

Current industry approaches in generating the COP range from manual *ad hoc* procedures by cut order planners to commercial software. However, many apparel manufacturers are still using rather primitive methods; they rely mainly on the expertise and subjective assessment of the planners to produce the plans. Therefore, the optimal COP cannot always be guaranteed. Commercial COP software is available for use, but the COP heuristics are usually kept confidential by the proprietors. Apart from generating a COP with the right quantity of garments with the right size and colour, there is little room for minimizing material, machine and labour costs.

This chapter attempts to offer near-optimal COP solutions to reduce both materials and labour and machine costs using a genetic optimization model based on adaptive evolutionary strategies. The objective is to assist the production management of the apparel industry in the COP decision-making process and improve the quality of the decisions. It has been pointed out that the COP problem is NP-completeness in nature and it is feasible to use a heuristic approach to solve the problem accordingly by using constructive heuristics with intuition start and fine-tuning the solution with another improvement heuristic (Jacobs-Blecha *et al.*, 1998).

5.1.2 Evolutionary algorithms

Recently, evolutionary algorithm (EA)-based solution approaches have been proposed for solving different types of optimization problems in different industries. EAs mimic the behaviour of chromosomes in the evolution of living organisms so as to derive solutions for real-world optimization problems. Fogel *et al.* developed a correspondence between natural evolution and the scientific method (Fogel *et al.*, 1966). In nature, individuals serve as hypotheses regarding the general perception of their environment. Their behaviour is an inductive inference regarding the unknown aspects of that environment. Validity is demonstrated by their survival over successive generations, during which individuals become successively better predictors of their surroundings.

In the same sense, in evolutionary algorithms, each individual can be viewed as a point in the search space of candidate solutions for the optimization problem. The fitness of an individual is defined by how well that individual solves the given problem. Individuals with progressively higher fitness will be obtained by evolution over successive generations. In other words, the adaptive change of chromosomes is explained by the principle of natural selection, and only those chromosomes that are best adapted to their environmental conditions are able to survive, i.e. the survival of the fittest. EAs thus constitute an efficient mechanism for finding highly fit individuals in optimization problems, and are regarded as global optimization tools for complex real-world problems (Yao, 1999). Such EAs are considered as a general concept for many real-world applications that are often beyond solution using traditional methods (Bäck and Schwefel, 1993; Bäck *et al.*, 1997).

Porter reviewed the various EAs which were developed for solving industrial optimization problems in the 1990s (Porter, 1998a). These EAs include genetic algorithms, non-adaptive and adaptive evolution strategies (ESs). EAs have gained more and more popularity in both research and application areas as they provide near-optimal or optimal solutions at the end of the optimization process and thus facilitate the choice of the best solution. In addition to their advantages in offering optimal solutions, EAs have been acknowledged for their flexibility and ease in hybridizing with domain-dependent heuristics in the field of industrial engineering and many other applications (Goldberg, 1989; Powell and Skolnic, 1993; Surrey *et al.*, 1995). In particular, there are successful applications of evolution strategies using chromosomes with binary strings to synthesize control policies for complex manufacturing systems (Porter, 1998b; Porter and Merzougui, 1997).

Other successful applications of EAs in marketing decision support systems for product line design (Alexouda, 2005), mechanical design components (Girand-Motean and Laton, 2002), dynamic shop floor scheduling problems (Käschel *et al.*, 2002), material flow in supply chains (Vergara, 2002), web searching (Lee and Tsai, 2003), competence set analysis (Huang *et al.*, 2006) and a detailed review on the area of other manufacturing applications in relatively recent years can also be found in Pierreval *et al.*, (2003).

Non-adaptive ESs perform well only after careful choice of probability of crossover and probability of mutation. Adaptive ESs provide a promising optimization tool since they require no *a priori* selection of mutation or crossover probabilities. In adaptive ESs, the genetic mutation operator has a self-adapting mechanism introduced by Porter (Porter, 1998b). The only difference between non-adaptive binary ESs and adaptive binary ESs is that the probability of mutation, P_m, is not pre-specified in the adaptive case. In addition, there are two major selection schemes in ESs, namely $(\mu+\lambda)$ and (μ,λ), where μ is the population size (which is the same as the number of parents) and λ $(\geq\mu)$ is the number of offspring generated from μ parents. In $(\mu+\lambda)$ ESs, the μ fittest individuals from the pool of $(\mu+\lambda)$ candidates are selected to form the next generation. In (μ,λ) ESs, the μ fittest individuals are selected from only the λ offspring to form the next generation. Experimental findings indicate that the $(\mu+\lambda)$ strategy performs as well as or better than the (μ,λ) strategy in many practical cases (Gehlhaar and Fogel, 1996). Thus, the $(\mu+\lambda)$ strategy was used in the selection for the adaptive ESs in this chapter. In addition, the promising performances of adaptive ESs over non-adaptive evolutionary algorithms are shown in their effectiveness in solving various problems, such as production planning (Porter and Leung, 1998), flow-shop sequencing (Zaheh and Porter, 1998), process planning in automated manufacturing systems (Porter and Leung, 1998) and the design of manufacturing systems (Tong, 2002).

The objective of COP is to minimize costs, including the costs of fabric, labour and machine operation. Indeed, the more garments marked in each of the lays, the more efficiently the fabric is used, though this increases the processing time involving the cutting machine and the labour working hours since more garment patterns need to be cut. Thus, a tradeoff to minimize costs exists between fabric cost and labour/machine operation cost under a pre-defined time frame. Solving such a problem by humans with an optimal solution thus becomes unfeasible. Jacobs-Blecha *et al.* stated that the COP problem is of an NP-complete nature (Jacobs-Blecha *et al.*, 1998). In this chapter, the use of adaptive ESs to solve the COP problem is proposed and a new encoding method with a shortened binary string is devised.

The outline of this chapter is as follows. Section 5.2 describes the model formulation of the COP problem. The genetic COP optimization procedures are described in Section 5.3. The proposed method is demonstrated by an illustrative example and various experiments in Section 5.4, in which the genetically optimized results are compared with those implemented by industrial practice. Finally, conclusions and recommendations for future work are outlined.

5.2 Formulation of the cut order planning (COP) decision-making model

In order to build the decision-making model for the COP, the following notations are addressed:

$G_{\alpha\beta}$ = number of garments in lay α with size β

$P_{\alpha\gamma}$ = number of plies in lay α with colour γ
$A_{\beta\gamma}$ = order quantity for size β with colour γ
$Q_{\alpha\beta\gamma}$ = plan order quantity in lay α for size β and colour γ
ℓ_{max} = maximum fabric length per lay
$L_{max'}$ = estimated maximum number of lays in the cut order plan
H_{max} = maximum allowed ply height
H_{min} = minimum required ply height if any
Y = fabric yield rate per dozen of garments
ε = fabric end allowance per ply
U_{α} = fabric utilization per lay
C_F = fabric cost per metre
C_L = labour cost per hour
C_E = electricity cost per kilowatt hour
T_C = cutting time per garment (min)
T_S = spreading time per metre (min)
T_P = preparation time per lay (min)
τ = demand time constraint from the sewing room (min)
W_C = cutting machine operation (Watts)
W_S = spreading machine operation (Watts)
Γ_F = total fabric cost for the cut order plan
Γ_L = total labour cost for the cut order plan
Γ_M = total machine cost for the cut order plan
Γ = total cost for the cut order plan
Φ = fitness of the cut order plan

Given a customer order consisting of certain quantities of garments with sizes β = 1,2,. . .,S and colours γ = 1,2,. . .,C, a certain number of fabric lays α = 1,2,. . .,L is determined for spreading and cutting. In each of the lays α = 1,2,. . .,L being cut, the number of garments $G_{\alpha\beta}$ for each size β = 1,2,. . .,S and the number of plies $P_{\alpha\gamma}$ for each colour γ = 1,2,. . .,C is determined. Hence, the quantity of garments allocated for a particular size and particular colour in a particular lay is the product of $G_{\alpha\beta} \times P_{\alpha\gamma}$ and denoted as $Q_{\alpha\beta\gamma}$ (α = 1,2,. . .,L; β = 1,2,. . .,S; γ = 1,2,. . .,C). In addition, for each of the cut order plans, the performance is evaluated in terms of the cost functions.

Equation 5.1a explains that the total material cost used for a production order depends on the total number of garments and fabric ply spread, which is determined by the cut order plan, the fabric length of each garment used (calculated by the fabric yield dozen per dozen divided by 12), and the fabric end allowance of each of the lays.

$$\begin{aligned}\Gamma_F &= \sum_{\alpha=1}^{L}\left\{\left[\sum_{\beta=1}^{S} G_{\alpha\beta}\frac{Y}{12}+\varepsilon\right]\sum_{\gamma=1}^{C} P_{\alpha\gamma}U_{\alpha}+\left[\sum_{\beta=1}^{S} G_{\alpha\beta}\frac{Y}{12}+\varepsilon\right]\sum_{\gamma=1}^{C} P_{\alpha\gamma}\left(1-U_{\alpha}\right)\right\}C_F \\ &= \sum_{\alpha=1}^{L}\left\{\left[\sum_{\beta=1}^{S} G_{\alpha\beta}\frac{Y}{12}+\varepsilon\right]\sum_{\gamma=1}^{C} P_{\alpha\gamma}\right\}C_F.\end{aligned} \quad [5.1a]$$

Equation 5.1b demonstrates the overall labour cost involved in a cut order plan, including the cost of the cutting worker who operates the cutting machine to cut the total number of garments in the plan, and the cost of the spreading worker who operates the spreading machine to spread the total fabric length determined by the total number of garments and plies according to the plan. As labour force is necessary to load the fabric to the spreading machine and remove the cut-pieces from the cutting machine after cutting, the amount of labour cost, which is proved to be proportional to the quantity of fabric lays, is considered in Eq. 5.1b.

$$\Gamma_L = \frac{T_P L + \sum_{\alpha=1}^{L}\left[\sum_{\beta=1}^{S} G_{\alpha\beta} T_C + \left(\sum_{\gamma=1}^{C} P_{\alpha\gamma} \sum_{\beta=1}^{S} G_{\alpha\beta}\frac{Y}{12} + \varepsilon\right) T_S\right]}{60} \times C_L. \quad [5.1b]$$

In Eq. 5.1c,

$$\Gamma_M = \frac{\sum_{\alpha=1}^{L}\left[\sum_{\beta=1}^{S} G_{\alpha\beta} T_C W_C + \left(\sum_{\gamma=1}^{C} P_{\alpha\gamma} \sum_{\beta=1}^{S} G_{\alpha\beta}\frac{Y}{12} + \varepsilon\right) T_S W_S\right]}{60 \times 1000} \times C_E \quad [5.1c]$$

the machine cost spent is based on the operation cost of both spreading and cutting machines in terms of machine working time and the specific operation Watt used. The total cost expense is

$$\Gamma = \Gamma_F + \Gamma_L + \Gamma_M \quad [5.1d]$$

and hence the fitness is

$$\Phi = \frac{10000}{\Gamma}. \quad [5.2a]$$

However, if any of the constraints 5.3, 5.4, 5.5 or 5.6 is violated, the fitness will be

$$\Phi = 0. \quad [5.2b]$$

The number of garments $G_{\alpha\beta}$ ($\alpha = 1,2,\ldots,L$; $\beta = 1,2,\ldots,S$) and the number of plies $P_{\alpha\gamma}$ ($\alpha = 1,2,\ldots,L$; $\gamma = 1,2,\ldots,C$) are subject to the following constraints:

$$H_{min} \le \sum_{\gamma=1}^{C} P_{\alpha\gamma} \le H_{max} \quad \forall\, \alpha = 1,2,\ldots,L \quad [5.3]$$

$$\sum_{\beta=1}^{S} G_{\alpha\beta} U_{\alpha} \frac{Y}{12} + \varepsilon \le L_{max} \quad \forall\, \alpha = 1,2,\ldots,L \quad [5.4]$$

$$\sum_{\alpha=1}^{L} Q_{\alpha\beta\gamma} \ge A_{\beta\gamma} \quad \forall\, \beta = 1,2,\ldots,S; \gamma = 1,2,\ldots,C \quad [5.5]$$

$$T_P L + \sum_{\alpha=1}^{L}\left[\sum_{\beta=1}^{S} G_{\alpha\beta} T_C + \left(\sum_{\gamma=1}^{C} P_{\alpha\gamma} \sum_{\beta=1}^{S} G_{\alpha\beta}\frac{Y}{12} + \varepsilon\right) T_S\right] \leq \tau \qquad [5.6]$$

$$\forall\, \alpha = 1,2,\ldots,L; \beta = 1,2,\ldots,S; \gamma = 1,2,\ldots,C$$

where the total number of plies $\sum_{\gamma=1}^{C} P_{\alpha\gamma}$ for all colours in each of the lays α is constrained by the physical cutter height H_{max} and the desired minimum number of plies H_{min}. The total length for the number of garments used $\sum_{\beta=1}^{S} G_{\alpha\beta} U_{\alpha} \frac{Y}{12} + \varepsilon$ in each lay α cannot exceed the cutting table length as denoted by ℓ_{max}. Moreover, in the case of lay $\alpha = L_{max'}$ that the total order quantity $\sum_{\alpha=1}^{L_{max'}} Q_{\alpha\beta\gamma}$ has not yet completed the order quantity $A_{\beta\gamma}$ ($\beta = 1,2,\ldots,S$; $\gamma = 1,2,\ldots,C$), this order plan fails and hence fitness equals zero as in Eq. 5.2b as it violates the inequality 5.5. Lastly, the total time used in cutting, spreading and preparation that constitutes the labour time as illustrated in Eq. 5.1b cannot exceed the demand time instructed from the sewing room, τ.

Thus, a genetic cut order plan is developed to find out the number of garments $G_{\alpha\beta}$ for each size $\beta = 1,2,\ldots,S$ and the number of plies $P_{\alpha\gamma}$ for each colour $\gamma = 1,2,\ldots,C$ in each of the lays $\alpha = 1,2,\ldots,L$ by adaptive evolution strategies so as to optimize the cost function in Eq. 5.1d with highest fitness in Eq. 5.2a.

5.3 Genetic COP optimization

In this section, two possible encoding methods are elaborated and a new encoding method which can shorten the binary string is demonstrated. Procedures for generating COP with an illustrative example and a genetic COP optimization process will be presented. In order to minimize the cost function Γ, a cut order planner needs to determine the number of lays L that the plan requires, as well as the number of garments $G_{\alpha\beta}$ for each size β and the number of plies $P_{\alpha\gamma}$ for each colour γ in each fabric lay α. The genetic cut order plan induction is to mimic how the industrial practice figures out the number of garments and plies in each lay for the plan using adaptive evolution strategies. Since the length of the binary string needs to be fixed for the evolutionary process with adaptive ESs, the estimated maximum number of lays, $L_{max'}$, which is the approximate maximum number of lays to complete the order, is introduced. Once the garment quantities of various sizes and colours required by the order are fulfilled in lay L (which $L \leq L_{max'}$), L would be the optimum number of lays used in completing the COP. However, in case of the binary string that the actual order cannot be completed until lay $L_{max'}$, zero fitness will be assigned to that particular binary string as inequality 5.2b as it violates inequality 5.5.

5.3.1 Encoding method of the binary string

In the genetic synthesis of the binary string representing the cut order plan, two possible kinds of encoding methods are considered due to search space discrepancy.

In encoding method 1, each binary string consists of $L_{max'}$ (S + C) binary sub-strings. Each binary sub-string represents the number of garments in S for different sizes, and the number of plies in C for different colours for a particular fabric lay α ($\alpha = 1,2,\ldots,L$). As each number of garment and ply could be chosen from the range $\left[1, \frac{12(\ell_{max} - \varepsilon)}{U_\alpha Y}\right]$ and $[H_{min}, H_{max}]$ respectively, the total number of combinations, N_{com1}, is used for the number of garments and plies in the plan represented by the binary string as

$$N_{com1} = \left(\frac{12(\ell_{max} - \varepsilon)}{U_\alpha Y} - 1\right)^{SL_{max'}} (H_{max} - H_{min})^{CL_{max'}}. \qquad [5.7]$$

In encoding method 2, the binary string is shortened with only $L_{max'}$ and binary sub-strings that comprise

$$N_{com2} = (H_{max} - H_{min})^{L_{max'}} \qquad [5.8]$$

different combinations. In this method, the great number of sizes and colours involved in the computing time thus will not hinder evolutionary progress in searching for the optimized solution. Consider the examples with $\frac{12(\ell_{max} - \varepsilon)}{U_\alpha Y} - 1 = 10$, $H_{max} - H_{min} = 10$ in the following four cases:

Case 1: S=1, C=1, $L_{max'}$ =1

Case 2: S=2, C=1, $L_{max'}$=1

Case 3: S=2, C=2, $L_{max'}$=1

Case 4: S=2, C=2, $L_{max'}$=2;

the total number of combinations for encoding method 1, N_{com1}, and encoding method 2, N_{com2}, as well as the number of binary sub-strings, can be compared, as shown in Table 5.1.

Table 5.1 clearly shows the rapid increase of N_{com1} with S, C and L, particularly when the number of lays, L, increases. Nevertheless, the computing time in searching for the optimized solution within such a huge search space with N_{com1} is crucial in the evolutionary progress. In order to evolutionarily generate the optimized solution with efficient running time, encoding method 2 is used in this chapter with the encoding details described on the next page.

Table 5.1 Comparison of the total number of combinations in two different encoding methods

	Case 1	Case 2	Case 3	Case 4
Encoding method 1: binary sub-strings	2	3	4	8
N_{com1}	100	1000	10 000	100 000 000
Encoding method 2: binary sub-strings	1	1	1	2
N_{com2}	10	10	10	100

The shortened binary string is presented, in which only the specific ply number $P_{\alpha\gamma'}$ of specific colour γ' is encoded as the binary sub-string for lay α in the binary string, as shown in Fig. 5.5. Indeed, $P_{1\gamma'}$ is selected from the minimum actual order quantity $\sum_{\beta=1}^{S} A_{\beta\gamma} > 0$ for the 1st lay and $P_{\alpha\gamma'}$ ($\alpha = 2,3, \ldots, L_{max'}$) is selected from the minimum remaining order quantity $\sum_{\beta=1}^{S}\left(A_{\beta\gamma} - \sum_{\alpha=1}^{L-1} Q_{\alpha\beta\gamma}\right) > 0$ for the Lth lay ($A_{\beta\gamma} - \sum_{\alpha=1}^{L-1} Q_{\alpha\beta\gamma} = 0$ instead when $\sum_{\alpha=1}^{L-1} Q_{\alpha\beta\gamma} > A_{\alpha\gamma}$ for each size β). The range of $P_{\alpha\gamma'}$ is bounded by the physical constraints of the ply height as shown in inequality 5.3, and the remaining $P_{\alpha\gamma}$ is bounded by $[\max(1,H_{min}),\min\left(\sum_{\beta=1}^{S} A_{\beta\gamma}, H_{max}\right)]$ when $\alpha = 1$ and $[\max(1,H_{min}),\min(\sum_{\beta=1}^{S}\left(A_{\beta\gamma} - \sum_{\alpha=1}^{L-1} Q_{\alpha\beta\gamma}\right), H_{max})]$ when $\alpha > 1$. Hence, the adaptive evolution strategy is used to find the $P_{\alpha\gamma'}$ within the above range for each lay so as to optimize the cost function as shown in Eq. 5.1d.

5.3.2 Procedures for generating COP

Then the specific ply number $P_{\alpha\gamma'}$ is used to generate the garment numbers $G_{\alpha\beta}$ for sizes $\beta = 1,2, \ldots, S$ as well as the remaining ply numbers $P_{\alpha\gamma}$ for the rest of the colours $\gamma = 1,2, \ldots, C$ except γ' in each lay. In general, $G_{\alpha\beta}$ is determined by the

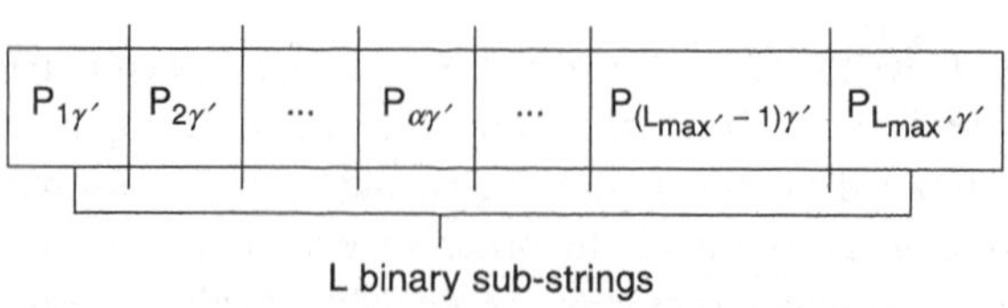

5.5 Configuration of binary strings for the cut order planning.

quotient $\Theta_{\alpha\beta\gamma'}$, as shown in Eq. 5.9 that $A_{\beta\gamma} - \sum_{\alpha=1}^{L} Q_{\alpha\beta\gamma}$ dividing $P_{\alpha\gamma'}$ with the consideration of the remainder $\Re$,

$$A_{\beta\gamma} - \sum_{\alpha=1}^{L} Q_{\alpha\beta\gamma} = \Theta_{\alpha\beta\gamma'} \times P_{\alpha\gamma'} + \Re, \qquad [5.9]$$

where $\sum_{\alpha=1}^{L} Q_{\alpha\beta\gamma} = 0$ when $\alpha = 1$ and $A_{\beta\gamma} - \sum_{\alpha=1}^{L} Q_{\alpha\beta\gamma} = 0$ when $\sum_{\alpha=1}^{L} Q_{\alpha\beta\gamma} \geq A_{\beta\gamma}$. Similarly, the remaining ply number $P_{\alpha\gamma}$ is determined by the minimum quotient min $\{\Theta'_{\alpha\beta\gamma}\}$ for $\beta = 1,2, \ldots, S$ in each particular lay α and colour γ derived from Eq. 5.10 when $A_{\beta\gamma} - \sum_{\alpha=1}^{L} Q_{\alpha\beta\gamma'}$, dividing $G_{\alpha\beta}$ for $G_{\alpha\beta} > 0$ with the consideration of the remainder $\Re'$,

$$A_{\beta\gamma} - \sum_{\alpha=1}^{L} Q_{\alpha\beta\gamma} = \Theta'_{\alpha\beta\gamma} \times G_{\alpha\beta} + \Re', \qquad [5.10]$$

where $\sum_{\alpha=1}^{L} Q_{\alpha\beta\gamma} = 0$ when $\alpha = 1$ and $A_{\beta\gamma} - \sum_{\alpha=1}^{L} Q_{\alpha\beta\gamma} = 0$ when $\sum_{\alpha=1}^{L} Q_{\alpha\beta\gamma} \geq A_{\beta\gamma}$. The details of determining the garment number $G_{\alpha\beta}$ by the specific ply number $P_{\alpha\gamma'}$, and hence the remaining ply number $P_{\alpha\gamma}$, are illustrated by the following example with $S = 3$, $C = 4$, $\gamma' = 4$ for both $\alpha = 1$ and $\alpha = 2$, as shown in Tables 5.2 and 5.3, respectively.

In this case, for $\alpha = 1$, if $P_{1\gamma'} = P_{14} = 7$, the number of garments is derived by Eq. 5.9 such that

$$G_{1\beta} = \begin{cases} \Theta_{1\beta 4} & \text{when } \Re \leq 5 \\ \Theta_{1\beta 4} + 1 & \text{when } \Re > 5 \end{cases}.$$

Since $\sum_{\alpha=1}^{L} Q_{\alpha\beta\gamma} = 0$ and $A_{14} = 1$, A_{14} dividing P_{14} gives the quotient $\Theta_{114} = 0$ with remainder $\Re = 1$, $G_{11} = 0$. Then, $G_{12} = 2$ and $G_{13} = 1$ could be drawn similarly to G_{11},

Table 5.2 Lay 1 cut order plan for the example with $S = 3$, $C = 4$, $\gamma' = 4$

No. of garments	$G_{11}=0$	$G_{12}=2$	$G_{13}=1$	$\sum_{\beta=1}^{3} A_{\beta\gamma}$	No. of ply
Col \ Size	1	2	3		
1	5	33	4	42	$P_{11}=4$
2	2	40	29	71	$P_{12}=20$
3	0	31	22	53	$P_{13}=16$
4	1	13	6	19	$P_{14}=7$

Table 5.3 Lay 2 cut order plan for the example with S = 3, C = 4, $\gamma' = 4$

No. of garments	$G_{21}=1$	$G_{22}=0$	$G_{23}=0$	$\sum_{\beta=1}^{3}\left(A_{\beta\gamma}-\sum_{\alpha=1}^{2-1}Q_{\alpha\beta\gamma}\right)$	No. of plies
Col \ Size	1	2	3		
1	5	25	0	30	$P_{21}=5$
2	2	0	9	11	$P_{22}=2$
3	0	0	6	6	$P_{23}=0$
4	1	0	0	1	$P_{24}=1$

which is shown in previous lines. According to Eq. 5.10, the number of plies $P_{1\gamma}$ is determined by the minimum quotient $\min\{\Theta'_{1\beta\gamma}\}$ across the size $\beta = 1,2,\ldots, S$ in lay 1 for each particular colour γ. The orders $A_{\beta\gamma}$ divide the number of garments $G_1\beta$ for $G_{1\beta} \neq 0$ such that

$$P_{1\gamma} = \begin{cases} \min\left\{\Theta'_{1\beta\gamma}\right\} & \text{for } \beta = 1,2,3 \quad \text{when } \Re' \le 5 \\ \min\left\{\Theta'_{1\beta\gamma}\right\}+1 & \text{for } \beta = 1,2,3 \quad \text{when } \Re' > 5 \end{cases}.$$

In drawing the number of plies P_{11}, the quotient Θ'_{111} is not included in the set $\min\{\Theta'_{1\beta 1}\}$ as $G_{11} = 0$ and is neglected. Thus P_{11} is determined by the quotient found by either G_{12} or G_{13}. As the quotient of $A_{21} = 33$ dividing $G_{12} = 2$ gives $\Theta'_{121} = 17$ with remainder $R' = 1$ while $A_{31} = 4$ dividing $G_{13} = 1$ gives $\Theta'_{131} = 4$ with remainder $R' = 0$, P_{11} is equal to the minimum quotient $\min\{\Theta'_{1\beta 1}\} = 4$ as remainder $R' = 0$. In the same sense, $P_{12} = 20$ and $P_{13} = 16$ can be drawn accordingly.

For $\alpha = 2$ related to the above example, if $P_{2\gamma} = P_{24} = 1$, the number of garments $G_{2\beta}$ is determined by

$$G_{2\beta} = \begin{cases} \Theta_{2\beta 4} & \text{when } \Re \le 5 \\ \Theta_{2\beta 4}+1 & \text{when } \Re > 5 \end{cases}.$$

Then, $G_{21} = 1$ as 1 divided by 1 gives the quotient $\Theta_{214} = 1$ with $\Re = 0$, $G_{22} = 0$ since $A_{24} - Q_{124} = 0$ as $Q_{124} = 7 \times 2 = 14 > A_{24} = 13$, and similarly $G_{23} = 0$. Next, the number of plies $P_{2\gamma}$ is determined by the minimum quotient $\min\{\Theta'_{2\beta\gamma}\}$ among the size $\beta = 1,2,3$ with actual orders $A_{\beta\gamma}$ divided by the number of garments $G_{2\beta}$ for $G_{2\beta} \neq 0$ such that

$$P_{1\gamma} = \begin{cases} \min\left\{\Theta'_{2\beta\gamma}\right\} & \text{for } \beta = 1,2,3 \quad \text{when } \Re' \le 5 \\ \min\left\{\Theta'_{2\beta\gamma}\right\}+1 & \text{for } \beta = 1,2,3 \quad \text{when } \Re' > 5 \end{cases}.$$

Drawing the number of plies P_{21}, G_{22} and G_{23} are neglected as they are equal to zero and thus P_{21} is determined by the quotient found by G_{21}. Hence, $P_{21}=5$ and similarly $P_{22}=2$ and $P_{23}=0$.

The general outline of the proposed approach is presented below:

- ***Step 1:*** Initialize parameter with population size with μ parents and λ offspring.
- ***Step 2:*** Randomly produce the binary string that represents $P_{\alpha\gamma}$ for $\alpha = 1,2, \ldots, L_{max}$, and assign a value of the probability of mutation, P_m, to each of the chromosomes in the population.
- ***Step 3:*** Decode the binary string and generate the according COP as illustrated in the previous section.
- ***Step 4:*** Evaluate the fitness, Φ, for each COP with Eq. 5.1 and 5.2 deduced from parent chromosomes.
- ***Step 5:*** Perform the mutation to give birth to λ offspring chromosomes.
- ***Step 6:*** Repeat Steps 3 and 4 for offspring chromosomes and assign new probability of mutation to the offspring such that if offspring fitness, Φ', is larger or equal to parent fitness, Φ, then the probability of mutation assigned to offspring, P'_m, is equal to parent's probability of mutation, P_m. Otherwise, if $\Phi' < \Phi$, then P'_m is assigned randomly.
- ***Step 7:*** Rank the pool of parents and offspring with the size $(\mu + \lambda)$ in terms of chromosome fitness and select the best μ chromosomes to be the next generation parents.
- ***Step 8:*** Repeat Steps 5, 6 and 7 until the target generation number is reached.

5.4 An example of a genetic optimization model for COP

The proposed genetic optimization model can be illustrated by considering a particular order with six sizes and nine colours with the order quantity $A_{\beta\gamma}$ ($\beta = 1,2, \ldots, 6$; $\gamma = 1,2, \ldots, 9$) as shown in Table 5.4. Validation was conducted to compare the results found by the industrial practice using commercial software and those by the proposed decision-making model using adaptive ESs with a population size of 100 runs for 100 generations and a population size of 1000 runs for 1000 generations respectively. The parameters adopted for the evolutionary algorithm after testing are: $\mu=50$, $\lambda=100$, and mutation rate = 0.003.

In this case, $S=6$, $C=9$, $Y=2.69$m, $\varepsilon=0.06$m, $\ell_{max}=10$m, $H_{min}=0$, $H_{max}=60$ and $L_{max}=20$ for inequalities 5.3 to 5.4. Thus, the number of combinations for this particular example as defined in Eq. 5.8 is $N_{com2}=(60-1)^{20}=2.61\times10^{35}$. According to constraint 5.4, the maximum number of garments per lay in this case is 45. The demand time constraint from the sewing room is $\tau=100$mins. The cost, time, and power-related parameters are defaulted as $C_F=\$30/\text{m}$, $C_L=\$4.17/\text{h}$, $C_E=\$0.27/\text{kWh}$, $T_C=0.173$ min/garment, $T_S=0.0324$ min/m, $T_P=4$ mins/lay, $W_C=3000$ Watt,

Table 5.4 Order quantity for the illustrated example

	Size 1	Size 2	Size 3	Size 4	Size 5	Size 6
Col 1	0	28	57	59	39	13
Col 2	1	47	109	103	74	34
Col 3	0	17	27	22	12	5
Col 4	1	74	152	163	116	22
Col 5	0	48	86	96	77	22
Col 6	0	10	15	16	4	1
Col 7	1	48	87	99	62	13
Col 8	0	76	150	161	125	46
Col 9	0	81	212	240	190	101

and $W_S = 2000$ Watt. Lastly, the fabric utilization, U_α, for each fabric lay can be determined based on Fig. 5.6, which demonstrates that in industrial practice the utilization rate will be improved when more garment patterns can be marked/drawn on the marker. Indeed, the fabric utilization in each lay depends on the total number of garments, $\sum_{\beta=1}^{S} G_{\alpha\beta}'$, used in that particular lay (in this chapter, the equations for the utilization are calculated as:

$$\text{(1) if } \sum_{\beta=1}^{S} G_{\alpha\beta} \le 20, \text{ then } U_\alpha = 0.6 + \log \frac{\sum_{\beta=1}^{S} G_{\alpha\beta} + 1}{2} \times \log 1.97;$$

$$\text{(2) if } \sum_{\beta=1}^{S} G_{\alpha\beta} > 20, \text{ then } U_\alpha = 0.9 + \frac{0.99 - 0.9}{(45-20) \times \left(\sum_{\beta=1}^{S} G_{\alpha\beta} - 20\right)}$$

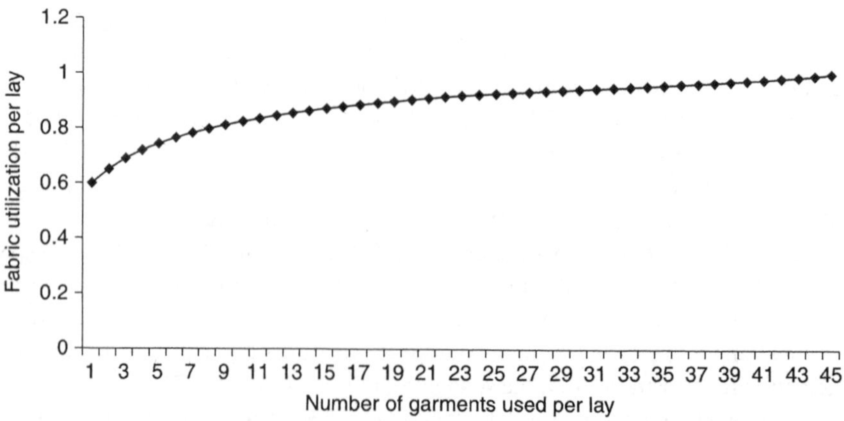

5.6 Fabric utilization rate versus the number of garments used per lay.

The evolutionary trajectories in this case for the best-of-generation and generation-average values of the fitness with the population size of 100 over 100 generations and population size of 1000 over 1000 generations are shown in Fig. 5.7 and 5.8 respectively. The fitness associated with the best cut order plan has the values of $\Phi-0.4549$ under the $100+100$ adaptive evolution strategy and $\Phi=0.4563$ under the $1000+1000$ adaptive evolution strategy. The fitness value of the best cut order plan decided by the industrial practice achieves $\Phi=0.4444$. The details of the cut order plans with the number of garments and plies in each of the lays decided by the industrial practice and evolutionarily synthesized are listed in the Appendix. Table 5.5 lists the detailed results between industrial practice and

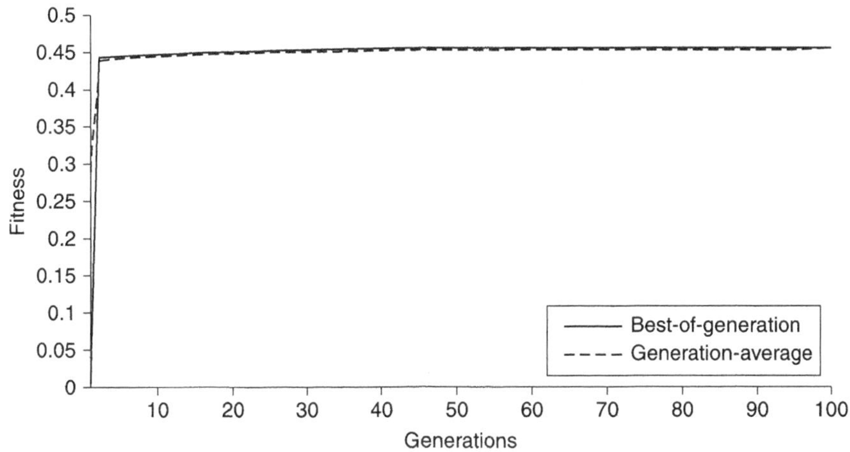

5.7 Best-of-generation and generation-average values of the fitness, over 100 generations.

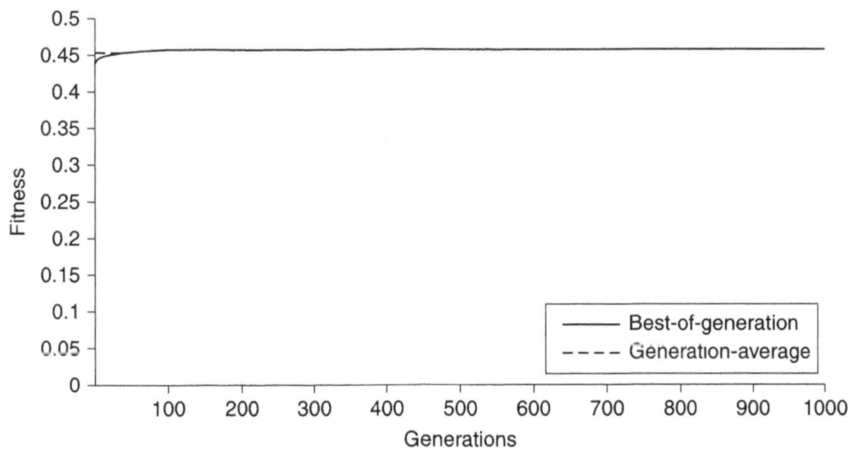

5.8 Best-of-generation and generation-average values of the fitness, over 1000 generations.

Table 5.5 Comparison of the results between industrial practice and proposed COP decision-making model using AESs

	Plan based on industrial practice	Best plan found by AESs (100 + 100)	Best plan found by AESs (1000 + 1000)
Number of lays used (L)	12	9	9
Fabric cost (Γ_F)	22 497	21 978	21 907.8
Labour cost (Γ_L)	6.52	6.77	6.85
Machine cost (Γ_M)	0.51	0.72	0.74
Total cost (Γ)	22 504.03	21 985.50	21 915.39
Fitness (Φ)	0.4444	0.4549	0.4563
Average number of garments per lay $\left(\frac{\sum_{\alpha=1}^{L}\sum_{\beta=1}^{S} G_{\alpha\beta}}{L}\right)$	10.33	24.22	25
Average number of plies per lay $\left(\frac{\sum_{\alpha=1}^{L}\sum_{\gamma=1}^{C} P_{\alpha\gamma}}{L}\right)$	20.67	14.67	14
Extra garments planned in COP $\sum_{\beta=1}^{S}\sum_{\gamma=1}^{C}\left[\sum_{\alpha=1}^{L} Q_{\alpha\beta\gamma} - A_{\beta\gamma}\right]$	72	50	33
Total lay length used $\left(\sum_{\alpha=1}^{L}\left[\sum_{\beta=1}^{S} G_{\alpha\beta}\frac{Y}{12}+\varepsilon\right]\sum_{\gamma=1}^{C} P_{\alpha\beta}\right)$	749.9 m	732.6 m	730.26 m
Total time used to complete the plan $\left(\sum_{\alpha=1}^{L}\left[\sum_{\beta=1}^{S} G_{\alpha\beta} T_C + \left(\sum_{\gamma=1}^{C} P_{\alpha\gamma}\sum_{\beta=1}^{S} G_{\alpha\beta}\frac{Y}{12}+\varepsilon\right)T_S\right]+T_P L\right)$	93.75 min	97.45 min	98.59 min

proposed COP decision-making model using AESs in terms of cost function, average fabric utilization, average lay length and the total time used to complete the plan.

The extra quantity of garments generated from the evolutionarily synthesized plans was 50 and 33 with the population size of 100 over 100 generations and population size of 1000 over 1000 generations respectively, much lower than the 72 extra garments generated by the industrial practice. Although the total time used to execute the plan by spreading and cutting was 97.45 min (100+100) and 98.59 min (1000+1000) when using adaptive ESs, which was longer than 93.75 min based on the industrial practice, the extra time used is within 5 min and acceptable under the demand time constraint from the sewing room (i.e. 100 min).

In addition to the illustrative example with S=6, C=9 as shown above, three other typical industrial cases with different sizes and colours were considered and compared in a similar way in terms of fitness, total lay length, extra quantity, and the total time used to complete the plan. The genetic optimized COPs are listed in Table 5.6. As illustrated in case 1, the fitness generated by adaptive ESs is 0.8077, which is better than the fitness of 0.7965 generated by the industrial practice. In addition, the number of extra garments (which may not be accepted by the customers) dramatically drops from 23 pieces to 3 pieces after using adaptive ESs. Moreover, the total length of fabric lay used shortens from 418.45 m to 412.64 m. Indeed, it can be shown that for all remaining cases, 2 to 4, the COPs found by adaptive ESs are able to achieve higher fitness values with a smaller extra quantity of garments and shorter total length of fabric lays, as in case 1; thus the fabric cost can be reduced. On the other hand, the average number of garments per fabric lay based on industrial practice is smaller than that generated by adaptive ESs, except in case 1. In case 1, the average number of garments per lay based on industrial practice is 22, compared with 22 and 21.5 based on adaptive ESs. The average number of fabric plies per lay based on industrial practice is in general larger than that obtained using adaptive ESs for all cases shown. Although the total operation (spreading and cutting) time used based on adaptive ESs is longer than that using industrial practice (except case 1 – ESs: 28.81 min, industrial practice: 29.17 min) in most cases, the longer operation time can be compensated by the great benefits obtained by reduced fabric cost and extra quantity of garments planned and produced. In fact, the extra operation time is acceptable as long as it does not exceed the time constraint requested by the sewing room.

The results described in this section were obtained by 100+100 or 1000+1000 adaptive evolution strategies, with each solution completed in less than 1 min and 4 min respectively. Nevertheless, humans need at least 15 min to figure out the plan depending on the order complexity with the number of sizes and colours incorporated. Thus, the evolutionarily synthesized plan introduced in this chapter is more effective in terms of time and cost in general when compared with the use of industrial practice in figuring out the plan by trial and error.

Table 5.6 Comparison of industrial practice (IP) and proposed COP decision-making model using 100 + 100 adaptive ESs

Case	S	C	Plan by	L	Avg. # of garment/lay	Avg. # of ply/lay	Total lay length (m)	Total time (min)	Order qty	Extra qty	Fitness
1	4	1	IP	2	22	40.5	418.45	29.17	1822	23	0.7965
			AESs	2	21.5	29.5	412.64	28.81		3	0.8077
2	7	2	IP	4	17.25	14.25	103.85	31.3	1023	34	3.2078
			AESs	2	71	7.5	100.56	35.82		25	3.3122
3	12	1	IP	3	29.33	49	919.02	57	4343	79	0.3626
			AESs	3	36	33	904.61	59.99		23	0.3684
4	8	2	IP	3	15.67	28	407.04	33.32	1307	33	0.8187
			AESs	3	22	21.33	401.64	36.43		19	0.8298

5.5 Conclusions

In the apparel industry, production orders tend to split into smaller orders with different product features in response to the growing requests for product customization, which greatly complicates the COP process. In the apparel manufacturing process, the effectiveness of COP extensively influences the overall material, machine and labour costs and thus, in turn, is critical to the overall system performance. In this chapter, a genetic optimization approach using adaptive ESs is developed to genetically synthesize the cut order plan in order to complete the order with minimized costs and the consideration of time constraint pre-determined by the downstream assembly departments. The production of extra quantities of garments caused by the COP can also be minimized. It can be shown in the illustrative examples that, since labour and electricity costs are not as significant as the fabric cost, the evolutionarily generated plan emphasizes minimizing the fabric cost under the time constraint set by the downstream sewing room. Even if the labour and electricity costs become significant, the evolutionarily generated plan will automatically be adjusted to accommodate such changes so as to minimize the costs. The evolutionary process of the proposed COP decision-making model can be improved further. Future research will focus on the combination of ESs and other heuristic search techniques, such as particle swarm optimization, ant colony optimization, etc., to improve the convergence speed and global optimization ability.

5.6 Acknowledgement

The authors would like to thank Earmarked Research Grant of Research Grants Council of Hong Kong (Project No. 529005) and The Hong Kong Polytechnic University (Project No. A-PG83) for financial support of this research project.

5.7 References

Alexouda G., 2005. A user friendly marketing decision support system for the product line design using evolutionary algorithm. *Decision Support System*, 38, 495–509.

Bäck T. and Schwefel H.P., 1993. An overview of evolutionary algorithms for parameter optimisation. *Evolutionary Computation*, 1(1), 1–24.

Bäck T., Hammel U. and Schwefel H.P., 1997. Evolutionary computation: comments on history and current state. *IEEE Transactions on Evolutionary Computation*, 1(1), 3–17.

Fogel L.J., Owens A.J. and Walsh M.J., 1966. *Artificial Intelligence through Simulated Evolution*, New York: John Wiley.

Gehlhaar D.K. and Fogel D.B., 1996. Tuning evolutionary programming for conformationally flexible molecular docking. *Proceedings of the 5th Annual Conference on Evolutionary Programming*, Cambridge, MA: MIT Press, pp. 410–429.

Girand-Motean L. and Laton P., 2002. A comparison of evolutionary algorithms for mechanical design components. *Engineering Optimisation*, 34, 307–322.

Goldberg D.E., 1989. *Genetic Algorithms Search, Optimisation, and Machine Learning*, Addison-Wesley, Reading, Massachusetts.

Huang J.-J., Tzeng G.-H. and Ong C.-S., 2006. Optimal fuzzy multi-criteria expansion of competence sets using multi-objectives evolutionary algorithms. *Expert Systems with Applications*, 30, 739–745.

Jacobs-Blecha C., Ammons J.C., Schutte A. and Smith T., 1998. Cut order planning for apparel manufacturing. *IIE Transactions*, 30, 79–90.

Käschel J., Teich T. and Zacher B., 2002. Real-time dynamic shop floor scheduling using Evolutionary Algorithms. *International Journal of Production Economics*, 79, 113–120.

Lee, W.P. and Tsai, T-C., 2003. An interactive agent-based system for concept-based web search. *Expert Systems with Applications*, 24, 365–373.

Pierreval H., Caux C., Paris J.L. and Viguier F., 2003. Evolutionary approaches to the design and organization of manufacturing systems. *Computers & Industrial Engineering*, 44, 339–364.

Porter B., 1998a. Evolutionary optimisation of industrial systems. industrial applications and practice: Users encyclopaedia, Anil Mital (Ed.), *International Journal of Industrial Engineering*, CD ROM.

Porter B., 1998b. Evolutionary production planning: a cautionary tale. *CIRP-Journal of Manufacturing Systems*, 27(2), 115–119.

Porter B. and Leung W.M., 1998. Evolutionary selection of process plans in automated manufacturing systems. *Proceedings of CIRP International Seminar of Intelligent Computation in Manufacturing Engineering*, Capri, Italy, pp. 91–96.

Porter B. and Merzougui T., 1997. Evolutionary synthesis of optimal control policies for manufacturing systems. *Proceedings of the IEEE 6th International Conference on Emerging Technologies and Factory Automation*, pp. 304–309.

Powell D. and Skolnick M.M., 1993. Using genetic algorithms in engineering design optimisation with non-linear constraints. *Proceedings of the Fifth International Conference on Genetic Algorithms*, pp. 424–430.

Surrey P.D., Radcliffe N.J. and Boyd I.D., 1995. A multi-objective approach to constrainted optimisation of gas supply networks. *The AISB-95 Workshop on Evolutionary Computing*, Sheffield, UK, pp. 166–180.

Tong C.M., 2002. *Evolutionary Design of Fuzzy-logic Controllers with Minimal Rule Sets for Manufacturing Systems*. Ph.D Thesis, The University of Hong Kong.

Vergara F.E., 2002. An evolutionary algorithm for optimising material flow in supply chains. *Computers & Industrial Engineering*, 43, 407–421.

Yao X., 1999. *Evolutionary Computation: Theory and Applications*. World Scientific, Singapore.

Zadeh N.N. and Porter B., 1998. Evolution strategies in flow-shop sequencing. *Proceedings of the World Automation Congress*, Anchorage, Alaska, USA, pp. 673–678.

5.8 Appendix: comparison between industrial practice and proposed COP decision-making model

Table A1.1 COP generated by industrial practice using commercial COP software

Lay #	Cut order plan
1	# of garment: size 1 – 0, size 2 – 4, size 3 – 6, size 4 – 6, size 5 – 2, size 6 – 1 # of ply: col 1 – 4, col 2 – 6, col 3 – 2, col 4 – 10, col 5 – 6, col 6 – 2, col 7 – 5, col 8 – 10, col 9 – 10
2	# of garment: size 1 – 0, size 2 – 4, size 3 – 6, size 4 – 6, size 5 – 2, size 6 – 1 # of ply: col 1 – 4, col 2 – 6, col 3 – 2, col 4 – 9, col 5 – 7, col 6 – 1, col 7 – 5, col 8 – 10, col 9 – 11
3	# of garment: size 1 – 0, size 2 – 0, size 3 – 2, size 4 – 2, size 5 – 4, size 6 – 1 # of ply: col 1 – 3, col 2 – 7, col 3 – 0, col 4 – 2, col 5 – 2, col 6 – 0, col 7 – 2, col 8 – 8, col 9 – 15
4	# of garment: size 1 – 0, size 2 – 0, size 3 – 2, size 4 – 2, size 5 – 4, size 6 – 1 # of ply: col 1 – 3, col 2 – 6, col 3 – 0, col 4 – 2, col 5 – 3, col 6 – 0, col 7 – 2, col 8 – 8, col 9 – 15
5	# of garment: size 1 – 0, size 2 – 1, size 3 – 2, size 4 – 0, size 5 – 3, size 6 – 1 # of ply: col 1 – 0, col 2 – 0, col 3 – 2, col 4 – 0, col 5 – 0, col 6 – 0, col 7 – 0, col 8 – 0, col 9 – 0
6	# of garment: size 1 – 1, size 2 – 0, size 3 – 4, size 4 – 2, size 5 – 0, size 6 – 4 # of ply: col 1 – 0, col 2 – 2, col 3 – 0, col 4 – 0, col 5 – 0, col 6 – 0, col 7 – 0, col 8 – 0, col 9 – 0
7	# of garment: size 1 – 0, size 2 – 0, size 3 – 3, size 4 – 4, size 5 – 5, size 6 – 0 # of ply: col 1 – 0, col 2 – 0, col 3 – 0, col 4 – 11, col 5 – 0, col 6 – 0, col 7 – 5, col 8 – 0, col 9 – 6
8	# of garment: size 1 – 0, size 2 – 0, size 3 – 0, size 4 – 1, size 5 – 2, size 6 – 1 # of ply: col 1 – 0, col 2 – 0, col 3 – 0, col 4 – 0, col 5 – 0, col 6 – 0, col 7 – 0, col 8 – 11, col 9 – 0
9	# of garment: size 1 – 1, size 2 – 0, size 3 – 0, size 4 – 0, size 5 – 3, size 6 – 0 # of ply: col 1 – 0, col 2 – 0, col 3 – 0, col 4 – 3, col 5 – 0, col 6 – 0, col 7 – 0, col 8 – 0, col 9 – 0
10	# of garment: size 1 – 1, size 2 – 3, size 3 – 2, size 4 – 4, size 5 – 1, size 6 – 0 # of ply: col 1 – 0, col 2 – 0, col 3 – 0, col 4 – 0, col 5 – 0, col 6 – 0, col 7 – 3, col 8 – 0, col 9 – 0
11	# of garment: size 1 – 0, size 2 – 0, size 3 – 1, size 4 – 3, size 5 – 0, size 6 – 5 # of ply: col 1 – 0, col 2 – 0, col 3 – 0, col 4 – 0, col 5 – 0, col 6 – 0, col 7 – 0, col 8 – 0, col 9 – 11
12	# of garment: size 1 – 0, size 2 – 0, size 3 – 0, size 4 – 2, size 5 – 7, size 6 – 1 # of ply: col 1 – 0, col 2 – 0, col 3 – 0, col 4 – 0, col 5 – 5, col 6 – 0, col 7 – 0, col 8 – 0, col 9 – 0

Table A1.2 COP with best fitness generated by proposed COP decision-making model using (100+100) Adaptive ESs

Lay #	Cut order plan
1	# of garment: size 1 – 0, size 2 – 5, size 3 – 8, size 4 – 8, size 5 – 2, size 6 – 1 # of ply: col 1 – 6, col 2 – 10, col 3 – 2, col 4 – 15, col 5 – 10, col 6 – 2, col 7 – 10, col 8 – 5, col 9 – 0
2	# of garment: size 1 – 0, size 2 – 7, size 3 – 11, size 4 – 6, size 5 – 8, size 6 – 3 # of ply: col 1 – 0, col 2 – 0, col 3 – 1, col 4 – 0, col 5 – 0, col 6 – 0, col 7 – 0, col 8 – 8, col 9 – 12
3	# of garment: size 1 – 0, size 2 – 0, size 3 – 5, size 4 – 6, size 5 – 14, size 6 – 4 # of ply: col 1 – 2, col 2 – 3, col 3 – 0, col 4 – 2, col 5 – 2, col 6 – 0, col 7 – 1, col 8 – 3, col 9 – 6
4	# of garment: size 1 – 0, size 2 – 0, size 3 – 0, size 4 – 2, size 5 – 15, size 6 – 2 # of ply: col 1 – 0, col 2 – 0, col 3 – 0, col 4 – 0, col 5 – 2, col 6 – 0, col 7 – 0, col 8 – 0, col 9 – 0
5	# of garment: size 1 – 1, size 2 – 0, size 3 – 14, size 4 – 5, size 5 – 12, size 6 – 12 # of ply: col 1 – 0, col 2 – 1, col 3 – 0, col 4 – 0, col 5 – 0, col 6 – 0, col 7 – 0, col 8 – 0, col 9 – 0
6	# of garment: size 1 – 1, size 2 – 0, size 3 – 1, size 4 – 5, size 5 – 10, size 6 – 0 # of ply: col 1 – 0, col 2 – 0, col 3 – 0, col 4 – 1, col 5 – 0, col 6 – 0, col 7 – 3, col 8 – 0, col 9 – 0
7	# of garment: size 1 – 0, size 2 – 0, size 3 – 2, size 4 – 11, size 5 – 2, size 6 – 1 # of ply: col 1 – 0, col 2 – 0, col 3 – 0, col 4 – 0, col 5 – 0, col 6 – 0, col 7 – 0, col 8 – 5, col 9 – 5
8	# of garment: size 1 – 0, size 2 – 0, size 3 – 3, size 4 – 4, size 5 – 7, size 6 – 0 # of ply: col 1 – 0, col 2 – 0, col 3 – 0, col 4 – 7, col 5 – 0, col 6 – 0, col 7 – 0, col 8 – 0, col 9 – 0
9	# of garment: size 1 – 0, size 2 – 0, size 3 – 5, size 4 – 10, size 5 – 0, size 6 – 5 # of ply: col 1 – 0, col 2 – 0, col 3 – 0, col 4 – 0, col 5 – 0, col 6 – 0, col 7 – 0, col 8 – 0, col 9 – 8

Table A1.3 COP with best fitness generated by proposed COP decision-making model using (1000+1000) Adaptive ESs

Lay #	Cut order plan
1	# of garment: size 1 – 0, size 2 – 5, size 3 – 8, size 4 – 8, size 5 – 2, size 6 – 1 # of ply: col 1 – 6, col 2 – 10, col 3 – 2, col 4 – 15, col 5 – 10, col 6 – 2, col 7 – 10, col 8 – 5, col 9 – 0
2	# of garment: size 1 – 0, size 2 – 7, size 3 – 11, size 4 – 6, size 5 – 8, size 6 – 3 # of ply: col 1 – 0, col 2 – 0, col 3 – 1, col 4 – 0, col 5 – 0, col 6 – 0, col 7 – 0, col 8 – 8, col 9 – 12
3	# of garment: size 1 – 0, size 2 – 0, size 3 – 5, size 4 – 6, size 5 – 14, size 6 – 4 # of ply: col 1 – 2, col 2 – 3, col 3 – 0, col 4 – 2, col 5 – 2, col 6 – 0, col 7 – 1, col 8 – 3, col 9 – 6
4	# of garment: size 1 – 0, size 2 – 0, size 3 – 0, size 4 – 2, size 5 – 15, size 6 – 2 # of ply: col 1 – 0, col 2 – 0, col 3 – 0, col 4 – 0, col 5 – 2, col 6 – 0, col 7 – 0, col 8 – 0, col 9 – 0
5	# of garment: size 1 – 1, size 2 – 0, size 3 – 7, size 4 – 3, size 5 – 6, size 6 – 6 # of ply: col 1 – 0, col 2 – 2, col 3 – 0, col 4 – 0, col 5 – 0, col 6 – 0, col 7 – 0, col 8 – 0, col 9 – 0
6	# of garment: size 1 – 1, size 2 – 0, size 3 – 1, size 4 – 7, size 5 – 14, size 6 – 0 # of ply: col 1 – 0, col 2 – 0, col 3 – 0, col 4 – 1, col 5 – 0, col 6 – 0, col 7 – 2, col 8 – 0, col 9 – 0
7	# of garment: size 1 – 0, size 2 – 0, size 3 – 2, size 4 – 11, size 5 – 2, size 6 – 1 # of ply: col 1 – 0, col 2 – 0, col 3 – 0, col 4 – 0, col 5 – 0, col 6 – 0, col 7 – 0, col 8 – 5, col 9 – 5
8	# of garment: size 1 – 0, size 2 – 0, size 3 – 7, size 4 – 8, size 5 – 15, size 6 – 0 # of ply: col 1 – 0, col 2 – 0, col 3 – 0, col 4 – 3, col 5 – 0, col 6 – 0, col 7 – 0, col 8 – 0, col 9 – 0
9	# of garment: size 1 – 0, size 2 – 0, size 3 – 7, size 4 – 13, size 5 – 0, size 6 – 6 # of ply: col 1 – 0, col 2 – 0, col 3 – 0, col 4 – 0, col 5 – 0, col 6 – 0, col 7 – 0, col 8 – 0, col 9 – 6

6

Optimizing marker planning in apparel production using evolutionary strategies and neural networks

W. K. WONG and X. X. WANG, The Hong Kong Polytechnic University, China and Z. X. GUO, Sichuan University, China

DOI: 10.1533/9780857097842.106

Abstract: Marker planning in apparel production is a kind of packing problem in the research field of engineering. The irregular shapes of pattern pieces of a garment make the marker planning problem more complex. Few approaches have been developed to solve these problems, although effectiveness of packing determines industrial resource utilization. This study constructs a packing approach that integrates a grid approximation-based representation, a learning vector quantization neural network, a heuristic placement strategy and an integer representation-based $(\mu + \lambda)$ – evolutionary strategy to obtain efficient placement of irregular objects. Real data are used to demonstrate the performance of the proposed methodology. The results are compared with those obtained by a genetic algorithm-based packing approach and those generated from industrial practice, demonstrating the effectiveness of the proposed approach.

Key words: irregular object packing, evolutionary strategies, neural network.

6.1 Introduction

Packing problems are combinatorial optimization problems that concern the allocation of multiple objects (patterns) in a large containment region without overlap, and the objective of the allocation process is to maximize the occupied space and minimize the 'wasted' space. In the literature, there are many approaches to tackling different packing problems, such as those based on the concept of 'no-fit polygons' (NFP) (Bennell *et al.*, 2001, Gomes and Oliveira, 2002; Li and Milenkovic, 1995; Oliveira *et al.*, 2000; Stoyan *et al.*, 1996), methods of bottom-left (BL) placement strategy (Dowsland and Dowsland, 1995; Oliveira *et al.*, 2000) and those based on linear programming compaction methods (Bennell and Dowsland, 2001; Gomes and Oliveira, 2006; Li and Milenkovic, 1995; Stoyan *et al.* 1996). In recent years, following the concept of phi-function proposed in Stoyan and Gil, (1976), Stoyan *et al.* constructed mathematical models of two- or three-dimensional packing problems as problems of mathematical programming to seek their local and global optimization solutions (Stoyan *et al.*, 2002; Scheithauer *et al.*, 2005; Bennell *et al.*, 2010; Stoyan and Chugay, 2009). It was reported that the phi-function based techniques showed superior performance to

NFP-based techniques. In a landmark paper, Burke *et al.* (2006) presented a new bottom-left-fill heuristic algorithm, which integrated a geometrical definition, a new technique of primitive overlap resolution, with hill climbing and tabu local search methods, for the two-dimensional (2D) irregular stock-cutting problem. Their experimental results on a wide range of benchmark problems showed that the new bottom-left-fill heuristic algorithm outperformed the other techniques of the previous studies.

It is well-known that packing problems are combinatorial optimization problems with a very large search space. In order to search for their global optimal solutions, mathematical programming techniques as a rule search for a huge number of local extrema and it takes a lot of computational time. Various meta-heuristic algorithms have been adopted as optimization tools to find good solutions fast. However, this very often leads to sacrifice of high-performance results. These meta-heuristic approaches include simulated annealing (Burke and Kendall, 1999; Gomes and Oliveira, 1999; Gomes and Oliveira, 2006; Heckmann and Lengauer, 1995; Oliveira and Ferreira, 1993; Wu *et al.*, 2003), tabu search (Bennell and Dowsland, 1999; Bennell and Dowsland, 2001; Blazewicz *et al.*, 1993), neural networks (Au *et al.*, 2006; Han and Na, 1996; Wong, 2003; Wong *et al.*, 2006; Wong *et al.*, 2009; Yuen *et al.*, 2009) and genetic algorithms (GA) (Babu and Babu, 2001; Bounsaythip and Maouche, 1997; Bounsaythip *et al.*, 1995; Fujita *et al.*, 1993; Guo *et al.*, 2008, 2008a; Hifi and Hallah, 2003; Hopper, 2000; Ismail and Hon, 1992; Jain and Gea, 1998; Jakobs, 1996; Song *et al.*, 2006; Wong, 2003a; Wong *et al.*, 2000; Yuen *et al.*, 2009a). Among these approaches, genetic algorithms are the most popular technique to solve irregular object packing problems (Hifi and Hallah, 2003).

Applications of genetic algorithms to irregular object packing problems based on geometric representation have been extensively studied. For packing approaches based on geometric representation, irregular objects are represented by polygons that are composed of a list of vertices. For instance, Fujita *et al.* (1993) developed an order-based genetic algorithm in combination with local minimization to solve convex polygon packing problems. Jakobs (1996) also used an order-based genetic algorithm to solve polygon packing problems. Bounsaythip and Maouche (1997) provided a binary tree approach for packing problems in the textile industry. When the above approaches were adopted, polygons were circumscribed by their bounding rectangles. In the packing process, low-level routines were adopted to find the smallest enclosing rectangle of the cluster using a special encoding technique (Bounsaythip *et al.* 1995), which describes the contour of a polygon relative to the enclosing rectangle by a set of integer values. Hopper (2000) proposed a genetic algorithm in combination with a bottom-left algorithm to solve both orthogonal and irregular nesting problems. Hifi and Hallah (2003) developed an approach which consists of a constructive heuristic and a hybrid genetic algorithm-based heuristic to two-dimensional layout problems for cases of regular and irregular shapes.

As reviewed in the previous paragraph, there are numerous approaches based on computational geometric description giving good performance. Nevertheless, it is hard to implement them due to their computational complexity for large and complex data sets. In order to overcome the drawback, a digitized representation approach called grid approximation (Ismail and Hon, 1992) was adopted and objects were represented by two-dimensional matrices. There are two advantages over the geometric representation: the first advantage is that there is no need to introduce additional routines to identify enclosed areas in objects, and the second one is that it is easier to detect overlap.

Although grid approximation has advantages, irregular object packing based on grid approximation is a complex task. As a result, very few attempts to develop efficient packing methods based on grid approximation for irregular objects have been reported in the literature. In Ismail and Hon's study (1992), rectilinear shapes were digitized and represented as a two-dimensional grid array. A multi-parameter binary string including relative positions of a shape was used to indicate shape sequences. The traditional single-point crossover operator and the basic gene-alter mutation operator (Goldberg, 1989) were adopted to generate new offspring. However, applying such genetic operators to the data structure may cause infeasible solutions (i.e. overlap). In view of the deficiencies of Ismail and Hon's method (1992), Jain and Gea (1998) designed a new concept of a 2D genetic algorithm chromosome as a two-dimensional matrix to describe the complete layout. Crossover and mutation operators were modified to suit this 2D genetic algorithm chromosome, while a new genetic operator called compaction was developed to increase the density of the layout. Nevertheless, this special encoding approach results in a very long parent chromosome and leads to a very extensive computation when it is applied to packing a large number of objects. Hence, it is impractical to implement Jain and Gea's algorithm (1998) for large-scale problems.

Although evolutionary strategy, like GAs, is also a powerful evolutionary algorithm that has been used successfully in solving various engineering problems (Quagliarella *et al.*, 1995) and usually shows faster convergence speed than GAs do (Bäck and Hoffmeister, 1991), it has not been investigated and used to solve packing and nesting problems in the current literature. It is desirable to investigate the performance of evolutionary strategy based on grid approximation for irregular packing problems. In this study, a new hybrid approach was developed which combines a $(\mu + \lambda)$ – evolutionary strategy, a learning vector quantization neural network, a grid approximation representation and a heuristic two-stage placement strategy, to increase the usability of the stock sheet. A $(\mu + \lambda)$ – evolutionary strategy is used to determine the packing information (i.e. the packing sequence of packing cells, objects' orientation, and packing rules selection), in which an integer representation is adopted to obtain higher computational efficiency than the 2D genetic chromosome in Jain and Gea's study (1998). A learning vector quantization neural network was also developed by a set of examples inspired by experienced packing planners to diminish the size of a search space by dividing the objects into three classes. A grid approximation representation technique was also employed to represent any shaped objects, including convex and concave. In contrast to the geometric algorithms reported in previous research studies, grid approximation simplifies the calculation process, and thus it is easier to judge whether objects overlap. A two-stage placement strategy was proposed to ameliorate the shortcomings of packing approaches based on enclosing rectangles.

The remainder of the chapter is organized as follows. A brief description of irregular object packing problems is given and a new heuristic placement method is presented in detail in Section 6.2. A $(\mu + \lambda)$ – evolutionary strategy is used to determine the packing sequence of packing cells in Section 6.3. The effectiveness of the proposed methodology is illustrated in Section 6.4. Conclusions are summarized in Section 6.5.

6.2 Packing method for optimized marker packing

The problem addressed in this study is to pack a set of irregular objects $\{p_1, p_2, \ldots, p_n\}$ onto a stock sheet of infinite length C_L and fixed width C_H without overlap. Hence, a general methodology which integrates a grid approximation-based heuristic placement approach, a learning vector quantization neural network, and an $(\mu + \lambda)$ – evolutionary strategy is developed to obtain a packing pattern with minimal length. In this case, the following assumptions are taken into consideration to construct the methodology:

- The stock sheet is a rectangle with a fixed width and an infinite length.
- Each object has only two orientations, 0° and 180°, since this study focuses on the marker planning process of the clothing industry. That is to say, the original object and the object obtained by a 180° counterclockwise rotation are allowed while an object is packed onto the stock sheet.
- The length and the width of each object are not larger than the size of the stock sheet.
- Each object can be placed at any position on the stock sheet.

6.2.1 Object representation

In this study, the digitized representation technique, grid approximation, proposed by Ismail and Hon (1992) was used to represent objects in any shapes, including convex and concave. In contrast to geometric algorithms, the major advantage of the grid approximation is that it is easier to detect overlap. By using this technique, each object is divided into a finite number of equalized cells, and the size of a selected cell is small enough to represent the objects. $P_L^{(i)}$ and $P_H^{(i)}$ denote the length and the width of an enclosing rectangle corresponding to the object p_i. $R_x^{(i)}$ denotes the length of a cell, and $R_y^{(i)}$ denotes the height of a cell for the object p_i. (In this chapter, $R_x^{(i)} = 1$ mm, and $R_y^{(i)} = 1$ mm.) The object with a two-dimensional matrix of size $A_H^{(i)} \times A_L^{(i)}$ is represented as follows:

$$A^{(i)} = \begin{pmatrix} a_{11}^{(i)} & a_{12}^{(i)} & \cdots & a_{1A_L^{(i)}}^{(i)} \\ a_{21}^{(i)} & a_{22}^{(i)} & \cdots & a_{2A_L^{(i)}}^{(i)} \\ \vdots & \vdots & \ddots & \vdots \\ a_{A_H^{(i)}1}^{(i)} & a_{A_H^{(i)}2}^{(i)} & \cdots & a_{A_H^{(i)}A_L^{(i)}}^{(i)} \end{pmatrix}, \qquad [6.1]$$

where $A_H^{(i)} = \dfrac{P_H^{(i)}}{R_y^{(i)}}$, and $A_L^{(i)} = \dfrac{P_L^{(i)}}{R_x^{(i)}}$.

For each entry, $a_{px,py}^{(i)} = \begin{cases} 1 & \text{if pixel (px, py) is occupied} \\ 0 & \text{otherwise} \end{cases}$.

In addition, each object examined in this study had only two orientations: 0° and 180°. The matrix representation of the rotated object (180° counterclockwise rotation) was obtained by simply modifying the matrix of the original object shown in the above-mentioned equation. Then the matrix of the rotated object becomes

$$A_{rotate}^{(i)} = \begin{pmatrix} a_{A_H^{(i)}A_L^{(i)}}^{(i)} & \cdots & a_{A_H^{(i)}2}^{(i)} & a_{A_H^{(i)}1}^{(i)} \\ \vdots & \ddots & \vdots & \vdots \\ a_{2A_L^{(i)}}^{(i)} & \cdots & a_{22}^{(i)} & a_{21}^{(i)} \\ a_{1A_L^{(i)}}^{(i)} & \cdots & a_{12}^{(i)} & a_{11}^{(i)} \end{pmatrix}_{A_H^{(i)} \times A_L^{(i)}}. \qquad [6.2]$$

Similarly to the object representation, the stock sheet with an infinite length and a fixed width was discretized into a finite number of equisized cells of size $R_x \cdot R_y$. Hence, the stock sheet with the length C_L and the width C_H were characterized by a matrix $\boldsymbol{U}$ of size $U_H \times U_L$ as follows:

$$U = [u_{px,py}], \qquad [6.3]$$

where $U_H = \dfrac{C_H}{R_y}$, and $U_L = \dfrac{C_L}{R_x}$.

For each entry, $u_{px,py} = \begin{cases} 1 & \text{if pixel (px, py) is occupied} \\ 0 & \text{otherwise} \end{cases}$.

6.2.2 Heuristic placement approach

The architecture of the proposed heuristic placement approach is shown in Fig. 6.1. First, the grid approximation is used to represent any shaped objects in

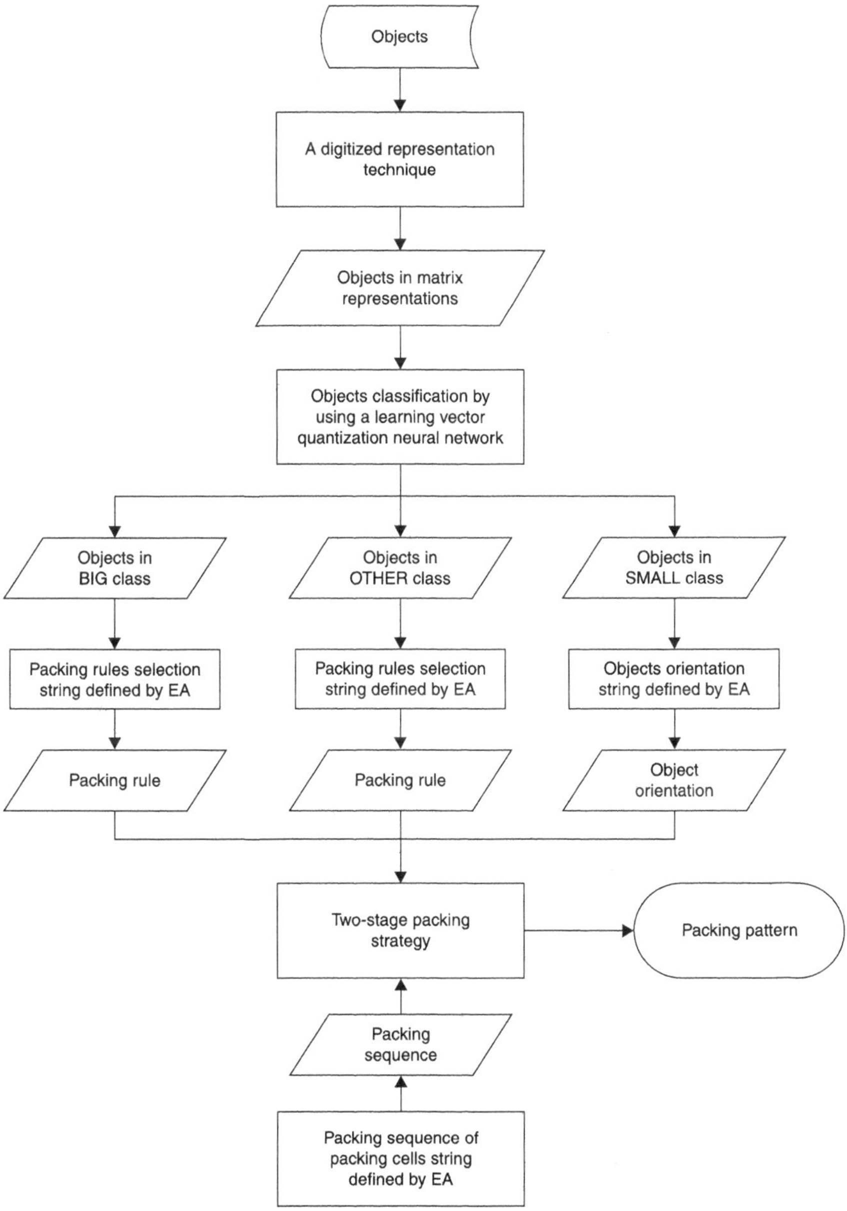

6.1 System architecture of packing materials.

two-dimensional matrices. Second, a learning vector quantization neural network is developed as a classification heuristic to divide the objects into three classes according to their relative sizes: BIG, SMALL and OTHER. Third, an evolutionary algorithm is used to determine the packing information (i.e. the packing sequence of packing cells, objects' orientation, and packing rules selection). Finally, a two-stage placement strategy is proposed for the construction of a packing pattern according to packing information, which is defined by the evolutionary strategy. Objects in the BIG and OTHER classes are packed onto the stock sheet according to the packing sequence of packing cells strings and packing rules selection strings defined by the evolutionary strategy. That is to say, the objects in the packing cells are placed by selecting rules from the 16 packing rules shown in Fig. 6.2, which

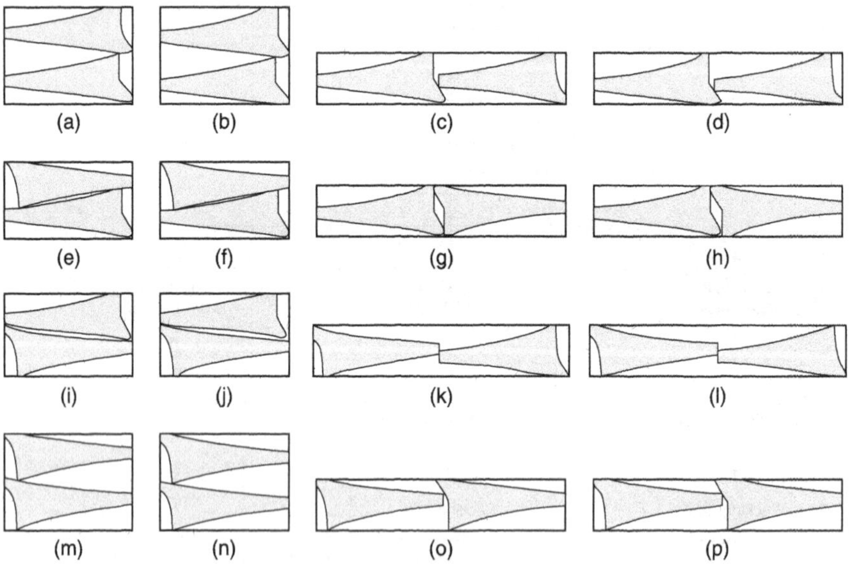

6.2 Packing rules. (a) Object 1 top, object 2 bottom. (b) Object 2 top, object 1 bottom. (c) Object 1 left, object 2 right. (d) Object 2 left, object 1 right. (e) Object I top, counterclockwise rotate 180, object 2 bottom. (f) Object 2 top, counterclockwise rotate 180, object 1 bottom. (g) Object 1 left, object 2 right, counterclockwise rotate 180. (h) Object 2 left, object 1 right, counterclockwise rotate 180. (i) Object 1 top, object 2 bottom, counterclockwise rotate 180. (j) Object 2 top, object 1 bottom, counterclockwise rotate 180. (k) Object 1 left, counterclockwise rotate 180, object 2 right. (l) Object 2 left, counterclockwise rotate 180, object 1 right. (m) Object 1 top, counterclockwise rotate 180, object 1 bottom. (n) Object 2 top, counterclockwise rotate 180, object 1 bottom, counterclockwise rotate 180. (o) Object 1 left, counterclockwise rotate 180, object 2 right, counterclockwise rotate 180. (p) Object 2 left, counterclockwise rotate 180, object 1 right, counterclockwise rotate 180.

are acquired by pattern planning experts through in-depth interviews with experienced pattern planners in the reference sites. Objects in the SMALL class are packed onto the stock sheet according to the packing sequence of packing cells strings and objects orientation strings defined by the evolutionary strategy. In other words, the objects might be rotated (180° counterclockwise rotation).

Object classification

A learning vector quantization neural network (Kohonen, 1990) is developed as a classification heuristic. The proposed network is trained by a set of examples inspired by experienced packing planners to diminish the size of a search space by dividing the objects into three classes according to their relative sizes: BIG, SMALL and OTHER. Once the network has been trained, it has the ability to classify various other kinds of objects that are similar to the training set, which makes the network powerful. For instance, according to the packing planners' experience, if the size of an object in the BIG class is three times larger than the size of an object in the SMALL class, and the length of an object in the OTHER class is four times larger than the width of an object in the OTHER class, BIG, OTHER and SMALL classes are classified. Without using a neural network, the experienced parameters such as three times and four times should be input into the system manually according to the packing planners' experience. That is to say, before using a neural network, the classification is based on the analysis of a great number of objects in practice. After the network has been trained by a large number of examples, instead of using packing planners' experience, the objects can be automatically classified by their relative sizes.

The BIG class is a class of bigger objects, while the SMALL class is a class of smaller objects (i.e. the size of an object in the BIG class is a multiplication of the size of an object in the SMALL class). On the other hand, the OTHER class is a class of objects that are very long but narrow or vice versa. Objects in the BIG class and the OTHER class are paired up to form packing cells. That is to say, each packing cell contains two objects that have the same or similar size. At the same time, each object in the SMALL class generates a single packing cell. The object packing sequence has thus been changed into the packing cells packing sequence, which decreases the size of the search space. For instance, it is assumed that the number of packed objects is 64 and the size of the search space is 64. However, after the procedure of object classification, if the number of objects in the BIG, SMALL and OTHER classes is 20, 8 and 36 respectively, then the size of the search space is reduced to 36. The key steps of the learning vector quantization neural network approach are presented below:

- ***Step 0:*** Initialize reference vectors, weight vectors, and learning rate $\alpha(0)$.
- ***Step 1:*** While the stopping condition is false, perform steps 2–6.

- ***Step 2:*** For each training input vector (i.e. the area of each piece and the narrow factor of each piece), perform steps 3–4.
- ***Step 3:*** Find ***J*** so that the Euclidean distance between the input vector and the weight vector for the jth output unit is a minimum.
- ***Step 4:*** Update the weight vector w_J as follows:

  if $T = C_J$, then $w_J\,(new) = w_J\,(old) + \alpha(X - w_J\,(old))$;
  if $T \neq C_J$, then $w_J\,(new) = w_J\,(old) - \alpha(X - w_J(old))$;

  where X denotes the training vector, T denotes the correct class for the training vector, and C_J denotes the class represented by the jth output unit.
- ***Step 5:*** Reduce learning rate α.
- ***Step 6:*** Test the stopping condition, which may specify a fixed number of iterations or the learning rate reaching a sufficiently small value.

Two-stage placement strategy

A two-stage placement strategy is proposed as an alternative to construct a packing pattern according to the packing information (i.e. the packing sequence of packing cells, objects orientation, and packing rules selection), which is defined by the evolutionary strategy. In this case, the enclosing rectangles of the packing cells are first examined, and then the packing cells are compacted directly. In particular, instead of implementing the compaction routine in a single step after all the enclosing rectangles of the packing cells are allocated, the compaction routine is done when each enclosing rectangle is placed. The advantage of this compaction routine is the ability to obtain a tight packing pattern, providing more space for the coming packing cells. It is obvious that the two-stage placement strategy improves the packing pattern quality without compromising the computational effort. The key steps of the two-stage placement strategy are presented as follows:

- ***Step 1:*** Place the coming packing cell C_{ij+1} at the uppermost and infinite right corner of the stock sheet. Due to the approximation of the packing cell by its enclosing rectangle at the first stage, the matrix of the stock sheet becomes

$$U(j+1) = U(j) + \begin{pmatrix} 0 & 0 & \cdots & A^{(i_{j+1})} \\ 0 & 0 & \cdots & 0 \\ \vdots & \vdots & \ddots & \vdots \\ 0 & 0 & \cdots & 0 \end{pmatrix}_{U_H \times U_L} = \begin{pmatrix} 0 & 0 & \cdots & A^{(i_{j+1})} \\ 0 & 0 & \cdots & 0 \\ \vdots & \vdots & \ddots & \vdots \\ UB^{(i_j)} & 0 & \cdots & 0 \end{pmatrix}_{U_H \times U_L} \qquad [6.4]$$

  with submatrices $A^{(i_{j+1})} = \left(a^{i_{j+1}}_{px,py}\right)_{A_H^{(i_{j+1})} \times A_L^{(i_{j+1})}}$ and $UB^{(i_j)} = \left(ub^{(i_j)}_{px,py}\right)_{B_H^{(i_j)} \times B_L^{(i_j)}}$, where $a^{(i_{j+1})}_{px,py} = 1$ and $ub^{(i_j)}_{px,py} = u_{px,py}$.

- ***Step 2:*** Shift the packing cell $C_{i_{j+1}}$ leftward and downward until it meets other packing cells and cannot be moved again. In view of the property of matrices, it is convenient to shift the packing cell by counting the empty cells in the matrix. Then the matrix of the stock sheet becomes

$$U(j+1)=\begin{pmatrix} 0 & 0 & \cdots & 0 \\ \vdots & \vdots & \cdots & \vdots \\ A^{(i_{j+1})} & 0 & \ddots & 0 \\ UB^{(i_j)} & 0 & \cdots & 0 \end{pmatrix}_{U_H \times U_L} . \qquad [6.5]$$

- ***Step 3:*** Represent the packing cell C_{ij+1} at the second stage by using its enclosing rectangle without approximating it, and then the matrix of the stock sheet is

$$U(j+1)=\begin{pmatrix} 0 & 0 & \cdots & 0 \\ \vdots & \vdots & \cdots & \vdots \\ UA^{(i_{j+1})} & 0 & \ddots & 0 \\ UB^{(i_j)} & 0 & \cdots & 0 \end{pmatrix}_{U_H \times U_L} \qquad [6.6]$$

with submatrices $UA^{(i_{j+1})}=\left(ua_{px,py}^{i_{j+1}}\right)_{A_H^{(i_{j+1})}\times A_L^{(i_{j+1})}}$,
where $ua_{px,py}^{(i_{j+1})}=u_{px,py}$.

- ***Step 4:*** Compact the packing cells by removing the vacant cells between these two matrices of packing cells, and then the matrix of the stock sheet becomes

$$U(j+1)=\begin{pmatrix} 0 & 0 & \cdots & 0 \\ \vdots & \vdots & \cdots & \vdots \\ 0 & 0 & \ddots & 0 \\ UB^{(i_{j+1})} & 0 & \cdots & 0 \end{pmatrix}_{U_H \times U_L} , \qquad [6.7]$$

with submatrices, $UB^{(i_{j+1})}=\left(ub_{px,py}^{(i_{j+1})}\right)_{UB_H^{(i_{j+1})}\times UB_L^{(i_{j+1})}}$ for each entry, $ub_{px,py}^{(i_{j+1})}=u_{px,py}$.
Furthermore, $UB_H^{(i_{j+1})}$ and $UB_L^{(i_{j+1})}$ satisfy the following conditions:

$$\begin{cases} UB_H^{(i_{j+1})} \le UB_H^{(i_j)} + UA_H^{(i_{j+1})} \\ UB_L^{(i_{j+1})} = \max\left\{UB_L^{(i_j)}, UA_L^{(i_{j+1})}\right\} \end{cases}.$$

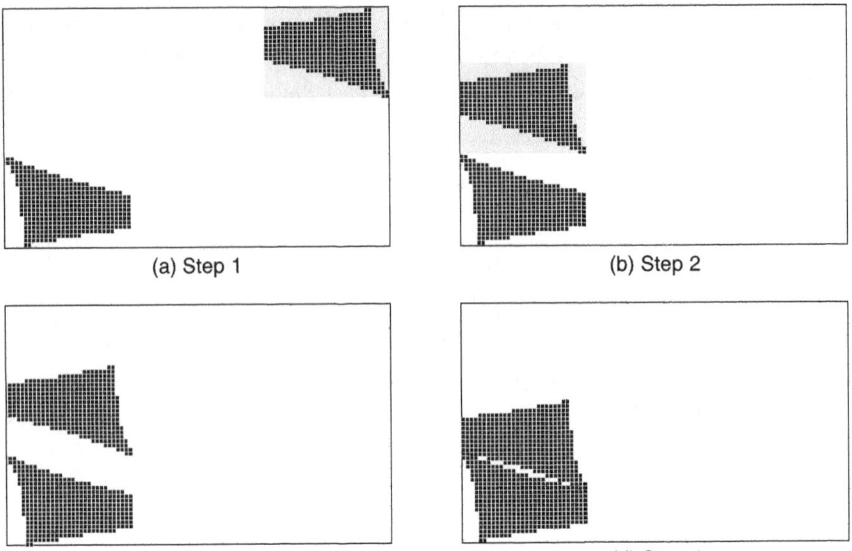

6.3 (a–d)Procedures of two-stage placement strategy: the object at the top right in Step 1 represents the coming packing cell C_{ij}+1.

An example of how the objects are placed according to the two-stage placement strategy is shown in Fig. 6.3.

6.3 Evolutionary strategy (ES) for optimizing marker planning

In this study, the $(\mu + \lambda)$ – evolutionary strategy (ES) was adopted. In contrast to the elitist strategy of genetic algorithms, with the aid of the $(\mu + \lambda)$ – ES, parents survive until they are superseded by better offspring (Bäck *et al.*, 1997). The following notation is used to facilitate the presentation:

μ = the population size of parents
λ = the population size of offspring
s_k = k th individual in the individual space
$f(s_k)$ = the fitness value of individual s_k $(k = 0,1,2,...,\mu + \lambda - 1)$
t = generation index $(t = 0,1,2,...)$

It is assumed that the current generation is t and the current population is represented by $\mathbf{X}(t)$, which is a population of μ individuals, and the general outline of the $(\mu + \lambda)$ – ES is illustrated in the block diagram in Fig. 6.4.

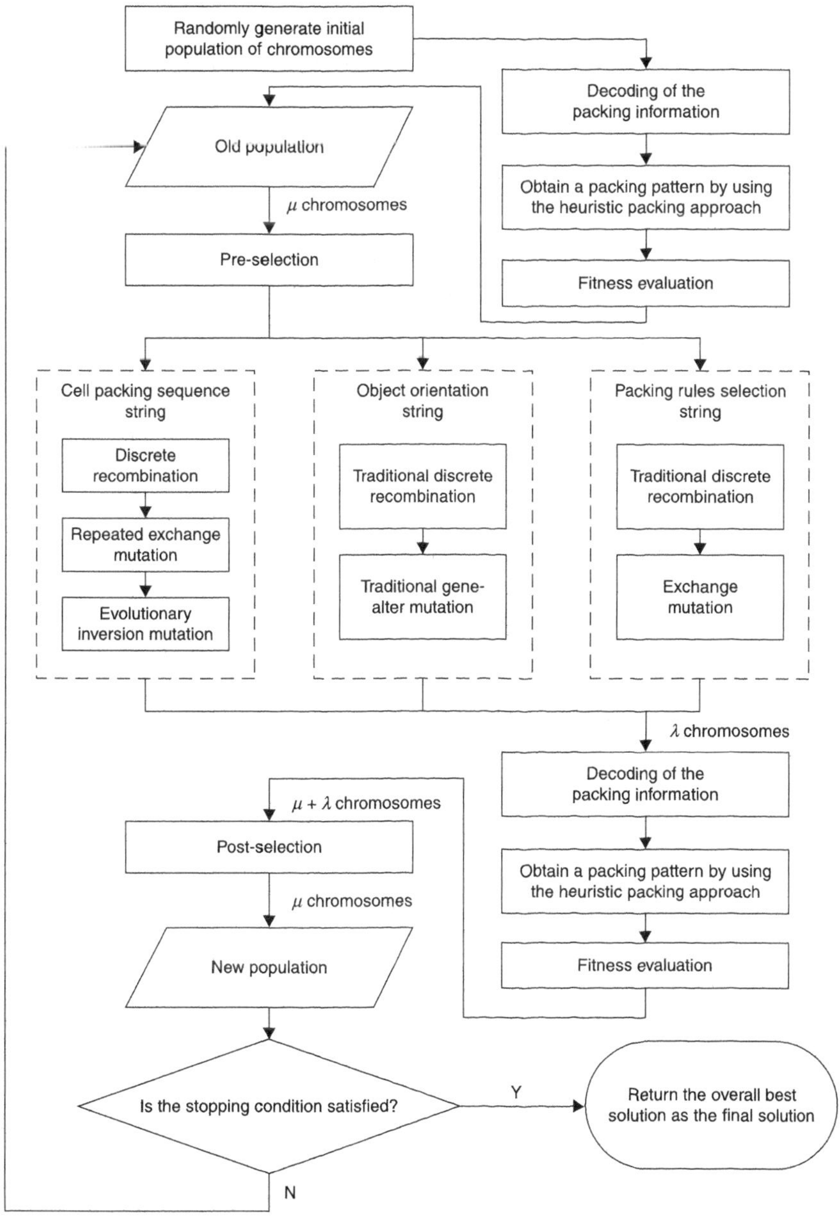

6.4 Block diagram of the $(\mu + \lambda)$ – ES.

- ***Step 1:*** Set $t = 0$ and generate an initial population of μ individuals randomly.
- ***Step 2:*** Generate a mating pool by pre-selection (see the selection operation section for details).
  Select individuals from the population according to a specified selection operation. The selected individuals are then placed into a mating pool.
- ***Step 3:*** Perform recombination and mutation.
  Pair up the individuals in the mating pool and generate $\lambda(\geq \mu)$ new-born offspring individuals using the operators of recombination and mutation. In this study, each chromosome consists of three portions. For the first portion of the chromosome, discrete recombination operators, repeated exchange mutation operators, and evolutionary inversion mutation operators are employed. For the second portion of the chromosome, traditional gene-alter mutation operators and traditional discrete recombination operators are developed. For the third portion of the chromosome, exchange mutation operators and traditional discrete recombination operators are developed.
- ***Step 4:*** Create a new population for the next generation by post-selection (see the selection operation section for details).
  Select μ best individuals from the combined population of parents (μ individuals) and offspring (λ individuals). All the selected μ individuals are then collected to form a new population known as $\mathbf{X}(t+1)$, which replaces $\mathbf{X}(t)$ and serves as the population of individuals for the next generation $t+1$.
- ***Step 5:*** Check the pre-specified stopping condition.
  In this case, the pre-specified stopping condition is satisfied when the pre-defined maximum number of generations is reached or no further increase in the fitness function values of the individuals is obtained. If it is satisfied, terminate the search process, and return to the best solution as the final solution. Otherwise, increase t by 1 and go to step 2.

6.3.1 Structure of the individuals

Although there are many different representations to implement evolutionary algorithms, the most natural representation for the object packing problem is integer representation. In this study, each chromosome, as shown in Fig. 6.5, consists of three portions. A set of bits in the first portion of the string is a set of integer numbers to indicate the packing sequence of packing cells, which are shown as $\Omega = (i_1, i_2, \ldots, i_n)$, i: index of the packing cell C_i. The order of a gene in an individual is the order to examine the packing cell that is identified by the gene. A set of bits in the second portion of the string is a set of $0-1$ binary decision variables to represent the object orientation (i.e. 0° or 180°) for each object in the SMALL class, and a set of bits in the third portion of the string is a set of integer numbers containing information to select packing rules for the BIG and OTHER classes. Since factors such as object orientation and packing rules selection in the second and third portions of the string complicate the packing problem, this new

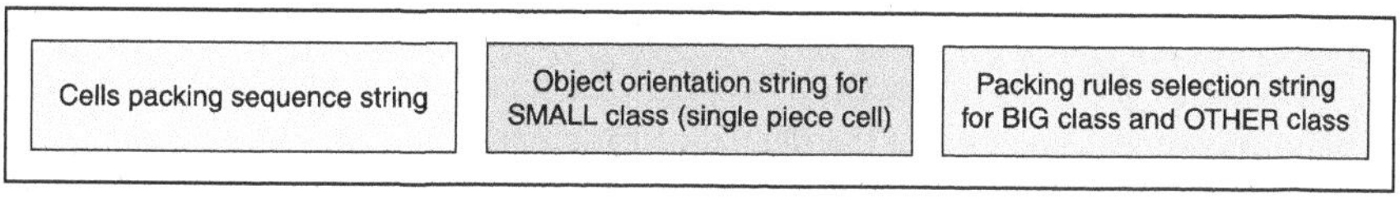

6.5 Chromosome structure.

chromosome structure could prevent potential or even detrimental squashing of the solution space. The length of the new chromosome is 3N, where N is the number of cells to be packed.

6.3.2 Selection operation

In this study, two selection schemes, pre-selection and post-selection, are implemented. The pre-selection scheme is stochastic, while the post-selection scheme is deterministic. For the pre-selection operation shown in Fig. 6.4, one of the best-known selection schemes, called the 'biased roulette wheel scheme' (Goldberg, 1989), was used. The probability of selecting an individual s_k from the current population **X(t)** is given by the following equation:

$$P_{select} = \frac{f(s_k)}{\sum_{k=0}^{\mu-1} f(s_k)}. \qquad [6.8]$$

In any generation, the individuals are selected by their respective selection probabilities governed by the above-mentioned equation. If the individual s_k represents a candidate solution, then the fitness function is $f(s_k) = 1/C_L$. Therefore, the candidate solutions with lower objective function values have higher selection probabilities. Through this connection, the optimal objective function value can be obtained by maximizing the fitness function values of the individuals. When the pre-selection process is completed, the individuals in the mating pool will then be paired up to generate λ new offspring by recombination and mutation operations.

In the case of the post-selection operation in Fig. 6.4, the combined population of parents (μ individuals) and offspring (λ individuals) are sorted by the fitness function values. The μ best individuals with higher fitness function values will survive while the λ remainder individuals with lower fitness function values will be discarded.

6.3.3 Recombination operation

The discrete recombination operator was used in this study. The procedure of the discrete recombination operator for the first portion of the chromosome is presented on the next page:

1. Select two parents randomly from the mating pool.
2. Randomly generate a decision string with the same length as the parent chromosomes. Each bit in the decision string can take a value of '1' or '2'. A value of '1' indicates that the corresponding components of the offspring chromosome are copied from the first parent chromosome; otherwise, '2' represents that the positions in the offspring chromosome are filled with the elements of the second parent chromosome.
3. Fill some positions with the offspring chromosome by copying corresponding elements of the first parent chromosome associated with a '1' in the decision string. That is to say, the same components appear in the same positions in the offspring chromosome as they do in the first parent chromosome.
4. With reference to the second parent chromosome, the components present in the offspring chromosome are omitted; otherwise, the remaining part is reserved.
5. The remaining positions in the offspring chromosome are filled with the reserved elements of the second parent chromosome in the same order whenever the decision string contains a '2'.

Consequently, each offspring chromosome consists of two portions: a set of bits in the first portion of the string preserves information from the first parent chromosome, and a set of bits in the second portion of the string incorporates information from the second parent chromosome. Figure 6.6 illustrates the

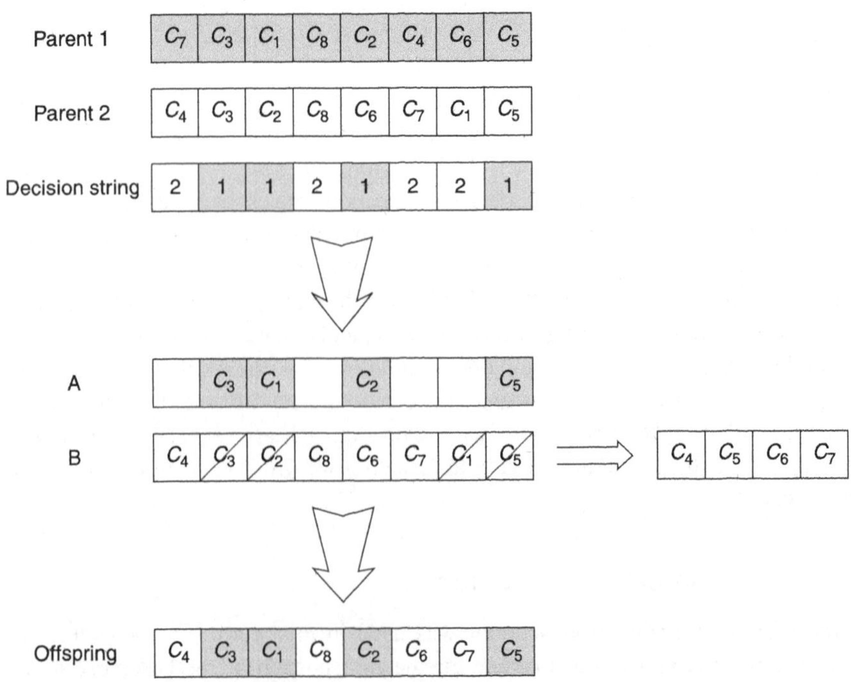

6.6 Discrete recombination operator.

mechanism of the recombination process graphically. For the second and third portions of the chromosome, the traditional discrete recombination operator is employed, in which each bit is randomly copied from either the first or the second parent chromosome.

6.3.4 Mutation operation

After the recombination process is completed, instead of using the traditional gene-alter mutation operation (Goldberg, 1989), for the first portion of the chromosome the repeated exchange mutation operation and the evolutionary inversion mutation operation are employed to prevent infeasible solutions in this study. In contrast to the recombination operator, the mutation operator is always regarded as a background operator. However, Bäck *et al.* (1997) suggested that the mutation operator becomes more productive as the ES converges. The repeated exchange mutation operator is used to introduce new schemata into the population in order to prevent premature convergence of the population, while the evolutionary inversion mutation operator is adopted to manipulate the local search process over the solution space like an uphill-climbing technique to improve the capability of the local search process. The algorithm regulates a balance between the exploration and exploitation of the solution space. The repeated exchange mutation operator has the following procedures:

- ***Step 1:*** Generate a random integer ω within a range of $[1, l]$ (where l is the length of the chromosome) to determine the number of exchanges.
- ***Step 2:*** Randomly choose two bits along the string and the two selected bits are exchanged.
- ***Step 3:*** Iteratively implement step 2 ω times.

Figure 6.7(a) shows an illustration of step 1 of the above-mentioned procedure.

The procedure of the evolutionary inversion mutation operation is outlined below:

- ***Step 1:*** Set *Loop_num = 0*. Generate a random integer: θ within a range of $[1, l]$ (where l is the length of the chromosome) to determine the number of loops.
- ***Step 2:*** Two cutting points are selected randomly along the length of the chromosome. The substring between these two cutting points is reversed and the remaining part of the chromosome is preserved.
- ***Step 3:*** If the fitness function value of the newly generated individual is higher than the original one, then the inversion operation in the above-mentioned step is implemented; otherwise, go back to the first step.
- ***Step 4:*** If *Loop_num* $\geq \theta$ is satisfied, terminate the process; otherwise, increase *Loop_num* by 1, then go to step 2.

Figure 6.7(b) illustrates an example of a simple inversion mutation process presented in step 2.

For the second portion of the chromosome, the traditional gene-alter mutation operator (Burke and Kendall, 1999) was adopted. For instance, if an offspring

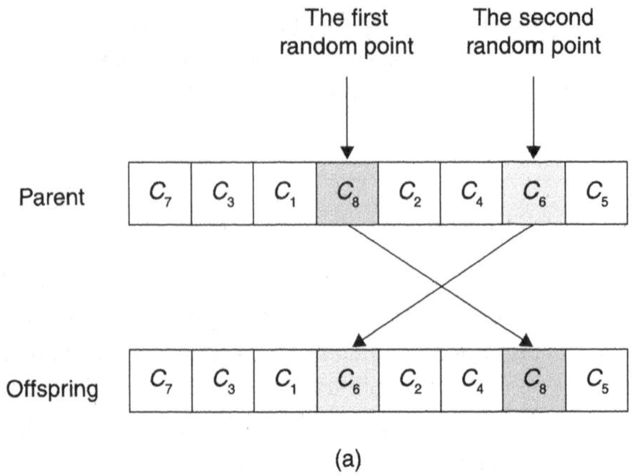

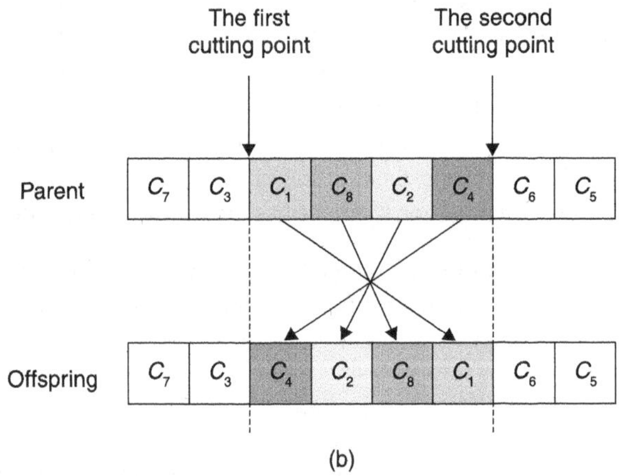

6.7 Mutation operators. (a) Exchange mutation operator. (b) Inversion mutation operator.

individual is encoded by the binary representation (0 1 1 0 0 1), then six random numbers ranging from 0.00 to 1.00 are drawn: (0.653, 0.231, **0.007**, 0.014, **0.003**, 0.024). If the mutation rate is 0.01, two random numbers in the above-mentioned array have their values smaller than the mutation rate. These two numbers will trigger the mutation operation to take place in the third and fifth bits of the string. The mutation operator causes the bits to change from 1 to 0 or 0 to 1 whenever the mutation operations are triggered. The resulting individual becomes (0 1 **0** 0 **1** 1). For the third portion of the chromosome, exchange mutation operator (Bäck and Hoffmeister, 1991) is employed. The procedure of the exchange mutation operator is to randomly choose two bits along the string, and then the two selected bits are exchanged.

6.4 Experiments to evaluate performance

In this section, eight real examples are used to evaluate the performance of the proposed methodology.[1] First of all, the results of the proposed methodology are compared with those obtained by the genetic algorithm (GA) with the elitist strategy and the heuristic placement (HP) approach (GA+HP approach). The GA+HP approach is the same as the proposed approach except that a GA with elitist strategy is used to replace the ES so that the performance of GA and ES can be compared in the problem investigated. Then the results are also compared with those derived by industrial practice (IP) in order to demonstrate the effectiveness of the proposed methodology.

Table 6.1 lists six real examples taken from a marker planning process of the clothing industry. In all experiments, the parameters adopted for the evolutionary strategy after testing were $\mu = 50$, $\lambda = 100$, recombination rate = 0.7, mutation rate = 0.03, and maximum number of generations = 500. In addition, the GA with the elitist strategy was also used to solve the examples for comparison purposes, and the genetic parameters adopted for the GA after testing were population size = 100, crossover rate = 0.7, mutation rate = 0.003, and maximum number of generations = 500. Due to space limitations, only example SWIM3 was used to evaluate the performance of the evolutionary strategy by the off-line performance measure:

$$\text{Off-line performance measure} = \frac{1}{T}\sum_{t=1}^{T} z_t^*, \qquad [6.9]$$

where z_t is the best objective function value among the candidate solutions in generation t, z_t^* is defined by the equation

$$z_t^* = \min\{z_1, z_2, \ldots, z_t\}. \qquad [6.10]$$

Table 6.2 shows that the average objective function value of the final solutions among the five runs for example SWIM4 is 138.85, which is less than the best solutions obtained by the GA. Table 6.2 also shows that the proposed algorithm has better off-line performance than those of the GA and also outperforms the GA in terms of quality of the final solution. The proposed algorithm is superior to the GA as a function optimizer.

Table 6.1 Data sets used in the illustrative examples

Problem name	Number of objects	Sheet width (inches)
SHIRT1	48	48
SHIRT2	64	48
SHIRT3	80	48
SWIM1	60	60
SWIM2	78	60
SWIM3	108	60

[1] The detailed given data of the eight experiments are available upon request.

Table 6.2 Comparison of the off-line performance by the proposed approach and the genetic algorithm

	GA	ES
Overall best solution among 5 runs	141.74	138.64
Average of the best solution among 5 runs	142.17	138.85
Best off-line performance among 5 runs	143.45	138.98
Average off-line performance among 5 runs	144.05	139.57

Notes: ES, evolutionary strategy; GA, genetic algorithm.

Each example listed in Table 6.1 was run five times by the ES and the GA while five trials were conducted by five marker planners. Table 6.3 summarizes the best results of the six packed stock sheets, and the results obtained by the proposed approach are marked in bold. The efficiencies of the packing pattern for the proposed approach, the GA+HP approach, and the IP are shown in the third, fourth and fifth columns of Table 6.3. The efficiency was measured as a quotient between the area of packed objects and the used rectangle area of the stock sheet (Gomes and Oliveira, 2006). The results indicate that the proposed methodology improves the efficiency of the packing pattern and shortens its length. Table 6.4 shows the details of the improvement percentage of each example. It reveals that the average improvement of the examples is 1.92% for the first comparison in column 2, and 9.99% for the second comparison in column 3. Finally, the packing patterns for each example generated by the proposed methodology, the GA+HP approach and the IP approach are presented in Fig. 6.8, 6.9 and 6.10 respectively.

Table 6.3 A summary of the results for the eight illustrative examples

Problem name	Number of objects	ES+HP sheet length (inches)	Efficiency (%)	Proposed methodology GA+HP Sheet length (inches)	Efficiency (%)	IP Sheet length (inches)	Efficiency (%)
SHIRT1	48	146.60	75.91	146.94	75.74	151.78	73.21
SHIRT2	64	193.72	76.61	201.32	73.71	203.21	73.03
SHIRT3	80	243.44	76.20	248.71	74.58	260.69	71.16
SWIM1	60	92.60	58.62	94.94	57.18	100.30	54.13
SWIM2	78	122.49	58.65	126.64	56.73	133.06	53.99
SWIM3	108	138.64	57.84	141.74	56.54	147.85	54.20

Notes: GA, genetic algorithm; HP, heuristic placement; IP, industrial practice.

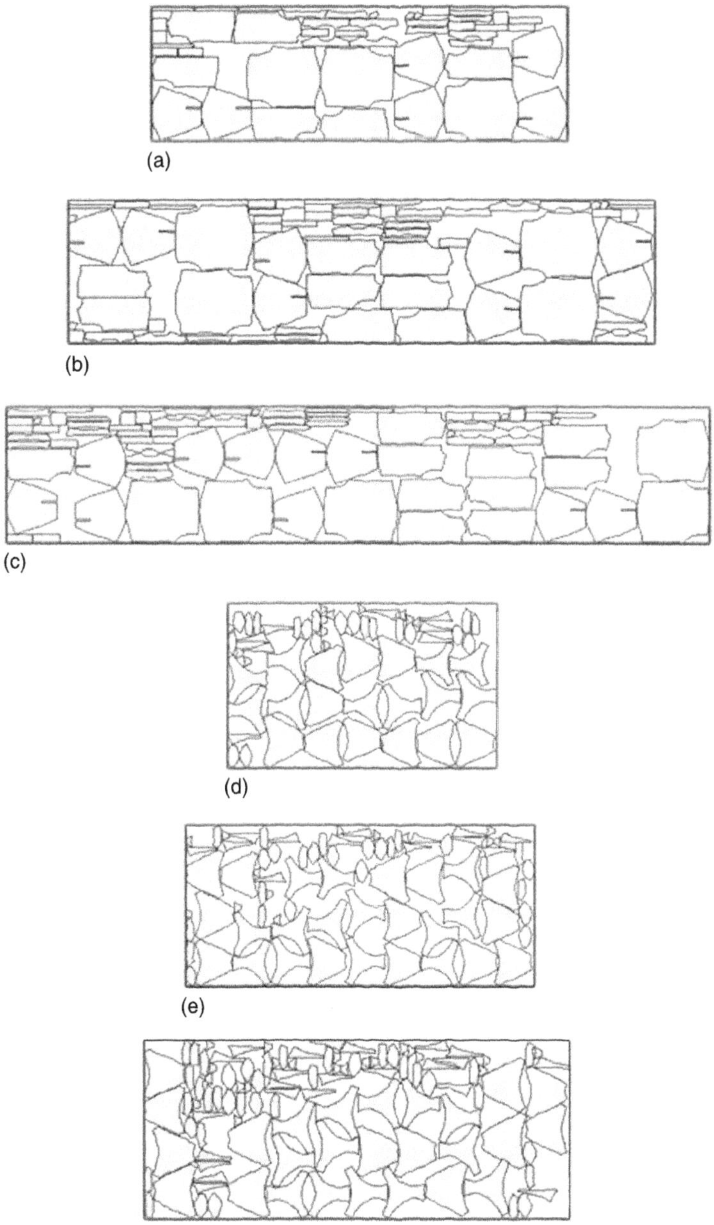

(a) (b) (c) (d) (e) (f)

6.8 The best packing pattern generated by the proposed approach for the illustrative examples: (a) SHIRT1, (b) SHIRT2, (c) SHIRT3, (d) SWIM1, (e) SWIM2 and (f) SWIM3.

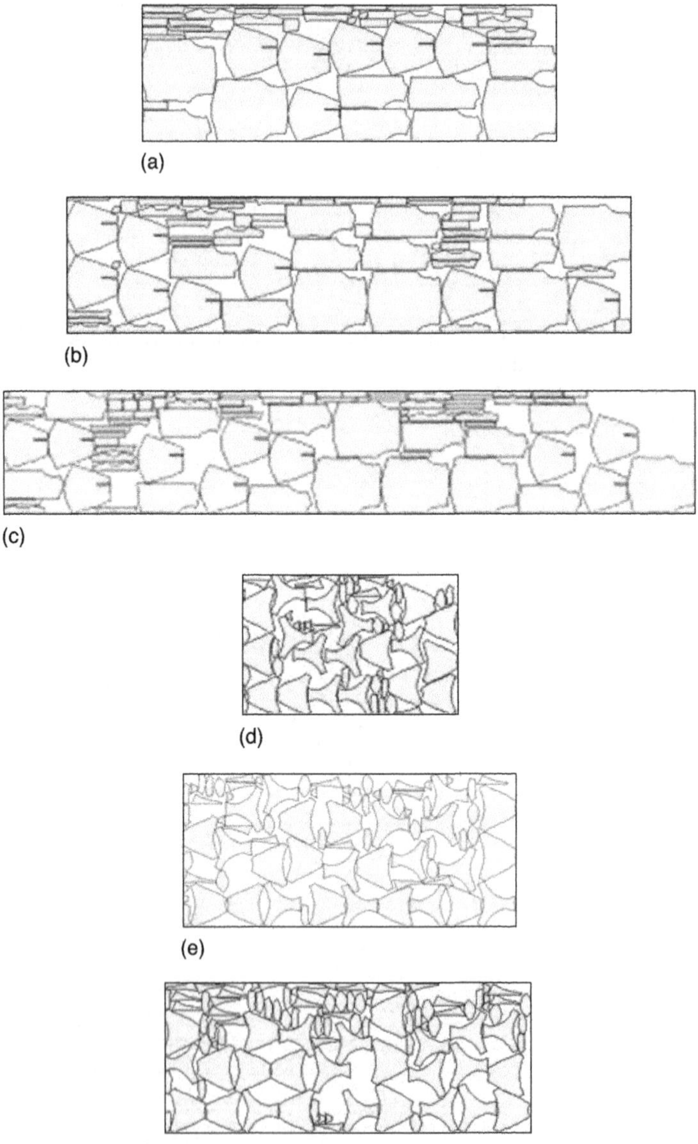

6.9 The packing pattern generated by the GA+HP approach for the illustrative examples: (a) SHIRT1, (b) SHIRT2, (c) SHIRT3, (d) SWIM1, (e) SWIM2 and (f) SWIM3.

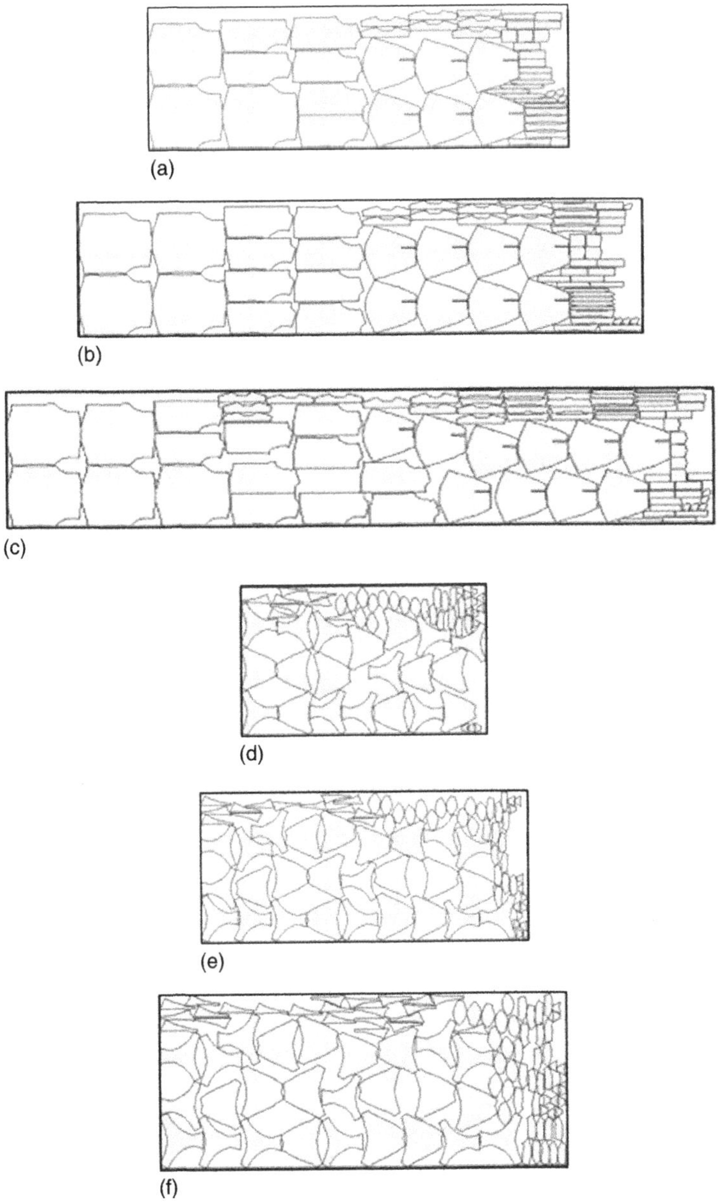

6.10 The packing pattern derived from the marker planner in the clothing industry for the illustrative examples: (a) SHIRT1, (b) SHIRT2, (c) SHIRT3, (d) SWIM1, (e) SWIM2 and (f) SWIM3.

Table 6.4 Method comparisons

Problem name	Improvement (proposed methodology vs. GA+HP) (%)	Improvement (proposed methodology vs. IP) (%)
SHIRT1	0.23	3.4
SHIRT2	3.78	4.67
SHIRT3	2.12	6.62
SWIM1	2.46	7.67
SWIM2	3.28	7.94
SWIM3	2.18	6.23

Notes: GA, genetic algorithm; HP, heuristic placement; IP, industrial practice.

6.5 Conclusion

In this study, a heuristic placement approach based on grid approximation, a learning vector quantization neural network, and an integer representation-based evolutionary strategy are proposed to establish an effective methodology for solving irregular object packing problems. This approach has many advantages. First, with the placement approach based on grid approximation, it provides the system designers with an easier way to detect whether overlap occurs. Second, the two-stage placement strategy improves the packing pattern quality without compromising the computational effort. Third, the formulation of optimal packing information can be accomplished easily by manipulating the composition of the integer string format. Fourth, a learning vector quantization neural network is developed as a classification heuristic to reduce the size of the search space. Fifth, adding factors such as object orientation and packing rules selection in the second and third portions of the string could prevent potential or even detrimental squashing of the solution space. Finally, the proposed evolutionary strategy can maintain a better balance between exploitation and exploration of the solution space by generating the evolution of the populations. The effectiveness of the proposed methodology is demonstrated through various experiments, and the results of this methodology are compared with those of the genetic algorithm using the heuristic placement approach and the results derived from marker planners in the industry. The results show that the proposed methodology provides an effective means to increase the usability of the stock sheet.

The proposed methodology can handle convex and concave shapes well and obtain the global optimization solutions. However, this study has not compared the performance of the proposed approach with the existing approaches in the literature. Based on various benchmark problems in open literature, future work will aim at the performance comparison of the proposed approach with various existing approaches, such as NFP techniques, phi-function techniques and the new bottom-left-fill heuristic algorithm of Burke *et al.*, (2006) Moreover, the proposed approach will also be fine-tuned, particularly in the parameter setting, which influences the optimization performance.

6.6 Acknowledgement

The authors would like to thank Earmarked Research Grant of Research Grants Council of Hong Kong and The Hong Kong Polytechnic University for financial support of this research project (Project No.529005).

6.7 References

Au, K.F., Wong, W.K. and Zeng, X.H., 2006. Decision model for country site selection of overseas clothing plants. *International Journal of Advanced Manufacturing Technology*, 29(3–4), 408–417.

Babu, A.R. and Babu, N.R., 2001. A generic approach for nesting of 2-D parts in 2-D sheets using genetic and heuristic algorithms. *Computer-Aided Design*, 33, 879–891.

Bäck, T. and Hoffmeister, F., 1991. Extended selection mechanisms in genetic algorithms, in *Proceedings of the Fourth International Conference on Genetic Algorithms*, Morgan Kaufmann, pp. 92–99.

Bäck, T., Fogel, D. and Michalewicz, Z., 1997. *Handbook of Evolutionary Computation*, IOP Publishing and Oxford University Press, New York.

Bennell, J.A. and Dowsland, K.A., 1999. A tabu thresholding implementation for the irregular stock cutting problem. *International Journal of Production Research*, 37(18), 4259–4275.

Bennell, J.A. and Dowsland, K.A., 2001. Hybridising tabu search with optimisation techniques for irregular stock cutting. *Management Science*, 47(8), 1160–1172.

Bennell, J.A., Dowsland, K.A. and Dowsland, W.B., 2001. The irregular cutting-stock problem—a new procedure for deriving the no-fit polygon. *Computers and Operations Research*, 28(3), 271–287.

Bennell, J., Scheithauer, G., Stoyan, Y. and Romanova, T., 2010. Tools of mathematical modelling of arbitrary object packing problems. *Annals of Operations Research*, 179(1), 343–368.

Blazewicz, J., Hawryluk, P. and Walkowiak, R., 1993. Using a tabu search approach for solving the two-dimensional irregular cutting problem. *Annals of Operations Research*, 41, 313–325.

Bounsaythip, C. and Maouche, S., 1997. Irregular shape nesting and placing with evolutionary approach. In: *Proceedings of the IEEE International Conference on Systems, Man and Cybernetics*, 4, pp. 3425–3430.

Bounsaythip, C., Maouche, S. and Neus, M., 1995. Evolutionary search techniques application in automated lay-planning optimization problem. In: *Proceedings of the IEEE Conference on SMC*, pp. 4497–4502.

Burke, E. and Kendall, G., 1999. Applying simulated annealing and the no fit polygon to the nesting problem. In: *Proceedings of the World Manufacturing Congress*, Durham, UK, pp. 27–30.

Burke, E., Hellier, R.S.R., Kendall, G. and Whitwell, G., 2006. A new bottom-left-fill heuristic algorithm for the two-dimensional irregular packing problem. *Operations Research*, 54(3), 587–601.

Dowsland, K.A. and Dowsland, W.B., 1995. Solution approaches to irregular nesting problems. *European Journal of Operational Research*, 84, 506–521.

Fujita, K., Akagji, S. and Kirokawa, N., 1993. Hybrid approach for optimal nesting using a genetic algorithm and a local minimisation algorithm. In: *Proceedings of the 19th Annual ASME Design Automation Conference*, pp. 477–484.

Goldberg, D.E., 1989. *Genetic Algorithms in Search, Optimization and Machine Learning*, Reading, MA: Addison Wesley.

Gomes, A.M. and Oliveira, J.F., 1999. Nesting irregular shapes with simulated annealing. In: *Proceedings of 3rd Metaheuristics International Conference*, Angra dos Reis, Brazil, pp. 235–239.

Gomes, A.M. and Oliveira, J.F., 2002. A 2-exchange heuristic for nesting problems. *European Journal of Operational Research*, 141, 359–370.

Gomes, A.M. and Oliveira, J.F., 2006. Solving irregular strip packing problems by hybridising simulated annealing and linear programming. *European Journal of Operational Research*, 171(3), 811–829.

Guo, Z.X., Wong, W.K. and Leung, S.Y.S., 2008. A genetic-algorithm-based optimization model for scheduling flexible assembly lines. *International Journal of Advanced Manufacturing Technology*, 36(1–2), 156–168.

Guo, Z.X., Wong, W.K., Leung, S.Y.S., Fan, J.T. and Chan, S.F., 2008a. A genetic algorithm based optimization model for solving the flexible assembly line balancing problem with work-sharing and workstation revisiting. *IEEE Transactions on Systems Man and Cybernetics Part C: Applications and Reviews*, 38(2), 218–228.

Han, G.C. and Na, S.J., 1996. Two-stage approach for nesting in two-dimensional cutting problems using neural network and simulated annealing. In: *Proceedings of the Institute of Mechanical Engineers, Part B, Journal of Engineering Manufacture*, pp. 509–519.

Heckmann, R. and Lengauer, T., 1995. A simulated annealing approach to the nesting problem in the textile manufacturing industry. *Annals of Operations Research*, 57, 103–133.

Hifi, M. and Hallah, R.M., 2003. A hybrid algorithm for the two-dimensional layout problem: the cases of regular and irregular shapes. *International Transactions in Operational Research*, 10, 195–216.

Hopper, E., 2000. *Two-dimensional Packing Utilising Evolutionary Algorithms and other Meta-heuristic Methods*, PhD thesis: University of Wales.

Ismail, H.S. and Hon, K.K.B., 1992. New approaches for the nesting of two-dimensional shapes for press tool design. *International Journal of Production Research*, 30, 825–837.

Jain, S. and Gea, H., 1998. Two-dimensional packing problems using genetic algorithms. *Engineering with Computers*, 14, 206–213.

Jakobs, S., 1996. On genetic algorithms for the packing of polygons. *European Journal of Operational Research*, 88, 165–181.

Kohonen, T., 1990. Improved version of learning vector quantization. In: *Proceedings of International Joint Conference on Neural Networks*, San Diego, CA, I, pp. 545–550.

Li, Z.Y. and Milenkovic, V., 1995. Compaction and separation algorithms for non-convex polygons and their applications. *European Journal of Operational Research*, 84, 539–561.

Oliveira, J.F. and Ferreira, J.S., 1993. Algorithms for nesting problems. In: Vidal, RVV. (Ed.). *Applied Simulated Annealing, Lecture Notes in Economics and Mathematical System*, 396, 255–273.

Oliveira, J.F., Gomes, A.M. and Ferreira, J.S., 2000. TOPOS – A new constructive algorithm for nesting problems. *OR Spektrum*, 22(2), 263–284.

Quagliarella, D., Périaux, J., Poloni, C. and Winter, G., 1995. *Genetic Algorithms and Evolution Strategies in Engineering and Computer Science: Recent Advances in Industrial Applications*, John Wiley and Sons, Chichester, UK.

Scheithauer, G., Stoyan, Y.G. and Romanova, T., 2005. Mathematical modeling of interactions of primary geometric 3D objects, *Cybernetics and Systems Analysis*, 41(3), 332–342.

Song, B.L., Wong, W.K., Chan, S.F. and Fan, J.T., 2006. A recursive operator allocation approach for assembly-line optimization problem with the consideration of operator efficiency. *Computers and Industrial Engineering*, 51(4), 585–608.

Stoyan, Y. and Chugay, A., 2009. Packing cylinders and rectangular parallelepipeds with distances between them into a given region. *European Journal of Operational Research*, 197(2), 446–455.

Stoyan, Y. and Gil, N., 1976. *Methods and Algorithms of Placement of 2D Geometric Objects* (in Russian). Ukrainian SSR Academy of Sciences. Naukova Dumka, Kiev.

Stoyan, Y.G., Novozhilova, M.V. and Kartashov, A.V., 1996. Mathematical model and method of searching for a local extremum for the non-convex oriented polygons allocation problem. *European Journal of Operational Research*, 92, 193–210.

Stoyan, Y., Terno, J., Scheithauer, G., Gil, N. and Romanova, T., 2002. Phi functions for primary 2D-objects. *Studia Informatica Universalis*, 2(1), 1–32.

Wong, W.K., 2003. A fuzzy capacity-allocation model for computerised fabric-cutting systems. *International Journal of Advanced Manufacturing Technology*, 21(9), 699–711.

Wong, W.K., 2003a. Optimisation of apparel manufacturing resource allocation using a generic optimised table-planning model. *International Journal of Advanced Manufacturing Technology*, 21(12), 935–944.

Wong, W.K., Chan, C.K. and Ip, W.H., 2000. Optimization of spreading and cutting sequencing model in garment manufacturing. *Computers in Industry*, 43(1), 1–10.

Wong, W.K., Au, K.F. and Zeng, X.H., 2006. Classification decision model for Hong Kong clothing manufacturing plant locations using artificial neural network. *International Journal of Advanced Manufacturing Technology*, 28(3–4), 428–434.

Wong, W.K., Zeng, X.H. and Au, W.M.R., 2009. A decision support tool for apparel coordination through integrating the knowledge-based attribute evaluation expert system and the T-S fuzzy neural network. *Expert Systems with Applications*, 36(2), 2377–2390.

Wu, T.H., Low, C.Y. and Tang, P.T., 2003. Nesting of two-dimensional parts in multiple plates using hybrid algorithm. *International Journal of Production Research*, 41, 3883–3900.

Yuen, C.W.M., Wong, W.K., Qian, S.Q., Chan, L.K. and Fung, E.H.K., 2009. Fabric stitching inspection using segmented window technique and BP neural network. *Textile Research Journal*, 79(1), 24–35.

Yuen, C.W.M., Wong, W.K., Qian, S.Q., Chan, L.K. and Fung, E.H.K., 2009a. A hybrid model using genetic algorithm and neural network for classifying garment defects. *Expert Systems with Applications*, 36(2), 2037–2047.

7

Optimizing fabric spreading and cutting schedules in apparel production using genetic algorithms and fuzzy set theory

W. K. WONG, C. K. KWONG, P. Y. MOK and W. H. IP,
The Hong Kong Polytechnic University, China

DOI: 10.1533/9780857097842.132

Abstract: Today's apparel industry must respond to an ever-changing fashion market. Just-in-time production is a must-go direction. The apparel industry generates more production orders, which are split into smaller jobs to provide customers with timely and customized fashion products. Production planning is even more challenging if the due times of production orders are fuzzy and resource competing. In this chapter, genetic algorithms and fuzzy set theory generate just-in-time fabric-cutting schedules in a dynamic and fuzzy environment. Real production data were collected to validate the proposed genetic optimization method. Results demonstrate that genetically optimized schedules improve the satisfaction of production departments and reduce costs.

Key words: genetic algorithms, fuzzy set theory, parallel machine scheduling, fabric cutting, apparel.

7.1 Introduction

Apparel production is a type of assembly manufacture that involves a number of processes. Fabric-cutting operation is done in a fabric-cutting department, which usually serves several downstream sewing assembly lines. Effective upstream fabric-cutting operation ensures the smoothness of downstream operations, and thus is vitally important to the overall system efficiency. Production scheduling of apparel production is a challenging task due to a number of factors. First of all, fashion trends are always unpredictable; thus just-in-time (JIT) production is employed to ensure a short production time-to-market. Moreover, in order to cope with the increasing demand for product customization, the quantity of garments per production order tends to be smaller, and thus the number of production orders processed by the manufacturer has become larger. In this chapter, JIT production scheduling of manual cutting department operation is investigated.

7.1.1 Just-in-time (JIT) scheduling

Production scheduling has been extensively studied, and previous literature has focused more on single regular measures, such as mean flow-time and mean lateness. Since the 1980s, the concept of penalizing both earliness and tardiness has spawned a new and rapidly developing line of research in the scheduling field

(Baker and Scudder, 1990). In a JIT environment, both earliness and tardiness must be discouraged, since jobs finished early increase inventory cost while late jobs lead to customers' dissatisfaction and loss of business goodwill. Thus an ideal schedule is one in which all jobs finish within the assigned due dates. The objectives of early/tardy (E/T) scheduling could be interpreted in different ways, for example minimizing total absolute deviation from due dates, job-dependent earliness and tardiness penalties, non-linear penalties, and so forth (see Baker and Scudder, 1990 for a comprehensive survey).

A main stream of E/T scheduling research is regarding the scheduling of a group of independent jobs with a common due date (De *et al.*, 1991, 1993, Hall and Posner, 1991; Hall *et al.*, 1991; Hoogeveen and van de Velde, 1991). The common due date is either a known property of the problem or a decision variable to be optimized along with the job sequence. The latter is equivalent to the former for the single-machine case when the common due date is large (long) enough (Hoogeveen and van de Velde, 1991; De *et al.*, 1991, 1993). Therefore, the former case of scheduling problem with a known due date can be divided into two classes: large due date (unrestrictive case) and small due date (restrictive case). Large due date problems are analytically solvable (Kanet, 1981; De *et al.*, 1993), while small due date cases are proven NP-hard even with linear E/T penalties (Hoogeveen and van de Velde, 1991; Hall *et al.*, 1991; De *et al.*, 1991). In the more complex case of small due date, researchers have so far obtained limited results for some special cases using various techniques such as explicit enumeration algorithms (Bagchi, *et al.*, 1986), branch and bound algorithms (Bagchi *et al.*, 1987; Szwarc, 1989) and pseudo-polynomial dynamic programming algorithms (Hall *et al.*, 1991, Hoogeveen and van de Velde, 1991). In the apparel industry, a single cutting department works on different production orders simultaneously in order to suit the needs of downstream sewing lines. In contrast to the above common due date cases, each production order, which is composed of a group of smaller jobs, has a distinct due time.

7.1.2 Parallel machine scheduling

The above-mentioned studies are mainly for single machine production scheduling. The scheduling of cutting department operation is similar to a traditional parallel machine scheduling (Mok *et al.*, 2007). Figure 7.1 shows an example of the configuration of the cutting department.

In parallel machine scheduling, a batch of jobs is scheduled to be processed by any one of a number of available machines so that the best overall system performance is achieved (Cheng and Sin, 1990). In cutting departments, fabric-cutting jobs that belong to different production orders are to be processed on one of the parallel spreading tables so that the demand from downstream sewing lines can be fulfilled in a timely manner. Research on parallel machine scheduling in the JIT context has received much attention in relatively recent years. Cheng and Chen (1994) showed that parallel machine scheduling problem is NP-hard when due

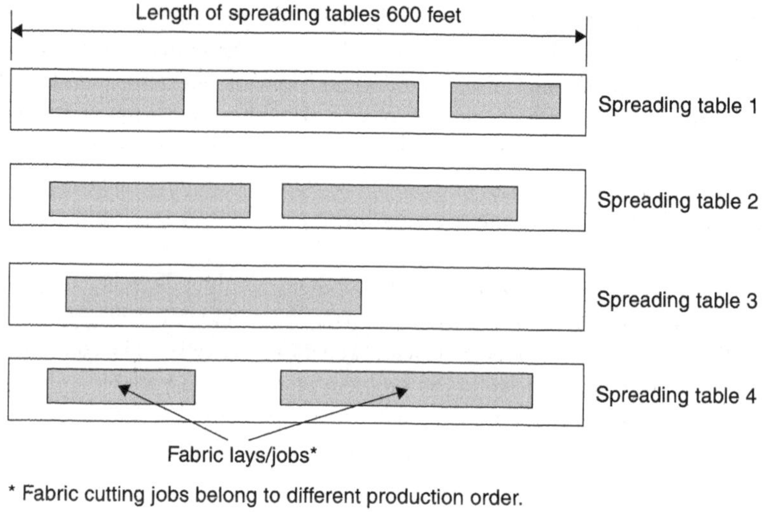

7.1 Layout of a fabric-cutting department consisting of four cutting tables with examples of fabric lays being spread.

date is a decision variable. Cheng *et al.* (1995) minimized the maximum weighted absolute lateness on parallel machine using genetic algorithms. Cheng *et al.* (1996) discussed the scheduling of multiple simultaneously available jobs on parallel machines with controllable processing times. Chen and Lee (2002) studied the parallel machine scheduling with a common due window using branch and bound algorithms. However, the above results assume all jobs with a common due date.

Moreover, fabric-cutting scheduling has the distinctive feature that two interdependent processes (spreading and cutting) must be scheduled simultaneously. The spreading operation must be completed before the cutting operation can start. The spreading operation can accordingly be viewed as a setup operation for the processes of cutting. In addition, fabric-cutting scheduling is a resource-constrained scheduling problem (see Section 7.2.3). Ventura and Kim (2003) investigated parallel machine scheduling with non-common due dates and additional resource constraints; however, all job processing times are assumed constant in their investigation. In a fabric-cutting scheduling problem, each job has its individual spreading and cutting processing times.

7.1.3 Fuzzy scheduling

The traditional production scheduling studies assumed that the due times are crisp values. In practice, it is sometimes allowable to complete jobs beyond certain due times in the apparel industry. This is because apparel manufacturers determine internally the due time windows of various production orders for different production departments, including cutting, sewing, pressing and packaging departments, based on the final delivery due dates and production capacity. Such internal due time windows are determined to ensure on-time delivery of final products and reduce work-in-progress. Fuzzy set theory has been applied to handle the scheduling problem in a fuzzy environment.

Fuzzy set theory (Zadeh, 1965) is an attractive framework for dealing with 'fuzzy' (uncertain) information, and there is indeed an increasing interest in fuzzy scheduling in academia and industry (Słowiński and Hapke, 2000). In fuzzy scheduling research, fuzzy numbers, an extension of the concept of confidence intervals, are used to model the imprecise time parameters. In this chapter, the production-order due-time windows are presented in the form of fuzzy numbers. Genetic algorithms are then used to optimize the cutting department production schedules such that the requirement by the downstream sewing lines for fabric cut-pieces for assembly can be maximally satisfied.

The outline of this chapter is as follows. Section 7.2 provides a general description of the fabric-cutting system, including model formulation, fuzzy due time definition, and job placement mechanism. The general methodology of genetic optimization of fabric-cutting scheduling with fuzzy due times is described in Section 7.3. The proposed method is demonstrated by two real production cases in Section 7.4, in which the genetically optimized results are compared with those implemented by industrial practice. Finally, conclusions and recommendations for future work are outlined.

7.2 Problem formulation in fabric-cutting operations

In a traditional fabric-cutting department, there are several key operations involved, which are shown in Fig. 7.2. The fabric-cutting operation studied in this chapter satisfies the following assumptions:

- The manual spreading carts for spreading and manual straight-knife cutters for cutting are always available throughout the scheduling period.
- Jobs (fabric lays) are always available to be loaded into the system and to be processed by any of the spreading carts and cutters on any of the parallel spreading tables.
- No job can be processed on more than one spreading table simultaneously.
- There is no precedence constraint on the jobs.

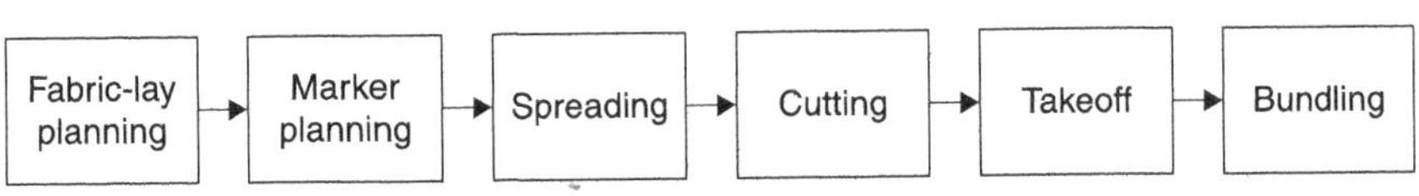

7.2 Workflow of a fabric-cutting department.

7.2.1 Efficient manual cutting systems

The system investigated in this chapter assumes an *efficient* manual cutting model configuration. In an efficient system, after spreading and cutting operations, fabric pieces are taken away from the spreading tables for bundling operations, which helps to make space for spreading new jobs. In an efficient fabric-cutting department, a group consisting of four operators is normally assigned to each spreading table. The group is divided into two sub-groups in which two operators are responsible for fabric spreading and the remaining two operators are responsible for cutting the fabric lay that has been spread. The division of labor allows operators to focus on their competent operations, thus improving the overall efficiency. Spreading operators continue to spread new fabric lays (jobs) once they have finished the present jobs. The purpose is to reduce delay due to the switching between spreading and cutting. Because of the limited length of spreading tables, idle time could occur if there were insufficient free area on the spreading table available for the new fabric lay. Cutting operators then cut the fabric lays according to the spreading schedule, that is, $\sigma_s=\sigma_c$, on each spreading table. Obviously, cutting idle time occurs when the cutting operators have finished the current job while the new job is still being spread and is not yet ready to be cut.

7.2.2 Fuzzy due times representation

As discussed in Section 7.1.1, both tardiness and earliness are discouraged in a JIT environment. A generic E/T model is represented as

$$f(S) = \sum_k (\alpha_k E_k + \beta_k T_k), \qquad [7.1]$$

where $E_k=\max(0, d_k-C_k)$ is the earliness of job k with completion time C_k and due time d_k, and $T_k=\max(0, C_k-d_k)$ is the corresponding tardiness. In Eq. 7.1, α_k and β_k are penalty weights for earliness and tardiness, respectively. JIT scheduling focuses on the best schedule to minimize the objective function $f(S)$.

In this chapter, the due times of different production orders are represented as trapezoidal fuzzy numbers (TrFN) with the following definition:

$$\mu_{\tilde{D}}(t) = \begin{cases} 0, & t \le d^A \\ \dfrac{t-d^A}{d^B-d^A}, & d^A < t < d^B \\ 1, & d^B \le t \le d^C. \\ \dfrac{d^D-t}{d^D-d^C}, & d^C < t < d^D \\ 0 & d^D \le t \end{cases} \qquad [7.2]$$

In the apparel industry, the factory manager determines departmental due time windows, rather than precise due time, of different production orders so as to ensure smoothness of downstream operations and on-time delivery of final products. Such due time windows represent the managerial preference regarding different values of production order completion time.

As shown in Fig. 7.3, d^A, d^B, d^C and d^D are crisp real numbers such that $0 \leq d^A \leq d^B \leq d^C \leq d^D$. The membership value of these fuzzy numbers expresses the degree of satisfaction associated with corresponding job completion time: complete satisfaction if the job is completed during the time interval of d^B to d^C; the degree of satisfaction increases linearly from time d^A to d^B and decreases linearly from time d^C to d^D; and complete dissatisfaction if the job is completed before $t=d^A$ or beyond $t=d^U$.

When the due dates are crisp, the weights α and β in Eq. 7.1 denote the decision-maker's view on how significantly each job's lateness or earliness affects the overall system. In the case of fuzzy due date, the steepness of change between complete satisfaction and complete dissatisfaction (i.e. the side slope) represents the same decision-maker's view.

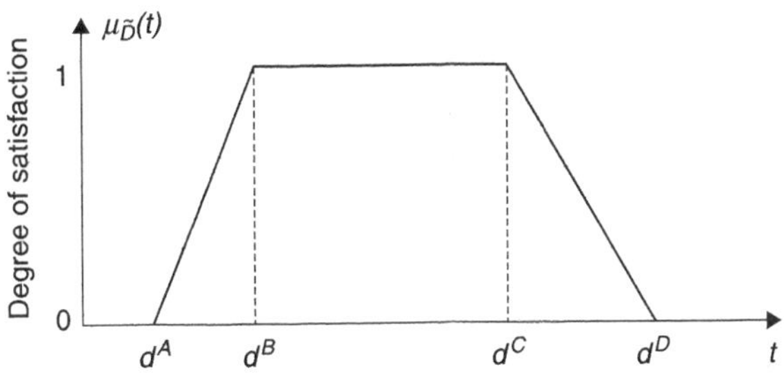

7.3 Trapezoidal fuzzy due date (d^A, d^B, d^C, d^D).

7.2.3 Job placement mechanism

The main objective of fabric-cutting scheduling in a JIT environment is to maximize the satisfaction of downstream production units. Minimizing production makespan (in other words, minimizing operator idle time) is another key issue. Since each fabric-cutting job involves both spreading and cutting operations, the job placement algorithm of manual cutting systems is described here to explain the way jobs are allocated to different spreading tables, and thus to calculate the makespan.

In a cutting department with multiple spreading tables, m, a first-come-first-serve rule is always applied when assigning a sequence of jobs to be processed by different spreading tables. For a given job sequence, σ, jobs are allocated to different spreading tables in accordance with the following placement algorithm:

1. Allocate the first m jobs, J_i ($i = 1, \ldots, m$), to the m spreading tables, set $i = m$.
2. If any spreading table has enough space for the job $J_{i+}1$ (free area > fabric length $\phi(J_{i+1})$), allocate J_{i+1} to the first available spreading table and set $i = i+1$.
3. If there is no spreading table available (free areas of all m tables < fabric length $\phi(J_{i+1})$), wait until enough spreading area is obtained by clearing up the cutting job J_j queues.
4. Repeat procedures 2 and 3 until all the jobs in the sequence are allocated.

According to the described job placement algorithm, individual schedules at different spreading tables are defined for a given job sequence. Thus, the system makespan time, that is, the maximal operation duration of the m spreading tables, can be calculated accordingly. Thus, using this placement algorithm, the parallel-machine (spreading table) scheduling problem becomes a single sequencing optimization problem with multiple objectives to maximize the degree of satisfaction of downstream sewing lines and reduce overall production makespan in the JIT context.

7.3 Genetic optimization of fabric scheduling

In apparel manufacturing, production planners assign a sequence of jobs (fabric lays) to different spreading tables for spreading, cutting and bundling. According to the job placement algorithm described in Section 7.2.4, the parallel machine scheduling optimization problem in the fabric-cutting department is reduced to a single sequencing optimization problem. The job sequencing problem is a permutation problem with n jobs, and the total number of possible solution is $n!$ (e.g. $n! = 1.24 \times 10^{61}$ for $n = 48$). The search space significantly expands as the number of jobs, n, increases, which makes it attractive to use genetic algorithms (GAs), a metaheuristic technique, to search for the best job processing sequence in a manual fabric-cutting department.

In the fabric-cutting scheduling problem, a group of jobs belonging to a defined set of production orders with different due times is to be processed on one of the parallel spreading tables. Earliness/tardiness scheduling with identical earliness and tardiness penalties for all jobs has been shown to be NP-complete (Baker and Schudder, 1990). In a more complex case when each job has its own earliness and tardiness weightings, it is implausible that an optimal schedule for the real-sized problem can be obtained by conventional time polynomial algorithms. However, GAs solve complex industrial optimization by iterations.

7.3.1 Individual representation

To apply GAs in solving an industrial optimization problem, it is usually assumed that a potential solution to the problem may be represented as a set of variables. These variables ('genes') are joined together to form a string of values ('chromosome'). The string can be of binary digits, integers or real numbers. Although the binary representation proposed by Holland (1975) is most widely employed, GAs are not restricted to binary representation. The choice of representation depends on the nature of the problem. In this job sequencing problem, integer chromosome representation is proposed to indicate the job processing sequences. An example of integer chromosome representation is shown in Fig. 7.4.

Chromosome:	3	7	10	1	2	5	8	4	6	9
Job sequence:	J_3	J_7	J_{10}	J_1	J_2	J_5	J_8	J_4	J_6	J_9

7.4 Chromosome representation.

7.3.2 Fitness evaluation

In GAs, a fitness function is defined to measure the fitness of each individual chromosome so as to determine which will reproduce and survive into the next generation. Given a particular chromosome, the fitness depends on how well that individual solves a specific problem. Maximizing degree of satisfaction of the downstream production units is the prime scheduling objective in JIT production.

In the genetic optimization of a fabric-cutting sequence problem, individual chromosomes represent a job processing sequence. Once a job sequence is defined, jobs are allocated to different spreading tables using the job placement algorithm described in Section 7.2.4. Thus, the completion times of individual jobs are evaluated accordingly. Such jobs belong to a set of production orders, and each of these production orders has its distinctive fuzzy due time. For a job J_k belonging to production order θ, θ has a fuzzy due time $\widetilde{D}_\theta$. If job J_k completes at time C_k, the degree of satisfaction with C_k with regard to fuzzy due time $\widetilde{D}_\theta$ is naturally expressed by means of number $\upsilon(C_k, \widetilde{D}_\theta)$ defined by

$$\upsilon(C_k, \widetilde{D}_\theta) = \widetilde{D}_\theta(C_k). \qquad [7.3]$$

Taking Fig. 7.5 as an example, jobs J_1 and J_2 are completed at time $C_1 = 42$ minutes and $C_2 = 65$ minutes, and the degrees of satisfaction achieved are 0.5 and 0.85 respectively with regard to a fuzzy due time of $\widetilde{D}(t) = (38, 46, 60, 94)$.

The JIT fabric-cutting schedule can be optimized using GAs such that the overall degree of satisfaction,

$$\Phi_{JIT}(\sigma) = \left(\sum_{\theta=1}^{p} \sum_{k=1}^{n} \upsilon(C_k(\sigma), \tilde{D}_\theta) \cdot x(J_k, \theta) \right) \cdot w_{DS}, \qquad [7.4]$$

is maximized. In Eq. 7.4, w_{DS} is the weight for degree of satisfaction, and $x(J_k, \theta)$ is the state value, which indicates whether or not job J_k belongs to

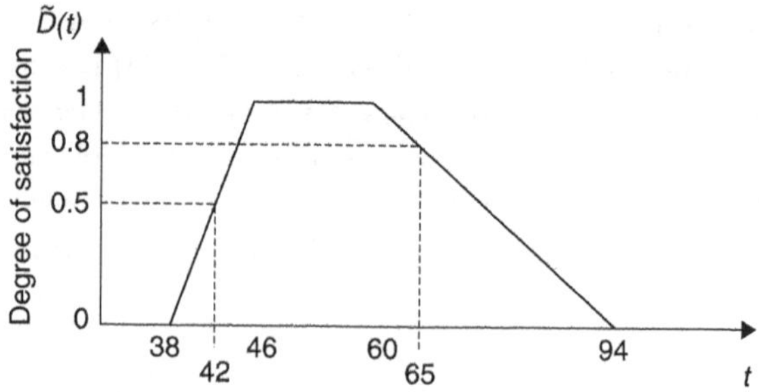

7.5 Degree of satisfaction evaluation.

production order θ. $x(\theta, J_k) = 1$ if job J_k belongs to production order θ; $x(\theta, J_k) = 0$.

In a fabric-cutting environment, it is very important that the production schedule should be optimized in such a way that the production makespan, the longest completion time among different spreading tables and operator idle times, is minimized. With the use of a job placement algorithm, a sequence of fabric-cutting jobs is assigned to different spreading tables and the production makespan is accordingly calculated. The fitness on production makespan of the corresponding individual chromosome is defined as

$$\Phi_{makespan}(\sigma) = \left({T_{target}}/{T_{makespan}}(\sigma) \right) \cdot w_T. \qquad [7.5]$$

where $T_{makespan}(\sigma)$ is the production makespan for sequence σ, T_{target} is the target completion time, and w_T is the weight of production makespan fitness. With reference to Eq. 7.5, a sequence with smaller makespan time results in larger makespan fitness.

Let Π denote the set of all feasible sequences. For a given sequence $\sigma\varepsilon\Pi$, the overall fitness is defined as

$$\underset{\sigma\in\Pi}{\Phi(\sigma)} = \Phi_{JIT}(\sigma) + \Phi_{makespan(\sigma)}, \qquad [7.6]$$

where $\Phi_{JIT}(\sigma)$, and $\Phi_{makespan}(\sigma)$ are the fitnesses for degree of satisfaction and production makespan, respectively. It is important to note that genetic optimization methodology can be applied for multi-objective optimization by defining the fitness function accordingly. For example, Wong *et al.* (2005) minimized the makespan while maximizing the cut-pieces fulfillment rates using GAs.

7.3.3 Genetic procedures

To optimize a fuzzy fabric-cutting schedule by GAs, the operation procedure begins by randomly generating an initial population of integer strings in which each string represents a job processing sequence, as shown in Fig. 7.4. Evolution is caused to occur in this population of strings in accordance with the genetic operations of crossover, mutation and selection. Applying genetic operations to the chromosome may cause lost features in some genes and result in infeasible solutions. In order to prevent such infeasible solutions in the job sequencing problem, uniform order-based crossover (see Fig. 7.6) and inversion mutation (see Fig. 7.7) are adopted. In the case of selection operation, standard biased roulette wheel selection with elitism (Goldberg, 1989; De Jong 1975) is employed. In the evolutionary process, the Darwinian fitness of each chromosome is evaluated by substituting into Eq. [7.7]. This evolutionary process is allowed to continue until no significant further improvement is obtained in the fitness of the fittest string. This fittest string thus provides the optimal job processing sequence for the given batch of fabric-cutting jobs. Figure 7.8 outlines the general methodology proposed in this investigation.

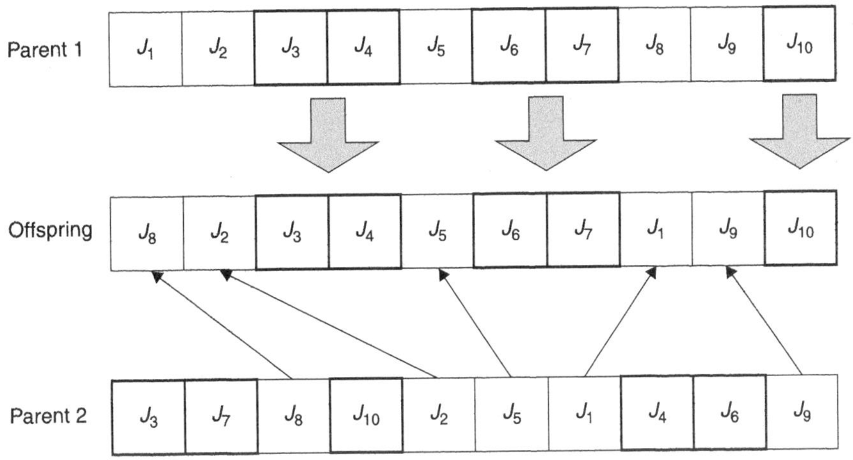

7.6 Uniform order-based crossover.

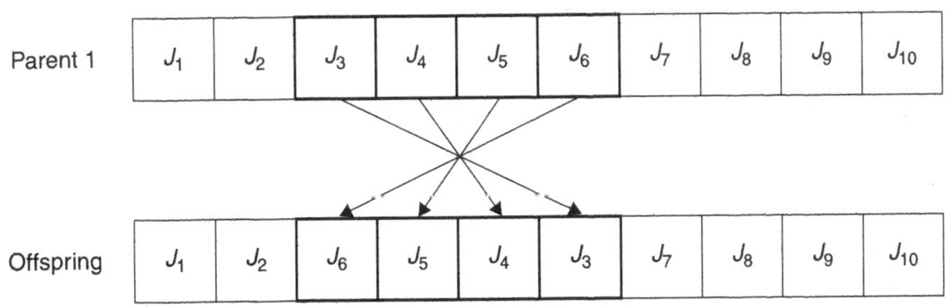

7.7 Inversion mutation.

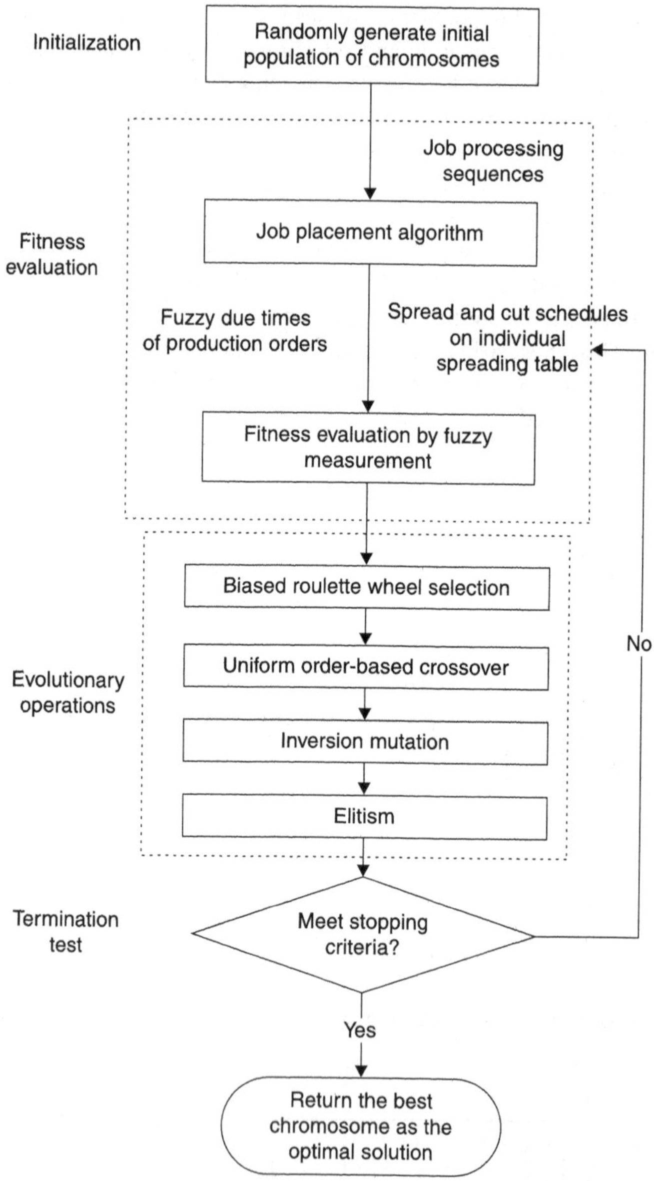

7.8 Methodology outline.

7.4 Case studies using real production data

Two sets of real production data, denoted as cases A and B, are used to demonstrate the proposed method. All the data listed in Table 7.1 were obtained from the

Table 7.1 Detailed job characteristic

(A)-Job (X_n)	1	2	3	4	5	6	7	8	9	10	11	12	13	14	15	16	17	18	19	20	21	22	23	24
Production order (ϕ)	4	1	3	7	6	8	8	8	8	7	5	9	2	8	6	2	9	6	2	6	6	2	4	8
Quantity of garments (χ)	30	116	114	66	15	224	224	224	300	118	300	10	200	300	98	14	4	200	42	52	42	140	13	21
Marker length (ϕ)	103	136	139	132	89	130	130	130	130	172	158	106	175	130	169	87	85	175	91	171	91	170	93	73
Spreading time (s)	50	90	90	57	30	161	161	161	209	104	233	20	170	209	87	29	19	170	60	53	60	121	28	34
Cutting time (c)	24	47	47	47	24	47	47	47	47	47	47	47	47	47	47	24	24	47	24	47	24	47	24	24
(A)-Job (X_n)	25	26	27	28	29	30	31	32	33	34	35	36	37	38	39	40	41	42	43	44	45	46	47	48
Production order (ϕ)	9	6	5	7	2	7	6	3	9	3	9	1	8	4	3	6	6	6	4	2	2	3	4	9
Quantity of garments (χ)	2	33	300	94	33	14	140	146	8	2	3	78	224	53	228	316	14	58	104	98	316	94	6	5
Marker length (ϕ)	68	91	158	132	91	137	170	140	81	73	72	105	130	171	148	170	87	170	171	169	170	132	101	81
Spreading time (s)	17	48	233	77	48	23	121	113	23	16	18	59	161	96	172	254	29	57	174	87	254	77	21	20
Cutting time (c)	24	24	47	47	24	47	47	47	24	47	24	47	47	24	47	47	24	47	24	47	47	47	24	24
(B)-Job (X_n)	1	2	3	4	5	6	7	8	9	10	11	12	13	14	15	16	17	18	19	20	21	22	23	24
Production order (ϕ)	2	1	1	3	2	2	2	2	2	2	3	4	5	4	3	1	4	1	1	3	1	2	3	3
Quantity of garments (χ)	33	140	316	224	3	8	316	4	14	5	21	94	118	94	116	13	146	33	30	300	200	140	224	224
Marker length (ϕ)	91	170	170	130	72	81	170	85	87	81	73	132	172	132	136	93	140	91	103	158	175	170	130	130
Spreading time (s)	48	121	254	161	18	23	254	19	29	20	34	77	104	77	90	28	113	48	50	233	170	121	161	161
Cutting time (c)	24	47	47	47	24	24	47	24	24	24	24	47	47	47	47	24	47	24	24	47	47	47	47	47
(B)-Job (X_n)	25	26	27	28	29	30	31	32	33	34	35	36	37	38	39	40	41	42	43	44	45	46	47	48
Production order (ϕ)	5	3	1	2	6	6	1	2	4	3	1	1	3	1	2	1	2	4	1	1	5	2	4	2
Quantity of garments (χ)	14	78	58	42	300	300	42	2	228	224	6	14	300	104	10	15	98	114	98	53	66	200	2	52
Marker length (ϕ)	137	105	170	91	130	130	91	68	148	130	101	87	158	171	106	89	169	139	169	171	132	175	73	171
Spreading time (s)	23	59	57	60	209	209	60	17	172	161	21	29	233	174	20	30	87	90	87	96	57	170	16	53
Cutting time (c)	47	47	47	24	47	47	24	24	47	47	24	24	47	24	47	24	47	47	47	24	47	47	47	47

fabric-cutting department of a Hong Kong owned apparel manufacturing company located in mainland China. These two-day spreading production schedules, in each of which 48 jobs were spread and cut by a manual cutting system, were recorded in the fabric-cutting department. The cutting department consists of four spreading tables, and the length of each one is 600 feet, as shown in Fig. 7.1.

The fuzzy due times of cases A and B are shown in Fig. 7.9 and 7.10. The genetic optimization procedure described in Section 7.3 is then used to optimize the production schedules. The schedules generated by GAs are maximized for the fitness function (Eq. 7.6). In the case of complete satisfaction, the degree of satisfaction is 1 when the job is finished exactly within the required time window. For 48-job sequences, the overall degree of satisfaction, Φ_{JIT}, is a real number being not greater than 48 when there is unit degree of satisfaction weighting, that is $w_{DS} = 1$. The target completion time (makespan) is $T_{target} = 1200$ min; however, the value of $T_{target}/T_{makespan}$ is a real number less than 1 since overtime is foreseen ($T_{makespan} > T_{target}$). The job sequence is optimized so that $T_{target}/T_{makespan}$ approaches 1. The makespan weighting is set as 24 because management considers that the

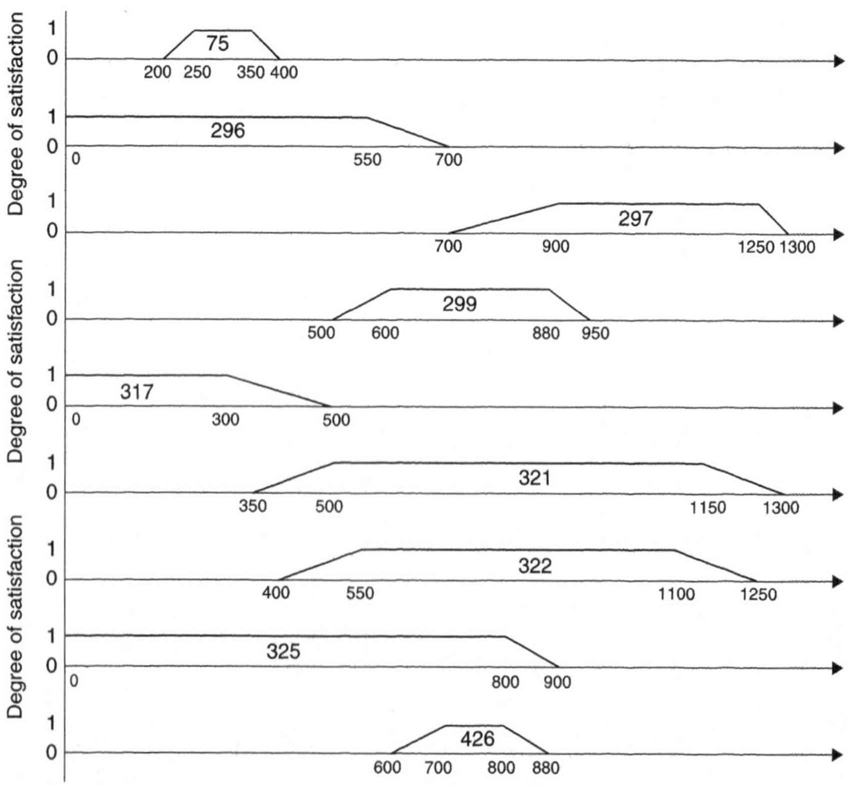

7.9 Fuzzy due times of production order (Case A).

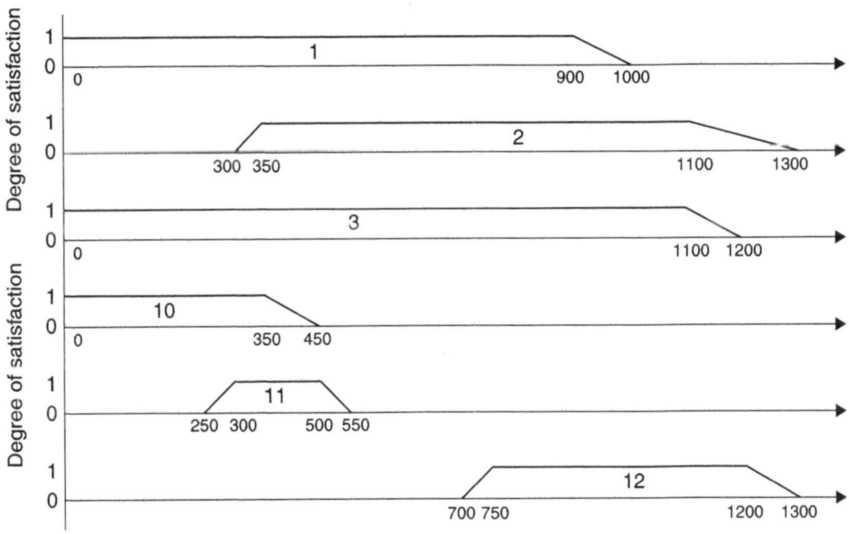

7.10 Fuzzy due times of production order (Case B).

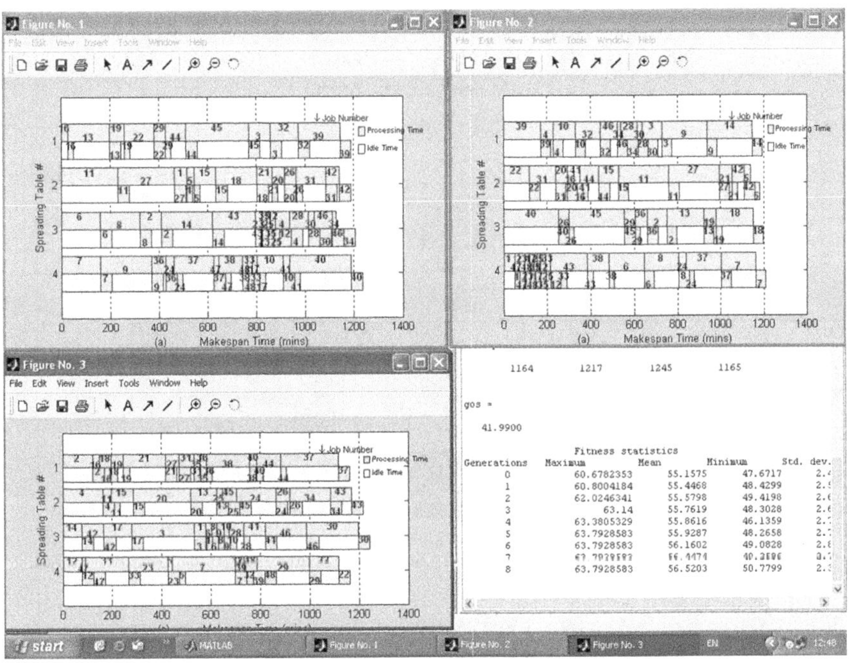

7.11 Matlab genetic optimization program.

customer satisfaction is twice as important as the production cost reduction (through idle time minimization). Therefore, the weights of fitness function (Eq. 7.6) are w_{DS}=1 and w_T=24.

Figure 7.11 depicts the genetic optimization program developed using MATLAB in this research. The production schedules generated by GAs with population size of 200 chromosomes, crossover probability of 0.7, mutation probability of 0.03, and over 200 generations are compared with those based on industrial practice in Fig. 7.12 and 7.13. Part (a) of the figures shows the production schedules adopted by industrial practice, and the genetically optimized schedules

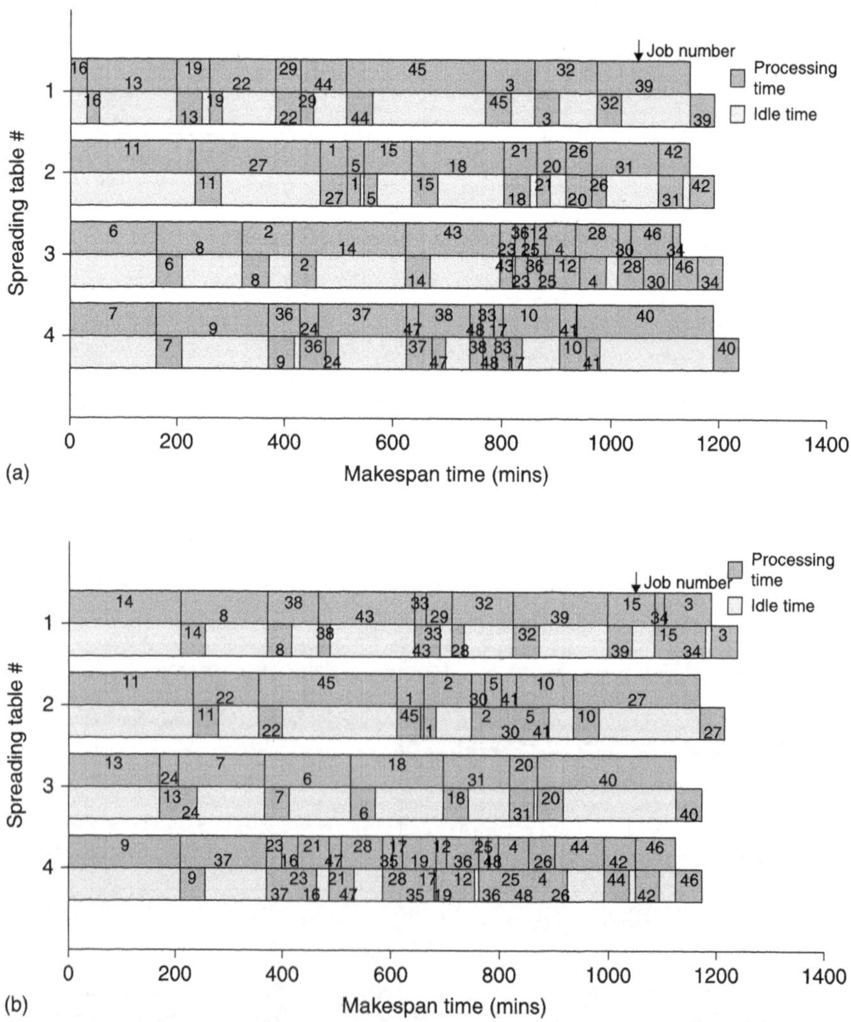

7.12 Case A. (a) Production schedule adopted by industrial practice. (b) Genetically optimized production schedule.

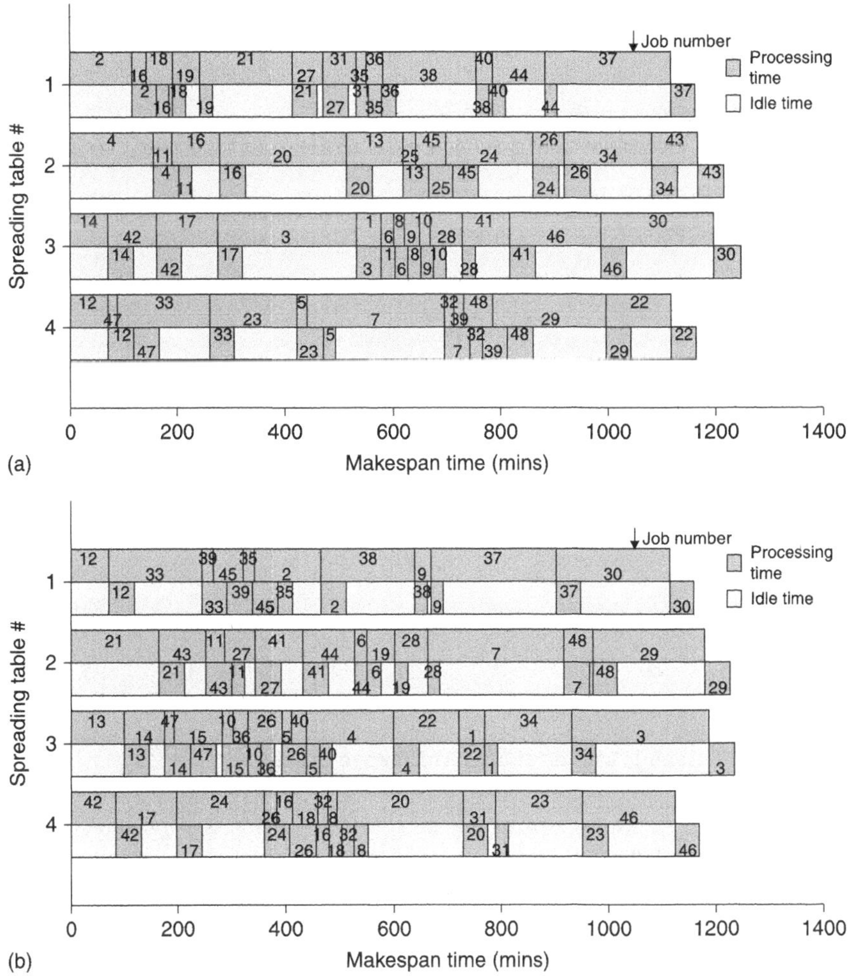

7.13 Case B. (a) Production schedule adopted by industrial practice. (b) Genetically optimized production schedule.

are shown in part (b). The evolutionary trajectory of cases A and B is shown in Fig. 7.14 and 7.15. In each of the production schedules, as shown in Fig. 7.12 and 7.13, the upper Gantt chart shows the spreading operations while the lower Gantt chart shows the cutting operations.

The performance of the genetically optimized production schedules is compared with that of industrial practice in Table 7.2. It is evident that the proposed genetic optimization method is effective in improving the system performance in two aspects. First of all, genetically optimized schedules significantly improve the overall degree of satisfaction, from 38.33 to 42.11 and from 41.99 to 45.53 in

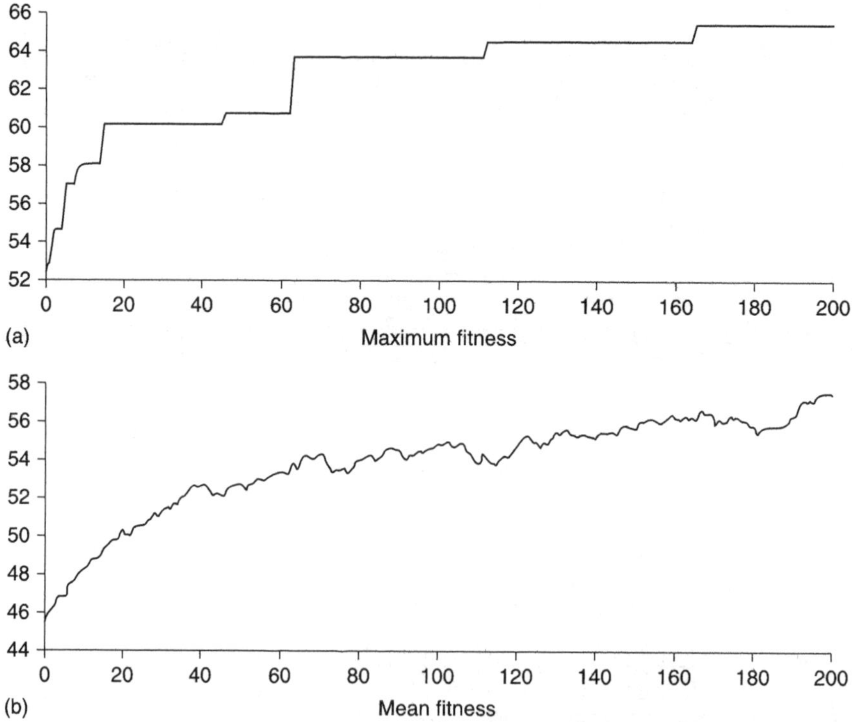

7.14 Genetic optimization performance of case A.

Table 7.2 Performance comparison of industrial practice and genetically optimized results

	Φ_{JIT}	$T_{makespan}$	$\Phi_{makespan}$	Φ_{total}
Ind (case A)	38.33	1237	23.28	61.61
GA (case A)	42.11	1236	23.30	65.41
Ind (case B)	41.99	1245	23.13	65.12
GA (case B)	45.53	1233	23.36	68.89

Note: GA, genetically optimized; Ind, industrial practice.

Table 7.3 Makespan time comparison

	Table 1	Table 2	Table 3	Table 4	Makespan
Ind (A)	1190	1188	1206	1237	1237
GA (A)	1236	1214	1171	1171	1236
Ind (B)	1164	1217	1245	1165	1245
GA (B)	1160	1227	1233	1170	1233

Note: GA, genetically optimized; Ind, industrial practice.

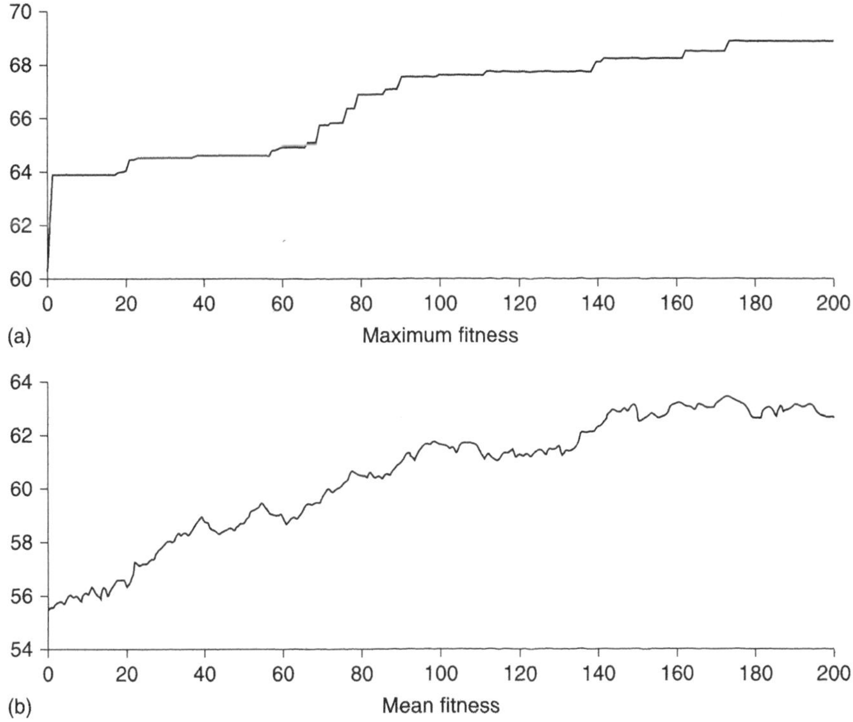

7.15 Genetic optimization performance of case B.

cases A and B, respectively. On the other hand, the improvement of satisfaction does not prolong production makespan. Instead, slight improvement of 1 min and 12 min was recorded when compared with industrial practice for the overall system makespan in cases A and B, respectively. Table 7.3 shows the detail of makespan time of different spreading tables with schedules adopted by industrial practice and those optimized genetically. In conclusion, the genetic optimization method generates production schedules which simultaneously improve the degree of satisfaction and production makespan.

7.5 Conclusions

In the apparel industry, production orders tend to split into smaller orders with different product features in response to growing requests for product customization. In order to shorten product time-to-market, apparel manufacturers work hard in the direction of just-in-time production. In the apparel manufacturing process, the effectiveness of fabric-cutting schedule planning extensively influences downstream assembly operations, and thus, in turn, is critical to the overall system performance. However, the demand from downstream operation departments may be fuzzy and resource-competing. In this chapter, genetic algorithms and fuzzy set theory have been used to generate just-in-time schedules for the fabric-cutting process in order to satisfy the fuzzy and resource-competing requests from downstream operating units. Two sets of real production data have been collected to validate the proposed genetic optimization method. Experimental results have demonstrated that the genetically optimized schedules simultaneously improve the internal satisfaction of downstream operation departments and reduce production cost.

The apparel manufacturing environment is typically dynamic. Apart from the uncertainties caused by the fuzzy and resource-competing internal demands, job processing times are fuzzy due to human factors, machine breakdowns, insertion of rush orders, and so on (Mok *et al.*, 2007). Research on the optimization of JIT schedules with fuzzy job processing time and production order due times is currently under investigation by the research team.

7.6 Acknowledgement

The authors would like to thank The Hong Kong Polytechnic University for financial support of this research project (Project No. G-YD75).

7.7 References

Bagchi, U., Sullivan, R.S. and Chang, Y.L., 1986. Minimizing mean absolute deviation of completion times about a common due date. *Naval Research Logistics Quarterly*, 33, 227–240.

Bagchi, U., Sullivan, R.S. and Chang, Y.L., 1987. Minimizing mean square deviation of completion times about a common due date. *Management Sciences*, 33, 894–906.

Baker, K.R. and Scudder, G.D., 1990. Sequencing with earliness and tardiness penalties: a review. *Operations Research*, 38(1), 22–36.

Chen, Z.L. and Lee, C.Y., 2002. Parallel machine scheduling with a common due window. *European Journal of Operational Research*, 136(3), 512–517.

Cheng, R., Gen, M. and Tozawa, T., 1995. Minmax earliness/tardiness scheduling in identical parallel machine system using genetic algorithms. *Computers & Industrial Engineering*, 29, 513–517.

Cheng, T.C.E. and Chen, Z.L., 1994. Parallel-machine scheduling problems with earliness and tardiness penalties. *Journal of Operational Research Society*, 45(6), 685–695.

Cheng, T.C.E. and Sin, C.C.S., 1990. A state-of-the-art review of parallel-machine scheduling research. *European Journal of Operational Research*, 47, 271–292.

Cheng, T.C.E, Chen, Z.L. and Li, C.L., 1996. Parallel-machine scheduling with controllable processing times. *IIE Transactions*, 28(2), 177–180.

De, P., Ghosh, J.B. and Wells, C.E., 1991. Scheduling to minimize weighted earliness and tardiness about a common due-date. *Computers & Operations Research*, 18(5), 465–475.

De, P., Ghosh, J.B. and Wells, C.E., 1993. On the general solution for a class of early/tardy problems. *Computers & Operations Research*, 20(2), 141–149.

De Jong, K.A., 1975. *An Analysis of the Behavior of a Class of Genetic Adaptive Systems*, Doctoral dissertation. University of Michigan, Ann Arbor, MI.

Goldberg, D.E., 1989. *Genetic Algorithms in Search, Optimisation, and Machine Learning*, Addison-Wesley, Reading, Massachusetts.

Hall, N.G. and Posner, M.E., 1991. Earliness-tardiness scheduling problems, I: weighted deviation of completion times about a common due date. *Operations Research*, 39(5), 836–846.

Hall, N.G., Kubiak, W. and Sethi, S.P., 1991. Earliness-tardiness scheduling problems, II: deviation of completion times about a restrictive common due date. *Operations Research*, 39(5), 847–856.

Holland, J.H., 1975. *Adaptation in natural and Artificial Systems*. University of Michigan Press: Ann Arbor, MI.

Hoogeveen, J.A. and van de Velde, S.L., 1991. Scheduling around a small common due date. *European Journal of Operational Research*, 55, 237–242.

Kanet, J.J., 1981. Minimizing the average deviation of job completion times about a common due date. *Naval Research Logistics Quarterly*, 28, 643–651.

Mok, P.Y., Kwong, C.K. and Wong, W.K., 2007. Optimisation of fault-tolerant fabric-cutting schedules using genetic algorithms and fuzzy set theory, *European Journal of Operational Research*, 177(3), 1876–1893.

Słowiński, R. and Hapke, M., 2000. *Scheduling under Fuzziness*, Physica-Verlag Heidelberg: New York.

Szwarc, W., 1989. Single machine scheduling to minimize absolute deviation of completion times from a common due date. *Naval Research Logistics Quarterly*, 36, 663–674.

Ventura, J.A. and Kim, D., 2003. Parallel machine scheduling with earliness-tardiness penalties and additional resource constraints. *Computers & Operations Research*, 30(13), 1945–1958.

Wong, W.K., Kwong, C.K., Mok, P.K., Ip, W.H. and Chan, C.K., 2005. Optimization of manual fabric-cutting process in apparel manufacturing using genetic algorithms. *International Journal of Advanced Manufacturing Technology*, 27, 152–158.

Zadeh, L.A., 1965. Fuzzy sets. *Information and Control*, 8, 338–353.

7.8 Appendix: nomenclature

A summary of the nomenclature used in this chapter is as follows.

n	number of jobs to be processed
$\boldsymbol{J}$	$\{J_1, J_2, \ldots, J_n\}$, set of jobs (fabric lays
m	number of spreading tables in the fabric cutting department
$\boldsymbol{M}$	$\{M_1, M_2, \ldots, M_m\}$, set of spreading tables in the cutting department
p	number of production orders to be processed
Θ	$\{\theta_1, \theta_2, \ldots, \theta_p\}$, set of production orders (PO)
$x(\theta, J_k)$	state value indicating whether or not job J_k belongs to production order θ. $x(\theta, J_k) = 1$ if job J_k belongs to production order θ, and $x(\theta, J_k) = 0$ otherwise.
i	job setup (spreading) index and $i=1, 2, \ldots, n$.
j	job processing (cutting) index and $j=1, 2, \ldots n$.
σ_s	setup (spreading) sequence of jobs
σ_c	processing (cutting) sequence of jobs
$\chi(J_k)$	quantity of apparel cut-pieces of job J_k

$\phi(J_k)$	length of fabric lay of job J_k
$s(J_i)$	spreading time for job J_i
$c(J_j)$	cutting time for job J_j
C_k	completion time for job J_k
$\tilde{A}$	fuzzy number A
$\widetilde{D}_{\theta_i}(t)$	fuzzy due time of production order θ_i, $i=1, 2, \ldots, p$

8 Optimizing apparel production systems using genetic algorithms

W. K. WONG, P. Y. MOK and S. Y. S. LEUNG,
The Hong Kong Polytechnic University, China

DOI: 10.1533/9780857097842.153

Abstract: In apparel manufacturing, it is difficult to achieve line balance because the production rate of each workstation is different. This difficulty is particularly prominent in a labour-intensive assembly process. The development of a line balancing technique using genetic algorithms is thus proposed for optimizing the assignment of operatives in an assembly line. The impact of different levels of skill inventory SI_n on the assembly makespan is also investigated in order to find out the optimal number of task skills an operative should possess in the apparel assembly process. Experimental results will be discussed to demonstrate the performance of the proposed genetic optimization approach.

Key words: genetic algorithms, optimization, line balance, apparel manufacture.

8.1 Introduction

In the apparel industry, the assembly process involves a set of workstations in which a specific task is processed in a pre-defined sequence. Before production, in order to achieve a balanced line, the sewing line supervisors assign one or more sewing operatives to each task based on the standard time required to complete the task. However, industrial experience shows that it is difficult to achieve a perfectly balanced line because the production rate of each workstation is different. Imbalance occurs due to various factors, including fluctuation in operative efficiency, frequent change of product style, order size, prior experience and some unexpected factors, such as absenteeism, machine breakdown, and so on. Line balancing control is required to smooth away the bottlenecks.

The line balancing problem is one of the most traditional problems which evolved from the concept of division of labour (Smith, 1776) and became popular because of Henry Ford's famous 'T-model' (Ford *et al.*, 1923). Despite its long history of development, line-balancing study is still an attractive research topic nowadays due to its relevancy to everyday industry manufacturing and the diversity in system configurations. Examples of detailed reviews on the topic have been provided by Ghosh and Gagnon (1989) and Erel and Sarin (1998). According to different system configurations, the assembly line can be classified as a single-model line, a mixed-model line, or a multi-model line. A single-model line only assembles one product, while multiple products are assembled in either mixed- or multi-model lines, but intermediate setup is required in the latter case. In addition to serial line assembly, flexibility can be improved by the introduction of parallelism, including parallel lines, parallel stations, and parallel tasks (Becker and Scholl, 2003). Apparel assembly, a kind of parallel-station line balancing problem, will be discussed in subsequent sections of this chapter.

Diverse techniques have been used in the line balancing control problem over the years. Early research mainly applied optimization techniques of dynamic programming (Held *et al.*, 1963, Kao, 1976, Schrage and Baker, 1978, Kao and Queyranne, 1982, Henig, 1986) and integer programming (Graves and Lamar, 1983, Talbot and Patterson, 1984, Gökcen and Erel, 1998). The Branch and Bound algorithm is one of the heuristic techniques, which has the longest history of application in the line balancing problem (Deutsch, 1971, Johnson, 1983, Scholl and Klein, 1997). Other heuristic techniques such as simulated annealing (McMullen and Frazier, 1998, Erel *et al.*, 2001), tabu search (Pastor *et al.*, 2002), and graphical method (Dolgui *et al.*, 2006) have also recently been applied in this attractive field. The rise of artificial intelligence (AI) computational techniques in the early 1990s also promoted their application to line balancing control. Elizabeth awnd Roger (1994) reviewed the AI-based systems and concluded that the results of most real-life problems have not been realized due to technical problems in implementation and the 'people problem', particularly in the human-centric apparel manufacturing process. Among various methods known in the AI domain, genetic algorithm (Kim *et al.*, 2000, 2000a; Dolgui *et al.*, 2002) is the most frequently adopted in line balancing control optimization.

However, in sewing assembly, workstations are tailored for specific tasks and are usually statically configured. Such constraints have hindered the direct application of line balancing research results obtained so far. In fact, the current solution to balancing sewing assembly lines relies heavily on the shop-floor expert's knowledge, experience and intuition. Experts' decisions may not be consistent under similar conditions and may thus be non-optimal. Small order sizes and frequent changes of style make optimal production control more difficult to achieve. In the 1990s, simulation technique was widely adopted by researchers to provide a scientific solution to control line balancing in apparel manufacture. Rosser *et al.* (1991) proposed a discrete event simulation model for manufacturing trousers, in which material flows and the problems resulting from the absence of supervision were considered. Oliver *et al.* (1994) developed a simulation system to solve the line balancing problem of an apparel bundle system. Fozzard *et al.* (1996) constructed an interactive simulation system using a multi-paradigm model with a knowledge-based approach to control the line balance of an apparel assembly line. Rotab (1999) developed a spreadsheet simulation model for a garment production system to minimize the average daily production cost, in which the minimum production cost for a suitable combination of repair men and backup machines could be identified. Emphasis has been put on the flow-charting process so as to simulate the efficiency using case-based reasoning technique. The above research projects were carried out under conditions of a steady-state manufacturing environment and discrete events, which may be unrealistic in practice. These constraints highlight the need for further study on effective algorithms to provide systematically an optimal solution to the problem of production control in thc apparcl assembly process.

The introduction of the Unit Production Hanger System (UPS), which is capable of automatically delivering a piece of cloth to a target workstation according to a planned workflow schedule, makes sewing operation configuration more flexible. A sewing assembly line equipped with UPS is similar to the traditional parallel stations system. It is essential to develop a 'smart' balancing solution for UPS sewing lines in order to take full advantage of its system flexibility. In addition, training the sewing operatives for multi-task handling is the approach of apparel manufacturers, such that a pool of multi-skilled operatives can be a better option for task reassignment in order to achieve a better line balancing result. However, few studies have ever been conducted to investigate the effect of skill inventory on operation efficiency in sewing assembly. Skill inventory SI_n represents the number of task skills each operator should have in the apparel assembly process. The objectives of this study are thus to search online optimal operative assignments in order to minimize the makespan using genetic algorithms (GA) and to compare the performance of different levels of skill inventory SI_n on the assembly makespan so as to search the optimal number of task skills an operator should possess in the apparel assembly process.

8.2 Problem formulation in sewing operations

In the apparel industry, sewing operators are usually trained to be multi-skilled. In other words, each operator is trained to master the skills of a set of tasks in which the operator's efficiency in completing the corresponding tasks depends on his/her skill level and previous experience. In this study, task set $\boldsymbol{T}_k$ and efficiency set $\boldsymbol{E}_k$ are determined by the skill inventory SI_n. In the example in Table 8.1, 14 operators are responsible for a production order composed of 6 tasks. The task set and efficiency set for operator $k=6$ are $\boldsymbol{T}_6=\{3, 4, 2, 5\}$ and $\boldsymbol{E}_6=\{100\%, 95\%, 90\%, 85\%\}$ when $SI_n=4$. Since operators are cross-trained with multi-skills, the operator may not achieve 100% efficiency at every task; therefore the actual task processing times vary among operators. For example, when operator k processes a task he/she is good at, $\alpha(k)=1$, he/she can achieve 100% efficiency ($e_{\alpha(k)}=100\%$) and the task processing time is the same as the task standard time, $PT_j=ST_j$. When operator k is processing his/her less competent task, $1<\alpha(k)\leq SI_n$, he/she can only achieve a lower efficiency, $e_{\alpha(k)}<100\%$. As a result, the task processing time is longer than the task standard time, $PT_j>ST_j$. The processing time for task j by operator k can be calculated by

$$PT_{j\in T_k} = ST_j/e_{\alpha(k)}. \quad [8.1]$$

Table 8.1 Operator's skill level (trained task with estimated efficiency in parenthesis $j(e)$) for different level of skill inventory

Skill level operator k	$\alpha(k)=1$	$\alpha(k)=2$	$\alpha(k)=3$	$\alpha(k)=4$	$\alpha(k)=5$	$\alpha(k)=6$
1	1 (100%)	2 (95%)	3 (90%)	4 (85%)	5 (85%)	6 (85%)
2	1 (100%)	2 (95%)	6 (90%)	5 (85%)	3 (85%)	4 (85%)
3	2 (100%)	1 (95%)	3 (90%)	4 (85%)	5 (85%)	6 (85%)
4	2 (100%)	1 (95%)	6 (90%)	5 (85%)	4 (85%)	3 (85%)
5	3 (100%)	4 (95%)	1 (90%)	6 (85%)	2 (85%)	5 (85%)
6	3 (100%)	4 (95%)	2 (90%)	5 (85%)	6 (85%)	1 (85%)
7	4 (100%)	3 (95%)	5 (90%)	6 (85%)	1 (85%)	2 (85%)
8	4 (100%)	3 (95%)	5 (90%)	6 (85%)	1 (85%)	2 (85%)
9	5 (100%)	4 (95%)	1 (90%)	2 (85%)	6 (85%)	3 (85%)
10	5 (100%)	6 (95%)	1 (90%)	2 (85%)	3 (85%)	4 (85%)
11	5 (100%)	6 (95%)	2 (90%)	1 (85%)	4 (85%)	3 (85%)
12	6 (100%)	3 (95%)	2 (90%)	1 (85%)	4 (85%)	5 (85%)
13	6 (100%)	5 (95%)	4 (90%)	3 (85%)	1 (85%)	2 (85%)
14	6 (100%)	5 (95%)	4 (90%)	3 (85%)	2 (85%)	1 (85%)

Skill inventory

↑ $SI_n=1$ ↑
↑ . . . . $SI_n=2$ . . . . ↑
↑ . . . . $SI_n=3$ . . . . ↑
↑ . . . . $SI_n=4$ . . . . ↑
↑ . . . . $SI_n=5$ . . . . ↑
↑ . . . . $SI_n=6$ . . . . ↑

8.3 Genetic optimization of production line balancing

In this chapter, genetic algorithms (GA) are used to optimize the operative assignment so that line balancing can be achieved through the minimization of overall operative idle time. The proposed method readjusts the operative assignment continuously, after every fixed time interval, according to the most updated system status in order to smooth out the bottlenecks in the assembly line. Eventually the overall production order completion time can be shortened by minimizing the operative idle time. This section is thus dedicated to describing the general genetic optimization methodology.

GA is a computational algorithm developed to mimic some of the processes observed in natural selection in the 1960s–1970s. GA is a metaheuristic for solving combinatorial optimization problems. In solving an optimization problem by GA, it is usually assumed that a potential solution to the problem may be represented as a set of variables. These variables ('genes') are joined together to form a string of values ('chromosome'). A fitness function is then defined to measure the relative merit of each string in solving the particular optimization problem. In genetic evolution, an initial population of chromosomes can be set by random initialization or heuristic method. Genetic variation is brought into the current population by the application of two genetic operators: crossover and mutation. Chromosomes are then selected as survivors of the next generation, and this selection is made in such a manner that fitter individuals have a higher tendency to be selected. The evolution process is continued such that the quality of the individual solutions improves in successive populations. In this way, GA can move to a successful outcome without the need to examine every possible solution to the problem in a drastically short time. The general procedure of GA is illustrated by the flow diagram in Fig. 8.1. The distinctive GA features employed in this line balancing optimization problem are described in detail in the following sub-sections.

8.3.1 Chromosome syntax

Although the binary representation proposed by Holland (1975) is the most widely accepted representation, solution strings are not restricted to binary in GA. Eiben and Smith (2003) commented that integer and real number strings are commonly used in various optimization studies. The choice of representation in GA is related to the nature of the problem. In the line balancing optimization problem, each operator possesses limited skills, which implies that each operator is only capable of handling limited tasks. For example, $SI_n=2$ implies that each operator is trained to master the skill of two tasks. In this chapter, integer chromosome representation is used. In an integer string, each gene represents the skill level, $\alpha_i(k)$, $k=1, 2, \ldots, n$, of each operator's current task, and the length of the chromosome is the number of operators. Therefore, the whole gene-code, which concatenates all operators' task skills, is represented as

$$\alpha_h = [\alpha_h(1)\ \alpha_h(2) \ldots \alpha_h(o)], \qquad [8.2]$$

where $h = 1, 2, \ldots, \mu$ (population size). Each operator's current task skill level, $\alpha_h(k)$, is not unconstrained, and must be within a range from 1 to SI_n, i.e. $1 \leq \alpha_i(k) \leq SI$, $\forall\ \alpha_i(k) \in \aleph$.

For example, five operators ($n=5$) are required to complete a production order. When skill inventory is 3, $SI_n=3$, chromosome α = [2 1 3 1 1] implies that operator 1 should process her second skilled task, operator 3 should process her third skilled task, and operators 2, 4 and 5 should process their first skilled tasks, respectively. Once skill levels, α, are defined, the operators' responsible tasks and the corresponding operation efficiency are obtained from the pre-defined lookup table provided by the operative training department, as shown in Table 8.1.

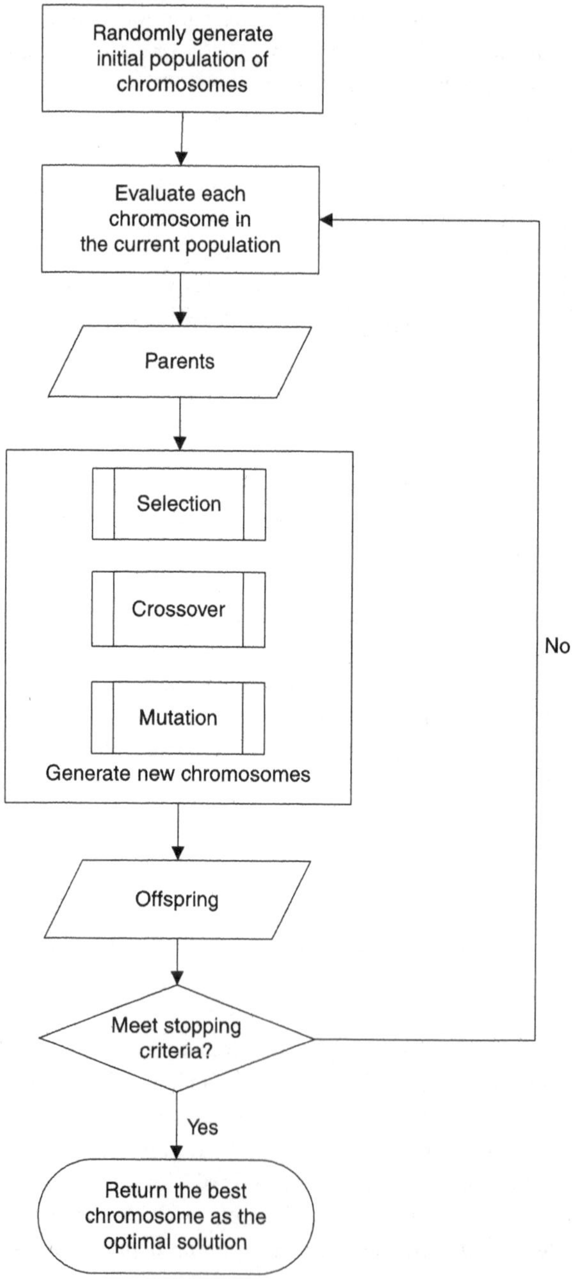

8.1 Flow diagram of genetic algorithms (GA).

8.3.2 Initial population

Initial population is generated randomly in this study. The initialization process is detailed as follows.

- ***Step 1***. Initialize parameters: index $h=1$, population size μ and population $\mathbf{P}=\{\varnothing\}$.
- ***Step 2***. Randomly produce an integer-number string, $\alpha_h=[\alpha_h(1)\ \alpha_h(2)\ldots\alpha_h(k)\ldots\alpha_h(o)]$, where $\alpha_h(k)$ is the skill level of operator k, and $1\leq\alpha_h(k)\leq SI$, $\alpha_h(k)\in\aleph$.
- ***Step 3***. If α_i is feasible, go to step 4, else go to step 2.
- ***Step 4***. If $h=\mu-1$, then $\mathbf{P}=\{\alpha_1, \alpha_2, \ldots, \alpha_{\mu-1}\}$ is the initial population and stop; else go to step 2.
- ***Step 5***. Set $\alpha_\mu=$ skill levels of theoretical operative assignment (which is calculated based on the standard time of different tasks; see Section 8.4 for an example), $\mathbf{P}=\{\alpha_1, \alpha_2, \ldots, \alpha_{\mu-1}, \alpha_\mu\}$.

In step 5 of the above procedure, the theoretical operative assignment is maintained in the initial population in order to speed up the optimization process. In the line balancing problem, the feasibility of each individual operative assignment is subject to various constraints. In the above routine, an individual is defined as a feasible solution in step 3 only when the following constraints are satisfied.

For $\alpha_h=[\alpha_h(1)\ \alpha_h(2)\ldots\alpha_h(o)]\in$P,
if

$$\boldsymbol{N}_t \subseteq \boldsymbol{T}_{\alpha_h} \tag{8.3}$$

then $\alpha_h=[\alpha_h(1)\ \alpha_h(2)\ldots\alpha_h(o)]$ is feasible, else $\alpha_h=[\alpha_h(1)\ \alpha_h(2)\ldots\alpha_h(o)]$ is not feasible. In Eq. 8.3, $\boldsymbol{N}_t$ is the set of tasks that have not been completed at time t for the current production order, $\forall \boldsymbol{N}_t\subseteq\boldsymbol{N}$. $\boldsymbol{T}\alpha_h$ is the task set of all operators with their current skill level setting, $\alpha_h=[\alpha_h(1)\ \alpha_h(2)\ \ldots\ \alpha_h(o)]$. If constraint (3) is not satisfied, it implies that $\alpha_h=[\alpha_h(1)\ \alpha_h(2)\ \ldots\ \alpha_h(o)]$ could never complete the production order, since there are some tasks in $\boldsymbol{N}_t$ that are not being processed by any of the operators in set $\boldsymbol{O}$. In addition, the total number of workstations employed for each task j ($j\in \boldsymbol{T}_{\alpha_h}$) of the current skill setting, α_h, must not exceed the available workstations for the corresponding task j, i.e.

$$\sum_j x_{ij} \leq |\mathbf{S}_j|, \qquad \forall j\in \boldsymbol{T}_{\alpha_h} \text{ and } x_{ij}\in \boldsymbol{M}. \tag{8.4}$$

8.3.3 Fitness function

In GA, fitness function is defined to measure the fitness of each individual chromosome so as to determine which will reproduce and survive into the next generation. Thus, given a particular chromosome, the fitness function returns a single numerical score, 'fitness', which is proportional to the 'ability' of the individual that the chromosome represents. The 'fitness' score assigned to each individual in the population depends on how well that individual solves a specific problem. In this line balancing optimization problem, minimizing operative idle time, which is equivalent to makespan minimization, would be the prime objective. Let **P** denote the set of feasible solutions. For a given sequence $\alpha \in \mathbf{P}$, fitness $\Phi(\alpha)$ can be defined as

$$\Phi(\alpha) = \frac{T_{target}}{T_{makespan}(\alpha)}, \quad [8.5]$$

where fitness $\Phi(\alpha)$ decreases as the makespan, $T_{makespan}(\alpha)$, increases. In Eq. 8.5, T_{target} is the target makespan. In GA, genetic operators such as crossover and mutation are responsible for bringing genetic variation into the population. However, applying such genetic operators may cause lost features in some genes and result in infeasible solutions. In the case when an infeasible solution results, that is, a solution that does not satisfy Eq. 8.3 and 8.4, the solution fitness is zero, i.e.

$$\Phi(\alpha) = 0. \quad [8.6]$$

8.3.4 Genetic operators

In GA, crossover and mutation are the two major genetic operators to provide genetic variations to the population by bringing in chromosomal changes. Crossover, as the name implies, exchanges information ('genes') among chromosomes. Mutation randomly alters some genes in chromosomes. In this chapter, traditional single point crossover (Holland, 1975), which is a powerful algorithm for both binary and integer chromosomes, is employed.

Single point crossover

Single point crossover follows the procedures below.

- ***Step 1.*** Randomly select two parents for mating from the population.
- ***Step 2.*** Generate a random integer within a range of $[0, l-1]$ (l is the length of the chromosome).
- ***Step 3.*** Split both parents at this point, thus producing two 'head' segments and two 'tail' segments.
- ***Step 4.*** The tail segments are then swapped over to produce two new full-length chromosomes.

The two offspring each inherit some genes from each parent from this single point crossover. Figure 8.2 shows a single point crossover that occurs after the third bits of two ten-bit parental chromosomes.

Crossover is not usually applied to all pairs of individuals selected for mating. Indeed, the crossover task is a random process with an application likelihood, which is called the probability of crossover: a typical probability of crossover is between 0.6 and 1.0.

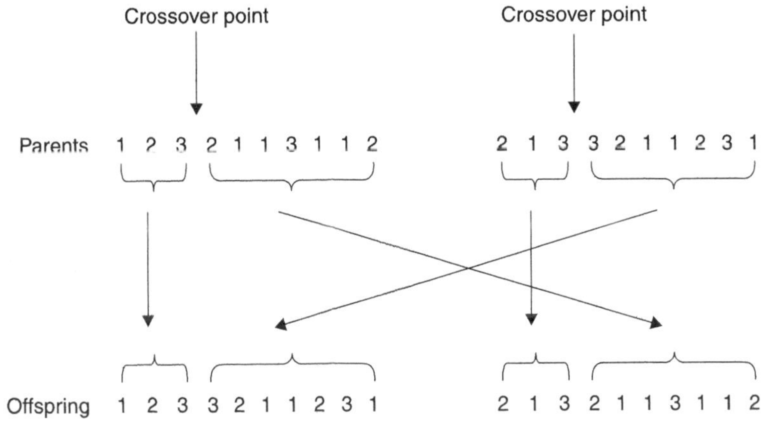

8.2 Single point crossover.

Random resetting mutation

In GA, mutation is another genetic operator that is applied to each offspring. Compared with crossover, mutation is only seen as a 'background' operator in GA. However, research has shown that, though mutation is of a generally low probability of use (typical value is between 0.0015 and 0.03), it is still a very important operator, as it becomes more productive, and crossover becomes less productive, when the population converges (Bäck *et al.*, 1997). In this line balancing optimization problem, random resetting mutation is used. Under random resetting mutation, with some small probability a new gene value is chosen at random from the set of permissible values in each position. Thus, for example, Fig. 8.3 shows an illustration in which the third gene is mutated such that a new gene value 1 replaces the original gene value 3.

8.3.5 Parent selection

In nature, different individuals compete for resources in the environment. Some are better than others. Those that are better are more likely to survive and propagate their genetic material. This process of natural selection is mimicked in GA by selection

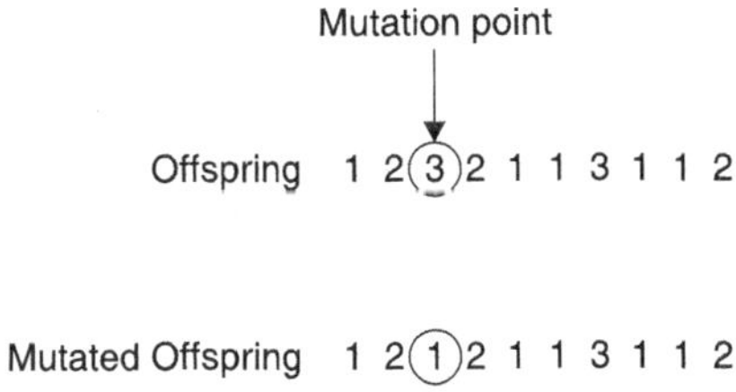

8.3 Random resetting mutation.

schemes in which parental chromosomes of high fitness have a greater chance than those of low fitness of producing offspring. One of the most widely used selection schemes is called the 'biased roulette wheel scheme', in which each current string in the population has a roulette wheel slot sized in proportion to its fitness (Goldberg, 1989). The biased roulette wheel scheme can be described as follows:

- ***Step 1.*** Sum the fitness of all the population members; call the result total fitness, $\Phi_{total}=\Sigma\Phi$.
- ***Step 2.*** Generate a random number, θ, between zero and total fitness, $\theta\in[0\ \Phi_{total}]$.
- ***Step 3.*** Return the first population member whose fitness, added to the fitness of the preceding population members, is greater than or equal to θ.
- ***Step 4.*** Repeat steps 2 to 3, until μ strings are selected from the parent pool.

In roulette wheel selection, the chance of a parent being selected is directly proportional to its fitness. In the example in Fig. 8.4, from a population of 10 chromosomes with a set of fitness evaluations totalling 80, 6 individuals are selected by the biased roulette wheel scheme, according to 6 random numbers generated from the interval of 0 and 80.

8.3.6 Elitism

Since the biased roulette wheel selection processes are based on the survival of the fittest and are random processes, there is no guarantee that some fit individuals will be selected. In order to improve the selection mechanism, De Jong (1975) proposed elitism in this job sequencing problem. Elitism is an addition to many selection methods that forces the GA to retain some of the best individuals in each generation. This elitist strategy copies the best individuals of each generation directly into the succeeding generation. Such individuals might otherwise be lost if they are not selected to reproduce, or if they are destroyed by crossover or

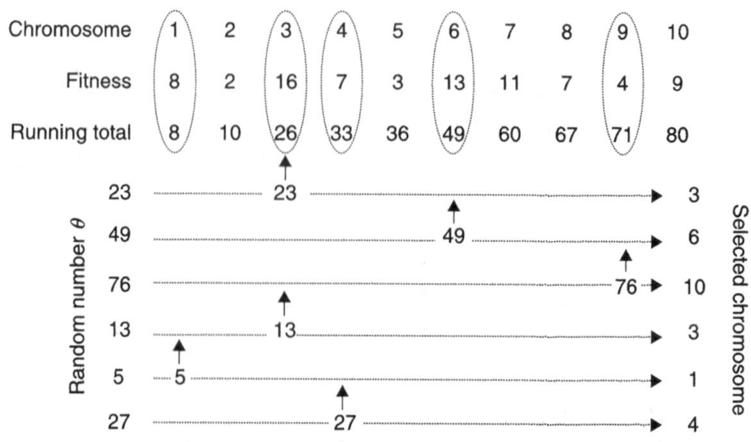

8.4 Biased roulette-wheel selection scheme.

mutation. This elitist strategy can increase the speed of domination of populations by the best individuals and provide an improvement of the GA's performance.

8.3.7 Evolution and termination criteria

After initialization, evolution occurs in accordance with the standard genetic operations of crossover, mutation and selection. The evolutionary process is allowed to continue until no significant further increase is obtained in the fitness of the fittest string or the defined maximum number of generations is reached. Thus, the fittest string generates the operative assignment which can finish the current production order with the minimized operative idle time and assembly makespan. The described genetic optimization procedure is repeated every fixed time interval so as to readjust the operative assignment according to system status. Such online rescheduling by GA is used to minimize the assembly makespan.

8.4 Experimental results

A case study about a Hong Kong-based high-priced shirt manufacturer is used to demonstrate the genetic line balancing optimization procedure. This manufacturer has one plant in China for component sewing (collar and cuffs) and the other in Hong Kong for six assembly processes (join shoulder, set sleeve, topstitch sleeve, join side-seam, set cuff and set collar). In this example, a production order with 3600 garments is to be assembled in the Hong Kong plant. The assembly process of each garment consists of the above mentioned six operation tasks, $N = \{1\ 2\ 3\ 4\ 5\ 6\}$, and each task description with standard time is given in Table 8.2. Fourteen operators in total are assigned to complete this production order. Based on the standard time of each operation, theoretical numbers of operators for each operation can be calculated and actual numbers of operators can be assigned. The operators' skill levels with the trained tasks and achievable efficiency are shown in Table 8.1, while the flow diagram of the assembly process is shown in Fig. 8.5.

Table 8.2 Operation breakdown

Task j	Task description	Standard time STj (s)	Theoretical no. of operator assignment	Actual no. of operators assigned	Theoretical operative assignment k
1	Join shoulder	25	1.54	2	1, 2
2	Set sleeve	36	2.21	2	3, 4
3	Topstitch sleeve	30	1.84	2	5, 6
4	Join side-seam	38	2.33	2	7, 8
5	Set cuff	45	2.70	3	9, 10, 11
6	Set collar	54	3.32	3	12, 13, 14
	Total cycle time	228	13.94	14	

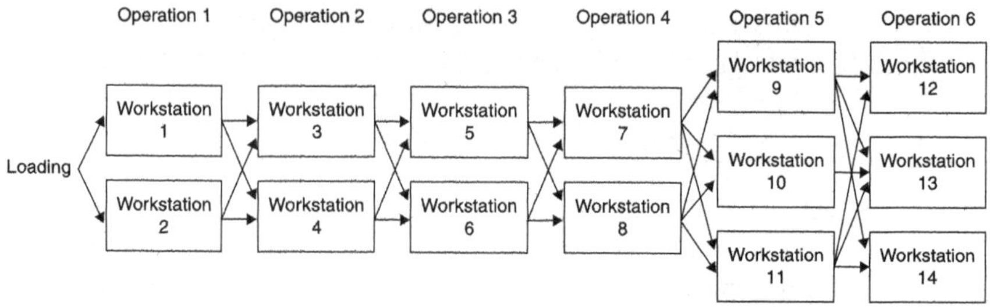

8.5 Flow diagram of an apparel assembly process.

This line balancing optimization problem has the following assumptions:

- Learning curve effect is not considered after shifting to another operation.
- The assembly system used for modelling is empty initially; in other words, there is no work in progress in each workstation.
- Number of workstations for each operation task is always sufficient.

In this study, the aim is to investigate whether genetic optimized operative assignment can reduce the apparel assembly makespan when compared with theoretical operator assignment. It is also intended to compare the performance of different levels of skill inventory, SI_n, on the makespan in order to determine the optimal number of task skills an operator should have in the assembly process. The proposed method is applied to adjust the operative assignment hourly so that the assembly makespan, $T_{makespan}$, is minimized. Each operative assignment is optimized by GA hourly with the following settings:

- Population size $\mu = 10$
- Maximum number of generations = 20
- Crossover probability = 0.7
- Mutation probability = 0.03

Figure 8.6 shows four sets of results (each with different seed number), in which the makespan of genetically optimized operative assignment based on different skill inventories, SI_n, is compared. The mean makespan of those four runs and the corresponding performance improvement are listed in Table 8.3. The target makespan, T_{target}, in Eq. 8.5 is set at 68 606 s, based on the theoretical operative assignment calculation in every genetic optimization. An example of genetic

Table 8.3 Mean makespan value of genetically optimized operative assignment with different level of skill inventories SI_n

Skill inventory SI_n	1	2	3	4	5	6
Makespan $T_{makespan}$	68606	68244	65086	66094	66700	65829
Fitness improvement	–	0.527%	5.131%	3.662%	2.779%	4.047%

optimization performance is shown in Fig. 8.7 for a particular simulation run when $SI_n = 3$ and for which the optimization was based on the system status at time $t=50\ 400$ s. Genetic optimization procedure can improve the assembly makespan, since all makespans of genetically optimized results are lower than those of the theoretical operative assignment, as shown in both Fig. 8.6 and Table 8.3. It is also indicated that skill inventory, $SI_n=3$, generates the shortest

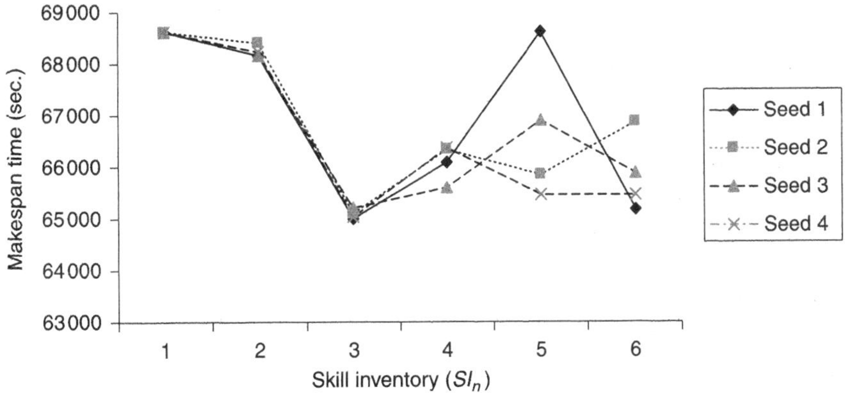

8.6 Makespan vs. skill inventory.

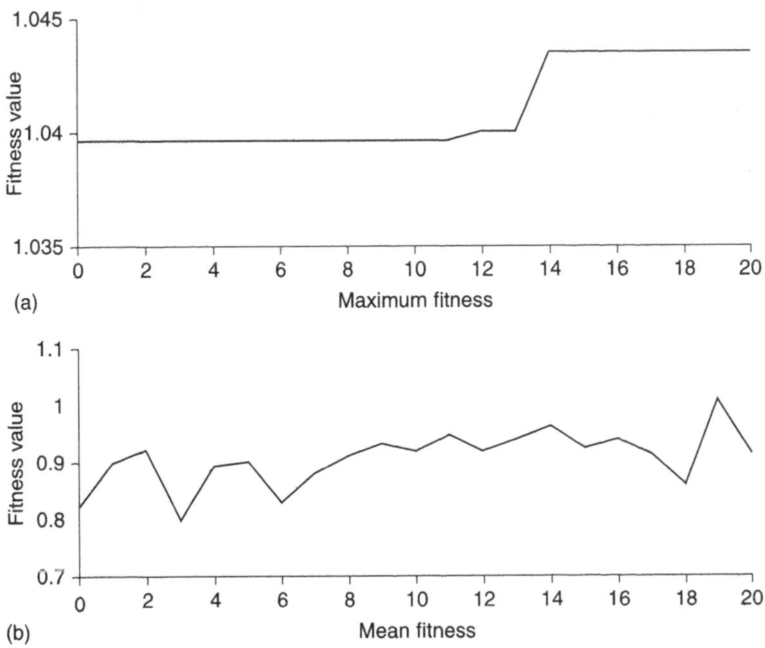

8.7 Genetic optimization performance of a particular run (seed 4) when optimization was based on system status at $t = 50400$ s.

Table 8.4 Optimal operative assignment when $SI_n = 3$

Optimal responsible	Operator k													
Task j														
Time range	1	2	3	4	5	6	7	8	9	10	11	12	13	14
$t = 0 \rightarrow 3600$	1	1	2	2	3	3	4	4	5	5	5	6	6	6
$t = 3600 \rightarrow 7200$	1	1	2	2	3	3	4	4	5	5	5	6	6	6
$t = 7200 \rightarrow 10800$	1	1	2	2	3	3	4	4	5	5	5	6	6	6
$t = 10800 \rightarrow 14400$	1	1	2	2	3	3	4	4	5	5	5	6	6	6
$t = 14400 \rightarrow 18000$	1	1	2	2	3	3	4	4	5	5	5	6	6	6
$t = 18000 \rightarrow 21600$	1	1	2	2	3	3	4	4	5	5	5	6	6	6
$t = 21600 \rightarrow 25200$	1	1	2	2	3	3	4	4	5	5	5	6	6	6
$t = 25200 \rightarrow 28800$	1	1	2	2	3	3	4	4	5	5	5	6	6	6
$t = 28800 \rightarrow 32400$	1	1	2	2	3	3	4	4	5	5	5	6	6	6
$t = 32400 \rightarrow 36000$	1	1	2	2	3	3	4	4	5	5	5	6	6	6
$t = 36000 \rightarrow 39600$	1	6	2	2	3	3	4	4	5	5	5	6	6	4
$t = 39600 \rightarrow 43200$	1	6	2	2	3	3	4	4	5	5	5	6	6	6
$t = 43200 \rightarrow 46800$	1	6	2	2	3	3	4	4	5	5	5	6	6	4
$t = 46800 \rightarrow 50400$	1	6	2	2	3	3	4	4	5	5	5	6	6	6
$t = 50400 \rightarrow 54000$	3	6	2	1	3	2	4	4	5	5	5	6	6	4
$t = 54000 \rightarrow 57600$	3	6	2	1	3	2	4	4	5	5	5	6	6	4
$t = 57600 \rightarrow 61200$	3	6	2	2	3	2	4	4	5	5	5	6	6	4
$t = 61200 \rightarrow 64800$	3	6	2	2	1	3	4	4	5	5	5	6	6	6
$t = 64800$ and thereafter	3	6	2	6	3	3	4	4	5	5	5	2	6	6

assembly makespan among all other skill inventories. In other words, operators mastering the skills of more than three tasks could not improve the system performance. Therefore, the optimal number of task skills each operator should have in the apparel assembly process is three. Table 8.4 lists the detail of genetically optimized operative assignments at different time intervals of a particular run when $SI_n = 3$.

8.5 Conclusions

In this chapter, genetic algorithms (GA) are used to optimize the operative assignment so that overall operative idle time and thus makespan can be minimized. The proposed method readjusts the operative assignment at fixed time intervals according to the most updated system status. The makespan of operative assignment based on different skill inventories, SI_n, is also compared, in which skill inventory $SI_n = 3$ generates the shortest assembly makespan. It has been shown that genetic optimization procedure can improve the assembly makespan, since all makespans of genetically optimized results are lower than those of the static theoretical operative assignment. It can also be concluded that the optimal number of operation skills each operative should have is three. The implication for the apparel manufacturers is that more resources put into training the sewing operatives to handle more than three operations cannot further improve the line balance and makespan of the apparel assembly process. Operative efficiency, complexity of fashion style, operational sequence and unexpected factors, including rush orders, machine breakdown, and so on, in a dynamic manufacturing environment having an impact on the planned operative assignment and the performance of the assembly line are now under investigation by the project team.

8.6 Acknowledgement

The authors would like to thank Earmarked Research Grant of Research Grants Council of Hong Kong and The Hong Kong Polytechnic University for financial support of this research project (Project A/C Code: B-Q730).

8.7 References

Bäck, T., Fogel, D.B. and Michalewicz, Z., 1997. *Handbook of Evolutionary Computation*, Oxford University Press, New York, and Institute of Physics Publishing, Bristol.

Becker, C. and Scholl, A., 2003. A survey on problems and methods in generalized assembly line balancing, *European Journal of Operational Research*, 168(3), 694–715.

De Jong, K.A., 1975. *An Analysis of the Behavior of a Class of Genetic Adaptive Systems*, Doctoral dissertation, University of Michigan, Ann Arbor, MI (University Microfilms No. 76-9381).

Deutsch, D.F., 1971. *A Branch and Bound Technique for Mixed-Product Assembly Line Balancing*, PhD dissertation, Arizona State University.

Dolgui, A., Ereemev, A., Kolokolov, A. and Sigaev, V., 2002. A genetic algorithm for allocation of buffer storage capacities in production line with unreliable machines, *Journal of Mathematical Modelling and Algorithms*, 1, 89–104.

Dolgui, A., Guschinsky, N. and Levin, G., 2006. A special case of transfer lines balancing by graph approach, *European Journal of Operational Research*, 168, 732–746.

Eiben, A.E. and Smith, J.E., 2003. *Introduction to Evolutionary Computing*, Springer, Berlin.

Elizabeth, S. and Roger, M.K., 1994. Knowledge-based reactive scheduling, *Production Planning and Control*, 5(2), 124–145.

Erel, E. and Sarin, S.C., 1998. A survey of the assembly line balancing procedures, *Production Planning and Control*, 9, 414–434.

Erel, E., Sabuncuoglu, I. and Aksu, B.A., 2001. Balancing of U-type assembly systems using simulated annealing, *International Journal of Production Research*, 39, 3003–3015.

Ford, H., 1923. *Mein Leben und Werk*, 27th Edition, Paul List Verlag, Leipzig.

Fozzard, G., Spragg, J. and Tyler, D., 1996. Simulation of a flow lines in clothing manufacturing Part 1: Model Construction, *International Journal of Clothing Science and Technology*, 8(4), 17–27.

Ghosh, S. and Gagnon, R.J., 1989. A comprehensive literature review and analysis of the design, balancing and scheduling of assembly systems, *International Journal of Production Research*, 27, 637–670.

Gökcen, H. and Erel, E., 1998. Binary integer formulation for mixed-model assembly line balancing problem, *Computers and Industrial Engineering*, 34, 451–461.

Goldberg, D.E., 1989. *Genetic Algorithms in Search, Optimisation, and Machine Learning*, Addison-Wesley, Reading, Massachusetts.

Graves, S.C. and Lamar, B.W., 1983. An integer programming procedure for assembly system design problems, *Operations Research*, 31, 522–545.

Held, M., Karp, R.M. and Shareshian, R., 1963. Assembly line balancing – Dynamic programming with precedence constraints, *Operations Research*, 11, 442–459.

Henig, M.I., 1986. Extensions of the dynamic programming method in the deterministic and stochastic assembly line balancing problems, *Computers and Operations Research*, 13, 443–449.

Holland, J.H., 1975. *Adaptation in Natural and Artificial Systems*, The University of Michigan Press, Ann Arbor, Michigan.

Johnson, N.V., 1983. A branch and bound algorithm for assembly line balancing problems with formulations irregularities, *Management Science*, 29(11), 1309–1324.

Kao, E.P.C., 1976. A preference order dynamic program for stochastic assembly line balancing, *Management Science*, 22, 1097–1104.

Kao, E.P.C. and Queyranne, M., 1982. On dynamic programming methods for assembly line balancing, *Operations Research*, 30, 375–390.

Kim, Y.K., Kim, Y. and Kim, J.Y., 2000. Two-sided assembly line balancing: a genetic algorithm approach, *Production Planning and Control*, 11, 44–53.

Kim, Y.K., Kim, J.Y. and Kim, Y., 2000a. A coevolutionary algorithm for balancing and sequencing in mixed model assembly lines, *Applied Intelligence*, 13, 247–258.

McMullen, P.R. and Frazier, G.V., 1998. Using simulated annealing to solve a multiobjective assembly line balancing problem with parallel workstations, *International Journal of Production Research*, 36, 2717–2741.

Oliver, B.A., Kincade, D.H. and Albrecht, D., 1994. Comparison of apparel production systems: a simulation, *Clothing and Textiles Research Journal*, 12(4), 45–50.

Pastor, R., Andres, C., Duran, A. and Perez, M., 2002. Tabu search algorithms for an industrial multi-product and multi-objective assembly line balancing problem with reduction of the task dispersion, *Journal of the Operational Research Society*, 53, 1317–1323.

Rosser, P.S., Sommerfield, J.T. and Tincher, W.C., 1991. Discrete-event simulation of trousers manufacturing, *International Journal of Clothing Science and Technology*, 3(2), 18–31.

Rotab, M.R.K., 1999. Simulation modeling of a garment production system using a spreadsheet to minimize production cost, *International Journal of Clothing Science and Technology*, 11(5), 287–299.

Scholl, A. and Klein, R., 1997. SALOME: A bidirectional branch and bound procedure for assembly line balancing, *INFORMS Journal on Computing*, 9, 319–334.

Schrage, L. and Baker, K.R., 1978. Dynamic programming solution of sequencing problems with precedence constraints, *Operations Research*, 26, 444–449.

Smith, A., 1776. *An Inquiry into the Nature and Causes of the Wealth of Nations*, 1st Edition, in *The Glasgow Edition of the Works and Correspondence of Adam Smith*, edited by R.H. Campbell, A.S. Skinner and W.B. Todd, Vol. II, Oxford University Press, Oxford.

Talbot, F.B. and Patterson, J., 1984. An integer programming algorithm with network cut for solving the assembly line balancing problem, *Management Science*, 30(1), 85–99.

8.8 Appendix: nomenclature

The following notation is utilized to search for optimal operative assignment for the apparel assembly process.

$\boldsymbol{M}$	set of workstations $\{1, 2, \ldots, m\}$
N	set of tasks $\{1, 2, \ldots, n\}$
$\boldsymbol{O}$	set of operators $\{1, 2, \ldots, o\}$
$\boldsymbol{S}_j$	set of workstations that are able to handle task j, $\boldsymbol{S}_j \subseteq \boldsymbol{M}(j = 1, 2, \ldots, n)$
$\lvert\mathbf{S}_j\rvert$	total number of workstations at which task j can be processed
x_{ij}	workstation state variable. $x_{ij} = \begin{cases} 1 & \text{if task } j \text{ is processed at workstation } i; \\ 0 & \text{otherwise} \end{cases}$
SI_n	skill inventory, which represents the number of tasks which each operator can handle
$\alpha(k)$	task skill level of operator$k$ ($k = 1, 2, \ldots, o$)
$\boldsymbol{T}_k$	$\{j: \alpha(k) \in [1\ SI_n]\}$ set of tasks which can be carried out by operator k
$\boldsymbol{E}_k$	$\{e: \alpha(k) \in [1\ SI_n]\}$ set of efficiency which operator k achieves for handling different tasks in $\boldsymbol{T}_k$
ST_j	standard time of task j, which is the time to complete task j with 100% operator efficiency
$PT_{j \in T_k}$	processing time of task j by operator k

9

Intelligent sales forecasting for fashion retailing using harmony search algorithms and extreme learning machines

W. K. WONG, The Hong Kong Polytechnic University, China
and Z. X. GUO, Sichuan University, China

DOI: 10.1533/9780857097842.170

Abstract: A hybrid intelligent (HI) model, comprising a data pre-processing component and a HI forecaster, is developed to tackle the medium-term fashion sales forecasting problem. The HI forecaster adopts a novel learning algorithm-based neural network to generate initial sales forecasts and then uses a heuristic fine-tuning process to obtain more accurate forecasts. The learning algorithm integrates an improved harmony search algorithm and an extreme learning machine. Experiments based on real fashion retail data and public benchmark data sets were conducted to evaluate the performance of the proposed model. Results demonstrate that the performance is far superior to traditional autoregressive integrated moving average (ARIMA) models and two recently developed neural network models.

Key words: fashion sales forecasting, harmony search, neural network, extreme learning machine.

9.1 Introduction

Sales forecasting is the foundation for planning various phases of a firm's operations (Boulden, 1958; Lancaster and Reynolds, 2002), which is a crucial task in supply chain management under dynamic market demands and greatly affects retailers and other channel members in various ways (Xiao and Yang, 2008). Without sales forecasts, operations can only respond retroactively, leading to poor production planning, lost orders, inadequate customer service, and poorly utilized resources (Fildes and Hastings, 1994). Recent research has shown that effective sales forecasting enables improvements in supply chain performance (Bayraktar *et al.*, 2008; Zhao *et al.*, 2002). Because of ever-increasing global competition, sales forecasting plays a more and more prominent role in supply chain management when the profitability and the long-term viability of a firm rely on effective and efficient sales forecasts. This chapter investigates the medium-term fashion sales forecasting problem to facilitate effective sales forecasting in fashion retail supply chains.

9.1.1 Fashion sales forecasting

The fashion industry is characterized by short product life cycles, volatile customer demands, tremendous product variety, and long supply processes

(Sen, 2008). Sales of most fashion items are strongly seasonal. Uncertain customer demands in a frequently changing market environment and numerous explanatory variables that influence fashion sales cause an increase in irregularity or randomicity of sales data. Such distinct characteristics increase the complexity of sales forecasting in the fashion retail supply chain. It is definitely desirable to develop forecasting models which are flexible and robust enough to handle these distinct characteristics of fashion sales data. Several studies have been reported to investigate fashion sales forecasting problems from different perspectives. Frank *et al.* (2004) proposed a multivariate fuzzy logic model to forecast women's casual sales. Thomassey and Happiette (2007) developed a neural network (NN)-based system to forecast sales profiles of new apparel items by extracting and analyzing available data with a self-organizing map NN-based clustering procedure and a probabilistic NN-based decision tree technique. Au *et al.* (2008) fulfilled fashion retail sales forecasting by developing an evolutionary NN (ENN) model, which adopted a genetic algorithm to determine an appropriate network structure for improving the generalization capacity of NNs. The ENN model is effective for sales forecasting of fashion items with features of low demand uncertainty and weak seasonal trends. Unfortunately, most fashion items are characterized by high demand uncertainty and strong seasonality. Sun *et al.* (2008) applied an NN model with extreme learning machine for fashion sales forecasting, and investigated the relationship between sales amount and some significant fashion product attributes such as color, size and price.

The studies in fashion sales forecasting mentioned above focus on forecasting sales volumes and sales profiles of fashion items, which is usually short-term forecasting. Due to the short life cycles and frequent replacements of fashion items, only forecasting sales of each item is not adequate in the fashion retail supply chain. In fact, the fashion retail enterprise usually makes sourcing budgets, on an annual, quarterly and monthly basis, by forecasting total sales amounts of fashion items in one fashion item category or in all categories of one city. Then the fashion designers determine which items need to be purchased or produced in each category. Each fashion item category consists of multiple items with some common attributes. In an enterprise, the categories are usually unchanged while the items in each category frequently change in different selling seasons. For instance, the short-sleeved T-shirt category consists of 200 items in this season, but 150 of them will probably be replaced by 150 new items in the next season. Based on soft computing techniques, Thomassey *et al.* (2005) developed a forecasting support system which involved medium-term sales forecasting at different sales aggregation levels. However, it is very difficult to apply the system in practice because it uses multiple soft computing techniques, and too many parameters for such techniques need to be set. Due to the lack of effective methodologies for fashion sales forecasting under dynamic market demands, medium-term sales forecasting in today's fashion retail supply chain mainly depends on subjective experience or simple linear models such as the autoregressive (AR) model and the moving average model.

To provide a flexible, robust and effective methodology for fashion sales forecasting, this chapter examines the sales forecasting problem based on the forecasting process in real-world fashion retailing, which forecasts the total sales amount of each fashion item category or each city (all categories) on a medium-term basis (annually, quarterly and monthly).

9.1.2 Techniques for sales forecasting

Various time-series forecasting models have been widely applied in sales forecasting, such as exponential smoothing models (Gardner; 2006, Geurts and Kelly; 1986 Harrison; 1967 Taylor; 2007), ARIMA models (Dalrymple; 1978 Goh and Law; 2002 Tang *et al.*; 1991), expert systems (Lo; 1994, Smith *et al.*; 1996), fuzzy systems (Chang *et al.*; 2008 Chen and Wang; 1999 Frank *et al.*; 2004) and NN models (Ansuj *et al.*; 1996 Chu and Zhang; 2003 Sun *et al.*; 2008 Thiesing and Vornberger; 1997 Zhang and Qi; 2005).

The exponential smoothing and ARIMA models are categorized as linear methods which employ a linear functional form for time-series modeling (De Gooijer and Hyndman; 2006). As such linear methods cannot capture features that commonly occur in many actual time-series data, such as non-linear patterns, occasional outlying observations and asymmetric cycles (Makridakis *et al.*; 1998), they are not suitable for fashion sales series characterized by strong non-linearity. Expert systems, fuzzy systems and NN models are heuristic methods, among which NNs are the most attractive alternatives for both forecasting researchers and practitioners, since a large number of research papers have reported successful experiments and practical tests and have shown that NNs exhibit better forecasting performances than some traditional approaches (Ansuj *et al.*; 1996; Chu and Zhang; 2003; Tang *et al.*;1991).

Ansuj *et al.* (1996) presented the use of a backpropagation (BP) NN model in analyzing the behavior of sales in a medium-sized enterprise and reported that the BP model generated more accurate forecasts than did ARIMA models with interventions. Thiesing and Vornberger (1997) developed an NN-based forecasting system to predict the weekly product demand in a German supermarket company. Alon *et al.* (2001) compared the performance of NN models with Levenberg-Marquardt learning algorithm and traditional statistical methods in forecasting US aggregate retail sales, and concluded that the NN model was able to effectively capture the dynamic non-linear trend and seasonal patterns, as well as the interactions between them. Chu and Zhang (2003) compared the performance of NN models and various linear models for forecasting aggregate retail sales and reported that the overall best model is the NN model built on deseasonalized time-series data. Chang *et al.* (2005) proposed an evolving NN forecasting model by integrating genetic algorithms and BP NN to generate more accurate forecasts than traditional statistical models and BP networks.

The previous studies usually adopted NNs with a gradient learning algorithm, such as BP, which is known to have slow convergence speed caused by the problem of local minima. In recent years, a new learning algorithm called extreme learning machine (ELM) has been proposed (Huang *et al.*, 2004), which tends to provide a better generalization performance and much faster learning speed than gradient learning algorithms. The ELM can also avoid many difficulties faced by gradient learning algorithms, such as the selection of stopping criteria, learning rate and learning epochs, due to its distinct learning mechanism. Sun *et al.*'s (2008) research in fashion sales forecasting demonstrated that the ELM-based NN had a much shorter training time and higher forecast accuracy than BP NNs. However, ELM determines the input weights and hidden biases randomly, which may lead to a higher number of hidden neurons and adversely affect the generalization performance of the network. Furthermore, the available historical sales data (training samples) for medium-term fashion sales forecasting are usually limited, and therefore the NN forecasting model is more apt to be over-parameterized and overfitted. Zhu *et al.* (2005) developed an evolutionary ELM by combining a modified differential evolution and an ELM, and concluded that higher generalization performance can be obtained by using an optimization technique to determine the optimal input weights and hidden biases.

To overcome the drawbacks of existing NN forecasting models, in this chapter a hybrid intelligent (HI) model comprising a data pre-processing component and a HI forecaster is developed to tackle the sales forecasting problems in the fashion retail supply chain. In the HI forecaster, it will be the first time that a novel metaheuristic optimization technique, harmony search (HS) algorithm (Mahdavi *et al.*, 2007), is integrated with ELM to construct a novel learning algorithm to obtain optimal NN weights and achieve better NN generalization performance. A heuristic fine-tuning process will also be presented and used in the HI forecaster to further improve the forecasting performance. The HI model will be able to effectively handle the non-linearity and irregularity of medium-term fashion sales caused by various realistic factors in the dynamic fashion retail supply chain, such as short product life cycles, volatile customer demands, and tremendous product variety.

The rest of this chapter is organized as follows. In Section 9.2, the proposed HI model for medium-term fashion sales forecasting is presented. Experimental design is presented in Section 9.3 concerning how numerical experiments are conducted to compare the forecasting performances of the proposed model and existing models. Section 9.4 presents and analyzes the experimental results. Section 9.5 further discusses the forecasting performance of the proposed model and its components based on extensive experimental results. Finally, conclusions and future work are described in Section 9.6.

9.2 Hybrid intelligent model for medium-term fashion sales forecasting

The HI model is composed of a data pre-processing component and an HI forecaster. Figure 9.1 shows the framework of the HI model. The data pre-processing component involves three processes, including detecting and removing outliers, interpolating missing data and data normalization. The pre-processed historical sale data are used as training samples of the HI forecaster generating the final sales forecast. The details of the HI model are given in the following sub-sections.

9.2.1 Data pre-processing

Data pre-processing has a significant impact on the performance of supervised learning models (Kotsiantis *et al.*, 2006) because unreliable samples probably lead to wrong outputs. Although fashion sales data are usually noisy and influenced by various unpredictable external factors, previous studies in fashion sales forecasting did not consider data pre-processing of sales data. Effective data pre-processing methods are applied in this study to avoid the effects of noisy and unreliable data.

In the fashion retail market, time series of sales of most item categories are strongly seasonal, such as knitted short-sleeved dresses (spring/summer) and coats (fall/winter). In this study, same-period time series, comprising sales data only from the same period of past years, are also used to observe the change trend

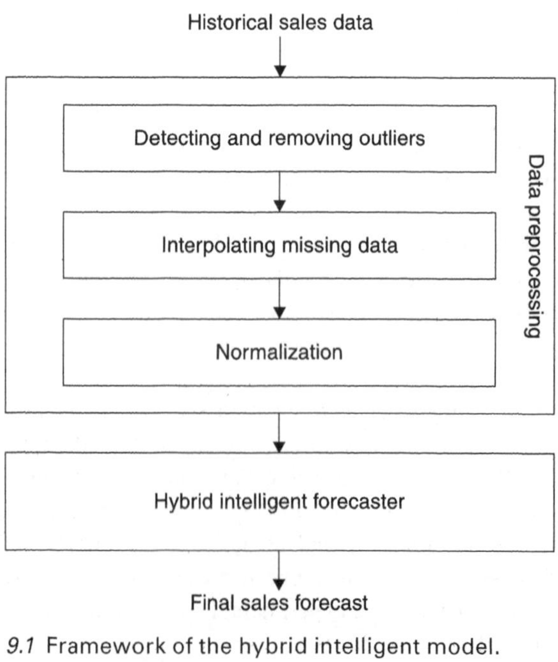

9.1 Framework of the hybrid intelligent model.

of fashion sales. Let $s_{i,j}$ denote the sales amount in jth month of ith year. The following sequence represents the original monthly time series S from the first month of ith year to the 12th month of $i+k$th year:

$$s_{i,1}, s_{i,2}, \ldots, s_{i,12}, s_{i+1,1}, s_{i+1,2}, \ldots, s_{i+1,12}, \ldots, s_{i+k,1}, s_{i+k,2}, \ldots, s_{i+k,12}.$$

The time series S involves 12 monthly same-period time series. Let S_j denote the same-period time series in j th month ($j = 1,2, \ldots, 12$). S_j can be represented as follows:

$$s_{i,j}, s_{i+1,j}, \ldots, s_{i+k,j}.$$

Detecting and removing outliers

An outlier is an observation that deviates so much from the rest of the observations as to arouse suspicion that the outlier was generated by a different mechanism. On the basis of extensive analyses on historical sales data of different fashion item categories, this study considers the observation $s_{i,j}$ in the same-period time series S_j of an item category as an outlier if it satisfies the following condition:

$$\text{abs}(s_{i,j} - \text{mean}(S_j)) > n \cdot \text{std}(S_j)$$

where mean($\cdot$) denotes the mean function, std($\cdot$) denotes the standard deviation function and abs($\cdot$) denotes the absolute value function. In this research, n is set to 3. The outlier needs to be removed and then to be handled as a missing observation.

Interpolating missing data

Incomplete data is an inevitable problem in handling most real-world data sources. The missing data need to be interpolated to maintain completeness and the change trend of time series. In this study, a missing observation is replaced by the mean of its latest two neighboring data in its same-period time series.

Normalization and de-normalization

Data normalization can speed up training time of NNs by starting the training process for each feature within the same scale. The z-score normalization method (Kotsiantis *et al.*, 2006) is adopted to normalize the input and output variables in this research. Taking the same-period time series S_j as an example, its normalized series S_j' is

$$S_j' = \frac{S_j - \text{mean}(S_j)}{\text{std}(S_j)}$$

The de-normalization process is described as follows.

$$S_j = \text{mean}(S_j) + S_j' \cdot \text{std}(S_j)$$

9.2.2 Hybrid intelligent forecaster

After the sales time series have been pre-processed, an HI forecaster is applied to generate medium-term sales forecasts. The essential feature of the HI forecaster is a novel learning algorithm-based NN forecasting. The HS-ELM learning algorithm is developed to improve NN generalization ability by integrating an HS algorithm with ELM. In addition, it is known that the number of hidden neurons has a large effect on NN performance (Zhang and Qi, 2005). To decrease the randomicity of NN outputs, the HI forecaster considers the forecasting outputs of multiple NNs with different numbers of hidden neurons. In the HI forecaster, the HS-ELM-based NN first generate multiple forecasting outputs by repeatedly running the network with different numbers of hidden neurons from 1 to $N_{\max hl}$ · $N_{\max hl}$ denotes the maximum number of hidden neurons. After the outputs of the proposed NNs have been de-normalized, a heuristic fine-tuning process is then used to analyze these outputs and generate the final sales forecast. The flow chart of the HI forecaster is shown in Fig. 9.2, and its details are described in the following sub-sections.

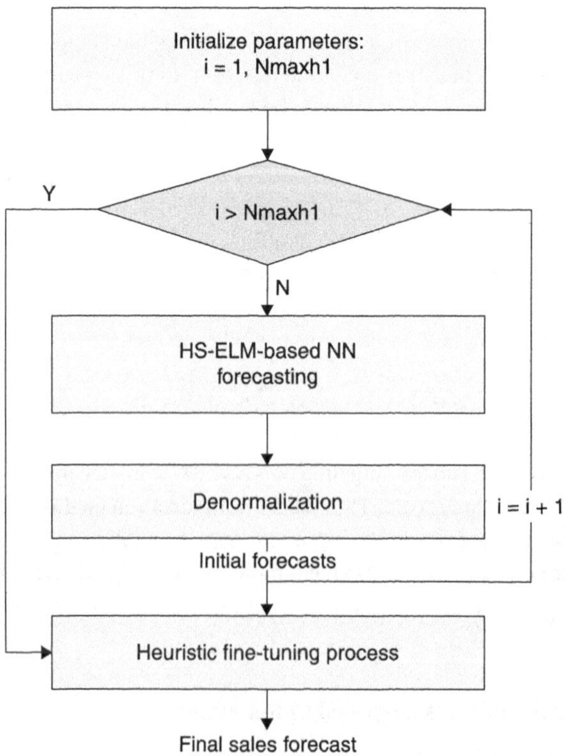

9.2 Flow chart of the hybrid intelligent forecaster.

Extreme learning machine

The ELM is a novel learning algorithm for single-hidden-layer feedforward NNs (SLFNs). Assume that SLFNs with L hidden neurons and activation function $g(x)$ are trained to approximate N distinct samples (u_i, y_i) with zero error means, where u_i is the input of samples and $u_i = [u_{i1}, u_{i2}, \ldots, u_{in}]^T \in R^n$; y_i is the output of samples and $y_i = [y_{i1}, y_{i2}, \ldots, y_{im}]^T \in R^m$. In ELM-based NNs, the input weights and hidden biases are generated randomly. The non-linear SLFNs can thus be converted into the following relationship:

$$H\beta = T, \quad [9.1]$$

where II = $\{h_{ij}\}$ $(i - 1, \ldots, N$ and $j - 1, \ldots, L)$ denotes the hidden-layer output matrix, $h_{ij} = g(w_j \cdot u_i + b_j)$ is the output of jth hidden neuron with respect to u_i; $w_j = [w_{j1}, w_{j2}, \ldots, w_{jn}]^T$ is the weight vector connecting jth hidden neuron and input neurons, and b_j denotes the bias of jth hidden neuron; $w_j \cdot u_i$ denotes the inner product of w_j and u_i; $\beta = [\beta_1, \ldots, \beta_j, \ldots, \beta_L]^T$ $(j = 1, \ldots, L)$ is the matrix of output weights and $\beta_j = [\beta_{j1}, \beta_{j2}, \ldots, \beta_{jm}]^T$ denotes the weight vector connecting the jth hidden neuron and output neurons; $Y = [y_1, y_2, \ldots, y_N]^T$ is the matrix of targets (desired outputs).

The determination of the output weights between the hidden layer and the output layer is to find the least-square solution to the given linear system. The minimum norm least-square (LS) solution to Eq. 9.1 is

$$\hat{\beta} = H^{\dagger}Y, \quad [9.2]$$

where $H^{\dagger}$ is the Moore–Penrose generalized inverse of matrix H. The minimum norm least-square solution is unique and has the smallest norm among all the least-square solutions.

HS-ELM learning algorithm

In this study, the HS-ELM learning algorithm is developed to train NNs, in which the improved HS algorithm (Mahdavi *et al.*, 2007) is adopted to search for optimal input weights and hidden biases of ELM instead of generating these weights and biases randomly. HS algorithm is a newly developed metaheuristic technique, which generates a new vector (individual) by considering all existing vectors, whereas the traditional evolutionary algorithm such as genetic algorithm (GA) only considers two parental vectors. This distinct feature of HS algorithm increases the algorithm's flexibility so that the algorithm can generate better solutions than conventional mathematical methods or GA-based approaches (Lee and Geem, 2004; Mahdavi *et al.*, 2007).

The following steps describe how the HS-ELM algorithm is implemented:

- ***Step 1:** Initialize algorithm parameters*. The parameters related to the problem and HS algorithm need to be specified in this step, including the possible ranges of values for all decision variables (input weights and hidden biases), the number of decision variables (*P*), the harmony memory size (*HMS*), harmony memory consideration rate (*HMCR*), pitch adjustment rate (*PAR*) and the number of improvisations (*NI*). The harmony memory (HM) and the *HMS* are similar to the genetic pool and the population size in the genetic algorithm respectively. *HMCR* usually ranges between 0.6 and 0.9 and *PAR* ranges between 0.1 and 0.5.

- ***Step 2:*** *Initialize the harmony memory*. The HM is generated randomly, and each HM member (solution vector), v, represents a distinct feasible solution of all decision variables. That is, v = $[v_1, v_2, \ldots, v_P]$. The decision variables are composed of all input weights and hidden biases.
- ***Step 3:*** *Calculate output weights and fitness of each individual*. For each individual in the HM, the corresponding output weights of the HS-ELM-based NN are analytically computed by Moore–Penrose generalized inverse (Huang *et al.*, 2004). Based on the individual and its output weights, the fitness of the individual is evaluated by comparing the sample output and the NN output according to a specified error criterion (accuracy measure), such as root mean square error, mean absolute percentage error.
- ***Step 4:*** *Improvise a new harmony*. After the fitness of all individuals in the population is calculated, two HS procedures are used to improvise a new harmony (generate a new solution vector). Generating a new harmony is called improvisation. A new harmony, v′ = $[v_1', v_2', \ldots, v_P']$, is generated based on the following two procedures.
  Memory consideration: The new variable value v_i' is selected from memory with probability *HMCR* or selected randomly from the allowed value range with probability (1 − *HMCR*).

$$v_i' \leftarrow \begin{cases} v_i' \in \{v_i^1, v_i^2, \ldots, v_i^{HMS}\} & \text{with probability } HMCR \\ v_i' \in V_i & \text{with probability } (1 - HMCR) \end{cases}$$

  Pitch adjustment: The decision variable obtained by the memory consideration should be pitch-adjusted with probability *PAR*:

$$v_i' \leftarrow \begin{cases} v_i' = v_1' \pm rand \cdot bw & \text{with probability } PAR \\ v_i' = v_1' & \text{with probability } (1 - PAR) \end{cases}$$

  where *bw* is an arbitrary distance bandwidth and *rand* is a random function generating a random number between 0 and 1. In this chapter, the values of *PAR* and *bw* are set according to the methods presented by Mahdavi *et al.*, (2007).
- ***Step 5:*** For the solution vector newly generated, its corresponding output weights and fitness are calculated by using the methods described in Step 3.

- ***Step 6:*** *Update the harmony memory*. If the new solution vector is better than the worst vector in the HM in terms of the objective function value (fitness), the new vector is included in the HM and the existing worst harmony is excluded from the HM. The HM is then sorted by the objective function value.
- ***Step 7:*** *Check termination criterion*. The HS in this study is controlled by a specified number of improvisations and a diversity measure. The diversity measure is satisfied if a specified percentage *PerHM* of HM members is the same in the current generation. If either of the two termination criteria is satisfied, the HS process is terminated. Otherwise, repeat Steps 4–6.

The input of NNs usually uses several latest sales in the existing literature (Au *et al.*, 2008; Sun *et al.*, 2008). The strong non-linearity and seasonality of sales data series increase the complexity of fashion sales forecasting. Due to the seasonal characteristic of fashion sales, this study attempts to investigate fashion sales series from a new perspective. By extensively analyzing the change trends of monthly sales data, it can be found that the patterns in the same-period time series are much simpler than the original pattern if the original monthly time series are strongly seasonal. In this research, for strongly seasonal monthly time series, we use the same-period time series to forecast the next month's sales. Furthermore, the output of the NN needs to be de-normalized, since the training samples are normalized data. The de-normalized output is the initial sales forecast.

Heuristic fine-tuning process

The initial sales forecasts from the HS-ELM-based NNs with different numbers of hidden neurons are transferred to the heuristic fine-tuning process. The initial forecasts can be unreasonable because the NN may be overfitted. Let PN denote the set of percent changes of two neighboring values in a same-period sales data series S_j, and pf denote the percent change of the forecast of the series S_j to its latest same-period observation. The initial forecast is considered unreasonable if one of the following conditions is met:

$$pf > \max(\text{PN}) \text{ at } pf > 0 \text{ and } \max(\text{PN}) > 0;$$

$$pf > abs(\min(\text{PN})) \text{ at } pf > 0 \text{ and } \max(\text{PN}) < 0;$$

$$abs(pf) > \max(\text{PN}) \text{ at } pf < 0 \text{ and } \min(\text{PN}) > 0;$$

$$pf < \min(\text{PN}) \text{ at } pf < 0 \text{ and } \min(\text{PN}) < 0;$$

where max(·), min(·) and abs(·) are maximum, minimum and absolute value functions, respectively. Lastly, all the reasonable initial forecasts are averaged as the final sales forecast.

9.3 Evaluating model performance with real sales data

To evaluate the performance of the proposed forecasting model, extensive experiments were conducted in terms of real fashion sales data, which forecast the total sales amounts of various item categories and cities on a monthly, quarterly or annual basis.

9.3.1 Fashion sales data

Real sales data were collected from one of the largest fashion retail companies in Hong Kong and Mainland China. They include monthly sales data of different cities and different item categories of each city from January 2001 through December 2008. The data from the last two years are out-of-sample data used to compare and evaluate the accuracy of forecasting models. For each out-of-sample observation, its previous sales data are used as training samples to set the forecasting model for making a one-step-ahead forecast.

9.3.2 Parameter setting for proposed model

Table 9.1 shows the parameters of the proposed model for experiments presented in this chapter, in which N_{inlay} denotes the number of input neurons and $N_{\max hl}$ denotes the maximum number of hidden neurons; $PAR_{\min}$ and $PAR_{\max}$ denote the minimum and the maximum of *PAR*, and $bw_{\min}$ and $bw_{\max}$ denote the minimum and the maximum of *bw*. Columns 2 and 3 show the parameters for monthly forecasting

Table 9.1 Parameters of hybrid intelligent models used in experiments

	Medium-term forecasting			
	Monthly		Quarterly	Annual
	One category	One city*		
N_{inlay}	2	12	4	2
$N_{max\ hl}$	10	50	15	10
HMCR	0.95	0.95	0.95	0.95
PAR_{min}	0.45	0.45	0.45	0.45
PAR_{max}	0.99	0.99	0.99	0.99
HMS	30	100	50	30
bw_{min}	1e-6	1e-6	1e-6	1e-6
bw_{max}	4	4	4	4
NI	1000	10000	5000	1000
PerHM	90%	90%	90%	90%

* One city means all item categories of a city.

of one or all categories of a city, respectively, while columns 3 and 4 show the parameters for quarterly and annual forecasting, respectively. The activation function $g(x)$ of NN is the sigmoidal function, i.e. $g(x) = \frac{1}{1+e^{-x}}$. In this chapter, the monthly forecasting of each fashion item category is fulfilled by using its same-period time series, whereas others are fulfilled by using their original time series directly.

9.3.3 Forecasting models used for comparison and their parameters

The forecasting performance of the proposed model is compared with that of six different models, including the extreme learning machine (ELME) model proposed by Sun *et al.* (2008), the ENN model proposed by Au *et al.* (2008), the ARIMA $^{(p,d,q)}$ model, the AR $^{(p)}$ model and the AR2 model. The AR2 model is the same as the AR $^{(p)}$ model except for using different forms of time series. The first four models use original time series while the last one uses the same-period series. The parameters of these models for different medium-term forecasting problems are shown in Table 9.2. For annual forecasting, the AR model is the same as the AR2 model, and the ARIMA model is not applicable because the available sample data are insufficient to estimate this model. The other parameters of the first two NN models are the same as the corresponding parameter setting in Sun *et al.* (2008) and Au *et al.* (2008).

9.3.4 Accuracy measures

No accuracy measure is generally applicable to all forecasting problems due to variation in forecasting objectives and data scales (De Gooijer and Hyndman, 2006; Hyndman and Koehler, 2006). Let Y_t denote the observation at time t and F_t denote the forecast of Y_t. Then define the forecast error $e_t = Y_t - F_t$. In this chapter,

Table 9.2 Parameters of different models used in experiments

		Medium-term forecasting		
		Monthly	Quarterly	Annual
ELME model	N_{inlay}	12	4	2
	$N_{max\ hl}$	50	15	10
ENN model	N_{inlay}	12	4	2
ARIMA	(p,d,q)	(12,0,12)	(4,0,4)	/
AR	p	12	4	3
AR2	p	3	3	/

the following three measures of forecast accuracy are adopted to calculate the fitness of each solution vector of the HI forecaster:

- Root mean square error (RMSE): RMSE is popular and often chosen by practitioners because of its ease of use and its theoretical relevance in statistical modeling. RMSE is expressed as follows:

$$\text{RMSE} = \sqrt{\text{mean}(e^2)}.$$

- Mean absolute percentage error (MAPE): this criterion is less sensitive to large errors than RMSE and can be expressed as

$$\text{MAPE} = \text{mean}\left(\frac{100e_t}{Y_t}\right).$$

- Mean absolute scaled error (MASE): To overcome the drawbacks of existing measures, Hyndman and Koehler (2006) proposed MASE as the standard measure for comparing forecast accuracy across multiple time series after comparing various accuracy measures for univariate time-series forecasting. MASE is expressed as follows:

$$\text{MASE} = \text{mean}\left(\left|\frac{e_t}{\frac{1}{n-1}\sum_{i=2}^{n}|Y_i - Y_{i-1}|}\right|\right).$$

MASE is less than one if it arises from a better forecast than the average one-step Naïve forecast computed in-sample. The Naïve model uses the last observation of the time series directly as the forecast. Conversely, it is greater than one if the forecast is worse than the average one-step Naïve forecast computed in-sample.

9.4 Experimental results and analysis

This section presents experimental results of three experiments, which involve monthly, quarterly and annual forecasting respectively. In each experiment, the sales amounts of the same four cities and four fashion item categories, respectively, are forecast. The cities selected are the four most important for the company's business. The four categories are knitted short-sleeved dresses (spring/summer), jean pants (spring/summer), coats (fall/winter) and tatting pants (fall/winter). Their sales, from the same city, are strongly seasonal and have more significant influence on the company's business than other categories.

9.4.1 Experiment 1: monthly forecasting

The monthly time series of sales for category 1 and city 1, respectively, are shown in Fig. 9.3 and 9.4, in which the last 24 observations from the last 2 years are

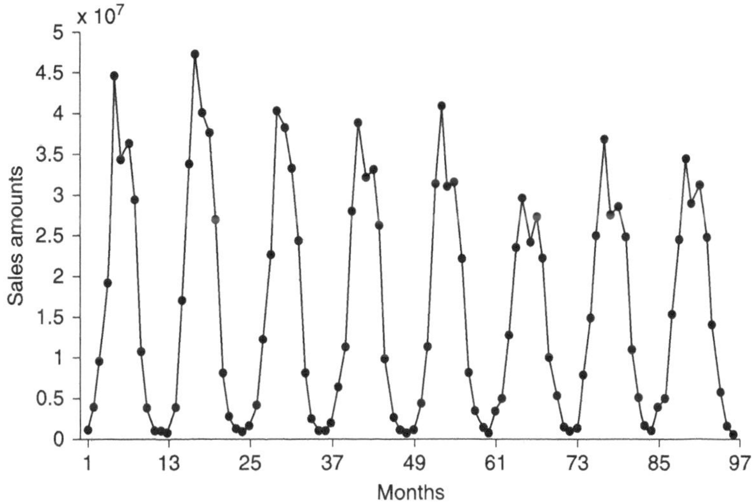

9.3 Monthly time series of sales for category 1 (January 2001–December 2008).

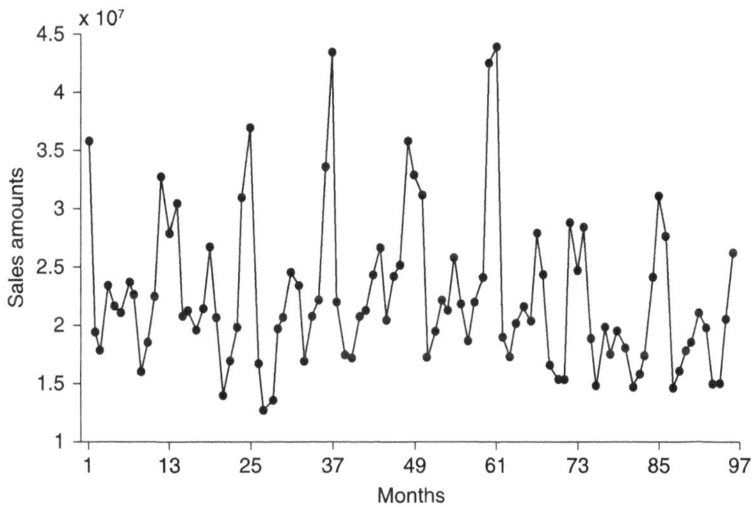

9.4 Monthly time series of sales for city 1 (January 2001–December 2008).

out-of-sample data for model comparison. It is clear that the time series of category 1 has stronger seasonality and less randomicity than that of city 1. The comparison of actual sales and out-of-sample forecasts of category 1 and city 1, generated by the proposed model, is shown in Fig. 9.5 and 9.6. Due to space limitations, this chapter does not present the figures of actual sales and forecasting results of other categories and cities.

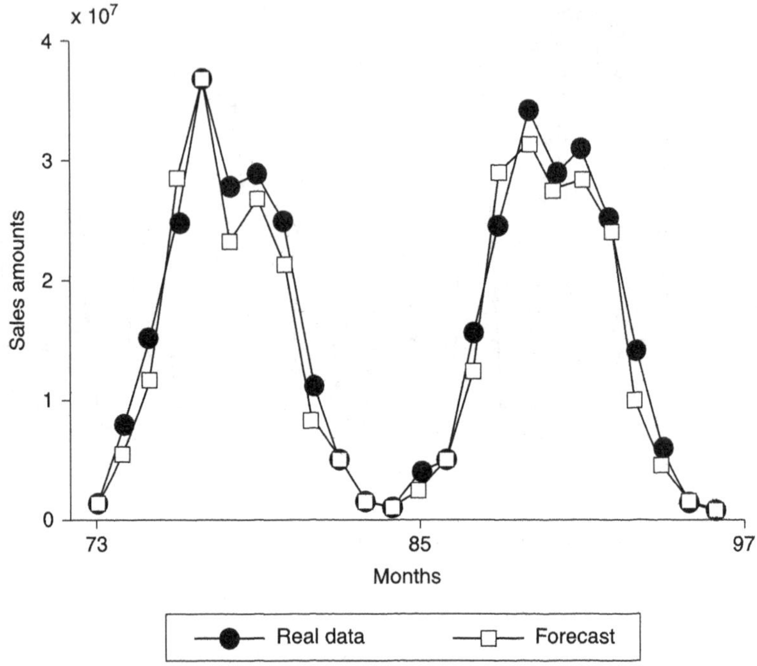

9.5 Monthly forecasting result generated by the proposed model (category 1).

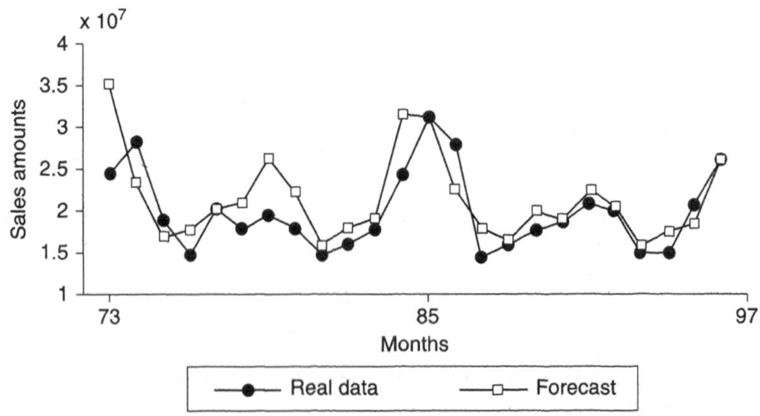

9.6 Monthly forecasting result generated by the proposed model (city 1).

The comparison of forecasting results of the proposed model and five other models is shown in Tables 9.3–9.5. Taking category 1 as an example, the proposed model produces smaller RMSE, MAPE and MASE, which shows that the proposed model generates better results whichever accuracy measure is used. For

Table 9.3 Comparison of monthly forecasting results (category 1 and city 1)

	Category 1			City 1		
	RMSE	MAPE	MASE	RMSE	MAPE	MASE
Proposed model	2.6E+06	19.3%	0.30	3.9E+06	14.6%	0.58
ELME model	3.5E+06	79.2%	0.39	3.9E+06	15.3%	0.58
ENN model	2.8E+06	57.6%	0.32	5.4E+06	24.8%	0.91
ARIMA	3.2E+06	31.8%	0.35	7.4E+06	27.5%	1.07
AR	2.6E+06	36.9%	0.31	4.9E+06	17.2%	0.67
AR2	3.4E+06	26.2%	0.37	5.8E+06	22.6%	0.91

Table 9.4 Comparison of monthly forecasting results (categories 2–4)

	Category 2			Category 3			Category 4		
	RMSE	MAPE	MASE	RMSE	MAPE	MASE	RMSE	MAPE	MASE
Proposed model	2.8E+06	25.6%	0.50	1.7E+06	37.0%	0.58	1.5E+06	58.1%	0.46
ELME model	2.4E+06	78.0%	0.46	2.4E+06	86.3%	0.81	2.6E+06	5209.9%	1.15
ENN model	2.5E+06	48.6%	0.48	2.1E+06	55.4%	0.71	2.9E+06	3464.8%	1.14
ARIMA	2.2E+06	38.1%	0.39	1.9E+06	35.5%	0.54	2.7E+06	6665.4%	0.92
AR	2.2E+06	32.7%	0.41	1.9E+06	41.3%	0.56	1.6E+06	582.9%	0.49
AR2	3.0E+06	31.5%	0.53	2.7E+06	53.4%	0.79	2.1E+06	84.0%	0.64

Table 9.5 Comparison of monthly forecasting results (cities 2–4)

	City 2			City 3			City 4		
	RMSE	MAPE	MASE	RMSE	MAPE	MASE	RMSE	MAPE	MASE
Proposed model	1.8E+07	17.7%	0.93	6.8E+06	15.2%	1.12	5.3E+06	15.5%	0.54
ELME model	1.8E+07	17.2%	0.88	8.0E+06	19.9%	1.39	6.1E+06	17.7%	0.63
ENN model	2.2E+07	17.6%	0.97	7.6E+06	16.5%	1.27	6.6E+06	21.4%	0.73
ARIMA	2.1E+07	25.1%	1.11	7.6E+06	19.5%	1.37	7.4E+06	24.0%	0.85
AR	2.0E+07	19.0%	0.95	7.0E+06	15.4%	1.14	6.2E+06	16.5%	0.60
AR2	2.1E+07	20.5%	1.03	1.0E+07	26.1%	1.88	7.6E+06	19.6%	0.74

other categories and cities, the RMSE, MAPE and MASE generated by the proposed model are usually the minimum value or very close to the minimum value. It is clear that the proposed model exhibits much better monthly forecasting performance than other models whichever accuracy measure is used.

9.4.2 Experiment 2: quarterly forecasting

Figure 9.7 and 9.8 show the quarterly time series of sales for category 1 and city 1 and their forecasting results generated by the proposed model. The change trends of forecasts generated by the proposed model and the real data are consistent, as shown in Fig. 9.7, but quite different, as seen in Fig. 9.8. This is because the quarterly time series of category 1 are regular and strongly periodic while the time series of city 1 is irregular and almost random. For instance, observations 25 and 26 in Fig. 9.8 deviate markedly from their historical data. Their forecasts do not match the real data very well because no univariate time series forecasting model can foresee these abnormal sudden changes.

The comparison of quarterly forecasting results of the proposed model and five other models is shown in Tables 9.6–9.8. For all forecasting cases except category 2, the RMSE, MAPE and MASE generated by the proposed model are the minimum value or very close to the minimum value. For category 2, the forecasts generated by the proposed model are superior to the two NN models and the ARIMA model but inferior to the two AR models. On the whole, similarly to the monthly forecasting results, the proposed model provides more accurate quarterly forecasting than other models.

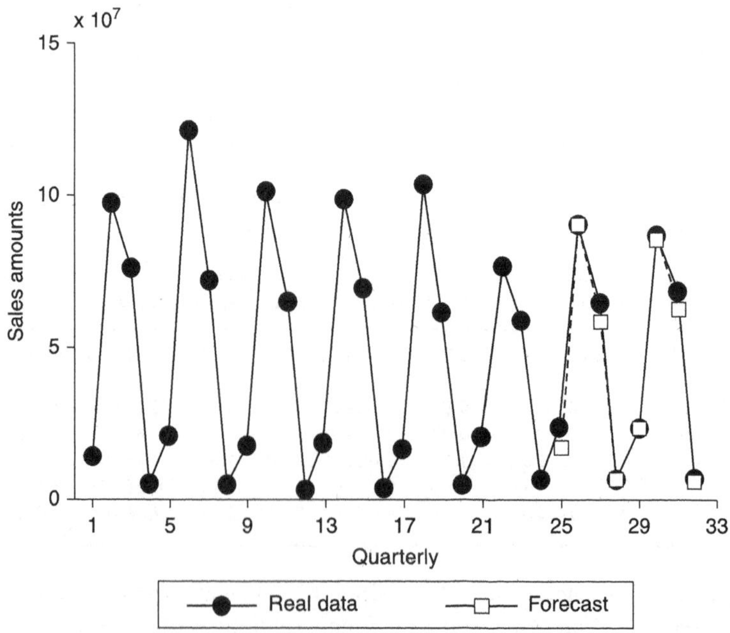

9.7 Quarterly forecasting result generated by the proposed model (category 1).

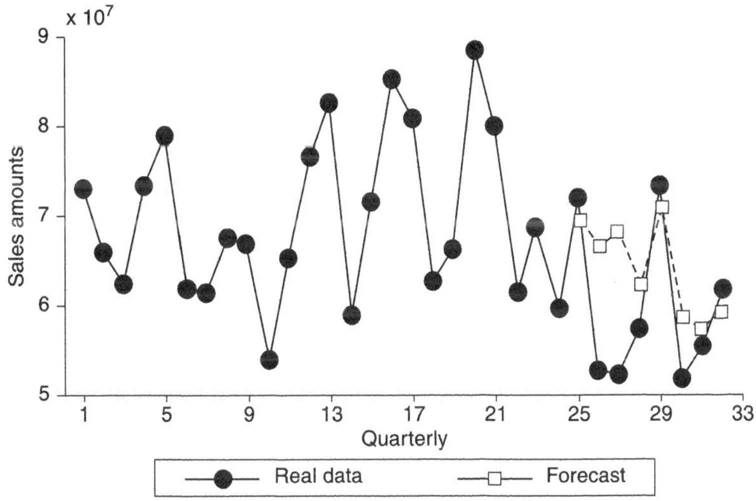

9.8 Quarterly forecasting result generated by the proposed model (city 1).

Table 9.6 Comparison of quarterly forecasting results (category 1 and city 1)

	Category 1			City 1		
	RMSE	MAPE	MASE	RMSE	MAPE	MASE
Proposed model	4.4E+06	11.9%	0.07	7.7E+06	11.0%	0.62
ELME model	6.0E+06	14.8%	0.09	1.0E+07	15.1%	0.85
ENN model	5.1E+06	14.3%	0.09	9.0E+06	12.1%	0.67
ARIMA	1.0E+07	15.3%	0.16	1.1E+07	15.5%	0.93
AR	5.4E+06	8.7%	0.08	7.8E+06	11.2%	0.65
AR2	5.2E+06	15.9%	0.09	8.2E+06	11.7%	0.69

Table 9.7 Comparison of quarterly forecasting results (Categories 2–4)

	Category 2			Category 3			Category 4		
	RMSE	MAPE	MASE	RMSE	MAPE	MASE	RMSE	MAPE	MASE
Proposed model	5.5E+06	17.2%	0.15	3.1E+06	15.1%	0.13	1.9E+06	16.2%	0.13
ELME model	7.3E+06	20.9%	0.20	3.6E+06	23.3%	0.23	9.0E+06	140.7%	0.38
ENN model	6.8E+06	20.3%	0.19	2.2E+06	14.4%	0.16	6.0E+06	232.1%	0.32
ARIMA	5.8E+08	27.2%	0.16	3.9E+06	20.2%	0.25	4.2E+06	40.5%	0.24
AR	4.4E+06	9.9%	0.10	3.2E+06	25.2%	0.23	4.1E+06	18.0%	0.19
AR2	5.2E+06	10.2%	0.12	4.0E+06	34.1%	0.28	5.5E+06	34.6%	0.22

Table 9.8 Comparison of quarterly forecasting results (cities 2–4)

	City 2			City 3			City 4		
	RMSE	MAPE	MASE	RMSE	MAPE	MASE	RMSE	MAPE	MASE
Proposed model	2.8E+07	9.4%	0.66	1.1E+07	10.7%	1.07	8.3E+06	9.4%	0.45
ELME model	3.6E+07	13.5%	0.94	1.5E+07	14.0%	1.54	1.4E+07	12.1%	0.62
ENN model	3.3E+07	11.1%	0.79	1.1E+07	10.6%	1.16	8.5E+06	9.0%	0.41
ARIMA	2.1E+07	7.6%	0.51	1.3E+07	13.9%	1.45	1.0E+07	10.2%	0.53
AR	3.0E+07	10.4%	0.74	1.2E+07	11.5%	1.28	7.0E+06	8.0%	0.38
AR2	3.9E+07	14.7%	1.03	1.3E+07	11.0%	1.21	1.2E+07	13.8%	0.64

9.4.3 Experiment 3: annual forecasting

The annual time series are strongly non-linear and highly irregular due to various uncertainties in fashion retailing. Figure 9.9 shows the annual sales series of category 1 and city 1 and their forecasting results generated by the proposed model.

It is very difficult to predict these irregular annual time series, especially when the sample data are insufficient. The comparison of annual forecasting results

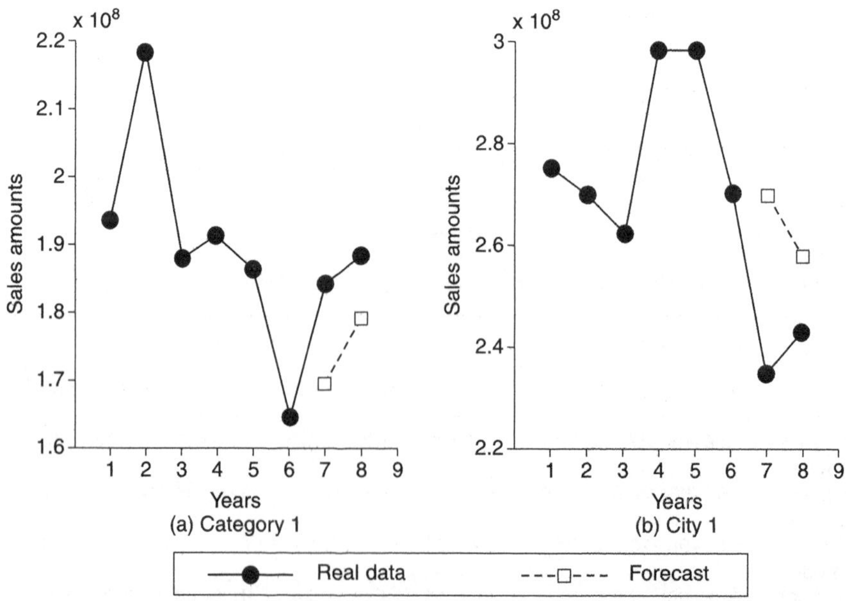

9.9 Annual forecasting result generated by the proposed model (category 1 and city 1).

generated by the proposed model and three other models is shown in Tables 9.9–9.11. It can be easily found from Tables 9.9–9.11 that, on the whole, the proposed model also exhibits superior performance over other models, although the superiority is not as prominent as that in experiments 1 and 2. In this experiment, the AR model and the ENN model provide better forecasting results in several cases. That is because NN models are prone to being over-parameterized when training samples are insufficient and the limited samples are not enough to model the strong non-linearity of annual sales series.

Table 9.9 Comparison of annual forecasting results (category 1 and city 1)

	Category 1			City 1		
	RMSE	MAPE	MASE	RMSE	MAPE	MASE
Proposed model	1.2E+07	6.5%	0.65	2.8E+07	10.4%	1.53
ELME model	4.5E+07	21.4%	2.27	8.1E+07	23.8%	3.65
ENN model	5.0E+06	2.3%	0.25	3.8E+07	15.9%	2.39
AR	1.2E+07	6.2%	0.66	3.2E+07	10.6%	1.57

Table 9.10 Comparison of annual forecasting results (categories 2–4)

	Category 2			Category 3			Category 4		
	RMSE	MAPE	MASE	RMSE	MAPE	MASE	RMSE	MAPE	MASE
Proposed model	1.7E+07	11.1%	1.21	4.1E+06	7.0%	0.57	1.4E+07	24.9%	3.03
ELME model	3.3E+07	22.2%	2.42	1.8E+07	31.4%	2.54	3.5E+07	61.2%	7.44
ENN model	2.1E+07	14.0%	1.53	2.5E+06	4.3%	0.35	1.6E+07	28.1%	3.41
AR	1.2E+07	7.7%	0.84	4.5E+06	7.7%	0.62	1.5E+07	26.9%	3.27

Table 9.11 Comparison of annual forecasting results (Cities 2–4)

	City 2			City 3			City 4		
	RMSE	MAPE	MASE	RMSE	MAPE	MASE	RMSE	MAPE	MASE
Proposed model	1.4E+08	13.5%	1.87	4.4E+07	12.7%	1.58	2.1E+07	4.8%	0.60
ELME model	1.7E+08	16.3%	2.26	6.7E+07	18.0%	3.43	4.1E+08	101.0%	17.13
ENN model	1.4E+08	13.9%	1.93	9.5E+07	27.1%	5.46	3.7E+07	10.9%	1.86
AR	1.2E+08	13.7%	1.84	3.6E+07	10.6%	1.31	4.5E+07	13.9%	1.76

9.5 Assessing forecasting performance

This section presents an in-depth discussion on the forecasting performance of the proposed HI model. The forecasting performance of the proposed HI model is first analyzed based on the experimental results presented in Section 9.4. Further analysis is then conducted to validate the superiority of the proposed model over other models based on public benchmark data sets. The effectiveness of the model's components, including the heuristic fine-tuning process, data pre-processing component and HI forecaster, is also analyzed in this section.

9.5.1 Performance comparison and analysis

Based on the three experiments presented in Section 9.4, Fig. 9.10 further shows the comparison of forecasting performances generated by different models, in which each bar indicates the number of best forecasts generated by its corresponding model in terms of a specified accuracy measure. For instance, the proposed HI model generates the best forecasting performance for 14 forecasting cases when RMSE is used as the accuracy measure. It is proved that the proposed model is able to provide much superior forecasting performances to other models. Its superiority would be more obvious if we did not consider the results of experiment 3, in which insufficient sample data probably weaken its performance.

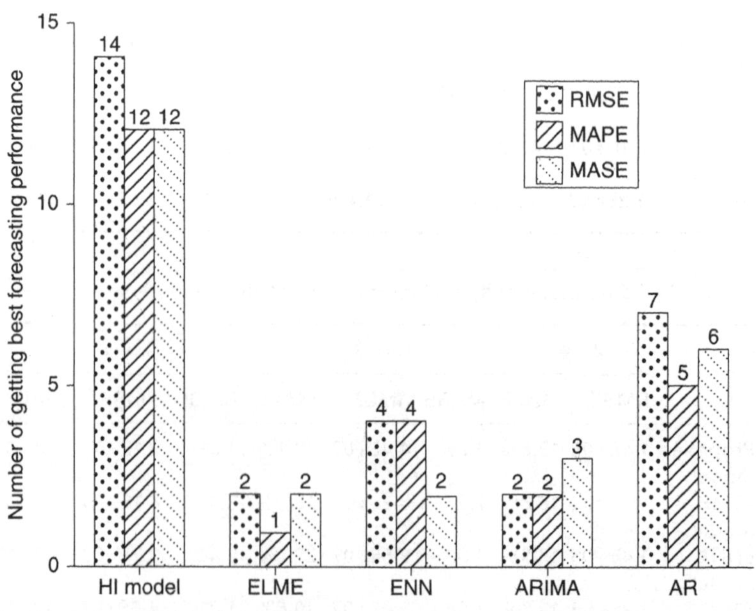

9.10 Comparison of forecasting performance of different models.

The proposed model uses a heuristic fine-tuning process to eliminate unreasonable forecasts, and the experimental results indicate that this is helpful to improve forecasting performance. Actually, for some forecasting cases in the experiments (e.g. the monthly forecasting of four categories), the MAPEs generated by ELME and ENN models are much greater than the MAPEs generated by traditional models. These abnormally large MAPEs are caused by unreasonable forecasts. The experimental results also revealed that different accuracy measures have effects on forecasting performance. For instance, for the monthly forecasting of category 2, the proposed model generates minimal MAPE but almost maximal RMSE and MASE. Therefore, it is important to select appropriate accuracy measures in practice.

9.5.2 Further analysis on forecasting performance of proposed model

It can be found from the experimental results in Section 9.4 that the ENN model and the AR model are the two major competitors for the proposed HI model, especially when annual forecasting was conducted. To further compare the annual forecasting performance of the HI model and the two other models, we made comprehensive simulation studies using public benchmark data sets with sufficient sample data. This chapter presents the forecasting results of seven sets of irregular annual time series from the well-known forecasting competition (Makridakis and Hibon, 2000). These time series included four industry data sets with 33 observations (series N188–191) and 3 finance data sets with 28 observations (series N359–N361), which were all irregular without seasonality. Each time series contained one or more outliers. The last six observations of each time series were used as out-of-sample data to compare the forecasting models.

Table 9.12 shows the annual forecasting results of the seven data sets based on the proposed HI model, the HI forecaster, the ENN model and the AR model. The HI forecaster is same as the HI model except that it does not contain the data pre-processing component. The parameter settings of these models were the same as those described in Section 9.3. It can be easily found from Table 9.12 that, for each time series, the HI model generates much better forecasts than the ENN and AR models. This indicates that, for the annual time series with sufficient samples, the HI model can demonstrate much better performance. The HI forecaster also gives much superior performance over the ENN and AR models on the whole, which means that the proposed HS-ELM learning algorithm is capable of obtaining good generalization performance. Moreover, the performance generated by the HI model is much superior to that generated by the HI forecaster. It implies that the data pre-processing component in the HI model is helpful to improve the forecasting performance, since the HI forecaster can be considered as an HI model without the data pre-processing component. That is, the data pre-processing component is able to tackle outliers and missing data well so that the forecasting performance generated by the HI model can be improved.

Table 9.12 Comparison of annual forecasting results (benchmark data sets)

Time series	Proposed model			HI forecaster			ENN			AR		
	RMSE	MAPE	MASE	RMSE	MAPE	MASE	RMSE	MAPE	MASE	RMSE	MAPE	MASE
N188	**1182**	**0.16**	**6.55**	1499	0.20	8.88	1876	0.26	11.14	1147	0.16	6.88
N189	**1514**	**0.12**	**3.65**	1551	0.12	3.69	2534	0.17	5.33	1952	0.13	4.21
N190	**606**	**0.06**	**1.97**	727	0.09	2.70	760	0.09	2.87	772	0.11	3.37
N191	**1553**	**0.13**	**3.24**	1773	0.16	3.86	1674	0.15	3.84	1847	0.14	3.37
N359	**3485**	**0.30**	**2.88**	3491	0.33	2.98	3626	0.33	2.94	3973	0.42	3.66
N360	**3643**	**0.59**	**5.73**	3925	0.67	6.02	4626	0.60	6.74	3701	0.73	6.16
N361	**2240**	**0.41**	**2.99**	2280	0.50	3.26	2409	0.54	3.38	3071	0.78	5.02

According to the forecasting results based on real fashion retail data and benchmark data from M3 competition, it can be concluded that the proposed model is widely applicable, since it is capable of generating accurate forecasts for a variety of time series with irregular patterns as well as strong seasonal patterns.

9.6 Conclusions

This chapter investigates the medium-term sales forecasting problem based on the real forecasting process in fashion retailing, which is helpful for fashion retail enterprises to facilitate medium-term sales forecasting and thus improve the performance and efficiency of the fashion retail supply chain. An effective HI model was developed to deal with the investigated problem, in which a data pre-processing component and an HI forecaster were presented. The data pre-processing component is used to detect and remove outliers, interpolate missing data and normalize sample data. The HI forecaster first generates multiple initial forecasts by HS-ELM learning algorithm-based NNs integrating an improved HS algorithm with an ELM algorithm, and then uses a heuristic fine-tuning process to generate the final sales forecasts based on the initial forecasts. The data pre-processing component, the HS-ELM learning algorithm, and the heuristic fine-tuning process introduced in this chapter are helpful to improve forecasting performance from different perspectives. The data pre-processing component is conducive to providing more reliable training samples. The HS-ELM learning algorithm is conducive to the improvement of NN generalization ability, while the fine-tuning process can further improve forecast accuracy by eliminating unreasonable initial forecasts and averaging multiple NN forecasts.

Extensive experiments were conducted to validate the proposed HI model in terms of real fashion retail data. The experimental results have shown that the HI model can tackle the medium-term sales forecasting problem effectively, which also demonstrates that the proposed model can provide much superior performance over traditional ARIMA models and two recently developed sales forecasting NN models. A further experiment was presented based on seven irregular annual data sets from M3 competition, which further validates the effectiveness of the proposed HI model and shows that the HI model is more powerful to tackle the time series with sufficient sample data. Furthermore, since the time series tackled in this chapter involve various patterns such as irregularity and seasonality, the proposed model is widely applicable and can be easily extended to solve other forecasting problems with similar time-series patterns.

The proposed model provides forecasts based only on historical sales data, which cannot reflect the effects of exogenous factors, such as weather and economic indexes, on fashion sales. Future research will focus on investigating multivariate HI forecasting models considering the effects of various exogenous changes on fashion sales. Moreover, it is also a worthwhile research direction to explore an effective intelligent model for short-term sales forecasting on the basis of the findings in this research.

9.7 Acknowledgement

The authors would like to thank The Hong Kong Polytechnic University for financial support of this research project (Project No A-PA9R).

9.8 References

Alon, I., Qi, M. and Sadowski, R. J., 2001. Forecasting aggregate retail sales a comparison of artificial neural networks and traditional methods. *Journal of Retailing and Consumer Services*, 8(3), 147–156.

Ansuj, A., Camargo, M., Radharamanan, R. and Petry, D., 1996. Sales forecasting using time series and neural networks. *Computers and Industrial Engineering*, 31(1–2), 421–424.

Au, K., Choi, T. and Yu, Y., 2008. Fashion retail forecasting by evolutionary neural networks. *International Journal of Production Economics*, 114(2), 615–630.

Bayraktar, E., Koh, S., Gunasekaran, A., Sari, K. and Tatoglu, E., 2008. The role of forecasting on bullwhip effect for E-SCM applications. *International Journal of Production Economics*, 113(1), 193–204.

Boulden, J. B., 1958. Fitting the sales forecast to your firm. *Business Horizons*, 1(1), 65–72.

Chang, P., Liu, C. and Lai, R., 2008. A fuzzy case-based reasoning model for sales forecasting in print circuit board industries. *Expert Systems with Applications*, 34(3), 2049–2058.

Chang, P., Wang, Y. and Tsai, C., 2005. Evolving neural network for printed circuit board sales forecasting. *Expert Systems with Applications*, 29(1), 83–92.

Chen, T. and Wang, M., 1999. Forecasting methods using fuzzy concepts. *Fuzzy Sets and Systems*, 105(3), 339–352.

Chu, C. and Zhang, G., 2003. A comparative study of linear and nonlinear models for aggregate retail sales forecasting. *International Journal of Production Economics*, 86(3), 217–231.

Dalrymple, D., 1978. Using Box-Jenkins techniques in sales forecasting. *Journal of Business Research*, 6(2), 133–145.

De Gooijer, J. and Hyndman, R., 2006. 25 years of time series forecasting. *International Journal of Forecasting*, 22(3), 443–473.

Fildes, R. and Hastings, R., 1994. The organization and improvement of market forecasting. *The Journal of the Operational Research Society*, 45(1), 1–16.

Frank, C., Sztandera, L., Vemulapali, B., Garg, A. and Raheja, A., 2004. A fuzzy forecasting model for women's casual sales, *National Textile Center Annual Report* (NTC Project: S01-PH10). USA.

Gardner, E., 2006. Exponential smoothing: The state of the art – Part II. *International Journal of Forecasting*, 22(4), 637–666.

Geurts, M. and Kelly, J., 1986. Forecasting retail sales using alternative models. *International Journal of Forecasting*, 2(3), 261–272.

Goh, C. and Law, R., 2002. Modeling and forecasting tourism demand for arrivals with stochastic nonstationary seasonality and intervention. *Tourism Management*, 23(5), 499–510.

Harrison, P., 1967. Exponential smoothing and short-term sales forecasting. *Management Science*, 13(11), 821–842.

Huang, G. B., Zhu, Q. Y. and Siew, C. K., 2004. Extreme learning machine: a new learning scheme of feedforward neural networks, *Proceedings of the International Joint Conference on Neural Networks* (IJCNN2004), pp. 25–29. Budapest, Hungary.

Hyndman, R. and Koehler, A., 2006. Another look at measures of forecast accuracy. *International Journal of Forecasting*, 22(4), 679–688.

Kotsiantis, S. B., Kanellopoulos, D. and Pintelas, P. E., 2006. Data preprocessing for supervised learning. *International Journal of Electrical and Computational Engineering*, 1(2), 111–117.

Lancaster, G. and Reynolds, P., 2002. *Marketing: Made Simple*, Oxford, UK: Elsevier.

Lee, K. and Geem, Z., 2004. A new structural optimization method based on the harmony search algorithm. *Computers and Structures*, 82(9–10), 781–798.

Lo, T., 1994. An expert-system for choosing demand forecasting techniques. *International Journal of Production Economics*, 33(1–3), 5–15.

Mahdavi, M., Fesanghary, M. and Damangir, E., 2007. An improved harmony search algorithm for solving optimization problems. *Applied Mathematics and Computation*, 188(2), 1567–1579.

Makridakis, S. and Hibon, M., 2000. The M3-Competition: Results, conclusions and implications, *International Journal of Forecasting*, 16(4), 451–476.

Makridakis, S., Wheelwright, S. and Hyndman, R., 1998. *Forecasting: Methods and Applications*, New York: Wiley.

Sen, A., 2008. The US fashion industry: A supply chain review. *International Journal of Production Economics*, 114(2), 571–593.

Smith, P., Husein, S. and Leonard, D., 1996. Forecasting short term regional gas demand using an expert system. *Expert Systems with Applications*, 10(2), 265–273.

Sun, Z., Choi, T., Au, K. and Yu, Y., 2008. Sales forecasting using extreme learning machine with applications in fashion retailing. *Decision Support Systems*, 46(1), 411–419.

Tang, Z., Dealmeida, C. and Fishwick, P., 1991. Time-series forecasting using neural networks vs Box-Jenkins methodology. *Simulation*, 57, 303–310.

Taylor, J., 2007. Forecasting daily supermarket sales using exponentially weighted quantile regression. *European Journal of Operational Research*, 178(1), 154–167.

Thiesing, F. and Vornberger, O., 1997. Forecasting sales using neural networks. *Computational Intelligence*, 1226, 321–328.

Thomassey, S. and Happiette, M., 2007. A neural clustering and classification system for sales forecasting of new apparel items. *Applied Soft Computing*, 7(4), 1177–1187.

Thomassey, S., Happiette, M. and Castelain, J., 2005. A global forecasting support system adapted to textile distribution. *International Journal of Production Economics*, 96(1), 81–95.

Xiao, T. and Yang, D., 2008. Price and service competition of supply chains with risk-averse retailers under demand uncertainty. *International Journal of Production Economics*, 114(1), 187–200.

Zhang, G. and Qi, M., 2005. Neural network forecasting for seasonal and trend time series. *European Journal of Operational Research*, 160(2), 501–514.

Zhao, X., Xie, J. and Leung, J., 2002. The impact of forecasting model selection on the value of information sharing in a supply chain. *European Journal of Operational Research*, 142(2), 321–344.

Zhu, Q., Qin, A., Suganthan, P. and Huang, G., 2005. Evolutionary extreme learning machine. *Pattern Recognition*, 38(10), 1759–1763.

10

Intelligent product cross-selling system in fashion retailing using radio frequency identification (RFID) technology, fuzzy logic and rule-based expert system

W. K. WONG and S. Y. S. LEUNG,
The Hong Kong Polytechnic University, China,
Z. X. GUO, Sichuan University, China and
Z. H. ZENG and P. Y. MOK,
The Hong Kong Polytechnic University, China

DOI: 10.1533/9780857097842.196

Abstract: This chapter presents a combined use of radio frequency identification (RFID) technology and a product cross-selling system to perform cross-selling and up-selling for the retail industry. A smart dressing system (SDS) enabled by RFID technologies and an intelligent product cross-selling system (IPCS) have been developed. Customers' in-store data can be collected using RFID-enabled SDS and used for promoting or cross-selling new products. The IPCS, integrating a rule-based expert system and a fuzzy screening technique, can process linguistic and categorical information to simulate fashion designers and recommend appropriate fashion product items for cross-selling. The proposed systems execute the selling strategies more effectively, which improves sales performance in the fashion retail industry.

Key words: information system, multi-criteria decision making, cross-selling, RFID, retailing, fuzzy logic, rule-based expert system.

10.1 Introduction

The competition in many product markets is becoming keener, as the retail market in particular is becoming highly saturated. Retailers well realize the importance of retaining existing customers and gaining new ones, since they are the two major factors for survival. However, customers tend to be switchers who are likely to switch from one retail store to another in response to attractive and competitive offers. The competition for customers in mature markets leads to a phenomenon in which each retailer becomes a revolving door of acquiring and losing customers. Retailers are adopting different strategies to retain customers. These include improving service quality, making better business decisions, and identifying customers' purchasing behaviour through analysing transaction data. As a result, different kinds of systems have been developed to cater for the needs of these retailers.

Some of these systems include geographical information systems (Nasirin and Birks, 2003; Tayma and Pol, 1995), inter-organizational information systems

(Lin *et al.*, 2003) and data mining systems (Bose and Mahapatra, 2001; Chen *et al.*, 2008). They enable retailers to make decisions in such areas as replenishment, inventory control, and marketing and promotion strategies. Through the use of various types of database marketing (Kamakura *et al.*, 2003) and data mining techniques (Hui and Jha, 2000; Lin and Hong, 2008; Padmanabhan and Tuzhilin, 1999), customers' purchasing behaviour can be analysed and new retail business knowledge can be discovered. However, one common feature of these systems is the reliance on the use of historical transactional data as input. Although transactional data are an important source of input, the data are unavailable before transactions are made. This chapter, however, demonstrates a research endeavour in which, apart from transactional data, customers' in-store data are collected and used for promoting or cross-selling new products to them.

Retailers are well aware that, as well as increasing the number of customers, they need to increase the profitability obtained from the customers they already have. In other words, increasing the number of transactions per customer may lead to growth in terms of both profits and customer loyalty. This has led to the use of cross-selling[1] and up-selling strategies[2] (Cohen, 2004; Loeb, 2003). To actualize these strategies, retailers inevitably have to make use of historical transaction data to identify customers' preference and to rely on the skills of sales staff inside the retail stores for successful execution. However, historical data could become outdated over time, rendering a poor reflection of customers' tastes. In addition, human performance in selling may also vary widely from one salesman to another.

Radio frequency identification (RFID) is a kind of technology for data collection by reading tags at a distance without contact. A RFID system consists of three major components, namely RFID tags (transponders), an antenna and a RFID reader, which is usually interfaced to a computer database where product information is held. Tags are attached to product items and, when they are brought close to an antenna, the tags are then activated and the product codes are transmitted to the RFID reader. By relating the product codes received to the product details stored in the computer database, users can identify the products and make use of the information for many business and management purposes. Many successful RFID applications have been reported over the last few years, particularly in production management (Guo *et al.*, 2009; Yin *et al.*, 2009), supply chain management (Angeles, 2005; Holmstrom *et al.*, 2010; Sarac *et al.*, 2010), and logistic and inventory control (Cakici *et al.*, 2011; Lefebvre *et al.*, 2007; Pei and Klabjan, 2010). In order to push business owners to adopt RFID technology, RFID cost-benefit analysis has become a topic of great focus. Many white papers have reported the benefits of using RFID in such applications as material and inventory tracking and logistics in supply chain management (SCM). Jones *et al.* (2005) reported that a faster and more cost-effective SCM system allowed a UK department store to track 3.5 million reusable trays, dollies and cages throughout its refrigerated food supply chain, leading to a reduction of almost 80% in the time used to read a stack of multiple trays while increasing data accuracy and reliability. Becker *et al.* (2010) proposed a model-based approach for evaluation of RFID benefits along business processes, which proved to be very helpful in improving the individual performance measurement of potential RFID investments in an automotive project. Lee and Lee (2010) presented a supply chain RFID investment evaluation model to enhance the understanding of RFID value creation and measurement, and ways to maximize the value of RFID technology in the supply chain.

Other application areas, including using the technology to interact with customers and improve retail sales, are comparatively fewer, although a smaller number of research outputs related to the retail business can still be located. For example, Brown and Russell (2007) conducted an exploratory study on the adoption of the RFID technology in the South African retail sector and Wamba *et al.* (2008) investigated the impact of the RFID technology and the Electronic Product Code (EPC) network on mobile B2B eCommerce in the retail industry. However, these research endeavours are not in the same realm as this chapter is attempting to report.

In the fashion retail business, the Prada store in New York seems to be the first documented case of using RFID application to interact with in-store customers (*RFID Journal*, 2002). In the store, RFID technology was used in the fitting rooms. This was achieved through using a near-range reader to detect the RFID tag on each garment. Therefore garments needed to be located at a specific location inside the fitting room so that the detection devices concealed behind walls could read the signals from the tags. Then production information, or a video clip showing a model on the catwalk wearing the garment, was provided to the customers inside the fitting rooms. The system used in the store seems to have been limited to the fitting room areas, and there was no integration with the overall store environment; for example, dressing mirrors located inside the store were not integrated into the system. In addition, there is little research relating to the content to be displayed through the RFID system inside the fitting room.

Much research was found on analysing transactional sales information in the retail business, but investigations into the utilization of product information on the cross-selling and up-selling activities on the retail shop floor, as well as sales performance, are limited. Utilizing product information to implement cross-selling and up-selling allows customers to be provided with fashion mix-and-match recommendations, in which two fashion items are matched to present a good and attractive aesthetic appearance. Generally, deciding which two fashion items can be matched is a subjective judgement by designers. They assess the effect of the mix-and-match performance from multiple perspectives, such as whether the colours of two fashion items are matched and how the silhouettes of two items fit in together. The procedure of fashion mix-and-match can be modelled as a decision-making process, as illustrated in Fig. 10.1.

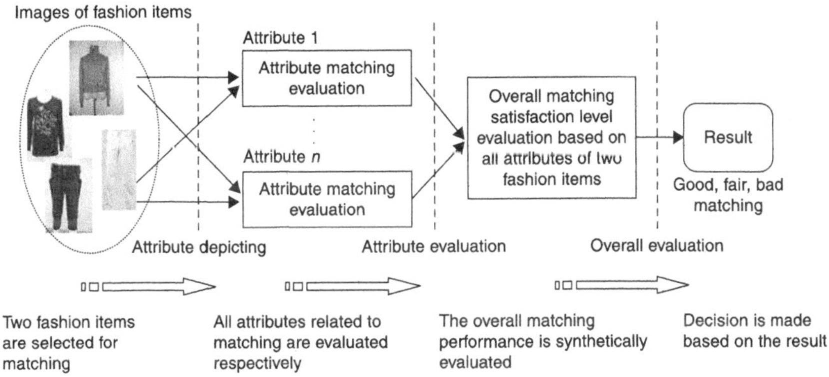

10.1 The fashion mix-and-match decision-making process of fashion designers.

Thus, the procedure of fashion mix-and-match recommendation is a decision-making process which involves the matching evaluations of multiple fashion attributes (multiple criteria), known as multiple criteria decision making (MCDM).

A variety of methods have been developed to solve MCDM problems, of which one of the most commonly used belongs to the classic method that uses mathematical functions to assist decision-makers to construct their preferences. The classic method includes multi-attribute value theory (MAVT) (Pictet and Bollinger, 2008; Simpson, 1996), multi-attribute utility theory (MAUT) (Gass, 2005; Khandelwal *et al.*, 2006), analytic hierarchy process (AHP) (Gass, 2005; Rohacova and Markova, 2009), and so on. MAVT and MAUT are difficult to use because the utility elicitation process is time-consuming and complex. The AHP is relatively easy to use and requires less cognitive skill than MAVT and MAUT. However, it cannot accommodate the variety of interactions, dependencies and feedback between higher and lower level elements. The expert system is a commonly used alternative for MCDM problems (Beynon *et al.*, 2001; Tsiporkova and Boeva, 2006) because it can simulate the performance of the expert and its knowledge base contains problem-related expertise. However, these methods generally assume that all criteria and their respective weights are expressed in crisp values. They cannot deal with problems with uncertain, vague and imprecise information. Unfortunately, the decision-making process for fashion mix-and-match involves various imprecise variables, such as the matching satisfaction levels of different products and the importance level of each attribute. The classic MCDM methods and expert systems are thus not appropriate for the fashion mix-and-match problem.

The fuzzy set theory introduced by Zadeh (1965) to handle problems involving a source of vagueness has been utilized for incorporating imprecise data into the decision framework (Benbernou and Warwick, 2007; Tong, 1982). It can be seen from Fig. 10.1 that the fashion mix-and-match problem mainly consists of two distinct decision-making phases: attribute evaluation and overall evaluation. Due to the complexity and fuzziness of these two phases, it is difficult to develop a precise mathematical model for the fashion mix-and-match. Moreover, some attributes of fashion items are categorical, such as colour, type of apparel, pattern, and so on. For example, the values for colour are black, red, white, and the like. These categorical attributes complicate the modelling of the attribute evaluation process by the fashion designers, because no computing method can be used directly on two categorical values. Therefore, it is infeasible to apply fuzzy logic methods directly to the fashion mix-and-match problem, even though there are many fuzzy rules existing in the overall evaluation. The rule-based expert system can effectively handle the large number of rules used for evaluating the matching degree of each fashion attribute. To handle various imprecise variables, it is desirable to combine the rule-based expert system with the fuzzy logic concept for fashion mix-and-match purposes.

This chapter demonstrates a combined use of RFID technology, expert system and fuzzy logic method to perform cross-selling and up-selling, which is implemented by two systems presented in this chapter. The first system is the smart dressing system (SDS), enabled by RFID technologies, which performs several functions including identifying product information, collecting customers' in-store preferences, and offering cross-selling and up-selling (mix-and-match) information. The second system is a hybrid intelligent system, called the intelligent product cross-selling system (IPCS), developed to match customers' selections with other fashion items for mix-and-match purposes. The SDS is therefore the front end which interacts with in-store customers while the IPCS is the back end responsible for evaluating and matching fashion items. These systems have been implemented in the real-life situation, and their potential and benefits are evaluated in this chapter.

The remainder of this chapter is organized as follows. Section 10.2 introduces the architecture and mechanism of the RFID-enabled SDS. Section 10.3 describes the IPCS and explains how to use product attributes of the fashion merchandise to generate cross-selling items. Section 10.4 presents an implementation of the two systems in a fashion retailing company in Hong Kong. Section 10.5 presents the experimental results of evaluating the effectiveness of the system on retail sales performance. Section 10.6 concludes the study and proposes further work.

10.2 Radio frequency identification (RFID)-enabled smart dressing system (SDS)

The SDS was developed in order to achieve a more integrated approach in utilizing fashion product information for cross-selling and to explore the potential of RFID in fashion retailing. The SDS is designed based on the current frequency allocation for RFID assigned by The Office of Telecommunication Authority (OFTA) of Hong Kong, and the frequency band is 920–925 MHz.

The system architecture of the RFID-enabled SDS system is shown in Fig. 10.2. The system consists of RFID-embedded dressing mirrors, smart fitting rooms, a

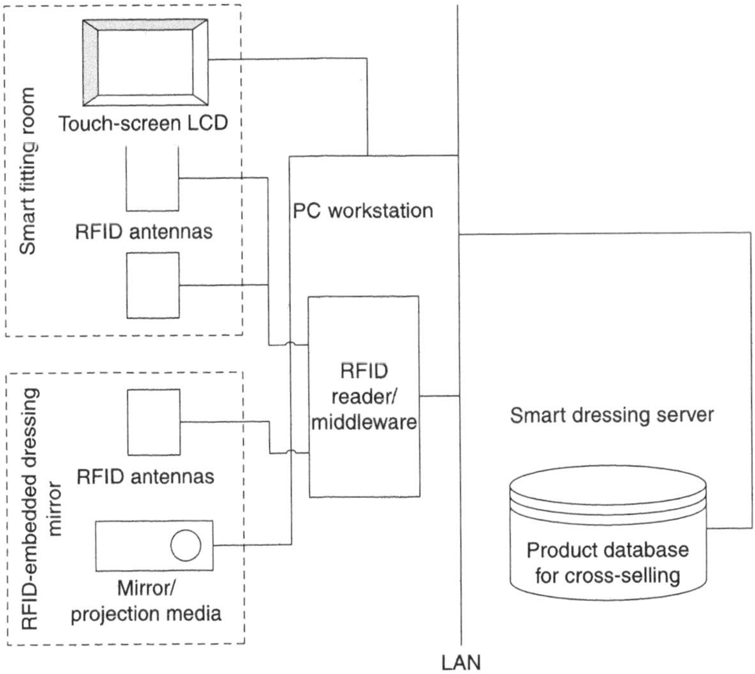

10.2 System architecture of RFID-enabled SFS for cross-selling in the fashion retail industry.

sales counter with a PC workstation connected to a server, RFID reader and middleware component inside a retail store, a smart dressing server and a product database for cross-selling.

Figure 10.3(a) shows a fashion retail shop equipped with the SDS. All fashion merchandise in the retail store has an ultra-high frequency RFID tag attached (Fig. 10.3(b)). The dressing mirror and fitting room are equipped with RFID antennas and projection devices. The RFID antennas are connected to RFID readers, which are connected to RFID middleware[3] and the smart dressing server, which forms an RFID data management platform to collect, filter and route raw RFID data from individual readers. It avoids network congestion by automatic data filtering of the vast amount of raw data entering the network. Any useless raw RFID data is filtered away to ensure that no 'noisy data' can enter the network, thus improving network efficiency. The RFID antennas are used to detect RFID tags in front of the dressing mirrors and inside the fitting rooms. When an item is brought in front of a dressing mirror or into a fitting room, the item can be detected and the antenna will convey the information to the RFID reader as well as the smart dressing server.

The system then delivers cross-selling (mix-and-match) recommendations to the customer, using a human-size display next to the dressing mirror (Fig. 10.3(c)).

If the customer is inside a fitting room, the recommendations will be displayed through touch-screen LCD monitor, which also allows the customer to interact with the system for more product information, such as colours, sizes, fabrics, and so on (Fig. 10.3(d)). If the customer is interested in the recommended items and wants to try them on, an intercom system is available to inform the sales staff, who will bring the clothes over (Fig. 10.3(e)).

(a)

(b)

10.3 (a) A fashion retail shop equipped with SDS. (b) A jacket with a smart tag attached.

(c)

(d)

10.3 Continued. (c) Smart dressing mirror displaying mix-and-match items based on the customer's selected item. (d) A customer inside the smart fitting room interacting with the system for more product details.

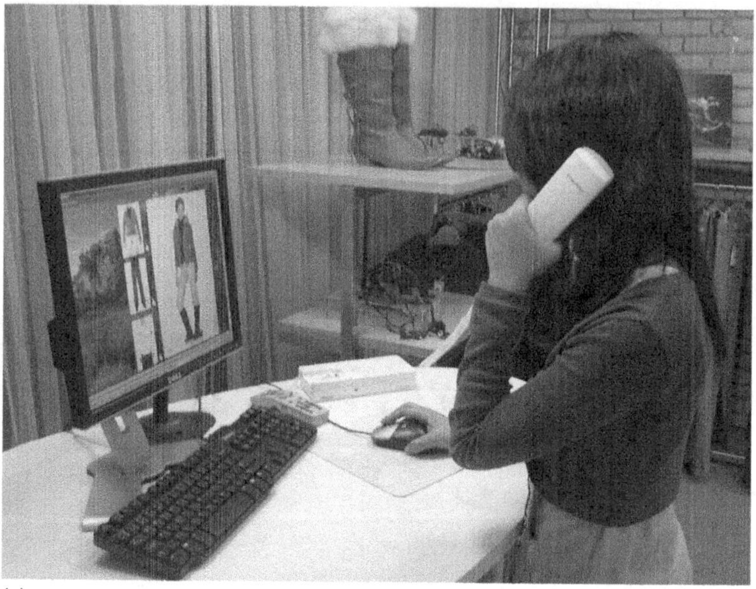

(e)

10.3 Continued. (e) A member of the sales staff is communicating with a customer inside the fitting room.

The store counter, being the control centre of the system, can synchronize with either the smart mirror or the smart fitting room system. Using the computer and the intercom systems at the store counter, the sales staff can know exactly what items are required by the customer inside the fitting room. The staff can then take the matching product items to the customer. In this way, the customer does not have the trouble of re-dressing, walking out of the fitting room, selecting the items, walking back and trying on again.

The store counter is also equipped with a hand-held scanning system whose purpose is to associate a barcode ticket with a smart tag. As many suppliers are not RFID enabled, fashion merchandise arriving at a store is only tagged with traditional barcode tickets. The hand-held scanning device reads the barcode and allows the system to generate a smart tag for an item. When a fashion item is sold at the store counter, the smart tag is removed and will be reused for other items.

10.3 Intelligent product cross-selling system (IPCS)

The smart dressing server involves a front-end sub-system and a back-end sub-system. The front-end sub-system, the RFID-enabled Smart Dressing System (SDS), is primarily used to interact with customers and allow the salespersons to provide service to them. The system can display the product details of selected items or recommend new fashion items to go with them through various display devices. The back-end sub-system, the Intelligent Product Cross-selling System (IPCS), is designed to assist fashion designers or stylists in streamlining the process of making the mix-and-match pairs. This is achieved through comparing the degree of importance of the characteristics (or attributes) of the fashion items with each other.

The system is designed to allow the input of the characteristics of the fashion merchandise in the form of data, which are stored in the product database. These characteristics, such as colour, pattern and product type, defined as product attributes throughout this chapter, are used to portray the fashion 'image'. These product attributes are identified through interviews and surveys with the fashion designers. Only those attributes that are important to fashion mix-and-match are identified as the product attributes. Nine product attributes were identified, as shown in Table 10.1. It should be mentioned that, although the 'price' attribute is an important factor for the customer in making purchase decisions in fashion retailing, price is not an important factor in fashion mix-and-match, and thus all nine identified attributes are related to the product features. Each day, the smart dressing server receives updated mix-and-match recommendations generated from the IPCS. These recommendations are then used for presenting to the customers.

The SDS described in Section 10.2 established an environment in which the customer can interact easily with the computer system and obtain the fashion mix-and-match recommendation generated by the IPCS. The SDS is the foundation for cross-selling fashion products and the IPCS is the kernel, which evaluates the matching performance of each fashion pair and provides well-matched fashion recommendations to customers.

Table 10.1 The attributes related to fashion mix-and-match and their level of importance

Attribute	Description	Degree of importance
Type	The categories of apparel items, such as skirt, jacket, etc.	*EH*
Colour	The overall harmonization of the combination of colours in creating the total look	*EH*
Size	The size of apparel	*VH*
Length	The length of apparel to create layers	*H*
Texture	The surface appearance of the materials	*H*
Pattern	The arrangement of design on/in the fabric	*M*
Silhouette	The overall outline or couture of the look in presenting the body figure	*H*
Occasion	The appropriateness of dressing in certain situations or conditions, such as formal, casual, etc.	*VH*
Trend	The general directions that govern what is in or out of the fashion trend	*H*

Note: EH, Extremely high; VH, very high; H, high; M, medium.

10.3.1 Overview of the IPCS architecture

Figure 10.4 illustrates the architecture of the IPCS. The IPCS is composed of a rule-based expert system for matching evaluations of product attributes, and a fuzzy screening module for generating final mix-and-match recommendations of fashion product items.

In the rule-based expert system, the fashion designers' experience and rules of thumb for matching fashion products were captured and programmed. The rule-based expert system, including an inference engine, was constructed for evaluating the matching performance of each product attribute and the overall performance of fashion pairs automatically. Since the experience and rules of fashion designers were subjective and involved vague and imprecise information, a fuzzy linguistic rating scale was devised to quantify their opinions. A fuzzy screening technique, called Fashion Matching Satisfaction Index (FMSI), was used to calculate the overall matching performance of each fashion pair. The pairs with the highest FMSIs were used for cross-selling to the customers in the shops. The following section describes the detailed mechanism of the proposed IPCS.

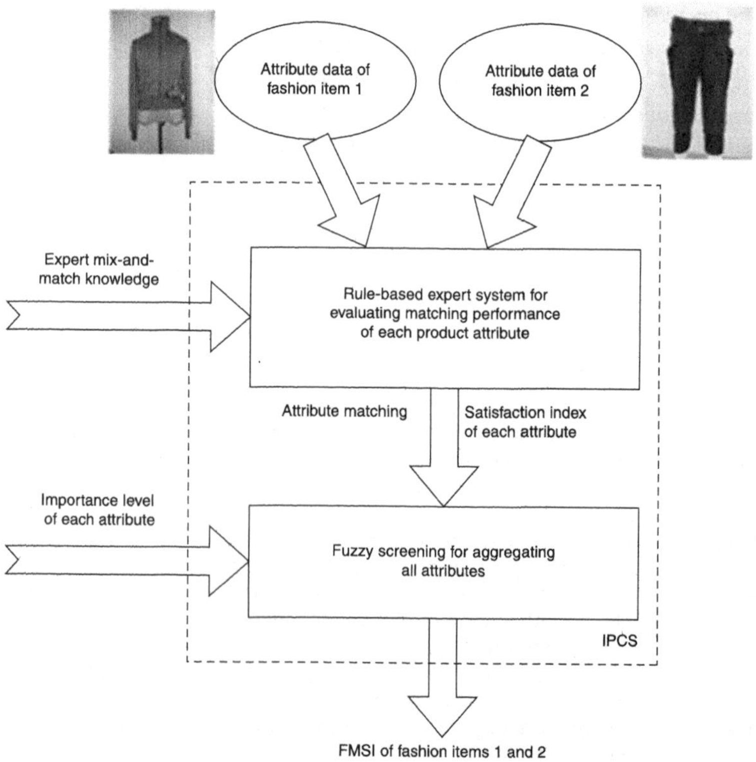

10.4 Architecture of the proposed intelligent product cross-selling system.

10.3.2 Intelligent product cross-selling based on rule-based expert system and fuzzy screening technique

In the IPCS system, there are two phases to evaluate the matching performance of paired merchandise: (1) individual attribute evaluation: assessing the matching performance of each individual attribute, such as colour, pattern and product type, of the paired merchandise (outfit); and (2) overall evaluation: inferring the overall performance of the pair (outfit) based on the evaluation of all attributes. The two phases are implemented by using a rule-based expert system and a fuzzy screening technique, respectively. One core component of the system is using linguistic rating scales to evaluate coordinated outfits, because it is computationally complicated to evaluate paired fashion merchandise with precise data. In this research, two variables are defined as fuzzy linguistic rating scales. One is the attribute matching satisfaction index (AMSI), denoted as $\widetilde{S}$, which is defined for the evaluation of the attribute matching satisfaction degree with respect to each product attribute of fashion pairs, such as 'black' colour of a jacket matching 'grey' colour of a pair of pants. The other one is the importance index of the product attribute denoted as $\widetilde{W}$, which is defined as representing the level of importance of each individual attribute in the matching decision. Each fuzzy rating scale can be represented by a number of linguistic terms, called fuzzy numbers.

Before the IPCS system was constructed, the two variables $\widetilde{S}$ and $\widetilde{W}$ were rated by fashion designers on a scale of 0 to 10. With this numerical scale, $\widetilde{S}$ and $\widetilde{W}$ can be determined by the optimal fuzzy partition using the heuristic cut and trial procedure (Carlsson and Fuller, 1995). Seven fuzzy numbers were used for each fuzzy rating scale of $\widetilde{S}$ and $\widetilde{W}$ and various linguistic terms are defined to represent the rating scales. The linguistic terms of the two fuzzy rating scales with the corresponding fuzzy numbers and membership functions are shown in Table 10.2.

A questionnaire based on the linguistic rating scale (Table 10.2) was then formulated to collect ten fashion designers' opinions about the level of importance of the said nine product attributes (see Table 10.1). Almost all attributes in

Table 10.2 Linguistic terms of fuzzy rating scales with fuzzy number representation

Linguistic terms of the satisfaction degree $\widetilde{S}$	Linguistic terms of the level of importance $\widetilde{W}$	Approximated value of corresponding fuzzy number
Perfect (*P*)	Extremely high (*EH*)	10
Very good (*VG*)	Very high (*VH*)	9
Good (*G*)	High (*H*)	7
Fair (*F*)	Medium (*M*)	5
Lightly bad (*LB*)	Low (*L*)	3
Bad (*B*)	Very low (*VL*)	1
Very bad (*VB*)	None (*N*)	0

Table 10.1 have the importance level of *H* (High) or above except the pattern attribute, rated as *M* (Medium).

The rule-based expert system, as shown in Fig. 10.5, consisting of a knowledge acquisition module, an expert knowledge base and an inference engine, is to compile the attribute data related to apparel and establish rules to conduct attribute evaluation. It has the ability of performing rule extraction, representation and inference. The knowledge acquisition module handles the interaction with experts, converts the knowledge of experts into rules in the format of symbolic representation, and adds or modifies rules for the expert knowledge base. The expert knowledge base is the core component to store the mix-and-match rules. The inference engine is to emulate the decision-making process of fashion designers based on mix-and-match rules stored in the expert knowledge base.

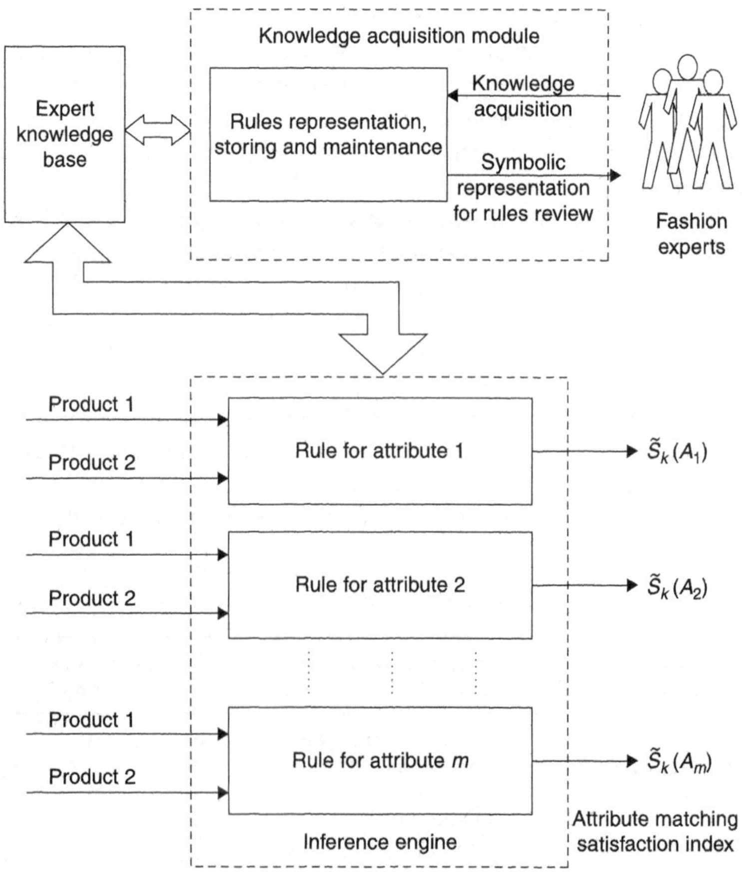

10.5 Rule-based expert system for evaluating the AMSI of each attribute.

The possible values of a product attribute are descriptive words; for example, the values for colour are black, red, and the like. In order to capture the matching rules, the possible values of each attribute should be identified and enumerated. Suppose that a set $A = \{A_1, A_2, \ldots, A_m\}$ denoting the m attributes of apparel is available. All possible values for the A_i $(i = 1, \ldots, m)$ are collected and enumerated as $A_i = \{A_{i1}, A_{i2}, \ldots, A_{ib_i}\}$, where b_i is the number of the enumerated values for A_i. Therefore, there are $b_i \times (b_i - 1)/2$ rules for attribute A_i. The number of rules for all attributes in sum is $\sum_{i=1}^{m} b_i \times (b_i - 1)/2$.

In the inference engine, the rules of fashion matching performance with respect to an AMSI $\tilde{S}$ could be expressed as an IF-THEN rule of the following form.

IF the value of attribute A_i of one fashion item is A_{i1} AND the value of attribute A_i of the other fashion item is A_{i2}, THEN the attribute matching satisfaction index of this paired fashion item in terms of this attribute is $\tilde{S}_k(A_i)$,

where A_{i1}, A_{i2} are the enumerated values of an attribute, $\tilde{S}_k(A_i)$ is one term drawn from $\tilde{S}$ (see Table 10.2), which is the linguistic rating scale for representing the AMSI.

After all the rules have been compiled, the inference engine is used for evaluating the satisfaction degree of each product attribute. The inference engine evaluates the matching performance of one fashion pair based on one individual attribute and then aggregates a total matching performance of all nine attributes using fuzzy screening technique to calculate the FMSI for each fashion pair.

As a large number of possible matches for multiple apparel items exists, detailed, consistent and precise evaluations of all possible apparel coordination are time-consuming and complicated. Fuzzy screening technique is used first to trim down the size of a problem by binding the space of promising alternatives so that unsatisfactory alternatives can be removed before the detailed evaluations, and then to generate mix-and-match recommendations for customers. For a fashion product pair C_j, on the condition that the AMSI and the importance level of each attribute are given, the FMSI of the fashion pair is calculated by the Łukasiewitz implication operator (Carlsson and Fuller, 1995). The detailed procedures of fuzzy screening technique are described as follows.

Let $C_1, C_2 \ldots, C_n$ denote n fashion pairs to be evaluated, and each pair has m attributes, $A_1, \ldots, A_m$, as criteria for calculating FMSI. Based on fashion experts' opinion (Table 10.2), the levels of importance for the attributes $A_1, \ldots, A_m$ are determined as follows:

$$\tilde{W}(A) = \{\tilde{W}_{A_1}, \tilde{W}_{A_2}, \ldots, \tilde{W}_{A_m}\} \qquad [10.1]$$

where $\tilde{W}_{A_j}$ pertains to the set of the linguistic rating scale $\tilde{W} = \{\tilde{W}_1, \ldots, \tilde{W}_t\}$, $\tilde{W}_1 < \ldots < \tilde{W}_t$.

First, for fashion pair C_i $(1 \leq i \leq n)$, utilize the rule-based expert system to evaluate the attribute matching satisfaction index, and obtain a collection of m satisfaction degree index corresponding to m evaluation criteria, that is:

$$\widetilde{S}_i(A) = \{\widetilde{S}_{i1}(A_1), \widetilde{S}_{i2}(A_2), \ldots, \widetilde{S}_{im}(A_m)\} \quad [10.2]$$

where $\widetilde{S}_{ij}(A_j)(1 \leq j \leq m)$ is the matching satisfaction index of attribute A_j, which pertains to the set of the linguistic rating scale $\widetilde{\mathbf{S}} = \{\widetilde{S}_1, \ldots, \widetilde{S}_t\}$, $\widetilde{S}_1 < \ldots < \widetilde{S}_t$ (see Table 10.2).

Then, according to the fuzzy screening approach, the FMSI, χ_i, of fashion pair C_i is calculated using the following equation:

$$\chi_i = Min_{j=1,\ldots m}\{\widetilde{W}_{Aj} \rightarrow \widetilde{S}_{ij}(A_j)\} \quad [10.3]$$

where $Min(\widetilde{S}_i, \widetilde{S}_k) = \widetilde{S}_i$, if $\widetilde{S}_i \leq \widetilde{S}_k$, otherwise $Min(\widetilde{S}_i, \widetilde{S}_k) = \widetilde{S}_k$. $\widetilde{W}_{Aj} \rightarrow \widetilde{S}_{ij}(A_j)$ is defined based on the Łukasiewitz implication operator given by $x \rightarrow y = Min\{1 - x + y, 1\}$, i.e.

$$\widetilde{W}_{Aj} \rightarrow \widetilde{S}_{ij}(A_j) = R\mathrm{Imp}(\widetilde{W}_{Aj}, \widetilde{S}_{ij}(A_j)) = \widetilde{S}_{b(ij)} \quad [10.4]$$

$$b(ij) = \begin{cases} t, & p \leq q \\ t - p + q, & p > q \end{cases} \quad [10.5]$$

where t is the number of the linguistic terms, $p(1 \leq p \leq t)$ is the index of $\widetilde{W}_{A_j}$ in $\widetilde{\mathbf{W}}$ and $q(1 \leq q \leq t)$ is the index of $\widetilde{S}_{ij}(A_j)$ in $\widetilde{\mathbf{S}}$.

Finally, after the FMSIs of all fashion pairs have been calculated using the above method, screen out the fashion pair for which FMSI, χ_i, is equal to or greater than the predefined minimum satisfaction degree, $\widetilde{S}^*$, and recommend it to the customer.

10.3.3 Validation on the IPCS for mix-and-match

To validate the performance of the proposed IPCS system on matching recommendations for cross-selling in a real-life environment, 48 fashion items of a fashion retailer, including a total of 538 expert rules, were used for experimental testing. These samples of fashion items belong to five product types, including dress, jacket, skirt, top and trousers. The distribution of apparel items in each product type and the potential 829 matching pairs are listed in Table 10.3.

To validate the performance of the system, another survey was conducted to collect the matching performance of these 829 pairs rated by 10 fashion designers.

Table 10.3 The number of fashion items in each type and their potential matching pairs

Total samples	The number of apparel items belonging to each type					Potential matching pairs
	Dress	Jacket	Skirt	Top	Trousers	
48	2	11	3	16	16	829

Table 10.4 Fashion matching results generated by IPCS system

	The FMSI level							Total
	P	*VG*	*G*	*F*	*LB*	*B*	*VB*	
Number of pairs	0	54	32	64	171	303	205	829
Ratio (%)	0	6.51	3.86	7.72	20.63	36.55	24.73	100

Notes: *P*, Perfect; *VG*, Very good; *G*, Good; *F*, Fair; *LB*, Lightly bad; *B*, Bad; *VB*, Very bad.

We divided the 829 pairs into seven groups (rated using a seven-level scale) on the basis of their FMSI produced by the program. Table 10.4 indicates the results of the mix-and-match recommendations generated by the IPCS system. The number of pairs in the *P* (*Perfect*) level was zero, which means that the matching rules in the expert system for *perfect* are very hard to meet. The numbers of pairs in the levels of LB, B and VB were 171 (20.63%), 303 (36.55%) and 205 (24.73%) respectively.

Each group was assigned to two fashion designers for the evaluation. A detailed comparison between the results generated by the proposed system and those provided by the fashion designers is summarized in Table 10.5.

In Table 10.5, it can be seen that the lowest percentage of the correct recommendations conducted by the system was 81.25 and the overall percentage was 94.09, indicating a high level of system accuracy meeting the practical requirements of the fashion retailer.

It can be seen from Table 10.6 that the performance of the system is very satisfactory. The system could achieve 87.04%, 91.86% and 99.33% accuracy

Table 10.5 Comparison between the result advised by the IPCS system and the evaluation result provided by the fashion designers

	The FMSI level						Total
	VG	*G*	*F*	*LB*	*B*	*VB*	
Expert system	54	32	64	171	303	205	829
Same result[a]	45	26	60	160	289	200	780
Designers							
Different result[b]	9	6	4	11	14	5	49
Correct ratio of the expert system (%)	83.33	81.25	93.75	93.57	95.38	97.56	94.09

Notes: [a]*Same result* means that the FMSI index of the pair evaluated by the fashion designers is same as the results generated by the IPCS system.

[b]*Different result* means that the FMSI index of the pair evaluated by the fashion designers is different from the results generated by the IPCS system.

P, Perfect; *VG*, Very good; *G*, Good; *F*, Fair; *LB*, Lightly bad; *B*, Bad; *VB*, Very bad.

Table 10.6 The screening performance of the IPCS system at the screening levels of VG, G and F

		The screening level S^*		
		VG	*G*	*F*
Designers	Recommended pairs	50	82	150
	Recommended pairs	54	86	150
IPCS System	Correct recommended pairs (%)	47 (87.04)	79 (91.86)	149 (99.33)
	Missed recommended pairs (%)	3 (5.56)	3 (3.49)	1 (0.67)
	Extra recommended pairs (%)	7 (12.96)	7 (8.14)	1 (0.67)

Notes: *VG*, Very good; *G*, Good; *F*, Fair.

when the minimum level of recommendation performance was set at level *VG*, *G* and *F* respectively. The numbers of pairs recommended by the fashion designers which were not recommended by the proposed system, called 'missed pairs', were only three, three and one, respectively, at three different screening levels, while the number of pairs recommended by the expert system which were not recommended by the fashion designers, called 'extra pairs', were seven, seven and one, respectively at three screening levels. The apparel pairs with very good ratings were exported to the product database of the SDS for cross-selling.

10.4 Implementation of the RFID-enabled SDS and IPCS

Based on the operation logic of the system, the layered technique for software design was employed (Seiter *et al.*, 2000) to develop the system architecture, in which there are three layers: user interface layer, application logic layer and data layer. The user interface layer receives commands from the users, transfers them to the application logic layer and returns results to the users. The application logic layer is composed of multiple logic processing functions. The object-oriented technique is employed and logic functions are developed module by module. The data layer, where there is a database management system using SQL Server, is responsible for data reading and writing.

Based on the theoretical architectures shown in Fig. 10.2 and 10.4, the SDS and the IPCS were developed and implemented in a fashion retailing company which has nine chain stores in Hong Kong. The product information and the subjective evaluation information of fashion items were input into the system via the back-end sub-system. Figure 10.6(a) and 10.6(b) show the interfaces of involving the product information, that is, attributes or features with the corresponding level of importance. Users can use this interface to input product features like colour, pattern, silhouette, and so on with their corresponding level of importance, such as extremely high, very high, and so on, which should be considered for evaluating the matching performance of fashion product items. Figure 10.6(c) is the interface to store the acquired knowledge and rules of fashion product mix-and-match using the fuzzy screening approach described in Section 10.3.2. Figure 10.6(d) is the interface for the user to input the product attributes of the fashion merchandise

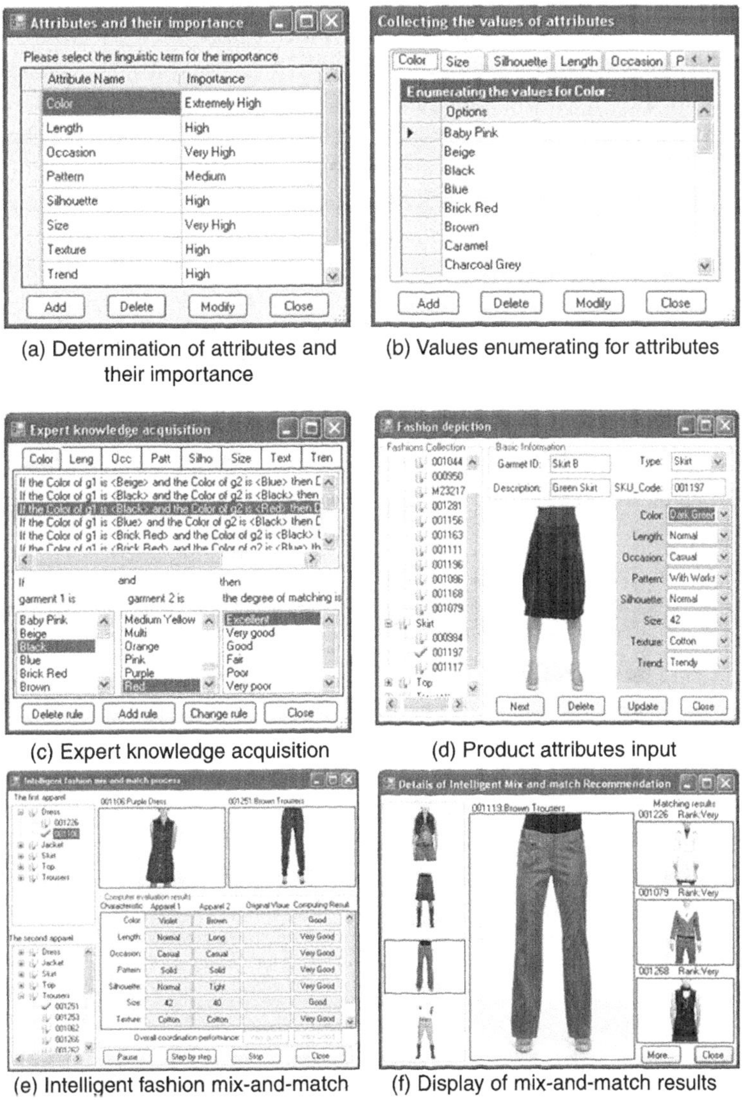

(a) Determination of attributes and their importance

(b) Values enumerating for attributes

(c) Expert knowledge acquisition

(d) Product attributes input

(e) Intelligent fashion mix-and-match

(f) Display of mix-and-match results

10.6 The client interfaces of the intelligent product cross-selling system. (a) Determination of attributes and their importance. (b) Value enumeration for attributes. (c) Expert knowledge acquisition. (d) Product attributes input. (e) Intelligent fashion mix-and-match. (f) Display of mix-and-match results.

which will be paired for matching performance evaluation. Based on the above input parameters, the product items for cross-selling can be generated automatically. In Fig. 10.6(e), a long vest in brown matched with a pair of pants in brown is automatically under evaluation by the system. The matching performance result of each attribute, such as colour, length, and so on, as well as overall matching performance, is shown in this figure. Figure 10.6(f) illustrates the recommended paired merchandise which can be used for cross-selling. The smart dressing server receives the updated mix-and-match recommendations generated from the IPCS, and these recommendations are then transmitted to the client PC workstations for presenting to the customers on the retail shop floor.

In Fig. 10.7, a pink jacket is selected and brought by a customer to the fitting room. As the jacket has a RFID tag attached, which is identified by the RFID-enabled SDS, a pair of pants is immediately recommended by the IPCS through a LCD monitor. To make the paired apparel more attractive to the customers, the fashion retailing company utilizes the IPCS by obtaining the matching result first and then arranging for a fashion model to dress up in the recommended pair for a photo-shoot. Figure 10.8 illustrates the mix-and-match recommendations generated by the IPCS through the smart fitting room and smart dressing mirror in a fashion chain store in Hong Kong. Figure 10.9 depicts a recently developed dressing mirror which can be movable, such that no renovation is required to embed the RFID antennas and accessories in the retail store.

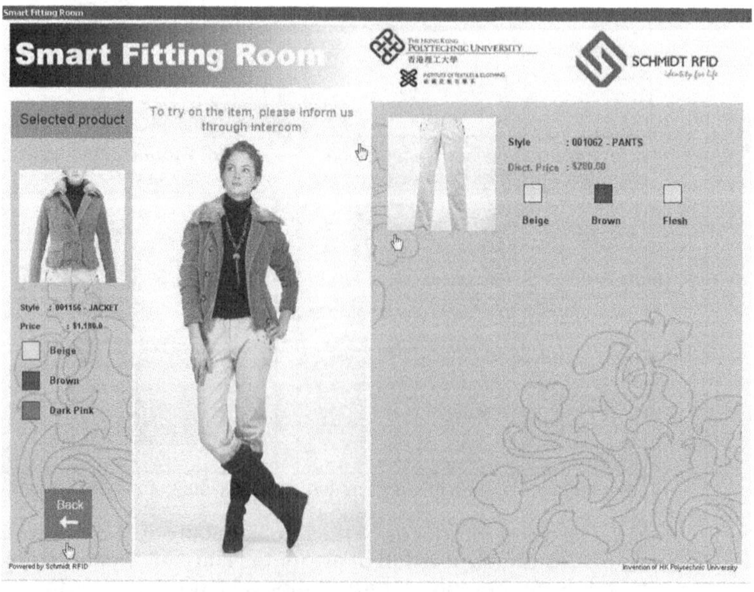

10.7 Mix-and-match recommendations in the fitting room by the smart dressing system.

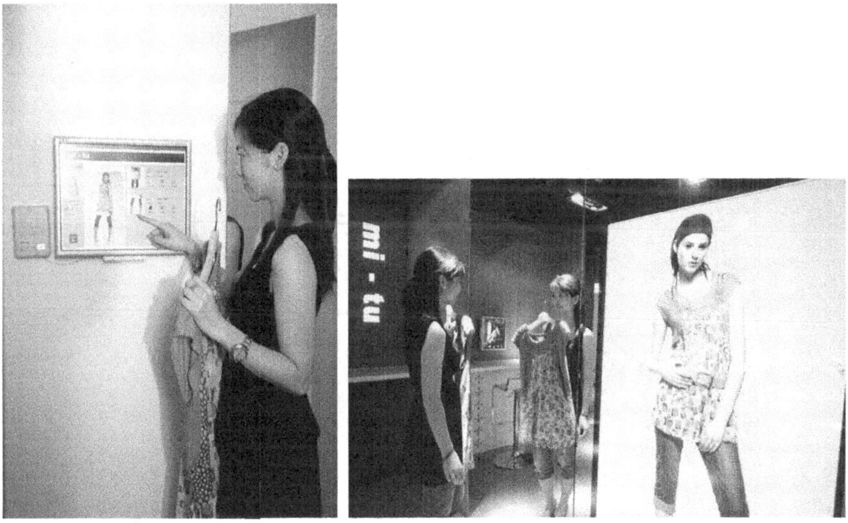

(a) (b)

10.8 Smart fitting room and smart dressing mirror integrated with the proposed IPCS in a fashon chain store in Hong Kong. (a) Smart fitting room. (b) Smart dressing mirror.

10.5 Evaluation of the RFID-enabled SDS

The RFID-enabled SDS was received by the fashion retail sector and developers after being publicized by the media, and the system was implemented in two of the stores of a fashion retailing company that runs nine chain stores located in major shopping malls in Hong Kong. In the stores, the fashion merchandise was tagged with RFID, and one ordinary dressing mirror and two out of the four fitting rooms were converted into smart devices using the RFID technology integrated with an IPCS for offering mix-and-match recommendations to customers.

Although the company reported that there was an improvement in sales of about 20% a few months after the installation, it is imperative to understand the contribution of the system towards the overall sales. In order to identify the sales improvement due to the cross-selling function of the system, three-month point-of-sale (POS) data after the installation were collected to evaluate the impact of the system on sales performance. As customers were not interviewed or asked whether or not the purchase was influenced by the system, an alternative approach was adopted: POS data were screened and those data recommended by the system for mixing and matching the detected items by the antenna within 30 minutes were counted as a successful application of the system. In Fig. 10.10, the total sales (ordinary sales and those initiated by the system) of the first three months after the installation are shown. The blue curve indicates the weekly change in total sales quantity and the pink curve provides the sold items which

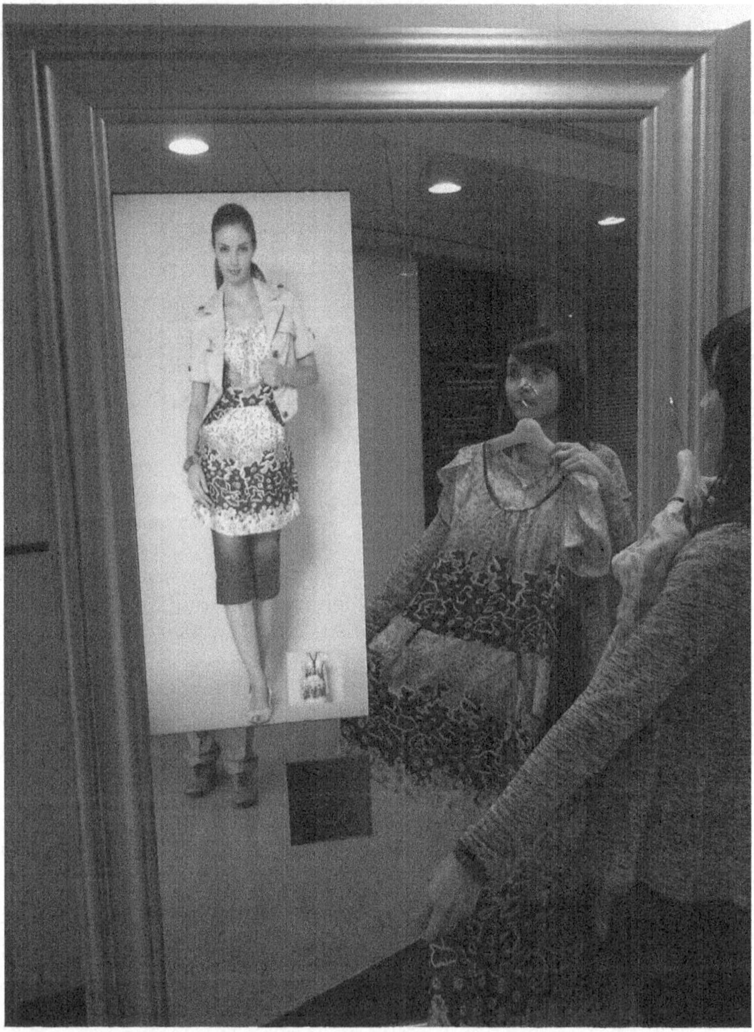

10.9 A movable smart dressing mirror.

were detected within the 30-minute limit. On average, the total sales remain more or less the same, but the sales due to the system (pink curve) rise in the last two months. This rise is shown more clearly in Fig. 10.11; it illustrates the proportion of the total sales due to the cross-selling function embedded in the dressing mirror and two fitting rooms of the system. In Fig. 10.11, there are two trend lines showing a two-stage rise in the system contributing to the total sales: in the initial period (i.e. the first month after system installation) about 11% of the total sales were due to the system, while in the last two months this contribution improved to over 20%.

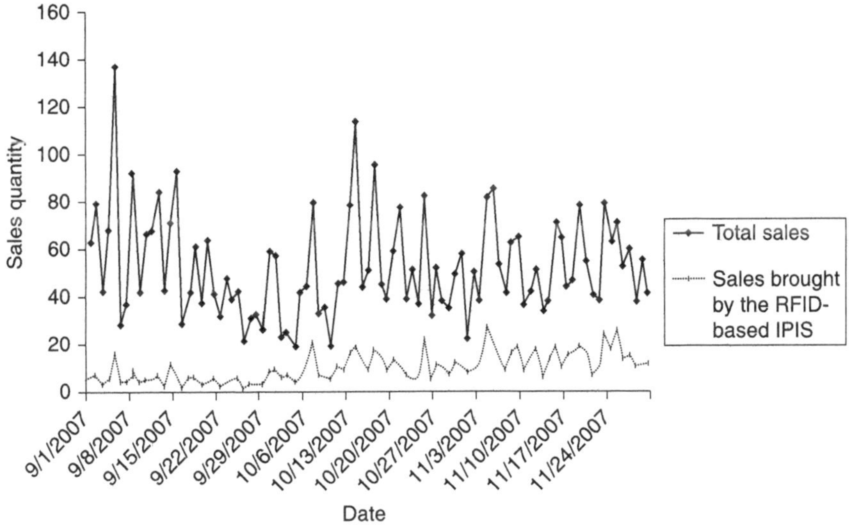

10.10 Comparison of the total sales with sales due to the installation of the RFID-based IPCS.

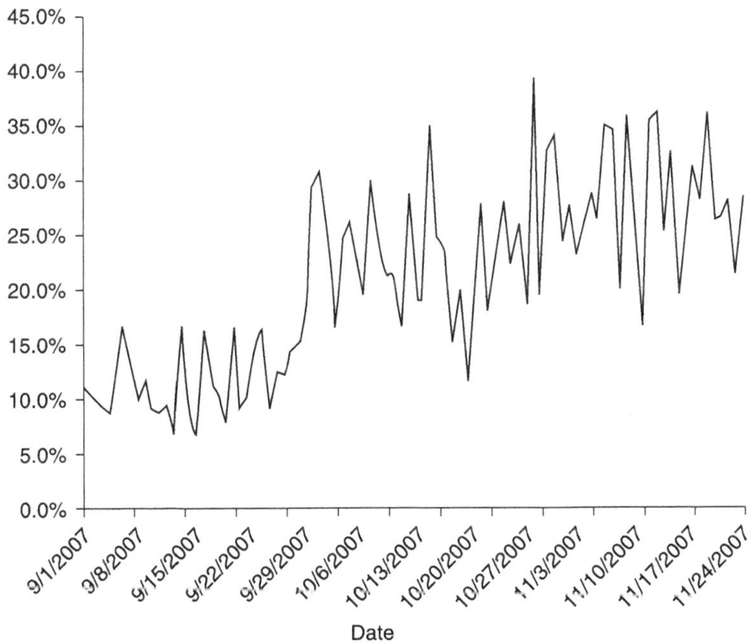

10.11 Proportion of the total sales due to the RFID-based IPCS.

The difference is due to the training of the sales staff. Although initial training was provided to all staff during the installation and the system was allowed to run for one month, in on-site observations it was found that few customers utilized the system and explored further details of the products, and sales staff were reluctant to encourage customers to use the system for cross-selling. It seems that they were not confident enough to rely on the technology for customer service. Management offered further training to familiarize the staff with the potential of the system and help them understand that the system was intended to assist their work rather than making the staff redundant. There was an obvious sales improvement, in which more than 20% of sales were due to the system.

As the cross-selling system is embedded in both the dressing mirror and the fitting rooms, it is also important to identify how each contributes to the sales individually. Figure 10.12 illustrates the breakdown of the sales quantities caused by the two fitting rooms and the dressing mirror as a result of the use of IPCS. In the first months, it was found that the sales generated by the dressing mirror were greater than those due to the fitting rooms. This is because of the fact that the human-sized visual display incorporated into the dressing mirror was more impressive to the customers; the cross-selling recommendations were easily recognized without the assistance of the sales staff. Unlike the dressing mirror, the visual display through LCD monitors in the fitting rooms was comparatively smaller, and customers did not feel compelled to use them if they were not encouraged and introduced by the sales staff.

After retraining had been provided to the sales staff about the importance of letting the customers know the mix-and-match recommendations from the fitting

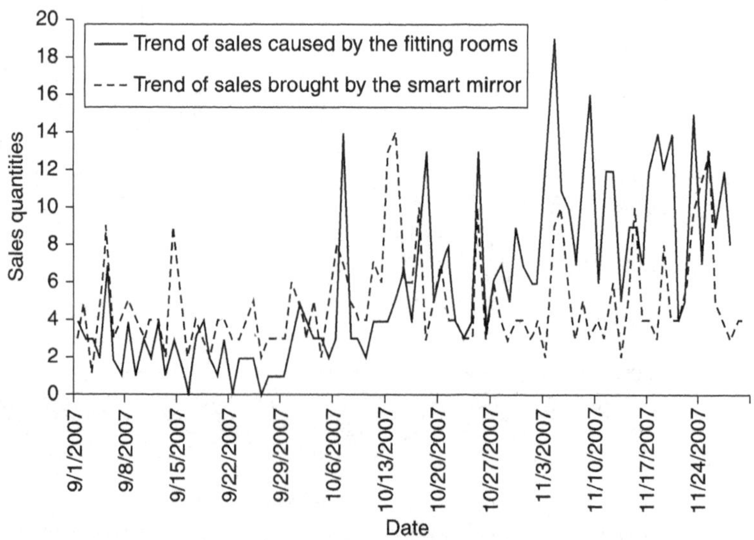

10.12 Trend of sales quantities due to the two fitting rooms and the dressing mirror with embedded RFID-based IPCS.

rooms, the sales based on the fitting rooms were greater than those based on the dressing mirror. It was found that the effectiveness and practicality of the system were also determined by the way in which the sales staff made use of the system in the cross-selling activities. When the sales staff perceive the system as their helping hands and use it effectively, they can recommend customers to try on more garments based on their selected items. When the research was carried out, there were a total of five dressing mirrors and four fitting rooms in each store, but the system had only been installed in one mirror and two fitting rooms. It is envisaged that more sales could result if all of them were equipped with the proposed system.

10.6 Assessing the use of RFID technology in fashion retailing

The more conventional use of RFID technologies is in the identification of products in logistics operations; this research, however, presented the use of RFID in cross-selling and up-selling of fashion items. This new approach can bring many benefits to fashion retailers in terms of business performance and customer services.

10.6.1 Early detection of customers' preference

Metropolitan fashion retailers usually know little about their customers in the conventional retailing process. This process usually comprises the following stages: 'walk-in', 'browse', 'fit' and 'go'. Usually the only piece of information a fashion retailer can collect from customers is their transaction and credit card details before customers 'go' out of the stores. With so little information to rely on, it is difficult for retailers to enhance their customer service/relationship. The SDS offers service to customers at the earlier stages of 'browse' and 'fit', even before a transaction is actualized. The very actions of selecting of one or several garments during the 'browse' (or selection) stage will have actually 'revealed' the preference of a customer. The SDS system allows the retailer to meet this immediate demand. A customer may be attracted to a style by its colour, fabric texture or the look. By the time the customer removes the item from a store rack and brings it to a dressing mirror for assessing or fitting, the mirror detects the items and shows how the style is dressed up in a human-sized display; it also recommends styles which can mix and match with the one which the customer is holding. Feedback from the stores using the system showed that customers bought not only their selected items but also the other items displayed and cross-sold on the screen.

10.6.2 Enriching customers' in-store purchase experience without changing the fitting process

The SDS system makes the fitting process more natural because it uses RFID technologies composed predominantly of ultra-high frequency (UHF) tags and readers. These enable the detection of the selected items at a distance and it is not necessary to bring the clothing item close to any reader. Generally the signals, unlike using a barcode system for which the line of sight is required, can be read during the try-on process. There is no change in the way in which a customer fits a piece of clothing, but the new approach allows retailers to have a computerized stylist advising their customers to mix and match.

10.6.3 Cross-selling and up-selling can be made possible using the smart fitting rooms

Customers who use the fitting rooms have been attracted by their selections (e.g., colours, fabric, style, etc.) and they want to determine whether or not they fit well into those outfits. Detailed product mix-and-match information together with prices and discounts can be offered to the customers at this stage. The smart fitting room is equipped with the same technology as the smart fitting mirror, but, in order to adapt to the small environment of a fitting room, the human-size display is replaced by a smaller interactive LCD touch-screen display (which is about the size of a desktop display). Thumbnail figures of the clothing items brought inside the fitting room are detected and shown on the screen. When the customer touches appropriate figures, the system gives further product details, including available colours, sizes, prices, and even promotions and discounts. At the same time, the screen recommends other styles that can go with the selected item in the same way as the smart dressing mirror outside.

10.6.4 New fitting and transaction experience

The system synchronizes with the system at the sales counter; staff can serve customers with matching clothing which a customer did not take into the fitting room in the first place. The customer inside a fitting room can avoid the hassle of putting on his/her own clothes and looking for the matching items from the store racks. In the final transaction stage, fashion retailers could utilize the RFID tags to replace barcodes at the till to generate invoices and finalize fund transfers. This could reduce the time customers wait in a queue for payment.

10.6.5 Standardized cross-selling and up-selling approach

The output of this research, SDS and IPCS, has enabled a more standardized approach in cross-selling and up-selling of fashion: the pre-determined ideas of the company's buyers or designers on how one fashion item matches with another or how several items are sold as coordinates can be conveyed to sales staff, who are in the first line for offering services, including styling advice, to customers. Customers may turn away due to such reasons as poor service or training of the sales staff; with the system, it would be possible to ensure that cross-selling and up-selling are executed as the original plans.

10.7 Conclusions

This chapter has presented the architecture of an intelligent system integrated with RFID technology for cross-selling activities in the fashion retail business. Two systems have been developed and applied in real-life situations. The first system is the Smart Dressing System (SDS), enabled by RFID technologies, which performs several functions, including identifying product information, collecting customers' in-store preferences, and offering cross-selling and up-selling (mix-and-match) recommendations. The second system is a hybrid intelligent system, called IPCS, developed to match customers' selections with other fashion items for mix-and-match purposes.

The success of the cross-selling capability of this new dress fitting system relies heavily on the back-end, which is a support incorporating not only the hardware but also the management involved in putting the right styles together based on fashion design/styling expertise and subsequent modelling and photo-shoots. With the collaboration of the case company and fashion design experts in the authors' institution, this research developed the IPCS, which is a system incorporating expert knowledge to carry out initial mix-and-match of the items before a season starts. The IPCS enables the design/styling team to focus on final judging and fine-tuning the mix-and-match outcomes, shortening the time needed for the initial matching. Utilizing product information to implement cross-selling is a multi-criteria decision making (MCDM) problem. However, the decision-making process for fashion mix-and-match involves various imprecise variables, such as the matching satisfaction levels of different products and the level of importance of each attribute, which cannot be solved directly by the ordinary rule-based expert systems that cannot deal with problems with uncertain, vague and imprecise information. The attributes of apparel items are categorical but the values of the attributes are literal. For example, the values for colour may be black, red, white, and the like. With the 'IF-THEN' rules base of the inference engine, the IPCS, combining fuzzy screening technique, specifically handles vague and imprecise information in the process of fashion mix-and-match. This application of the knowledge-based attribute evaluation expert system provides an innovative approach to processing linguistic information for similar decision-making problems.

After roll-out of the first prototype, further enhancement and commercialization have been licensed to developers. This gives room for the researchers of this chapter to focus on the back-end development and the intelligence part of the system. The future direction will focus on improving the functionalities of the IPCS. Currently, it is able to match any selected items with all the available items in a store and produce a score/index for each pair. In a real-life situation, coordinating several items to create a total look is common; thus an important research area is to explore the possibility of enhancing the ability of the inference engine to evaluate three or more items together.

Research can also be extended to incorporate the analysis of consumer buying behaviour and business intelligence based on the captured data. Fashion items which have been tried on most or least can be identified and the data can be compared with the sales of these items for further analysis. The data obtained can be used to improve a number of analyses, including customer preferences and visual merchandising performance.

10.8 Acknowledgement

The work described in this chapter was fully supported by a grant from the Research Grants Council of the Hong Kong Special Administrative Region, China (Project No. PolyU 5226/08E).

10.9 Notes

1 Cross-selling refers to selling of additional items to a customer in relation to the item(s) that the customer has purchased.

2 Up-selling is a process through which a customer is persuaded (usually by a salesman) to purchase an upgrade of the item which he/she intends to purchase.

3 The middleware is used to allow seamless connections of different kinds of antennas and readers produced by different manufacturers.

10.10 References

Angeles, R., 2005. Rfid technologies: Supply-chain applications and implementation issues. *Information Systems Management* 22(1), 51–65.

Becker, J., Vilkov, L., Wei, B. and Winkelmann, A., 2010. A model based approach for calculating the process driven business value of RFID investments. *International Journal of Production Economics* 127(2), 358–371.

Benbernou, R. and Warwick, K., 2007. year fuzzy multi-criteria decision approach for enhanced auto-tracking of seismic events, *IEEE International Conference on Signal Processing and Communications* (ICSPC 2007), pp. 1331–1334.

Beynon, M., Cosker, D. and Marshall, D., 2001. An expert system for multi-criteria decision making using Dempster Shafer theory. *Expert Systems with Applications* 20(4), 357–367.

Bose, I. and Mahapatra, R., 2001. Business data mining – a machine learning perspective. *Information and Management* 39(3), 211–225.

Brown, I. and Russell, J., 2007. Radio frequency identification technology: An exploratory study on adoption in the South African retail sector. *International Journal of Information Management* 27(4), 250–265.

Cakici, O.E., Groenevelt, H. and Seidmann, A., 2011. Using RFID for the management of pharmaceutical inventory – system optimization and shrinkage control. *Decision Support Systems* doi: DOI: 10.1016/j.dss.2011.02.003.

Carlsson, C. and Fuller, R., 1995. On fuzzy screening system, *Proceedings of EUFIT' 95 Conference*. Aachen: Verlag Mainz, Aachen, Germany.

Chen, Y., Huang, T. and Chang, S., 2008. A novel approach for discovering retail knowledge with price information from transaction databases. *Expert Systems with Applications* 34(4), 2350–2359.

Cohen, M., 2004. Exploiting response models – optimizing cross-sell and up-sell opportunities in banking. *Information Systems* 29(4), 327–341.

Gass, S., 2005. Model world: The great debate – MAUT versus AHP. *Interfaces* 35, 308–312.

Guo, Z.X., Wong, W.K., Leung, S.Y.S. and Fan, J.T., 2009. Intelligent production control decision support system for flexible assembly lines. *Expert Systems with Applications* 36(3), 4268–4277.

Holmstrom, J., Framling, K. and Ala-Risku, T., 2010. The uses of tracking in operations management: Synthesis of a research program. *International Journal of Production Economics* 126(2), 267–275.

Hui, S.C. and Jha, G., 2000. Data mining for customer service support. *Information and Management* 38(1), 1–13.

Jones, P., Clarke-Hill, C., Hillier, D. and Comfort, D., 2005. The benefits, challenges and impacts of radio frequency identification technology (RFID) for retailers in the UK. *Marketing Intelligence and Planning* 23(4), 395–402.

Kamakura, W., Wedel, M., de Rosa, F. and Mazzon, J., 2003. Cross-selling through database marketing: A mixed data factor analyser for data augmentation and prediction. *International Journal of Research in Marketing* 20, 45–65.

Khandelwal, N., Krueger, K., Berger, B., Carpenter, M. and Butz, B., 2006. Developing hospice drug formulary using Multi-Attribute Utility Theory (MAUT) method and the evaluation of their economic impact. *Value in Health* 9(6), A356–A357.

Lee, I. and Lee, B.-C., 2010. An investment evaluation of supply chain RFID technologies: A normative modeling approach. *International Journal of Production Economics* 125(2), 313–323.

Lefebvre, L.A., Lefebvre, É., Bendavid, Y., Wamba, S.F. and Boeck, H., 2007. The potential of RFID in warehousing activities in a retail industry supply chain. *Journal on Chain and Network Science* 5(2), 101–110.

Lin, C. and Hong, C., 2008. Using customer knowledge in designing electronic catalog. *Expert Systems with Applications* 34(1), 119–127.

Lin, Q., Chen, Y., Chen, J. and Chen, Y., 2003. Mining inter-organizational retailing knowledge for an alliance formed by competitive firms. *Information and Management* 40(5), 431–442.

Loeb, W.F., 2003. Better customer service through technology. *Stores* 85, 104.

Nasirin, S. and Birks, D., 2003. DSS implementation in the UK retail organisations: A GIS perspective. *Information and Management* 40(4), 325–336.

Padmanabhan, B. and Tuzhilin, A., 1999. Unexpectedness as a measure of interestingness in knowledge discovery. *Decision Support Systems* 27(3), 303–318.

Pei, J. and Klabjan, D., 2010. Inventory control in serial systems under radio frequency identification. *International Journal of Production Economics* 123(1), 118–136.

Pictet, J. and Bollinger, D., 2008. Extended use of the cards procedure as a simple elicitation technique for MAVT. Application to public procurement in Switzerland. *European Journal of Operational Research* 185(3), 1300–1307.

RFID Journal, 2002. Learning from Prada. http://www.rfidjournal.com/article/view/425 (accessed 24 June 2002).

Rohacova, I. and Markova, Z., 2009. The Analysis of AHP method and its potential use in logistics. *ACTA Montanistica Slovaca* 14(1), 103–112.

Sarac, A., Absi, N. and Dauzere-Peres, S., 2010. A literature review on the impact of RFID technologies on supply chain management. *International Journal of Production Economics* 128(1), 77–95.

Seiter, L., Mezini, M. and Lieberherr, K., 2000. Dynamic component gluing, in: Czarnecki, K., Eisenecker, K. and Eisenecker, U. (Eds.), *Generative and Component-Based Software Engineering: First International Symposium, GCSE'99*. Berlin Heidel-berg: Springer, Erfurt, Germany, pp. 134–146.

Simpson, L., 1996. Do decision makers know what they prefer? MAVT and ELECTRE II. *Journal of The Operational Research Society* 47(7), 919–929.

Tayma, J.F. and Pol, L., 1995. Retail site selection and geographic information systems. *Journal of Applied Business Research* 11, 46–54.

Tong, R., 1982. Fuzzy-sets and multi-criteria decision-making. *Human Systems Management* 3, 266–268.

Tsiporkova, E. and Boeva, V., 2006. Multi-step ranking of alternatives in a multi-criteria and multi-expert decision making environment. *Information Sciences* 176(18), 2673–2697.

Wamba, S., Lefebvre, L., Bendavid, Y. and Lefebvre, E., 2008. Exploring the impact of RFID technology and the EPC network on mobile B2B eCommerce: A case study in the retail industry. *International Journal of Production Economics* 112(2), 614–629.

Yin, S.Y.L., Tserng, H.P., Wang, J.C. and Tsai, S.C., 2009. Developing a precast production management system using RFID technology. *Automation in Construction* 18(5), 677–691.

Zadeh, L.A., 1965. Fuzzy Sets. *Information and Control* 8, 338–353.

Index

activation function, 28
adaptive evolution strategies, 86, 87
adaptive resonance theory (ART2), 47
analytic hierarchy process (AHP), 45
annual forecasting, 188–9
  Categories 2–4 comparison, 189
  Category 1 vs City 1, 189
  Cities 2–4 comparison, 189
  result generated by proposed model (Category 1 and City 1), 188
apparel management
  artificial intelligence techniques, 13–39
    evolutionary optimisation techniques, 21–6
    feedforward neural network (FNN), 26–32
    fuzzy logic, 32–8
    overview, 13–17
    rule-based expert systems, 17–21
apparel manufacturing plant
  location selection using neural networks, 41–54
    classification methods using artificial neural network, 42–3
    classification using supervised ANN, 49–52
    classification using unsupervised ANN, 47–9
    decision models classification for clothing plants location, 43–7
    performance of BP with different number of hidden neurons, 54
    performance of LVQ with different number of hidden neurons, 54
apparel production
  cut order planning (COP) optimisation using evolutionary strategies, 81–105
    best fitness generated by decision-making model using (100+100) adaptive ESs, 104
    best fitness generated by decision-making model using (1000+1000) adaptive ESs, 105
    decision-making model formulation, 87–90
    genetic optimisation, 90–5
    genetic optimisation model sample, 95–100
    industrial practice using commercial software, 103
    overview, 81–7
  fabric spreading and cutting schedules by genetic algorithms and fuzzy set theory, 132–50
    case studies using real production data, 142–9
    genetic optimisation of fabric scheduling, 138–42
    problem formulation in fabric-cutting operations, 135–8
  genetic algorithms, 153–67
    experimental results, 163–6
    problem formulation in sewing operations, 155–6
    production line balancing, 156–63
  marker planning optimisation using evolutionary strategies and neural network, 106–29
    packing method for optimised marker packing, 109–16
    performance evaluation experiments, 123–8
  order planning scheduling using genetic algorithms, 55–80
    experiment, 66–74
    Gantt charts, 77–80
    nomenclature, 76
    order scheduling, 61–6
    problem formulation, 57–9
    uncertain completion and start times, 59–61
apparel supply chain
  cutting room, 3–9
  key decision points, 1–12
  plant locations selection, 1–2
  production scheduling and assembly line balancing control, 2–3
  retailing, 10–12
ARIMA models, 172
artificial intelligence (AI)
  apparel management applications, 13–39

evolutionary optimisation techniques, 21–6
feedforward neural network (FNN), 26–32
fuzzy logic, 32–8
overview, 13–17
definition, 13–14
techniques classification, 14–17
uses, 14
rule-based expert system, 17–21
artificial neural network (ANN), 16
classification methods, 42–3
supervised classification, 49–52
unsupervised classification, 47–9
classification results of seven sites of five cases, 49
classification results using ART2, 49
five cases of weights of four factors, 48
resultant suitability indices of the five cases, 48
tentative scores for seven sites, 48
assembly line balancing control, 3
assembly sewing process, 3
attribute matching satisfaction index (AMSI), 207
autoregressive (AR) model, 172

backpropagation (BP) NN model, 172
backpropagation network, 28–9, 42–3, 49–50
correct classification percentage, 50
backward chaining, 20–1
biased roulette wheel scheme, 119
binary string
encoding method, 91–2
configuration for the cut order planning, 92
total number of combinations in two different encoding methods, 92

case-based reasoning system, 15
case studies
production data, 142–9
detailed job characteristic, 143
fuzzy due times of production order (Case A), 144
fuzzy due times of production order (Case B), 145
genetic optimisation performance of case A, 148
genetic optimisation performance of case B, 149
industrial and genetically optimised production schedule (Case A), 146
industrial and genetically optimised production schedule (Case B), 147
industrial practice vs genetically optimised results, 148
makespan time comparison, 148
Matlab genetic optimisation program, 145
chromosome syntax, 157–8
clothing plant
classifying decision models for location, 43–7
learning process of artificial neural network, 45
site selection, 44
coding *see* genetic representation
completion time, 60
computerised cutting system, 8
cross-selling, 11–12
crossover operation, 64–5
uniform-order crossover operator, 65
customer order, 6, 84, 88
cut order planning (COP), 3–7, 81–5
apparel production using evolutionary strategies, 81–105
best fitness generated by decision-making model using (100+100) adaptive ESs, 104
best fitness generated by decision-making model using (1000+1000) adaptive ESs, 105
decision-making model formulation, 87–90
genetic optimisation, 90–5
genetic optimisation model sample, 95–100
industrial practice using commercial software, 103
overview, 81–7
fabric lay composed of fabric plies after spreading, 6, 84
marker paper, 5, 83
marker planning process using commercial computing software, 83
marker planning using commercial computing software, 5
workflow activities of a fabric-cutting department, 82
workflow of activities of a fabric-cutting department, 4
cutting room, 3–9
cutting scheduling, 8–9
operating procedures of a computerised cutting system, 9

data pre-processing, 174–5
detecting and removing outliers, 175
interpolating missing data, 175
normalisation and de-normalisation, 175
database, 18
decision-making model, 87–90
defuzzification, 36–7
discrete recombination operator, 119–20
illustration, 120

early/tardy (E/T) scheduling, 133
elitism, 162–3
evolution, 163
evolution strategy (ES), 24–5
best fitness generated by decision-making model using (100+100) adaptive ESs, 104

best fitness generated by decision-making model using (1000+1000) adaptive ESs, 105
cut order planning (COP) optimisation in apparel production, 81–105
decision-making model formulation, 87–90
flowchart, 24
genetic optimisation, 90–5
genetic optimisation model sample, 95–100
industrial practice using commercial software, 103
marker planning optimisation in apparel production, 106–29, 116–22
chromosome structure, 119
mutation operation, 121–2
population size of parents and offspring, 117
recombination operation, 119–21
selection operation, 119
structure of individuals, 118–19
overview, 81–7
packing method for optimised marker packing, 109–16
performance evaluation experiments, 123–8
best packing pattern generated by the GA+HP approach, 126
best packing pattern generated by the proposed approach, 125
illustrative data sets, 123
method comparison, 128
off-line performance by the proposed approach *vs.* genetic algorithm, 124
packing pattern derived from the marker planner, 127
results of the six packed stock sheets, 124
evolutionary algorithm (EA), 86–7, 112, 118
evolutionary computation, 15–16
evolutionary NN (ENN) model, 171
evolutionary optimisation technique, 21–6
evolution strategy (ES), 24–5
genetic algorithm (GA), 22–3
harmony search (HS), 25–6
seeking mechanism, 21–2
flowchart, 22
exchange mutation operator, 121
expert system, 15, 172
explanation facility, 18
exponential smoothing models, 172
extreme learning machine (ELM), 29–30, 173, 177
intelligent sales forecasting for fashion retailing, 170–94
assessing forecasting performance, 190–3
evaluating model performance with real sales data, 180–2
experimental results and analysis, 182–9
hybrid intelligent model for medium-term fashion, 174–9
fabric cutting
schedule in apparel production by genetic algorithms and fuzzy set theory, 132–50
case studies using real production data, 142–9
fuzzy scheduling, 134–5
genetic optimisation of fabric scheduling, 138–42
JIT scheduling, 132–3
problem formulation in fabric-cutting operations, 135–8
fabric lay dimension, 6
fabric scheduling, 138–42
fitness evaluation, 139–40
degree of satisfaction evaluation, 140
genetic procedures, 140–2
inversion mutation, 141
methodology outline, 142
uniform order-based crossover, 141
individual representation, 138–9
chromosome representation, 139
fabric spreading
fabric scheduling, 138–42
fitness evaluation, 139–40
genetic procedures, 140–2
individual representation, 138–9
problem formulation in fabric-cutting operations, 135–8
department worflow, 135
efficient manual cutting systems, 136
fuzzy due times representation, 136–7
job placement mechanism, 137–8
trapezoidal fuzzy due date, 137
schedules in apparel production by genetic algorithms and fuzzy set theory, 132–50
case studies using real production data, 142–9
Fashion Matching Satisfaction Index (FMSI), 206
fashion retailing, 10, 11
assessing RFID technology usage, 219–20
cross-selling and up-selling using smart fitting rooms, 220
early detection of customers preference, 219
enriching customers in-store purchase experience, 219–20
new fitting and transaction experience, 220
standardised cross-selling and up-selling approach, 220
IPCS using RFID technology, fuzzy logic and rule-based expert system, 196–222
intelligent product cross-selling system (IPCS), 204–12
RFID-enabled SDS and IPCS implementation, 212–15
RFID-enabled SDS evaluation, 215–19
RFID-enabled smart dressing system (SDS), 200–4

fashion sales forecasting, 10, 170–2
evaluating model performance with real sales data, 180–2
accuracy measures, 181–2
different models parameters used in experiments, 181
forecasting models used for comparison and their parameters, 181
hybrid intelligent models parameters used in experiments, 180
parameter setting for proposed model, 180–1
sales data, 180
experimental results and analysis, 182–9
experiment 1: monthly forecasting, 182–5
experiment 2: quarterly forecasting, 186–8
experiment 3: annual forecasting, 188–9
harmony search algorithms and extreme learning machines, 170–94
assessing forecasting performance, 190–3
sales forecasting techniques, 172–3
hybrid intelligent model for medium-term fashion, 174–9
data pre-processing, 174–5
framework, 174
hybrid intelligent forecaster, 176–9
feedforward neural network (FNN), 16, 26–32
hidden layer, 26
neuron, 27
fitness function, 63–4, 159–60
forecasting performance assessment, 190–3
comparison and analysis, 190–1
different models, 190
further analysis, 191–3
annual forecasting results comparison (benchmark data sets), 192
forward chaining, 20
fuzzification, 38
fuzzy complement, 35
fuzzy intersection, 35
fuzzy logic, 16–17, 32–8
IPCS in fashion retailing, 196–222
radio frequency identification (RFID)-enabled smart dressing system (SDS), 200–4
RFID-enabled SDS and IPCS implementation, 212–15
RFID-enabled SDS evaluation, 215–19
uses, 32–3
fuzzy logic system, 35–8
fuzzy rules evaluation, 37–8
input data fuzzification, 36–7
output data fuzzification, 38
fuzzy numbers, 207
fuzzy rule, 35
evaluation, 37–8
fuzzy scheduling, 134–5
fuzzy screening technique, 207–10, 209
fuzzy set theory, 33–5
fabric spreading and cutting schedules in apparel production, 132–50
case studies using real production data, 142–9
genetic optimisation of fabric scheduling, 138–42
problem formulation in fabric-cutting operations, 135–8
linguistic variables and hedges, 34
operations, 34–5
representation, 33–4
fuzzy union, 35

gene-alter mutation operator, 121–2
generation, 23
genetic algorithm, 22–3, 86, 107
apparel production order planning scheduling, 55–80
experiment, 66–74
experimental results, 163–6
flow diagram of an apparel assembly process, 164
makespan vs skill inventory, 165
mean makespan value of genetically optimised operative assignment, 164
operation breakdown, 163
optimal operative assignment, 166
optimisation performance based on system status at t=50400s, 165
fabric spreading and cutting schedules in apparel production, 132–50
case studies using real production data, 142–9
genetic optimisation of fabric scheduling, 138–42
problem formulation in fabric-cutting operations, 135–8
flowchart, 23
Gantt charts, 77–80
nomenclature, 76
optimising apparel production systems, 153–67
problem formulation in sewing operations, 155–6
order scheduling, 61–6
problem formulation, 57–9
production line balancing, 156–63
chromosome syntax, 157
elitism, 162–3
evolution and termination criteria, 163
fitness function, 159–60
genetic algorithms flow diagram, 158
genetic operators, 160–1
initial population, 159
parent selection, 161–2
uncertain completion and start times, 59–61
genetic operator, 64–5, 160–1
random resetting mutation, 161
single point crossover, 160–1
illustration, 161

genetic optimisation, 90–5
encoding method of the binary string, 91–2
generating procedures, 92–5
lay 1 cut order plan, 93
lay 2 cut order plan, 94
model sample for COP, 95–100
best-of-generation and generation-average values of the fitness over 100 generations, 97
best-of-generation and generation-average values of the fitness over 1000 generations, 97
fabric utilisation rate *vs.* the number of garments used per lay, 96
industrial practice *vs.* proposed COP decision-making model using 100+100 adaptive AES, 100
industrial practice *vs.* proposed COP decision-making model using AES, 98
order quantity, 96
genetic representation, 61–2
chromosome representation, 62
grid approximation, 108, 109–10

harmony search (HS), 25–6
flowchart, 25
intelligent sales forecasting for fashion retailing, 170–94
assessing forecasting performance, 190–3
evaluating model performance with real sales data, 180–2
experimental results and analysis, 182–9
hybrid intelligent model for medium-term fashion, 174–9
heuristic fine-tuning process, 179
heuristic methods, 172
heuristic placement approach, 111–16
object classification, 113
packing rules, 112
system architecture of packing materials, 111
two-stage placement strategy, 114–16
HS-ELM learning algorithm, 177–9
hybrid intelligent forecaster, 176–9
extreme learning machine, 177
flow chart, 176
heuristic fine-tuning process, 179
HS-ELM learning algorithm, 177–9
hybrid intelligent (HI) model, 174–9

improvisation, 26, 178
inference engine, 18
inference technique, 19–21
initial population, 159
intelligent product cross-selling system (IPCS), 204–12
attributes related to fashion mix-and-match and their level of importance, 205
overview, 206
RFID technology, fuzzy logic and rule-based expert system, 196–222
fashion mix-and-match decision-making process of fashion designers, 199
radio frequency identification (RFID)-enabled smart dressing system (SDS), 200–4
RFID-enabled SDS and IPCS implementation, 212–15
RFID-enabled SDS evaluation, 215–19
rule-based expert system and fuzzy screening technique, 207–10
AMSI evaluation, 208
linguistic terms of fuzzy rating scales with fuzzy number representation, 207
validation for mix-and-match, 210–12
fashion items and potential matching pairs, 210
fashion matching results, 211
IPCS system result vs evaluation result provided by fashion designers, 211
screening performance at screening levels VG, G and F, 212
inversion mutation operator, 121

just- in-time (JIT) scheduling, 132–3

knowledge acquisition facility, 18
knowledge base, 15, 18
knowledge-based system, 15
knowledge inference mechanism, 15

labour cost, 89
labour force, 89
learning algorithm, 28
learning vector quantisation neural network, 30–2, 43, 108–9, 112, 113–14
architecture abbreviation notation, 51
correct classification percentage, 51
structure, 31
linguistic hedge, 34
linguistic variable, 34
location factor, 45
hierarchical representation for clothing manufacturing site selection, 46

marker, 7
marker planning, 7–8
evolutionary strategies and neural network, 106–29
packing method for optimised marker packing, 109–16
performance evaluation experiments, 123–8
maximum defuzzifier, 38
mean absolute percentage error (MAPE), 182
mean absolute scaled error (MASE), 182
mean of maxima defuzzifier, 38
monthly forecasting, 182–5
Categories 2-4 comparison, 185
Category 1 vs City 1, 185
Cities 2-4 comparison, 185

monthly time series of sales for category 1, 183
monthly time series of sales for city 1, 183
result generated by proposed model (Category 1), 184
result generated by proposed model (City 1), 184
Moore-Penrose, 177
multi-attribute utility (MAU), 45–7
grouping and suitability indices for locating clothing manufacturing sites, 47
mutation operation, 121–2
exchange and inversion mutation operator, 122
inversion mutation operator, 65

Naïve model, 182
network architecture, 27–8
neural network (NN), 16
apparel manufacturing plants location selection, 41–54
classification methods using artificial neural network, 42–3
classification using supervised ANN, 49–52
classification using unsupervised ANN, 47–9
decision models classification for clothing plants location, 43–7
marker planning optimisation in apparel production, 106–29
packing method for optimised marker packing, 109–16
performance evaluation experiments, 123–8
best packing pattern generated by the GA+HP approach, 126
best packing pattern generated by the proposed approach, 125
illustrative data sets, 123
method comparison, 128
off-line performance by the proposed approach *vs.* genetic algorithm, 124
packing pattern derived from the marker planner, 127
results of the six packed stock sheets, 124
performance of BP with different number of hidden neurons, 54
performance of LVQ with different number of hidden neurons, 54
neural network (NN)-based system, 171
non-adaptive evolution strategies, 86, 87

offspring chromosome, 120
optimisation
genetic algorithms for apparel production systems, 153–67
experimental results, 163–6
problem formulation in sewing operations, 155–6
production line balancing, 156–63
optimised marker packing, 109–16
heuristic placement approach, 111–16
object representation, 109–10
order scheduling, 61–6
apparel production using genetic algorithms, 55–80
experiment, 66–74
Gantt charts, 77–80
nomenclature, 76
problem formulation, 57–9
uncertain completion and start times, 59–61
genetic algorithms
fitness and selection, 63–4
genetic operators, 64–5
initialisation, 62–3
representation, 61–2
termination criterion, 65–6
uncertain arrival times, 73–4
case 1 of experiment 3 results, 73
case 2 of experiment 3 results, 74
uncertain order, 71–2
case 1 of experiment 2 results, 72
case 2 of experiment 2 results, 72
uncertain processing time, 66–71
case 1 of experiment 1 data, 67
case 2 of experiment 1 data, 67
case 3 of experiment 1 data, 68
case 1 of experiment 1 results, 68
case 2 of experiment 1 results, 71
case 3 of experiment 1 results, 71
Gantt charts for case 1 of experiment 1, 70
solutions for all cases of three experiments, 69

packing cell, 114–15
parallel machine scheduling, 133–4
fabric-cutting department layout consisting of four cutting tables, 134
parent selection, 161–2
biased roulette-wheel selection scheme, 162
pitch adjustment rate, 178
plant location, 1–2
point-of-sale (POS), 215–16
post-selection operation, 119
pre-selection operation, 119
probabilistic network, 43, 51–2
architecture abbreviation notation, 52
correct classification percentage, 52
probability density function (PDF), 43
problem formulation, 57–9
probability distribution of processing time, 58
relationship between C_i and its satisfactory level, 58
production planning and scheduling (PPS), 2
production scheduling, 2

quarterly forecasting, 186–8
Categories 2–4 comparison, 187
Category 1 vs City 1, 187
Cities 2–4 comparison, 188

result generated by proposed model (Category 1), 186
result generated by proposed model (City 1), 187

radio frequency identification (RFID), 11–12
IPCS in fashion retailing, 196–222
RFID-enabled SDS and IPCS implementation, 212–15
client interfaces of IPCS, 213
mix-and-match recommendations in fitting room by smart dressing system, 214
movable smart dressing mirror, 216
smart fitting room and smart dressing mirror, 215
RFID-enabled SDS evaluation, 215–19
total sales due proportion to RFID-based IPCS, 217
total sales vs sales due to installation of RFID-based IPCS, 217
trend of sales quantities due to two fitting rooms and dressing mirror, 218
RFID-enabled smart dressing system (SDS), 200–4
fashion retail shop equipped with SDS and jacket with smart tag, 202
sales staff communicating with customer inside fitting room, 204
smart dressing mirror in mix-and-match items and customer in smart fitting room, 203
system architecture for cross-selling in fashion retail industry, 201
random neural network, 16
random resetting mutation, 161
recurrent neural network, 16
retailing, 10–12
RFID antenna, 11
RFID reader, 11
RFID tag, 11–12
root mean square error (RMSE), 182
rule-based expert system, 17–21
inference techniques, 19–21
IPCS in fashion retailing, 196–222
radio frequency identification (RFID)-enabled smart dressing system (SDS), 200–4
RFID-enabled SDS and IPCS implementation, 212–15
RFID-enabled SDS evaluation, 215–19
rule-based knowledge representation, 19
structure, 17–18
architecture, 18
rule-based knowledge representation, 19
run, 23

sewing operations
problem formulation, 155–6
skill level for different level of skill inventory, 156
single-hidden-layer feedforward NNs (SLFNs), 177
single point crossover, 160–1
smart dressing system (SDS), 200–4
solution vector, 25
spreading scheduling, 8–9
operating procedures of a computerised cutting system, 9
start time, 60–1
probability distributions of processing time, 60

trapezoidal fuzzy numbers, 136
two-stage placement strategy, 114–16
procedures, 116

ultra-high frequency (UHF), 219
up-selling, 11–12
user interface, 15, 18